Praise for *The Brain Fix*

"Ralph Carson has drawn our attention to a subject of greatest importance—our brains and how we are not taking care of them. He has distilled this subject into an assessible, informative book that everyone should have—this is a must-read."

—**Emmett Bishop, MD, FAED, CEDS**, Medical Director, Adult Services, Eating Recovery Center, Former President of the International Association of Eating Disorders Professionals

"You will never have to ask another 'Why' or 'What if' question again after reading *The Brain Fix*. Dr. Carson provides all of the information anyone would need to optimize their brain power. The use of humor and down-to-earth versions of complex mechanisms help the reader identify with how the brain is something we can change for the better."

—**Vicki Berkus, MD, PhD, CEDS**, Past President and Senior Advisory Board Member of the International Association of Eating Disorders Professionals

"In *The Brain Fix*, Dr. Ralph Carson demonstrates his exceptional skills in clarifying the intricacies and mysteries of brain function and nutrition science for both the non-scientist and the knowledgeable professional. His breadth of knowledge and ability to share it in a refreshingly easy and cogent style make this work, simply put, required reading."

—**S. Roy Erlichman, PhD, LMFT, CAP, CEDS**, Past President, Board of Directors of the International Association of Eating Disorders Professionals, Certified Addictions Professional and Certified Eating Disorders Specialist

"A brilliant, understandable, and useful how-to manual on brain health. This book should be on the desk of every clinician who treats patients as well as any individual interested in his/her long-term well-being and brain health."

—**Bonnie Harken,** Managing Director, the International Association of Eating Disorders Professionals Foundation Inc.

"*The Brain Fix* is the ultimate guide to healing your brain and body. Dr. Carson has eloquently outlined a comprehensive review of neuroscience—from apples to zinc, sleep to exercise, yoga to massage. Neuroscience is delineated through practical tools that clinicians and patients alike can easily use in healing and recovery. By specifically highlighting addictions and eating disorders, Dr. Carson offers patients and clinicians a comprehensive resource aimed

—**Kevin Wandler, MD**, Professor & Chief, E
College of Medicine, Depa
Internal Medicine, Direc

"Dr. Carson has done it again. This outstanding book on the brain takes you on a journey that is invaluable. Understanding brain functioning in this simple but scientifically correct book is ideal for anyone who deals with people, wants to understand behavior, or has a brain themselves. It is a must-read."

—**Machiel N. Kennedy, MD**, Board of the American Society Bariatric Physicians

"Einstein said, 'If you can't explain it simply, you don't understand it well enough.' In *The Brain Fix*, Ralph Carson demonstrates the depth and breadth of his understanding of brain science and nutrition by explaining the requirements for brain health in clear and simple language. This book is a gift for anyone interested in a healthier brain and a healthier life."

—**Anita Johnston, PhD**, Author, *Eating in the Light of the Moon*, Director, 'Ai Pono Eating Disorders Program, Hawaii, Consultant, Moonpointe & Focus Center for Eating Disorders, Tennessee, Consultant, EATFED, Australia

"Whether you are looking for an understanding of glycemic index, the truth about carbs, what happens when you drink or smoke, or how best to take care of yourself and prevent premature aging, Ralph gives specific doable advice. This is a must-have book on the shelves of anyone interested in the effects of nutrition."

—**Carolyn Costin**, Founder, Monte Nido & Affiliates, Author of *The Eating Disorder Sourcebook: 8 Keys to Recovery from an Eating Disorder, 100 Questions and Answers About Eating Disorders*, and *Your Dieting Daughter*

"Dr. Carson's book, *The Brain Fix*, combines the latest scientific research on brain neurology and nutrition in a powerful yet simple to understand format. Dr. Carson has produced a book that not only explains problems physically and psychologically, but provides practical tools that do not require massive changes in your lifestyle. I highly recommend this book."

—**A. David Wall, PhD**, Psychologist, Remuda Ranch

"This book is a gift to the healing community."

—**Mary Bellofatto, MA, LMHC, CEDS, NCC, TEP**, President of the Board, the International Association of Eating Disorders Professionals

"This book debunks myths and illuminates truths about the brain, body, and living in good health. It presents a generous dose of hope about how we can improve our brains, our bodies, and our lives."

—**Michael E. Berrett, PhD**, CEO and Cofounder, Center for Change and Coauthor, *Spiritual Approaches in the Treatment of Women with Eating Disorders*

"I consider this a must-read for anyone in recovery or anyone who is striving for a happier, healthier life. This book is informative, motivating, and most of all, hopeful."

—**Cathy Reto, PhD**, Director, Pine Grove Women's Center

Improve Your Memory, Moods, and Mind

THE
Brain
Fix

What's the Matter with Your Gray Matter

Ralph E. Carson, LD, RD, PhD

Health Communications, Inc.
Deerfield Beach, Florida

www.hcibooks.com

Library of Congress Cataloging-in-Publication Data
is available through the Library of Congress.

The information contained in this book is not intended as a substitute for the advice/and or medical care of the reader's physician. The author of this book does not endorse the use of any treatment without seeking the advice of a medical professional.

ISBN-13: 978-0-7573-1629-6 (paperback)
ISBN-10: 0-7573-1629-8 (paperback)
ISBN-13: 978-0-7573-1609-8 (e-book)
ISBN-10: 0-7573-1609-3 (e-book)

Publisher: Health Communications, Inc.
　　　　　3201 S.W. 15th Street
　　　　　Deerfield Beach, FL 33442-8190

Cover design by Larissa Hise Henoch
Interior design and formatting by Dawn Von Strolley Grove

Contents

Introduction: No Matter the Problem, Your Brain Is Very Fixable

OFTENTIMES THE WORK WE CHOOSE to do in this world is born out of our own personal journey. That's the thought I contemplated when I embarked on this project to explore the many ways to help the brain heal from the diseases and situations we often encounter that can injure it.

Along my life's journey, brain injuries from mild to fatal have affected many of my loved ones. When I was a teenager, my mother passed away suddenly and unexpectedly from a cerebral hemorrhage (which causes bleeding in the brain) at the age of forty-four. Her mother was diagnosed with dementia in her early sixties. Several of my close family members struggled with alcoholism, nicotine, and other drugs of abuse that can harm the brain. And my sister died at a too-young age from a devastating form of brain cancer called glioblastoma multiforme.

I originally planned to attend medical school. So in the early 1970s, I pursued a premed degree at Duke University. Perhaps because of heavy competition (or from being a poor standardized test-taker—I had a high grade-point average but a poor score on the medical college admission test), I didn't qualify at any of the medical schools to which I applied.

So instead, I went on to study pathology at Duke University Medical School. I was fascinated with the human brain and became intrigued with how little we knew about its function at the time. (As we'll see later in the book, much of what we *thought* we knew about the brain's ability to heal was wrong.)

I later earned a doctoral degree in nutrition from Auburn University. Since then, I have spent my entire career investigating how lifestyle behaviors affect brain function, psychological disorders, and neurological healing. In particular, I've spent a great deal of time counseling people with eating disorders and addictions, both of which can leave an impact on the brain's ability to work properly.

While most people realize that nutrition, exercise, and sleep affect our bodies from the neck down—contributing to diseases such as heart disease, diabetes, cancer, and arthritis—fewer understand how these factors affect the health of the mind and brain, too. The typical American lifestyle encourages inflammation to run rampant, and the inflammatory chemicals that erode tissues and upset well-balanced processes in your body also affect your brain. Cardiovascular disease affects millions of Americans, and when blood isn't flowing properly through your arteries, it can affect your brain's health too.

Furthermore, while it's easy to envision how strokes and head injuries can injure your brain, not as many people have a good grasp on how more subtle insults can harm it. These include addictions, obesity, eating disorders, and lifestyle choices. Even anxiety and depression, which are very common in our society, can leave your brain in need of healing.

As a result, most of us have something going on in our lives that could harm our ability to think clearly. Thus, this book is intended for *everyone* who has a brain.

I will talk a fair amount about addiction, obesity, and eating disorders in these pages simply because I have spent more than thirty years treating them. If you are trying to get past any of these problems, this book is for you.

But if you've ever struggled with depression or anxiety, this book is for you, too. If you've watched older relatives disappear into a mental fog because of Alzheimer's or other types of dementia and you want to avoid their outcome, this book is for you. And if you've simply fallen into a sedentary lifestyle and unhealthy diet like so many other Americans, this book is also for you.

All of us can reap the rewards of giving our brains a tune-up.

"But what can *I* do to fix my brain?" you might ask.

On one hand, your brain is the most complex of organs. It's locked away in your skull like a treasure in a safe. It's not a relatively simple body part like a bone, which you can strengthen with more calcium and vitamin D. It has billions of cells that work together to become more than the sum of their parts. Your brain gives you the consciousness, reason, and higher thinking ability that make you human. It's a creation that mankind has barely begun to comprehend, even with our wisest of philosophers and our most high-tech MRIs, PET scans, and other imaging devices.

This is all true. Your brain *is* special. But the same rules that govern the health of the rest of your body apply to it, too. Helping your brain heal isn't especially difficult, even when it has become dysfunctional from a lifetime of injuries, insults, and lack of proper care. In these pages, I'll be sharing with you many of the discoveries that leading experts have made in recent years for better understanding how the brain works in illness and good health.

Though I've experienced a great deal of success during my career in helping people turn away from addictions and other health threats, my goal when I began was to find a *cure* for them and work myself out of a job. I often tell people that aside from antibiotics and chemotherapy, medicine isn't able to cure disease. Instead, the body cures itself if we give it the supplies it needs. Good nutrition, the right supplements, the right amount of exercise and sleep, and the proper mental outlook can bring balance back to your body and brain.

Needless to say, given that so many people still don't have this information, I have work yet to do. I consider this book to be part of my mission.

We are all challenged to make the best of our time on Earth, and the one goal we universally seek is happiness. What makes me happy is guiding people toward better health by sharing what I have learned over these many years. By restoring your brain to its peak-possible condition, *you'll* be able to enjoy a happier life, too.

Your brain is quite fixable; it's not stuck in place, unchangeable. Your brain is mysterious, but you can still understand it well enough to steer it back to health. The same is true of your mind, which goes hand in hand with your brain. My hope is that when you become more familiar with your own brain, you'll be encouraged to use the simple tools that I offer in "The Brain Fix Toolbox" sections throughout the book in your daily life.

With your "fixed" brain you can improve your quality of life by thinking more clearly, enjoying a sharper memory, feeling happier and less stressed, and being in control of your habits. These improvements can occur quickly—and they can be long-lasting. By making these changes now, you'll have a better chance of preserving all these qualities even later in life when dementia and difficulty thinking clearly tend to become a concern for many people.

PART 1

The Brain in Illness and Health

1

If Your Brain Can Get Off Track, It Can Be Fixed, Too

FOR NEARLY TWO DECADES, a man named Terry Wallis lay in bed mute and virtually unresponsive after a car crash. Year by year the calendar marched forward, yet Wallis stayed in a state of minimal consciousness. The impact of the crash had simply sheared apart the nerves in his brain that had previously allowed him to speak, move, and live a normal human life.

At one time, scientists wouldn't have held much hope for his recovery. The brain, they felt, simply wasn't "plastic." To understand plasticity, first think of a stone that you've plucked from a riverbed. You can't squish it, stretch it, or do much of anything to change it, at least with just your hands. The stone is what it is, and it can remain that way forever.

And to put it simply, common wisdom once held that the brain was similar in some regards to this piece of rock. The experts felt that once neurons—the brain cells that do our thinking—died or became damaged, they couldn't be replaced. As a result, the brain's ability to recover from injuries was extremely limited, or so they thought.

Of course, we could make new memories and learn new skills, so *something* that involved change was going on in our brains. However, our capacity to attain new memories and abilities was believed to come from the brain rewiring *existing* cells rather than growing *new* ones. And once nerve cells became too damaged to function, they were thought to be lost forever. So any continuing function in the brain after damage must have been a result of the organ tapping into already-existing reserves.

The notion that the brain couldn't heal itself had critical repercussions when it came to treatment. Doctors would counsel patients to surrender to their disabilities and learn to live with the disappointing reality that they would never get better.

That was then. As we're learning nowadays, the brain isn't like an unchangeable stone. It's actually more like a blob of the Silly Putty you remember from childhood. You can squish Silly Putty, tug on it, and poke holes in it. But when you're done, you can put it back in its original shape, spread it thin, and use it to pick up an image from the comics page. Of course, your brain can't recover from as much abuse as you can inflict on Silly Putty, but it *does* have a remarkable ability to regain vital functions even after trauma or years of mistreatment. This means that it's *plastic.*

Throughout our lives, our brains remain flexible and responsive to the outside world by constantly changing. As we form memories and learn from our experiences, the brain changes itself and learns new tricks. Even in his severely injured state, Wallis's brain was mending. By 2003, doctors had discovered convincing evidence that his brain was healing itself by forming new connections. He was speaking, moving, and remembering more, while scans of his brain showed that neural cells were becoming denser and neural fibers were growing. Though his case is extreme, we can see how it applies to our own lives. Many other examples of the plasticity and malleability of the brain are easy to find:

- Particular areas of our brains evolve in response to particular new demands (such as juggling or learning to type, for example).
- Images of the brains of blind Braille readers show that regions that are normally responsible for *vision* get taken over by the sense of *touch.*
- People who smoke marijuana heavily often have lower numbers of a certain type of chemical receptor in their brains compared to nonusers. But after they stay away from marijuana for a month, brain scans show a marked increase in activity in the areas that had been affected.

I've been around many individuals in treatment centers who didn't have obvious injuries—like from brain trauma—that we could see with the naked eye. However, they showed subtle but clear evidence of healing over time that was visible in their behaviors, on questionnaires they filled out, and on scans of their brains. This let us know that *something* had gone wrong in their brains that was being fixed.

On monthly visits to treatment centers, I repeatedly met with patients who had passed through detox but couldn't comprehend the simplest of explanations or remember what people had told them for more than an hour. Their restlessness and irritability was evident as they fidgeted, zoned out, or abruptly got up and walked away from conversations. Yet given time, avoidance of drugs, and support, they were able to regain their focus, memory, and learning skills, which indicated an obvious change in their brains. This would also show up on high-tech SPECT scans of blood flow in their brains. In addition, I've seen:

- Multiple patients who experienced sexual, physical, or emotional trauma and were in a constant state of psychic numbing that left them frozen and unable to communicate. In time, they became free from this paralyzing mental block as the reaction in the fear center of their brain diminished.
- People who could not "feel" their feelings or put them into words showed that when their brain healed, they were able to light up areas in their brain on scans that corresponded to acknowledging feelings.
- Individuals who felt hopeless due to treatment-resistant depression showed more brain wave activity—as measured on EEG—in their left prefrontal cortex. This is the brain's center of happiness.
- Others who were morbidly obese and couldn't control their voracious appetite became capable of showing a more balanced response in the hunger center of their brain.
- And while working with people with anorexia who had an inability to accurately assess their appearance (despite the number on the scale and the emaciated appearance in the mirror), I've noted that given time and therapy, the area of the brain that connected their external reality to their internal acceptance—called the insula —could be resurrected.

We have clear evidence that the brain continually adapts and reorganizes itself through its plasticity. Like a chunk of Silly Putty that can go back to its old shape, plasticity implies that the brain can rewire itself and return to a fairly normal state of functioning after harmful or destructive changes. Plasticity in adults is not only *possible*, it is even *essential* for learning, memory, and mood regulation. The connections between cells in the brain are capable of rerouting. And synapses—the tiny gaps over which nerve cells "talk" to each other—are constantly being regulated and altered. In addition, the concentrations and availability of chemical messengers, such as neurotransmitters, as well as growth factors and other chemicals, are always changing.

Simply put, the brain is always changing. This means you have plenty of opportunities to help make changes for the better. Because the brain can heal and recover from trauma, the proper advice for patients whose brains have encountered hardship is to inform them of everything possible they can do to stimulate plasticity and provide hope for fixing their brain.

That's also the message you'll find in this book. Given that we're going to be talking about the brain throughout this entire book, we should first learn the basics about it.

Your Brain 101: What's that Gray Thing Doing in There?

Experts think that the brain—which weighs about 2.8 pounds or so—contains roughly 100 billion neurons, which are nerve cells. We're largely going to be concerned with the neurons in this book, but the brain also contains many other cells that support the neurons, including astrocytes and oligodendrocytes (some of the Brain Fix steps will address these cells, too).

The brain's neurons have long, spindly branches called dendrites that pick up signals from other cells. "Branches" is a particularly apt word, since these can look like tiny trees. Neurons also have a structure called an axon that sends signals *out*. Parts of the neurons are covered with a fatty protective coating called myelin, which acts like the insulation around an electrical wire.

The crucial job of neurons is to communicate with each other and with your body. Because nerves can talk to each other, you can:

- Form memories
- Learn new skills and information
- Tell your body parts to move
- Pick up clues about your surroundings through your eyes, ears, skin, nose, and tongue
- Rest easily knowing that your brain keeps your temperature, fluid levels, and countless chemical processes operating smoothly

A brain that's working well requires neurons that are communicating well. But when neurons aren't sending their signals to each other efficiently, it can cause problems with your mood, memory, and mental sharpness. Since much of the information in this book is geared toward keeping your neurons communicating properly, let's take a moment to understand how they talk to each other.

When neurons communicate, the axon of one neuron sends signals to a part of another neuron. These two neurons don't actually touch each other, though. Instead, they're separated by a minuscule space called a *synaptic cleft*. When a neuron decides it needs to send a message to another cell, an electrical charge first runs down its length. Tiny tunnels open and close in the wall of the cell, allowing ions, such as sodium and potassium, to flood in and out of the cell. This creates the electrical charge. When the charge reaches the end of the axon, the axon releases chemicals called neurotransmitters into the synaptic gap. These neurotransmitters can cross the gap, where the neighboring cells can pick them up. The neurotransmitter then causes the other cells to act accordingly.

Neurotransmitter sounds like a ten-dollar word, but it's merely a substance that helps a neuron transmit messages (thus, *neuro* plus *transmitter*). Neurotransmitters, by definition, are (1) created in one cell, called the presynaptic cell, and (2) released by the presynaptic cell in large enough amounts to cause a measurable effect on another cell, called the postsynaptic cell. Also, when an artificial version of the neurotransmitter is given to a person, it mimics the natural release. And a specific mechanism removes the neurotransmitter from the synaptic cleft. Examples of neurotransmitters include:

- **GABA**

  This chemical inhibits signaling. Popular prescription sleeping pills activate GABA. Antipsychotic drugs affect it, too. This neurotransmitter helps reduce anxiety and plays an important role in sedation.

- **Serotonin**

  Serotonin helps you feel calm and centered. If your levels get low, you may wind up with depression. A form of antidepressant called a selective serotonin reuptake inhibitor—or SSRI—raises serotonin levels. The hormone estrogen can have an impact on serotonin levels, which may explain irritable moods linked to PMS.

  Serotonin gets a lot of recognition in our society—probably due to the popularity of SSRI antidepressants—and it deserves a closer look here. In the emotional center of the brain, called the limbic system, nerves communicate via one nerve throwing out a neurotransmitter across the synapse to be caught by a second nerve. When the neurotransmitter serotonin is used during communication and it attaches to its receptor on the second nerve, you feel calmer.

  However, when we're exposed to intense stress, the amount of available serotonin becomes depleted. In an attempt to preserve serotonin, the nerve that's producing the stuff starts to "reabsorb" the serotonin floating around in the synapse. This leaves less available to attach to the receptor of the receiving neuron. As less serotonin attaches to these receiving neurons, your mood becomes down or depressed. The SSRI drugs (Prozac is a well-known example) were designed to reduce this absorption of serotonin—also known as *reuptake*. This keeps serotonin available near the receptors on the neurons that are picking it up, and it allows us to remain in an overall state of calmness.

  The fact that the synapses between the nerves are flooded with excess serotonin might lead you to believe that an antidepressant would immediately reverse the symptoms of depression. That's not true, though. Therapists and patients alike know all too well that it takes anywhere from three to four weeks for mood to lift after a person starts the medication. (This has led some researchers to theorize that SSRIs may have the ability to stimulate nerve cell growth.)

But you don't have to take an antidepressant to boost your serotonin levels. Later in the book, you'll learn many other ways to improve your serotonin on your own without taking a medication.

- **Glutamate**

This neurotransmitter *accelerates* neurons' signals. It plays a role in arousal and wakefulness. Having glutamate on hand can increase your mental sharpness and improve your memory. However, if levels get too high, it kills neurons. A handful of scientists—but not all—speculate that the food additive monosodium glutamate (MSG) may be a concern for brain health.

- **Dopamine**

Dopamine heightens the sense of pleasure that comes from food and sex. It also helps make drug and alcohol abuse feel rewarding to users. Dopamine also plays a role in muscle control and function, which becomes disturbed in the neurodegenerative Parkinson's disease.

- **Norepinephrine**

Norepinephrine, also called noradrenaline, is made from dopamine. It plays a role in our fight-or-flight reaction to stressful situations and leads to a state of high arousal that can contribute to anxiety. Too much can cause high blood pressure, and low levels may set the stage for fatigue and depression.

- **Epinephrine**

Epinephrine, or adrenaline, is produced by the adrenal glands on the kidneys. It helps control attentiveness and mental focus. Having high levels can contribute to sleep problems and anxiety.

- **Acetylcholine**

This plays an important role in memory and other brain abilities. Having low levels of acetylcholine is linked to Alzheimer's disease.

- **Histamine**

This neurotransmitter causes allergic reactions and is involved in the release of epinephrine and norepinephrine. Antihistamines counteract its stimulatory effect and are often associated with producing sleep.

Returning to our discussion on synapses, these areas are of great interest to scientists because changes in their number and function affect learning, memory, and behaviors. Changes in the number of synapses in particular brain regions—or the way they do their job—often play a role in brain disorders and abnormal behaviors.

Meanwhile, a complex system of blood vessels laces through the brain. Blood carries oxygen and fuel to the brain by coursing through arteries. Blood also carries waste out of the brain through veins. Blood vessels can change for the worse. If arteries become narrowed and stiff because of fatty plaque buildup in their walls, these changes can result in lack of blood flow to the brain. If the brain is starved for fuel and oxygen, it's not going to work at its best.

You can think of your brain as having an inner core that's more primitive and an outer layer—the cortex—that is more highly evolved. The area below the cortex busies itself with matters of basic survival. It spurs you to eat, find sources of warmth, and reproduce. Parts of this area make sure you breathe and sleep properly and that your blood is circulating as needed, without you having to consciously control these processes. Deeper parts of your brain judge incoming information from your surroundings that could be a threat.

The outer portion of your brain handles many of the higher-level thinking skills that make us human. This area makes decisions and controls impulses that may not be a great idea to act upon. The frontal lobe—which rests behind your forehead—is the most highly evolved part of your brain. It handles planning, reasoning, and self-conscious awareness. Just behind this lobe is the parietal lobe, which processes sensory information like taste, smell, touch, and temperature. Your temporal lobes—located on the sides of your brain just above your ears—handle language issues. And your occipital lobe, at the back of your head, helps you see.

Your *thalamus* serves as a kind of gatekeeper between the old and new parts of your brain. It keeps unwanted information from overwhelming your cortex, but lets important information through for further processing.

The brain is a voracious eater, requiring a constant flow of glucose—or blood sugar—to keep it running. A system called the *blood-brain barrier* keeps some chemicals in your body—whether those your body makes naturally or those you put into it—from getting into your brain. But some substances *can* get into your brain and reduce its ability to work properly, or even injure it.

Like a hedge that sprouts new branches that are pruned afterward into the desired shape, the brain's plasticity helps it adapt to changing situations. Messages can be embedded or erased in the brain in response to feelings, emotions, thoughts, behaviors, and actions. The cellular structure in the brain is capable of much change, too. Let's take a closer look at how the brain is capable of changing in the direction of healing.

The Brain: Shifting, Healing, and Improving

The cortex of the brain is a thin layer that covers the outer surface of part of the organ. It's responsible for many aspects of our human reason, and it serves as the foundation of our consciousness. To stay maintained, the cortex requires neurons to regenerate.

Scientists discovered that nerve cells replace themselves using stem cells called *amplified progenitor cells*. These stem cells remain available in your brain from birth. They're *undifferentiated*, meaning that they have not yet been stimulated to turn into a specific kind of functional cell. Think of them as raw materials that are waiting around to be converted into different types of cells.

These stem cells are housed in the short-term memory center of the brain called the hippocampus. More clusters of stem cells are located around the ventricles. (The ventricles are like a series of canals through which cerebrospinal fluid continually flows.) Stem cells were first identified in adult primates' brains in 1967. Since that time, research has confirmed that new neurons continue to be created in the human brain throughout adulthood. New neurons continuously develop from the hippocampus and around the ventricles, and they eventually become woven into the existing neural networks of different brain regions. Not only can nerve cells regenerate, they can adapt their function to take on critical roles that were once performed by the damaged tissue they replace.

The stem cell is stimulated to divide asymmetrically. This means that it makes a replica of itself and another specialized neural cell. It can also create support cells known as *glia*. Cells continue to go through a series of changes until they become functioning nerve cells while they migrate to various regions of the brain, where they turn into the particular type of cell that's needed.

For example, the left prefrontal cortex is the place in the brain that produces feelings of contentment and happiness. Newly formed cells that migrate through the brain to depleted areas here help restore happiness and reduce depression.

Within the layers of neurons that coat the outer surface of the brain (making it resemble the layers of phyllo dough in the Greek dessert baklava), cells divide repeatedly and add to their number of offspring. Like the chips and transistors in a supercomputer, the added neurons and circuits support the capacity for sophisticated computation.

If you were to accept the erroneous notion that your brain is incapable of healing, you might feel a sense of helplessness when your brain isn't working at its best, which could lead you to feel even more dejected. But again, it's not true. You have constant regeneration, which allows for reasoning, planning, mood stability, and decision-making. One should have an unending train of new brain cells, which is consistent with our ability to store new memories.

A number of chemicals in the brain assist this process of regeneration. Neurogenesis—or the creation of new neurons—is aided by a number of growth factors that act much like fertilizer on a newly planted garden. Some of the more well-known growth factors include:

- Neurotrophins. These signal cells to grow, develop specialized function, and divide. They're especially crucial for the survival of cells that work with your fight-or-flight system and your sensory nerves.
- Insulin-like growth factor. This acts much like the hormone insulin. It helps repair damaged tissue and encourages cells to grow and divide.
- Brain-derived neurotrophic factor (BDNF). If amplified progenitor cells from the hippocampus and frontal cortex are simmered in BDNF in the lab, the cells turn into neural cells involved in memory and cognition. Neurotrophic factors spur the survival,

development, and function of nerve cells. They can also prevent a natural process called *apoptosis*, which you can think of as a pre-programmed form of cell suicide. In addition to supporting the survival of existing neurons, BDNF also encourages the growth of synapses through a process called *dendritic sprouting*. This sprouting is where branches from existing nerves make new connections with other nerves. Antidepressants are capable of increasing BDNF, which is another way that antidepressants known as selective serotonin reuptake inhibitors (SSRIs) do their job.

When our lives spin out of control, stress has a profound effect on the lives of neurons and their branches. Nerve cells can shrink and die in response to stress, for example. In monkeys that are stressed for even one hour, cell survival decreases. The hormones that our bodies unleash during stress—such as cortisol—are toxic to neurons. This implies that the sustained periods of the fight-or-flight response that we cycle into during stress are destructive to our brain. This process is similar to what we see with degenerative diseases such as Alzheimer's and Parkinson's.

Does it surprise you that a mundane problem such as stress can have a harmful impact on your brain? So do a lot of other everyday issues that are less dramatic than a head injury from a car crash. Drugs of abuse can slow down the rate of new cell growth. So can aging. And so can physical disease that affects the rest of your body. Your brain cells can die from lack of environmental stimulation—also known as loneliness. Many elements of an unhealthy diet can also harm your brain cells.

That's why later we will learn about the importance of keeping a lid on excess calories, big loads of carbohydrates, saturated and trans-fatty acids, and damaging free radicals, and making a priority of getting enough healing omega-3 fatty acids.

Diet is just the *starting* point for helping your brain bounce back from all the harmful elements in your surroundings. Other crucial steps for fixing your brain include exercise, meditation, sleep, therapy (such as cognitive behavioral therapy) to change the way you think and act, and keeping an enriching environment in which you make your brain learn and remember new skills.

Believe that Your Brain Can Heal, and Let the Healing Begin

As I mentioned, I've spent much of my career helping people recover from various addictions. But even if you *aren't* addicted to any drug of abuse, the steps that these people need to take will likely apply to you to some degree as well.

During addiction, nerve cells can be destroyed, dendrites connecting the nerves are rerouted, neurotransmitters are depleted, and the protective myelin coating on nerves dwindles during years of abuse. Some of these changes are due to stress, trauma, and poor nutrition. The first step that people who are addicted need to take is to completely stop the further destruction of brain tissue. This means they need to take a total and complete break from using drugs or alcohol.

Recovering from any addiction is often a very difficult, challenging, and drawn-out process. People don't typically recognize the problem and solve it overnight. Long before they can start constructive treatment, they need to break through their denial and admit they have a problem.

Even after they accept that their behavior is inappropriate, they typically keep resisting the treatment they need. Often they have a feeling that the addiction is not *that* severe, and it will go away if they simply abstain from their drug or behavior of choice. If they do commit to treatment, too many times they only adhere to what they think recovery should look like, instead of aiming for true and lasting recovery. If the individual never connects with the *final* stage of recovery—which is emotional commitment and total surrender—the potential for long-term recovery is small. Unfortunately, many people who are addicted will either find themselves relapsing, becoming addicted to other substances or activities, or fighting their cravings tooth and nail for the rest of their lives.

"But I'm not addicted to anything. What does all this have to do with me?" some readers will rightfully ask. Well, the *rest* of us face threats to our brain health that are serious, too. And we can have just as much difficulty changing lifestyle concerns that threaten our brains.

Many of us find ourselves struggling with issues that threaten our brain health year after year. Or even decade after decade! Some people go their entire lives without fixing their unhealthy diets, their excess weight, or the way they react to stressful or challenging situations. In the meantime, they can often easily see the effects that their choices are having on their bodies, such as diabetes, heart disease, or even cancer. But they might not fully appreciate how the impact on their brain is draining away their quality of life.

Right now, you could be suffering from a brain that needs fixing, too.

How often do you feel stressed and unhappy, even though everything in your life is going pretty well? How often do you feel fatigued? Do you get the sense that your mind could be working more quickly and productively? That your memory could be sharper? Maybe you do, but even if you don't, that doesn't mean you're not overdue for a brain fix. Many of us go through our lives without fully realizing how our choices are slowing down our brain and mind. After all, you'll never view your brain like you can see your belly or your muscle tone. Who knows what it's doing hidden away inside your skull? As far as your *mind* goes, that's an even more difficult entity to get to know.

It's time to assess your brain and familiarize yourself with it, no matter who you are. The tools in this book for fixing your brain will be very useful for people with addictions and eating disorders—and I have a special chapter near the end of the book just for these readers. But for everyone else, it's also time for you to make the changes that will allow your brain to live up to its highest potential. If you suspect that you:

- Aren't getting as much out of life as you could
- Aren't making the best choices for your health
- Could be happier and more productive if you gave your brain the chance to thrive as fully as it could . . .

. . . then it's time to shed your old habits, develop new ways of thinking and acting, and take heart that your brain *is* changeable. You can indeed push your brain to make new connections. You can ask it to learn new skills. You can expect it to adapt to overcome injuries and damage. You can fix your brain.

Throughout this book, I'll put most of my focus on things you can do all on your own—*without* the help of a doctor or therapist. After all, as I said earlier in the book, medications—with a few exceptions—don't produce a cure, and that's what we're seeking here. You don't necessarily need any medications to fix your brain (but make sure to adhere to your doctor's advice when they are prescribed). That's because the key to healing your brain is to take advantage of its plasticity and its ability to adapt and heal *itself*. Hope and belief are two of the most important tools to help brain healing take place. Up to 70 percent of successful treatments may result from just believing that the plan will work. Only *you* can provide this belief.

It's also up to you to deploy many of the other tools that will heal your brain. You'll need:

- Proper nutrition to feed your body and brain the necessary nutrients and raw materials. When you're trying to build your muscles, you require good nutrition in addition to strength-training exercises. In the same way, the foods we choose to eat have a significant influence on how our brain heals from problems. Your brain only has so much reserve. The combination of abuse (including stress, addiction, or eating disorders) and neglect (such as poor eating, exercise, and sleeping habits) takes a toll on mental function. Fortunately, if you get the proper nutrients, nerves can be regenerated, neurotransmitters can be replaced, and brain functioning can reach its optimal level. New research has revealed to us how to design a food plan that maximizes the healing of the brain and speeds its recovery. Your diet will need to give your brain protection from further damage, which vitamins, minerals, antioxidants, and phytonutrients can provide. Your foods must also put building materials like omega-3 fats and protein into your system, along with fuel in the form of the right kinds of carbohydrates.
- You'll also need appropriate amounts of exercise. Our bodies are built for movement. And when you don't give your body the physical activity it requires, fat can build up. The hormones and other chemicals that swirl through your bloodstream can swing far out of their normal ranges. Inflammation can increase throughout your body, burning up tissues and organs like an out-of-control

fire. And your brain, which taps into the same blood supply as the rest of your body, can pay the price.

- Odds are good that you'll need to make sleep more of a priority. Americans are, as a whole, a sleep-deprived bunch of people. Yet effective healing takes place during certain stages of sleep. If you're not sleeping, you're missing out on a crucial brain-repairing tool. Your brain fix will likely require that you improve your quality of sleep to ensure that you're getting enough of these periods of restorative snoozing.

- In addition, you will probably benefit from learning to better control stress and depression. Good nutrition and exercise will provide a nice start to improving your mood and your outlook. But other steps, such as meditation and yoga, can also do wonders for alleviating stress and depression.

These are all tools that you can easily use on your own. I'll show you how. But bringing in outside help can help you fully achieve the repair job you're planning for your brain. Working with a good counselor or therapist may be helpful or even necessary. A consultation with a dietitian or nutritionist would be useful to establish a sound dietary plan that fits your individual lifestyle and food preferences.

There's a lot of truth to the saying that "You are what you eat," but when it comes to your brain, you are what you *think*. Every experience can change the brain. So it makes sense, when necessary, to learn how to lead your thoughts to more productive and healthy places. A therapist can guide you to recognize negative, unrealistic, unhelpful thoughts and replace them with constructive thoughts. At the same time, the therapist can show you how to identify and replace unhealthy behaviors with more appropriate ones. This is called cognitive behavioral therapy, or CBT. Through CBT, we have the capacity to change the way we view our circumstances.Therapy must be aimed at improving specific thoughts and feelings that are holding you back. It helps to *repeat* your new healing thoughts and emotions over and over, and it further helps that these feel *genuine*. During the course of therapy, the brain actually changes.

A physician can also prescribe medications that help you keep your brain working properly (though these aren't a substitute for the changes you also need to make on your own). As we've discussed, SSRI antidepressants can treat depression and anxiety, but they can also physically repair damage in your brain. Working with a mental health provider who can diagnose and prescribe the proper medications can be an important way to regain control over your thought processes and help your brain heal. You may also want to work with a physician to get on medication regimens to lower high blood pressure, cholesterol, or blood sugar if these issues are a problem and you can't fix them on your own.

Nutritional advice from a registered dietitian (RD) or licensed nutritionist can be invaluable. They can help design a food plan that addresses your individuality and special health needs (diabetes, weight, age, culture, etc). Advice on how to shop and prepare foods, as well as answering difficult questions on food choices, are all within the realm of their expertise.

 ## THE BRAIN FIX TOOLBOX
Tools for Launching a Healthy Outlook

Starting now, each chapter will end with a recap of the most important points you should put into action in your daily life. For now, the main takeaway messages to remember are:

- Remember that your brain doesn't remain in one place. In fact, it changes every single day! Levels of chemicals go up and down, and connections between nerves evolve. As a result, you can encourage changes that put your brain in a *healthier* place.

- The same steps that are important for your health from the neck down—eating right, getting enough exercise, and sleeping enough—are especially crucial for your health *above* your neck!

- Stress, depression, loneliness, and lack of stimulation are common problems that make our brains work less effectively (and can even damage our brains). To truly fix your brain, you will probably need to take steps to change your outlook and the way you react to stressful situations. You may also need to give your brain more challenges to chew on.

- All of the changes you need to make to fix your brain—whether it's losing weight or turning away from a drug—are within your power. No matter how long you've been keeping up an unhealthy habit, you can make a change. Believing that you can make this change is an important first step.

- Don't be afraid to bring in outside help, whether it's a physician or a mental health counselor. Many of the Brain Fix strategies are steps you can take on your own, but sometimes there's no substitute for a professional teammate.

2

Know Your Brain's Worst Enemies

YOUR BRAIN HAS A LEVEL OF responsibility that's unmatched by any other organ. It keeps all manner of physical processes regulated, many without your awareness. It keeps your temperature and blood pressure within a tight range, and it controls your hunger, thirst, blood pressure, and breathing.

Your brain stores the memories you've gained over the decades of your lifetime. It almost instantaneously provides a library's worth of facts whenever you need them. Your brain is responsible for the skills you need to do your job. It provides the impulses necessary for controlling your muscles, whether you're walking around, playing basketball, or leaning down to delicately pluck a four-leaf clover. It stays alert and ready for threats to your safety.

I could continue for *days* listing what your brain does to maintain your health and quality of life. Our brains do more for us every second than we can probably fully appreciate. But in short, you *are* your brain. And your brain *is* you.

Given that your brain touches nearly every aspect of your existence from moment to moment and is tightly interconnected with so many processes in your body, many factors can harm your brain. As a result, some of the steps you should take to protect your brain may not seem obviously crucial for your brain health. "How does obesity affect my *brain*?" you might ask. You might wonder the same thing about stress. Or high cholesterol. Or salt in your diet. But these and many other factors within your body, and outside you in your environment, certainly do influence whether your brain works well or malfunctions.

The overview in this chapter will offer a quick primer on common issues that affect your brain health, some of which may not be apparent at first glance. By understanding *why* it's important to prevent or treat these problems, you may be more likely to want to follow the many recommendations you'll find throughout *The Brain Fix*.

Vascular Diseases

Your entire body—including your brain—is connected to a system of plumbing called the cardiovascular system. Your heart lies at the center of this system.

Your heart pumps out blood that carries oxygen, fuel in the form of glucose and fat, hormones, enzymes, and a chemical supply company catalog's worth of other substances. This blood pulses out to your body through large arteries. These lead to smaller and smaller arteries as the blood heads out to more distant territory.

These "pipes" in your cardiovascular plumbing must stay open and clear to let blood circulate. Ideally, the blood isn't carrying high levels of inflammatory chemicals or substances that encourage the blood to clot excessively. And hopefully the blood isn't under such high pressure that it damages the organs connected to the arteries (in much the same way you don't want clogs in your home's pipes or water pressure so high that it causes your faucets to explode).

Unfortunately, these "pipes" can become damaged and inflamed. A substance called plaque can build up in the walls of arteries, causing them to become narrowed and stiff. If major arteries in your neck that carry blood to your brain become narrowed, your brain can become starved for fuel and oxygen. This can hamper your thinking and memory, and it can injure or even kill brain cells.

If a clot forms in your bloodstream and gets hung up in a narrowed artery in your brain, it can cause a transient ischemic attack (TIA, also known as a "ministroke") or even a full-fledged stroke. Strokes are a major threat to brain health in America. They can be fatal, and many stroke survivors are left with lingering cognitive problems and disability.

So-called vascular dementia can occur by itself or along with Alzheimer's disease. It can develop after a series of blockages in blood vessels in the brain, even tiny ones. According to the Alzheimer's Association, early symptoms of vascular dementia often include impaired judgment and inability to make plans.

In the heart, narrowed arteries can cause chest pain, and a clot that completely blocks an artery can cause a heart attack. This type of plumbing problem can also cause erectile dysfunction if it occurs in the penis or pain and damage in the legs if the arteries leading to them become narrow.

Regardless of which organs are affected by unhealthy arteries, here's something important to keep in mind: *they're all connected to the same plumbing system*! If arteries in your heart, your neck, or your legs become diseased, you have reason to worry about your brain's health. Along the same lines, the steps you take to protect your heart or your cardiovascular system in general will be *crucial* for protecting the flow of blood to your brain.

The following issues are major sources of damage within the cardiovascular system, which is why the Brain Fix plan is aimed at preventing or treating them:

- High blood sugar and insulin (including the levels of blood sugar and insulin seen with prediabetes and diabetes)
- High "bad" LDL cholesterol and low "good" HDL cholesterol
- High blood pressure
- Obesity
- High sodium consumption
- Lack of exercise

Stress, Anxiety, and Depression

Multiple times during each day, you encounter events that could possibly threaten your safety or well-being. These include other cars pulling up to a four-way stop while you're driving, unexplained loud noises in another room, or a worrisome e-mail from your boss in your inbox at work.

Your brain is the key organ that copes with these stressors, since it interprets whether these issues are threatening to your survival. And your brain determines your physical and behavioral response to these factors. Your brain may prompt your endocrine system to produce more cortisol, the so-called stress hormone, if you feel threatened. (Your endocrine system is a set of glands scattered throughout your body; major ones include the hypothalamus and pituitary in your brain, and your adrenal glands on your kidneys.)

The cortisol serves as a chemical messenger that gets multiple body systems switched over to fight the threat or flee from it (even if it's more of a minor hassle like someone taking a long time in the checkout line in front of you, a screaming child on an airplane, or that e-mail from your boss).

Your cortisol level may increase by as much as *five times* when you're facing a stressful event. It increases blood flow to your muscles, raises your blood pressure, and boosts oxygen and glucose to your brain so you can think faster. Sounds like a wonderful hormone, right? Well, it *is* useful momentarily. But chronic worry, stress, and even depression cause us to pump out cortisol continuously.

Over the long term, cortisol causes a decrease in blood flow, oxygen, and glucose to the brain. This can lead to loss of neurons, shrinkage of the brain, and trouble thinking. Cortisol can also affect brain cells' ability to communicate, in part by impacting neurotransmitters, brain circuits, the branching of dendrites, and neuron regeneration.

In people with Alzheimer's disease, cortisol levels are directly related to the level of cognitive impairment. More cortisol equals more trouble thinking, in other words. In addition, chronic psychological stress is linked to faster shortening of telomeres, which are caps on the ends of chromosomes. (Yes, stress directly affects even your genetic material!) This leads to accelerated aging.

Stress causes regions of your brain to undergo *remodeling*, such as the amygdala (which leads to an increased fear response), the hippocampus (leading to impaired memory), and the prefrontal cortex (leading to changes in your decision-making and attention).

Your brain is resilient, and it will make every effort to repair itself when it can. But over time, repeated stressful episodes—or situations that shouldn't be a big deal, but lead you to overreact with an unnecessary burst of cortisol—can cause changes in your brain that lead to less mental flexibility and more difficulty paying attention, remembering events, and learning new information.

That's why the Brain Fix plan emphasizes changes in your lifestyle that will help you better resist stress and anxiety and their frequent traveling companion of depression. These include:

- Keeping your blood sugar steady to ensure that your cognitive power stays sharp and you feel refreshed. This will help you handle stress better.
- Getting enough sleep.
- Getting regular exercise, which helps you cope better with stress. Exercise can also treat depression and help you sleep better.
- Practicing natural stress-relieving mental exercises such as meditation and yoga.

Alzheimer's Disease

If you're going to fix your brain—and keep it well repaired—you'll want to make the changes that protect it from dementia. The most common form of dementia is Alzheimer's disease. Roughly 13 percent of Americans over the age of sixty-five have Alzheimer's. After age eighty-five, nearly half have it. Given that our population is living longer than previous generations did, and the Baby Boomers are reaching their senior years now, by the year 2040 our nation is expected to have ten times more beds in nursing homes compared to hospitals!

Alzheimer's is an inflammatory condition. During Alzheimer's, glial cells—which are there to support neurons—become activated. As a result, the glial cells change their shape and become cells called macrophages. They start churning out inflammatory chemicals and other substances. These chemicals affect the production of a substance called beta amyloid protein. This accumulates in clusters called plaques, which ultimately destroy neurons. Plaques develop quickly and cause relatively focused damage to nearby neurons.

However, the amyloidal plaques don't just affect neurons in their immediate vicinity. They also increase the activity of astrocytes, which are cells in the nervous system that support your brain's function. Astrocytes can become hyperactive throughout the brain. As a result, plaques can affect distant areas of the brain via the astrocytes.

In addition to the plaque, tangles can form within neurons in structures called the microtubules. The microtubules' job is to convey nutrients and other necessary substances within the neuron. These tangles interrupt the flow of these necessary chemicals inside the neuron, eventually causing cell death.

After the plaques and tangles appear, they seem to irritate the brain, causing the release of chemicals that can kill brain cells. As the disease grows worse, more neurons die, leading to worsening symptoms. Damage begins in the hippocampus and parts of the brain that control language, memory, and your ability to perceive the world around you.

Cholesterol raises beta amyloid production, so lowering your cholesterol might reduce the production of these plaque-building proteins. In addition, you'll find other steps throughout *The Brain Fix* that might protect you from Alzheimer's (like avoiding big crests in your body's insulin levels. That's the next topic!).

Poor Blood Sugar Control

America is facing an unprecedented wave of type 2 diabetes. About 26 million Americans already have this disease, while 79 million have *pre*diabetes, meaning they're at higher risk of getting diabetes.

During type 2 diabetes, the body doesn't respond well to its natural supply of insulin from the pancreas. Your pancreas naturally releases this hormone after you eat, and the resulting increase in blood sugar from eating can make its way into your body's cells.

If you have this disease, the insulin can't do its job, so blood sugar levels stay high, which is harmful. The pancreas pumps out more insulin to try to get the blood sugar to fall, and this excess insulin in your blood causes its own problems. Eventually, the pancreas can get tired from all this work and start to malfunction. (Type 1 diabetes is an autoimmune disease in which the immune system destroys cells in the pancreas. It's not considered to be preventable like the more common type 2 diabetes. From now on, "diabetes" refers to type 2.)

The high blood sugar that occurs with diabetes is toxic to brain cells. Plus, it damages blood vessels, which reduces the flow of blood and sets the stage for blockages in the vessels. This can lead to declines in mental sharpness and memory if it occurs to vessels in the brain. High insulin also encourages beta amyloid plaques, which, as mentioned earlier, are harmful to brain cells. Having too much insulin circulating may also lead to the accelerated death of neurons in the brain.

Research has found that people with metabolic syndrome—a cluster of symptoms including high blood pressure, insulin resistance, and obesity around the midsection—have a higher risk of cognitive impairment. So implementing steps that keep your blood sugar regulated could help prevent declines in your brainpower. That's why you'll find many solutions in *The Brain Fix* to prevent high blood sugar, diabetes, and prediabetes, such as:

- How to eat a diet that provides the nutrients your brain needs without a lot of extra calories that lead to weight gain, which is a major risk factor for diabetes.
- How to work regular physical activity into your life. Exercise helps keep your body's cells sensitive to the effects of insulin, which is good for your blood sugar. Exercise is also crucial for helping you stay fit.

Traumatic Brain Injury

Your brain is not a physically durable organ. In fact, it has the consistency of yogurt or tofu. Imagine what would happen at the supermarket if you just tossed containers of yogurt into your cart, then piled cases of sodas and big cans of food on top of them. They'd be easily damaged. The same is true for our brains. About 1.7 million Americans develop traumatic brain injuries every year. These include concussions, which are a form of mild brain injury. Symptoms of concussion typically include confusion, blurry vision, difficulty concentrating, nausea, and memory problems.

Even a mild injury that doesn't knock you out can be responsible for substantial damage to your brain. A strike to your head can cause fragile brain tissue to bounce against the inner walls of your skull. This can tear tiny blood vessels, leading to bleeding and scarring in the brain. Even an incident that simply causes your head to whip or spin quickly can cause a brain injury.

A head injury can cause a decrease in blood flow to the brain, as well as impairment of communication between brain cells. Neurotransmitters that excite the neurons—such as glutamate—increase. This leads nerve cells to rapidly fire off and become so excited that they become injured. The brain suddenly starts working in a frenzy just as blood flow is reduced, robbing it of the oxygen and glucose it needs.

Some damage from brain injury is reversible, such as the alterations in the way the neurons are working. However, long-term effects of head injuries can include psychiatric problems, loss of long-term memory, and a higher risk of Alzheimer's disease.

It's important to get prompt medical care for traumatic brain injuries, even concussions. Afterward, people need plenty of rest and recuperation. More severe cases of brain injury may require physical and occupational therapy. Following the diet and lifestyle approaches throughout the Brain Fix plan are also crucial for recovering from brain injury.

The Legal Drugs: Tobacco and Alcohol

If you've ever tossed back a little too much alcohol, or you've seen someone else do it, you probably aren't surprised to learn that alcohol affects the brain. Drinking can cause slowed reaction times, slurred speech, difficulty following what's going on around you, and poor coordination. But alcohol has more of an impact on your brain than just these immediate symptoms.

Even drinking alcohol at a moderate level leads to lower brain volume. If people drink more alcohol on a regular basis, their brain volume decreases even more. Since women are more sensitive to alcohol and absorb it faster, they have slightly more brain shrinkage.

Your brain is able to repair *some* of the damage. However, if you drink heavily for too long, your brain becomes less able to regenerate and respond to the damage. Alcohol consumption has many specific effects in your brain that you may not have realized:

- It causes the neurotransmitter glutamate to become less effective. This leads you to feel sluggish.
- It destroys omega-3 fatty acids. These are used as a building block in the membranes of your nerve cells (which are the walls surrounding each neuron). The omega-3s are also important for good cell-to-cell communication.
- Alcohol locks onto receptors in the brain that are intended to serve as attachment points for a substance called GABA. This keeps the GABA from attaching to receptors, which causes it to flood the brain. As a result, the excess GABA causes these receptors to become less sensitive or even decrease in number.
- The symptoms of drinking that are so familiar are due to very precise changes in the brain. Alcohol affects the cerebral cortex, slowing down how you process the information coming in from your eyes. Your behaviors become less inhibited, and your usual judgment becomes poorer. It damages your cerebellum, causing problems with your fine motor skills.

Over the long term, drinking too much alcohol causes a lingering impact on your brain's limbic system. This can leave you anxious and depressed.

Having a little alcohol—just a maximum of a drink or two a day—may be beneficial for your heart health. But alcohol's powerful effects on your brain's health mean that you should be very wary of the dangers of excessive drinking. If you drink too much—even if it's just a *little* too much—getting a lid on your alcohol consumption may be an important element of your Brain Fix plan.

As far as smoking goes, *any* amount is too much. Cigarettes contain thousands of chemicals, and many of them are toxic to your body and brain. The tobacco in cigarettes (and other types of smoking products) impairs, changes, and damages your brain. Smoking can cause loss of brain volume in regions that are responsible for attention, memory, higher-level thinking, and learning. It has a particular effect on a part of the brain called the medial orbital frontal cortex, which leaves you less able to control impulses and make decisions. Smoking has even been found to lower people's intelligence!

In addition:

- The more cigarettes people smoke per day and the more years they smoke, the thinner their brain's cerebral cortex becomes.
- Your brain gets to grab a substantial portion of the oxygen in each breath you take. That's because it needs a considerable supply of oxygen to keep its cells working properly. However, chemicals in tobacco smoke clog up your lungs, preventing sufficient oxygen from reaching your bloodstream. As a result, your brain gets less oxygen, which leads brain cells to die prematurely.
- A substance in tobacco called NNK causes white blood cells in the brain to trigger inflammation, which harms healthy neurons.
- Secondhand smoke is linked to a *doubled* risk of having major depression. Breathing other people's smoke may also increase the risk of memory problems and dementia after the age of fifty.
- Nicotine can kill cells in a part of the brain called the fasciculus retroflexus, which is responsible for willpower and self-control.

Nineteen percent of American adults still smoke cigarettes. Maybe you're one of them. If so, you're probably aware of the many well-known reasons why you should quit, such as to reduce your risk of lung cancer and heart disease. I don't want to be yet another person who's beating you over the head with more stern warnings that you should stop. Just keep in mind that if you stop smoking, it will have a positive impact on your brain.

The book's last chapter is dedicated to changing your mind-set and finally conquering ingrained behaviors, such as smoking, overeating, and other issues that are making your brain less healthy.

The Not-So-Legal Drugs

Illicit drug use is common in America. In 2009, 8.7 percent of Americans ages twelve and older had used an illicit drug in the previous month. In many cases, these drugs are illegal because they're harmful to your health, including your brain health. Let's take a look at some drugs that are more commonly used and abused.

Marijuana

Your brain has a neurotransmitter called anandamide, which latches onto cannabinoid receptors on neurons and triggers them to behave in a certain way. Does that make you think of *cannabis*? If so, you're onto something important.

Cannabinoid receptors are scattered throughout the brain in spots like your hippocampus, hypothalamus, and cerebellum. A chemical called THC in marijuana is the main substance in the plant that affects the brain. THC can work like anandamide—or keep it from doing its own job. This can affect your motor coordination, mood, and short-term memory. It can also make you paranoid (incidentally, these are all major symptoms of marijuana use).

Marijuana suppresses anandamide receptors in different parts of your brain. These receptors normally help keep a lid on your brain's dopamine, thus preventing you from lapsing into an eternal state of ecstasy that would keep you from living a normal life. Thus, this drug leaves your dopamine system unopposed, which is why people sometimes find everything around them so amusing after smoking marijuana.

In addition, marijuana can:

• Increase your heart rate and blood pressure.
• Increase the distance between nerves in a synapse. This means messages need longer to travel across the synaptic gap, which can slow your movements. Your brain tries to make up for this by pumping out more neurotransmitter chemicals. When you come down off the marijuana and the distance in the synapses shrinks, you're left with excess neurotransmitter. You may feel irritable, keyed-up, and have trouble sleeping.
• Cause changes in your personality, difficulty motivating yourself to take action, and trouble concentrating.
• Cause a permanent drop in IQ points if you use it daily for a long period.
• Increase the risk of depression and suicidal thoughts in young people who smoke it regularly.

- Have a toxic effect on your brain if you use it heavily. Research has found the hippocampus and amygdala to be smaller in long-time pot users. These areas handle emotion, memory, learning, fear, and aggression.

As far as illicit drugs go, our society tends to regard marijuana with a special fondness and tolerance. However, this is not the benign drug that many people make it out to be. And the symptoms that many people find so enjoyable—the mellowness, absentmindedness, and sensation of being easily amused—are signs that the brain is being affected in a worrisome way.

Opioids

Your body produces natural painkillers called *endorphins*. These signal nerves in your spinal cord to stop sending pain messages to your brain after they're no longer useful in alerting you to an injury. A variety of drugs are similar in structure to these natural painkillers, including morphine, codeine, heroin, and oxycodone.

Opioid drugs can become addictive because they bind to receptors in the emotional part of the brain, causing the release of the feel-good, euphoria-spurring neurotransmitter dopamine. This gives the person a sense of pleasure and well-being. But if you start taking a prescription opioid to treat pain—say your leg is severely injured in an accident—the injured cells in your leg eventually change to protect themselves from the effects of the painkiller.

The cells become even more sensitive to pain, and this hypersensitivity to the pain can last even after the injury heals. Meanwhile, the function of GABA receptors becomes ramped down. These receptors play a role in reducing anxiety and fostering a sense of well-being. This can lead a person to want to take larger amounts of the drug to feel good. After about two weeks, people may become dependent on the drug.

The same thing can happen with people taking illicit opioid drugs. They need more and more to get the same pleasurable effect. If they try to stop taking the drug, they develop withdrawal. Their bodies cannot respond to their natural painkilling endorphins because they now have a lower number of receptors for them. However, receptors in the brain that play a role in discomfort and a sense of unhappiness are still working just fine! As a result, during withdrawal, everything hurts— including the user's eyes and hair. The mere act of digesting food can be painful. Their heart rate goes up and their ability to sleep goes down. They're restless, anxious, depressed, and feel like they have the worst flu that's ever struck them.

As a result, they may go seeking some other drug to help them feel better. Or they may go back to opioids. That's why recovering from opiate addiction is often so tough. But recovery is necessary for restoring brain health. Other changes in the brain linked to opiate use include:

- The creation of substances called peroxynitrites. These trigger inflammation and damage to DNA and proteins in neurons. Phytonutrients in fruits and vegetables, however, may keep these substances from forming or encourage them to decompose more quickly.
- Decreases in attention, memory recall, concentration, movement, and vision tasks.
- Difficulty sleeping.
- Changes in the body's breathing patterns, including breathing while asleep.

Methamphetamines and Cocaine

Methamphetamine ("meth") and cocaine (including crack) belong to a large class of drugs called stimulants. They have a similar effect on mood, and people can abuse these or become dependent on them easily. In animals—and maybe humans—methamphetamine and cocaine are toxic to neurons that produce dopamine and serotonin.

When a person uses meth, his or her brain will start churning out dopamine. This may continue for twelve hours or more until the body can break down the meth and get rid of it. In the meantime, the dopamine is latching onto receptors in the brain and turning on a sensation of euphoria. Eventually, the dopamine levels fall, leading to a "crash" that leaves the user feeling worn-out, depressed, and unmotivated.

Cocaine use also causes the release of large amounts of dopamine. When one neuron releases too much of this neurotransmitter, the next cell isn't able to handle it. And the cell that created it can't soak it back up. As a result, the dopamine lingers in this space, continuing to send its signal. At this time, the user feels euphoric. But the drug eventually wears off and the brain gets rid of the excess dopamine after two to four hours. As a result, the user crashes into depression. Unlike the quick burst of euphoria, this crash lasts longer because the brain needs time to replace its dopamine stores.

These drugs can cause lingering harmful effects in the brain. For example, cocaine can:

- Cause high blood pressure that can lead to a stroke.
- Damage the structure called the fasciculus retroflexus. This area houses your sense of self-control. If it's damaged, the user just doesn't care about his or her usual concerns, like paying bills, taking care of the kids, or obeying laws. This damage also leads to paranoia. The damage isn't permanent, but it can linger for some time.

Eating Disorders

People with eating disorders tend to have striking changes in their physical appearance. They grow thin, and their malnutrition can affect their skin coloring, hair texture, and facial features. But eating disorders such as anorexia also involve—or sometimes cause—changes in the brain:

- People with anorexia have been found to have wider ventricles (which are natural channels and open spaces in the brain through which fluid constantly flows) and wider sulci (the spaces between the outer folds of the brain that give it its familiar "brainlike" appearance).
- People with anorexia may have loss of brain tissue. In one study, people with anorexia had an average gray matter volume of about 648 milliliters, compared to 680 milliliters in healthy people without anorexia. People who'd had anorexia the longest had the

greatest decrease in gray matter volume. (Gray matter is a type of brain tissue.) Once they began eating again and their body weight went up, their brains started growing bigger. As a result, it appears that anorexia causes these changes, not vice versa.

* In people with anorexia, eating worsens their anxiety, and refusing to eat relieves it. These individuals may have an abnormal serotonin system (serotonin is the natural neurotransmitter that acts to calm you and keep you from being depressed). This may make them more likely to restrict their eating. The dopamine in their brains may also not work correctly. This may keep them from feeling the usual reward that most of us feel after we eat.

In sum, a *lot* of problems can affect your brain health—some that seem obvious (like taking illegal drugs), and some that might not be so immediately apparent (like having high blood sugar linked to obesity).

The pessimistic person might look at all these factors that can keep the brain from working well and say, "What hope do I have of turning back this tide of problems that could knock my brain out of kilter?" But for each of these problems you'll find many solutions. *All* of these insults to your brain can either be prevented (for example, by keeping a healthy weight, eating a plant-based diet, exercising regularly, and never starting to smoke) or treated (such as resting after a brain injury, taking an antianxiety medication, and meditating to treat depression).

The rest of *The Brain Fix* will now show you how!

THE BRAIN FIX TOOLBOX

- In general, problems that affect your body affect your brain, too. These include high blood pressure, diabetes, high cholesterol, heart disease, smoking, and eating disorders. What hurts you from the neck down will hurt you from the neck up, too.

- The steps that help you prevent chronic diseases—the commonsense approaches like eating a sensible diet, not becoming overweight, and getting enough sleep—will also fix your brain and keep it well repaired.

- Problems that affect your mind or mood can also have very real effects on the structure and function of your brain. For example, illicit drugs, or even prescription drugs that are abused, leave the brain in need of healing. Stress and depression also make a visible mark on structures in the brain. To fix your brain, you'll want to take steps to fix all these issues.

PART 2

Diet and
Supplements

3

Antioxidants: For Good Brain Health, Sometimes You Have to Go Out on a Limb

MORE THAN TWO THOUSAND YEARS ago, Hippocrates—often honored as the father of medicine—pronounced, "Let food be your medicine, and medicine be your food." Even before *his* time, wise folks were already realizing that prevention is better than treatment. Just look at a Chinese proverb credited to Chi Po in 2500 BC that warned: "Taking medicine only when you are sick is like digging a well only when you are thirsty; it is already too late." Traditional Asian folk medicine hews to the belief that certain foods seem to benefit healing, reduce symptoms, or make one feel better. A common assumption was that a Creator would not expose mankind to diseases without supplying natural remedies necessary for their cure.

When ancient cultures noticed positive outcomes from their natural medicine, they passed on this information to younger people. When the benefits of these treatments persisted from generation to generation, they became woven into folklore that exists to this day.

Long ago, healing foods were thought to be endowed with unique and mystical powers sent by gods. Nowadays, foods with healing properties are subject to more scrutiny. Scientists can analyze compounds in plants in the lab or look at the eating habits of thousands of people—or even hundreds of thousands—to see if certain foods may raise our risk of disease or protect us from illness.

We now know that the foods you eat play a vital role in repairing your brain or keeping it in good condition. Just as a poor diet of junk food and fast food, with nary a fruit or vegetable crossing your plate, will cause your body to function poorly and break down, eating this way will affect your brain in much the same manner.

So why haven't you already heard more about the effects of healthy eating regarding your brain health? Well, a big reason is because no one is making much money on natural brain-healing treatments. To be able to make health claims, a pharmaceutical or nutraceutical company needs to invest a minimum of $4.8 million and fifteen years of research. About one in one thousand new products makes it past the clinical trials to measure a product's safety and efficacy. Only one in five of those will be approved for sale. Once a natural product has made it to where its manufacturer can make health claims, any other company can make the same claim without ever having to spend a cent or expend one second of its time! You cannot patent a food (the category that most botanicals are placed in); therefore, it is possible for *anyone* to sell the very same botanical product and capitalize on the hard work and research of others.

So that's one reason why you don't hear a lot about the simple, natural steps you can take to help heal your own brain: there aren't many companies in the business of marketing and promoting brain-healing options. In addition, the Food and Drug Administration (FDA) allows only a handful of limited health claims for foods, including:

- Calcium and vitamin D to prevent osteoporosis
- Foods low in sodium to reduce the risk of high blood pressure
- Foods low in saturated fat and cholesterol to reduce the risk of heart disease
- A diet rich in fruits, vegetables, and fiber-containing grain products to reduce the risk of cancer
- Soy protein for reducing the risk of heart disease
- Potassium for reducing the risk of high blood pressure and stroke
- Fluoridated water for reducing the risk of cavities

Finally, if you pay attention to the stream of news headlines as they pass by, you might have gotten the notion that foods—or nutrients found in foods—don't help prevent or treat *anything*. In recent years, we've heard that:

- Vitamin E doesn't decrease heart disease or cancer, and it may even cause heart failure.

- Echinacea doesn't prevent or fight colds.
- Green tea doesn't reduce the risk of heart disease.
- Fiber doesn't prevent colon cancer.
- Garlic doesn't reduce LDL cholesterol.
- Ginkgo doesn't improve memory.
- Ginseng doesn't improve well-being.
- Duct tape doesn't cure warts.

As a result, it would be understandable if you told yourself, *Why should I even bother doing anything to improve my health? Some study is just going to show that what I'm doing isn't helpful and may even be harmful.*

This being said, however, numerous studies on fruits and vegetables *do* support their value in health. There are more than 300,000 research papers on the importance of increasing fruit and vegetable consumption. Consider that each year Americans have 935,000 heart attacks, 795,000 strokes, and that 76 million adults have high blood pressure. If more people consumed a diet rich in fruits and vegetables, these numbers could be greatly reduced!

When we talk about heart disease, stroke, high blood pressure, and high cholesterol, remember that *all* these factors have a major effect on your brain's health. Maintaining good circulation through your arteries is key for good brain functioning. So helping your brain heal and thrive requires taking steps that are good for your cardiovascular system. And the foods you eat—or avoid—play a crucial role in determining how well your circulatory system works. This has been proven many times:

- A study from 2011 that followed more than 313,000 European men and women for about eight years found that those eating eight or more servings of fruits and vegetables daily had a 22 percent lower risk of fatal heart disease compared to those who ate less than three servings. Each daily serving was linked to a 4 percent lower risk.
- A 2007 study that combined earlier studies found that people who bumped up their consumption of fruits and vegetables from less than three to more than five servings each day could lower their risk of coronary heart disease by 17 percent, providing "strong support" for recommending that we eat at least five servings daily.

- Green leafy vegetables and vitamin C–rich fruits and vegetables may be especially good for preventing coronary heart disease, according to a 2001 study from the *Annals of Internal Medicine*.
- Eating more dark yellow and green leafy vegetables may help prevent type 2 diabetes in overweight women, according to a 2004 study. People with diabetes have a markedly higher risk of heart disease and stroke.

The antioxidants in fruits and vegetables may reduce the oxidation of the bad LDL cholesterol that clogs arteries and boosts heart attack risk (we'll see later how this gunk in the arteries becomes even more dangerous when free radicals "oxidize" it).

Strokes are a major killer of nerve cells in the brain. According to the American Heart Association, roughly 7 million Americans have survived a stroke, often with significant lingering brain injury. A Brain Fix diet plan, however, can help protect you from this threat. For example, another study including 258,000 people that involved eight earlier studies found that people who ate more than five servings of fruits and vegetables had a 26 percent lower risk of stroke than people who ate less than three daily.

A diet rich in fruits and vegetables is a cornerstone for reducing high blood pressure, which is an important factor that triggers strokes. And if you do suffer a stroke, this diet may help limit its devastating impact. Rats that were fed a diet high in fruits and vegetables had less brain cell loss and better recovery of movement after a stroke, for example. The antioxidant and anti-inflammatory components of fruits and vegetables may decrease injury to nerve cells and death from a stroke.

History Teaches Us Why Plants Are Crucial for Brain Health

So how do fruits and vegetables contribute to health? For starters, they're excellent sources of vitamins and minerals. But you could actually obtain these from a multiple vitamin and mineral supplement. Why bother with the whole piece of fruit? It's true that the vitamin C you obtain from an orange is no different than what you get in pill form.

Well, fruits and vegetables are excellent sources of fiber, but so are bran or psyllium supplements. Plant foods contain fructose and various sugars, but these don't provide more energy than other carbohydrates. And water in fruits and vegetables is simply H_2O, just like you get from a tap.

To understand what makes fruits and vegetables so valuable to your brain, you have to look deeper. And you have to focus on their less visible ingredients. Their overwhelming benefit comes from the vast array of chemicals they contain called *phytonutrients*. These mostly provide antioxidant and anti-inflammatory benefits for your body and brain.

Researchers are still trying to figure out all the ways that phytonutrients can help keep us healthy. Originating from the Greek word *phyto*, which means "plant," phytonutrients aren't essential for our lives, as are traditional nutrients like vitamins, minerals, protein, carbohydrates, and fats. But what they do is represent ammunition against a hostile world, which plants know all about.

In plants, phytonutrients provide defenses against yeast, molds, parasites, bacteria, fungi, and viruses. Nature itself can provide a hostile environment with constant fluctuations, from floods to droughts. The sun shines down with damaging radiation, and plants can't put on sunscreen or uproot themselves and find shade. Nor can they avoid pollutants and toxins in the environment. Add to this the challenge of competing plants, and it is easy to see why plants face unending threats to their existence. Only the hardiest of plants will end up surviving and flourishing, and it's due in part to the chemicals they contain.

Plants—and later, humans and other animals—have been making use of these life-preserving chemicals since the dawn of time. About 4.5 billion years ago, the only gases in our atmosphere were hydrogen, methane, and carbon dioxide. What was missing that humans would need for life? That's right—oxygen. The sky had a distinct lack of oxygen until a tiny plant called cyanobacteria appeared on the scene. Unlike us, it *didn't* have a brain. But it was able to convert carbon dioxide, sunlight, and water into carbohydrates through a process called photosynthesis. At the same time, it released oxygen into the atmosphere.

Humanity's thanks to cyanobacteria—which we now call "blue-green algae"—is long overdue. While oxygen enables us to breathe (and thus live), it comes with a downside. The oxygen that cyanobacteria created reacted with the surrounding gases and produced free radicals that could destroy the very plant that produced the oxygen. It took another two billion years before the cyanobacteria "learned" how to produce antioxidants to protect themselves from the free radicals that promoted oxidation. The protective antioxidant was contained in the pigment that gave the plant its color. About 500 million years ago, multicelled plants began appearing with a variety of pigments, and thus a variety of antioxidants.

When animals ate the plants, the protection the plants contained was now passed on to them. The same is true now. Herbivores—which are plant-eating animals—consume a generous amount of these plants. When they do, they incorporate the same phytonutrient protection against pathogens and environmental threats. Plants are available to humans, too, as sort of nature's medicine chest, stocked with antibacterial, antiviral, antimicrobial, anticlotting, antipain, and antiaging chemicals. Experts often say that phytonutrients "boost, stimulate and modify" the immune system. These chemicals are pretty much "anti-anything" that is bad for us. In other words, they provide a "cure looking for a disease."

So if you want a healthy body and brain, you'll want to bump up the amount of this protection you get. Even though plants contain chemicals that answer many of our needs, they're especially crucial for protecting you from the free radicals that are constantly attacking your brain and the arteries that feed it.

Freeing Yourself from the Danger of Free Radicals

Every minute of our lives, the oxygen we breathe is combining with the food we eat to produce energy. That's good. Energy keeps us going. But this process also produces free radicals. That's both good and bad. These free radicals are found within white blood cells, and they serve to wipe out disease-causing germs such as invading bacteria and viruses. Furthermore, free radicals are crucial to our immune systems' ability to rid our bodies of cancer cells.

But free radicals are also a devastating weapon that can be turned against us. To limit the destruction that free radicals can cause in our bodies, our cells are equipped with a system of antioxidant enzymes that keep the radicals in check.

However, a lot of factors in our environment can produce more free radicals than this system is able to handle. These include pollution, tobacco smoke, addictive drugs, industrial chemicals, stress, obesity, food additives such as nitrates, pesticides, infections, sunlight, and radiation from x-rays. Even exercise and the mineral iron can add to our free radical load!

To understand a free radical and how it creates destruction, visualize an atom with electrons circulating around its nucleus. As long as the electrons are available in pairs, they are neutral and harmless. But if a single electron is removed, the remaining electron seeks a companion. This atom is now called a free radical (also known as a reactive oxygen species, or ROS). Since they're missing an electron, these atoms try to take one from another. Thus, a free radical is an atom or molecule that's zipping around in search of an electron to steal from another.

They're *relentless* in their pursuit of electrons. When a free radical takes an electron from another atom, *that* atom can then go searching for another atom to rob. This can disrupt the normal activity in a cell.

The effect of free radicals in the body is called *oxidation*. When oxidation becomes excessive, it damages cells, which can affect their structure and function. Over time, heavy oxidation can result in more than fifty chronic degenerative diseases like Alzheimer's disease, atherosclerosis, cancer, diabetes, chronic obstructive pulmonary disease, arthritis, and skin aging.

Some examples of *how* free radicals trigger disease may be helpful at this point. Rusting is a prime example of oxidation. If you leave a shovel out in the rain or allow water to puddle in an unseasoned cast-iron pan, you know what happens: it'll soon be blotchy with rust. Even though it's much softer and squishier than a pan or shovel, your brain is very vulnerable to this kind of deterioration, too! The iron in your brain is a prime target for free-radical damage—and it also provides a good reason for you to take steps to protect yourself from this damage.

Free radicals also injure the cells that line blood vessels. This allows cholesterol to collect at the site, which can cause arteries to grow narrow.

If blood vessels leading to your brain grow narrow, this can lead you to have trouble thinking and remembering things. If a blood clot attaches in the tightened artery, it can cause a stroke.

In addition, the DNA within cells that guides their function can also become mutated by free-radical damage. The altered cells can then multiply as a cancerous tumor, which then migrates and causes a drain on the body that eventually leads to death.

Picture a vandal entering a furniture manufacturing plant and changing the blueprints so that chairs are built with two less legs. The two-legged chairs are mass manufactured and transported all over the country. No one has a need for a two-legged chair any more than they need mutated cells that don't work well. With a worthless product, the company can no longer survive. And with too many "worthless" cancer cells, people can't survive either. About 22,000 Americans developed cancer in the brain or other parts of the nervous system in 2011, and about 13,000 died of these cancers.

In addition, the ends of chromosomes in your DNA—called telomeres—are shortened by free-radical damage. The shorter the telomere becomes, the shorter the life of the cell. Once a telomere gets too short, cell reproduction and functioning stops. This accelerates aging, dementia, arthritis, graying of the hair, wrinkles, and other problems.

As I mentioned earlier, your body does have a system of enzymes that help limit damage from free radicals. (By the way, some of these enzymes contain minerals such as copper, zinc, selenium, and manganese, and this serves as a reminder of why minerals are important in our diet.) Just one molecule of certain types of antioxidant enzyme has the ability to neutralize up to a million free radicals! However, as you get older, your supply of protective enzymes diminishes, and those that remain aren't as effective

Clearly, the free-radical defense system your body tries to keep going isn't foolproof. To add *another* layer of protection, you should also keep your body brimming with antioxidants at all times.

Antioxidants: Your Weapon Against Oxidation from Free Radicals

Antioxidants don't eliminate the creation of free radicals, or even reduce their production (that would be impossible). Free-radical production is unavoidable, and since these play a necessary role in your body's function, you wouldn't even *want* to eliminate them. What we need to focus on instead is which substances we can put into our bodies that are most powerful at scavenging free radicals that are already zipping around in there and causing damage from your brain down to your toes.

Antioxidants work by neutralizing these free radicals. Remember: once a free radical attempts to become stable by grabbing electrons from other molecules, it causes *those* molecules to become unstable in turn. This sparks a chain reaction that can cause major cell damage. The antioxidant steps in to donate an electron to make the free radical stable again. Then the free radical gets passed along an assembly line or bucket brigade of antioxidants that continue to neutralize one another until they are eradicated from the body or the antioxidant is sacrificed as a consequence of loaning an electron.

Think of all this like heating your home with a wood-burning fireplace that doesn't have a screen or glass doors. Over time, hot sparks and cinders fly out and burn tiny holes in your carpet. Eventually, the carpet can no longer do its job, which is to cover the floor in an attractive manner. The same thing happens to your brain and other tissues when free radicals "burn" tiny holes throughout. But if you place a metal mesh curtain across the opening to keep in the sparks—which represents our antioxidant shield—your carpet will stay fresh and new.

However, free radicals come in many varieties. Various free radicals must be dealt with in different types of tissues, including epithelial cells that line organs and other structures, such as blood vessels, collagen in your skin, and even your hair follicles. Free radicals also travel in different substances in your body, such as fat and water. One type of antioxidant won't defend you equally as well across all these playing fields. As a result, you want to make sure you get a rich blend of antioxidants that can address different types of free radicals in different locations.

We've talked a lot about the importance of antioxidants to combat free radicals in general. Here's why they're especially important in your brain. The brain is very vulnerable to free-radical oxidation for three reasons:

- The predominant fuel source for the brain is carbohydrate—in particular, blood sugar, also known as glucose. Carbohydrates are very efficient at producing energy in the presence of oxygen. Since the brain needs lots of oxygen to burn glucose, it is capable of producing a *large* number of free radicals.
- Much of the brain's weight is composed of unsaturated fatty acids. *Unsaturated* means these fatty acids have a bond in their chemical structure that is available for molecules like oxygen to attach to. Think about leaving an open bag of potato chips on the counter, exposed to the room air, before you leave for vacation. When you come back, they'll be rancid (in other words, oxidized). This ruins the quality of the chips. For the same reason, the high oxygen content of the brain makes it vulnerable to becoming "rancid" as well. Antioxidants, however, stabilize and maintain the integrity of these fatty acids that account for a good deal of your brain's structure. In other words, they keep your brain fresh!
- Since the brain requires a great deal of the body's total blood flow, it doesn't just have a constant source of oxygen. It also has a healthy amount of something else found in the blood: iron. And remember, what does iron do very easily? That's right—it rusts. Rusting is a textbook example of oxidation, and the high iron content of your brain makes it highly susceptible to this deterioration.

In your brain, the free radicals zipping around can easily damage neurons. Eventually this can result in memory loss, slow learning, and poor coordination. A young, healthy brain has a ready supply of natural antioxidants that neutralize these damaging free radicals. But as we get older, the level of our antioxidant enzyme shield diminishes, and our brains become an easy target for injury. If you subject your brain to an addiction, an eating disorder, or the other factors discussed earlier that act as free-radical factories, you'll be at risk of additional damage.

Another destructive process that goes hand in hand with our discussion of free radicals is *inflammation*. Remember those sparks popping out of the fireplace in the analogy given earlier? This also provides a good way of understanding inflammation. Your body contains an inner fire that can be a force of good, but it can also rage out of control and severely damage your body and brain. Eating fruits and vegetables and other antioxidant-rich plant foods can help keep *it* harnessed, too.

Dampening the Fire of Inflammation

Inflammation can strike throughout your body. Whenever you have a condition containing the letters "-itis," it means some kind of tissue is inflamed:

- Bursitis (involving a tissue in a joint called the bursa)
- Bronchitis (lung)
- Cystitis (bladder)
- Arthritis (joint)
- Nephritis (kidney)
- Endocarditis (heart)
- Vasculitis (blood vessels)
- Rhinitis (nose)
- Hepatitis (liver)
- Tonsillitis (tonsils)

Even tissues in and around your brain can become inflamed, such as with meningitis. But just like free radicals have a useful role in your body for attacking invaders, inflammation is *intended* to be a force for good. Inflammation helps your body heal from injuries and infections. It also helps you replace damaged tissues after these problems occur.

Your body's inflammatory response begins with a signal of pain to alert your defenses to where the injury is located. An army of white blood cells rallies and travels to the site of the injury through your bloodstream. This causes the tissue to become red. Fluids can escape their normal channels, which causes swelling. As your body tries to repair the damage, blood forms clots in the area. New tissues are generated and scarring develops.

The symptoms of inflammation—including the accumulation of white blood cells, pain, redness, swelling, and scarring—can be very helpful when they're really needed. But *none* are welcome when they become a constant condition in our lives.

Nevertheless, inflammation often silently smolders away in our body and brain without us feeling it anywhere in particular. When inflammation becomes chronic—persisting over time at a slow burn—it isn't protecting your tissues from damage. Now *it* is damaging cells and organs and leading to disease. Inflammation is no longer the solution but the cause of the problem.

Factors that trigger inflammation include infections from viruses and bacteria (that's a *good* use of the inflammatory response). But other situations that crop up in our everyday lives unleash inflammation that leads to harm over time. Free radicals cause inflammation, for example. These include free radicals that result from:

- Your body naturally turning fuel into energy
- Ultraviolet rays from the sun
- Pollution
- Drugs (including tobacco)
- Stress
- Insulin resistance (a problem that can lead to diabetes)
- Excess fat around your midsection

When your ankle is inflamed after you sprain it, you know it. It's hot, red, and painful. However, your brain has no pain receptors. You could literally poke your brain tissue with a fork and not feel a thing—but please don't! (Headache pain, by the way, comes from nerves in blood vessel walls being stretched to their maximum capacity. Your brain itself isn't hurting.) So inflammation can affect your brain without causing any pain in your head.

High levels of inflammation in your body are associated with problems with so-called executive thinking. This is the kind of higher-level thinking that makes us intelligent humans, such as planning, decision making, and self-control.

A 2010 study found that people with the highest levels of C-reactive protein, which is a marker of inflammation, needed seven more seconds to complete a cognitive test. These people also had changes in their brain that added up to the equivalent of twelve additional years of aging.

Our mood can affect our levels of inflammation. For example, research has found that depressed men have higher levels of inflammatory chemicals (in one study, men with depression had 46 percent higher C-reactive protein compared to men without depression). Anxiety can also cause levels of inflammatory chemicals to rise. So can hostility.

Just as antioxidants in your food fight free-radical damage, they can also help reduce inflammation. For example, researchers found that in baboons, vitamin E and coenzyme Q_{10} were associated with a drop in C-reactive protein. A study in older people found that getting more antioxidants (in the form of supplements) was also associated with better C-reactive protein levels. Which brings us to an important topic when discussing antioxidants: where should we get them?

The Best Way to Get Antioxidants Is in Their Natural Containers—Not Bottles

During the past two decades, Americans have gained more recognition of the importance of antioxidants in their diet. However, in some cases antioxidant nutrients have been overhyped and misused. Many nutritionists are optimistic about the role of antioxidants in disease prevention, yet we're realistic that we still need to learn a lot more about how they work.

The three most popular antioxidants that are taken in supplement form are:

- Beta-carotene
- Vitamin E
- Vitamin C

Promotional materials from supplement makers often would have you think that you need an ever-increasing dose of specific antioxidants because free radicals are responsible for *all* the ills that plague mankind. However, research supports the notion that a judicious amount of antioxidants is healthy—but taking high doses of particular antioxidants is not necessarily a good idea. To get the proper array of antioxidants in your system to protect your brain from free radicals, moderation, balance, and variety are best. (But nutritional experts often have little monetary reward for taking this stance.)

Within the past few years, numerous studies have questioned the wisdom of taking megadoses of vitamin C (such as more than 500 milligrams a day), vitamin E (more than 250 to 440 IU per day), and beta-carotene (more than 22 to 30 milligrams a day).

When the National Institutes of Health put high doses to the test, the results were disconcerting. These antioxidant vitamins, when used at more than the recommended dietary intake, didn't reduce heart attacks, strokes, cancer, or Alzheimer's disease—or even lead to longer lives. In fact, in some cases, megadoses actually *increased* the risk of death.

Problems arise with antioxidants when overexcited consumers buy into the hype of supplement pushers. Antioxidants in high doses may do some good in some cases but can also be harmful. We can't always predict which will be the case ahead of time.

Excessive antioxidants can cause problems through four main ways:

- High doses of antioxidants can act like *pro*-oxidants, which encourage widespread free-radical production and damage. That's because antioxidants protect one another from oxidation, and if one is lacking, another can become a pro-oxidant. It's useful to remember that antioxidants must be neutralized themselves.
- An overabundance of antioxidants can prevent cancer cells from self-destructing through a natural process called *apoptosis. All* cells are programmed to die on schedule, which is a normal part of life. Injured cells that are allowed to survive are more likely to become cancerous instead of being replaced by healthy ones. Rapidly multiplying cancer cells can use antioxidants to their advantage to fuel their growth. Taking too many antioxidants at the wrong time essentially arms the bad guys with the weapons they need to stay alive and multiply.
- High doses of a single antioxidant may disturb the body's balance by keeping you from absorbing other antioxidants. These

protective chemicals need to work as a team, and if you've ever played a team sport, you know that having one member who's superstrong or superfast can ultimately destroy the team's ability to succeed as a whole.

- And finally, studies suggest that excess vitamin C, vitamin E, and beta-carotene can increase the production of "bad" LDL cholesterol from the liver.

There is no consensus in the scientific community for *any* doses of supplemental antioxidants that the public should take. This leaves consumers confused and often at the mercy of supplement suppliers, who may muddy the waters with pseudoscientific claims. They frequently sell their products by scaring consumers with threats of illnesses due to antioxidant deficiencies, or by floating promises of "super" health and longevity by taking these supplements.

My goal, however, isn't to bash the use of supplemental antioxidants or to question their existence. Instead, I just hope that this chapter convinces you of the importance of antioxidants for your brain health—and steers you toward getting them from a variety of natural foods rather than pills.

Though large doses of antioxidants may be toxic (and have just a single effect), the antioxidants in *whole* foods provide a variety of health benefits, and you should consume them every day.

Mix Your Phytochemicals to Fix Your Brain

Plant sources contain *thousands* of antioxidant compounds. You want a blend of many antioxidants, since certain types work in certain situations, and not all antioxidants are the optimal one for a specific body tissue. Remember that you're trying to keep many different types of free radicals from damaging different substances in your body and brain.

It's as if you're trying to catch a zoo full of escaped animals before they can rampage through your town. One type of net isn't going to catch everything from snakes and birds to tigers and elephants. You'll need to outfit your friends with many kinds of nets—big, small, and made of different materials.

Antioxidants perform best when they are working together. To carry this analogy further, when you really need someone with a big elephant-catching net, having thirty people outfitted to catch monkeys really isn't going to do the job.

The antioxidants and other healthful nutrients in foods work in a fine balance, which scientists are just beginning to understand. When you're repairing and protecting your brain, the best approach is to get antioxidants through foods like fruits and vegetables, where they exist in the proportions that nature intended. With this approach, you don't have to worry about whether one antioxidant is getting out of balance because you're getting too much. You don't have to track all the thousands of antioxidants to ensure you're not missing any.

For example, experts think beta-carotene has five hundred or so siblings collectively known as *carotenoids*. Perhaps fifty or so are found in common foods, including alpha-carotene, gamma-carotene, cryptoxanthin, lutein, lycopene, and zeaxanthin. These act synergistically with beta-carotene to give you that well-armed group of protectors who are working together to "net" that army of free radicals before they can rampage through your body.

Meet the Phytochemical Superstars

Here are just a few key players from the multitude of phytonutrients contained in fruits and vegetables that are supported by studies to improve brain health. A host of research gives us all the encouragement we should need to eat a variety of plant-based foods to stack the deck for brain healing:

Resveratrol is found in high concentrations in grape skin, grape seeds, and red wine. The grape plant uses resveratrol for protection against fungus. Resveratrol increases an enzyme called heme oxygenase, which breaks down a substance called heme. This is a powerful pro-oxidant in the blood that destroys nerve cells. So resveratrol protects nerve cells—including those in your brain.

Resveratrol also increases the activity of your body's natural antioxidant enzymes, such as superoxide dismutase and glutathione peroxidase. Resveratrol helps protect the brain from free-radical damage and degenerative diseases such as Alzheimer's, Huntington's, and Parkinson's. Resveratrol may also be useful in treating depression, since it has been found to be a potent monoamine oxidase (MAO) inhibitor. MAO helps break down and remove the neurotransmitters norepinephrine, dopamine, and serotonin from the brain. If you keep MAO from doing this task, more of these chemicals will linger. Some antidepressants are also classified as MAO inhibitors.

Lycopene is found in tomatoes, pink grapefruit, watermelon, papaya, apricot, and guava, and is a powerful memory-boosting phytonutrient. The protective effect of lycopene may come from preventing a lack of oxygen in the brain. And by scavenging free radicals, it may protect neurons. As a powerful antioxidant, lycopene may be useful as a treatment for neurodegenerative diseases.

Quercetin is one of the major flavonoids. It has a much stronger antioxidant activity than vitamin C. It is most commonly found in apples, onions, cherries, citrus fruits, leafy vegetables, broccoli, red grapes, and raspberries. Studies have found that quercetin contributes significantly to protecting neurons from oxidative damage.

Myoinositol is found naturally in cantaloupe, citrus fruits, dried beans, lentils, whole grain products, oats, and nuts. It helps nerves send messages and may protect against nerve damage. Several studies report that it may act as an antianxiety agent and help you sleep better.

Anthocyanins are found in berries, including wild blueberries, bilberries, cranberries, elderberries, raspberries, and strawberries. These phytochemicals can boost your neural and cognitive function. They can protect brain cells from free-radical damage and the resulting cognitive losses that can come with this damage. These chemicals can also help reduce the signs of aging and improve your memory and coordination in your later years.

Boron is found in avocados, beans, apples, red grapes, bananas, broccoli, celery, and carrots. Having the right amount of boron is associated with better brain function. Too little boron results in decreased brain activity, attention, and short-term memory. People who get too little boron have also been found to have poorer response times on tasks that require manual dexterity and eye-hand coordination.

Surprising Foods that Pack an Antioxidant Punch

Although fruits and vegetables are powerful sources of antioxidants, other plant foods that you might not immediately categorize as a fruit or vegetable can also give your body an antioxidant boost. These include:

- Berries, such as blackberries, blueberries, and strawberries
- Beans, including kidney beans and black beans
- Prunes
- Soy
- Coffee
- Olive oil
- Pecans

Supplements do have their place, and that is to fill any shortages you still have *after* you eat an ample amount of antioxidant-rich foods. But most Americans are a long, long, long way from getting enough antioxidant-rich foods.

With hundreds of fruits and vegetables to choose from, you might expect Americans to take advantage of this assortment of more than 25,000 health-building phytonutrients. They're not. Most people consume two to three vegetables daily, and those are often iceberg lettuce, French fries, and ketchup. (These aren't brimming with healthy antioxidants, by the way.) A study published by the Centers for Disease Control and Prevention in 2010 found that only 33 percent of adults ate fruit at least two times a day, and only 26 percent had vegetables at least three times a day.

The ultimate question is *why* do we eat the way we do when we know better? It's not hard to find the message that fruits and vegetables are healthy, and junk food and fast foods are harmful. It's as if we have a map that leads us to better health—and the brainpower to understand it—but we choose to throw the map away and follow our own route elsewhere on most days.

We often like to play the blame game when it comes to our fitness and eating habits, and it seems that there is no better scapegoat for our nutritional shortcomings than the fast-food industry. Yet McDonald's has offered apples and fruit yogurt, Wendy's a fruit bowl entrée, Arby's has put apples into their chicken salad, and Chick-fil-A has provided fresh fruit sides. You can find antioxidant fruits and vegetables these days without having to look too hard.

And you don't have to become a vegetarian to reap the rewards that fruits and vegetables offer you. You don't have to hack through the rain forest with a machete to find unusual fruits with "miracle" antioxidant power (nor do you have to buy their very expensive juice in the supermarket). You just need five to nine servings of fruits and vegetables every day. That's five to nine *servings*—not five to nine entire grapefruits or heads of lettuce. One serving equals:

- A half-cup of fresh fruit
- One medium-sized fruit
- A cup of leafy vegetables
- A half-cup of cooked or raw vegetables

Have a fruit or vegetable with every meal and snack. Stick an apple or banana in your pocket or purse to enjoy in the afternoon instead of a candy bar. If you have to stop at a fast-food restaurant for a meal, skip the burgers and fries and get a salad or other vegetable-based meal. When you go shopping at the supermarket, be sure to spend a significant amount of your time—and grocery money—in the produce section.

Go for a variety of plants, and don't just stick with your favorites every day. Remember that your brain is hungry for *all* the phytonutrients in these plants, not just the set that's available in a particular vegetable. And keep in mind that deep and bright colors are your sign that a fruit or vegetable is a good source of these antioxidants and other protective chemicals. Your shopping cart—and plate—should look like a rainbow of purple, blue, red, yellow, orange, and green.

THE BRAIN FIX TOOLBOX

- Be sure to put an ample variety of antioxidants into your system each and every day. Look to brightly colored fruits and vegetables as your main source of antioxidants.

- Get at least five servings of fruits and vegetables every day. Go for a variety, which will provide different antioxidants to tackle different challenges within your body. Simply eating five apples a day wouldn't be sufficient.

- Taking antioxidants in the form of a multivitamin supplement is not a bad idea, but these should be in *addition* to what you get from plant foods in your diet.

4

Sugar: The Most Important Nutrient
for Brain Healing

HUMANS DON'T HAVE TO LEARN to enjoy sweet foods. Our brains seem to have a desire for them from the day we're born. In fact, we use sugar even earlier in our development!

During pregnancy, the fetus uses only glucose (also known as blood sugar) for fuel. That's because the placenta between the mother and baby keeps fat from passing through. Breast milk is also sweet, since nursing mothers produce 70 grams of carbohydrate per day in their breast milk, which adds up to 280 calories. That's more calories than you'll find in a candy bar.

It's not surprising, then, that babies appear to come into the world with a strong preference for sweets. They'll smile when offered a drink that tastes sweet, but cry if it is bitter. Our taste buds that pick up sweetness are at the front of the tongue, where they are best situated to quickly tell us which foods are safe. This could be nature's way of protecting us from eating harmful foods, since no natural poison is sweet. Sweetness also signals that a plant food is ripe and at its peak nutritional density.

In addition, sweetness has traditionally told humans that a food is a good source of calories. Long ago, when survival meant finding edibles that provided more calories than you had to burn while searching for food, our ancestors wanted to hit the calorie jackpot as often as possible.

In the Paleolithic era, perhaps better known as "caveman times," the hunter-gatherers' main source of concentrated sweetener was honey. If they were lucky, they could also find fruits and berries that provided sugar.

Once mankind began cultivating foods ten thousand years ago, our ancestors enjoyed an influx of carbohydrates due to the introduction of wheat, tubers, beans, and corn. Among the first foods we began to cultivate deliberately were cane and beets, which both provided sugar. Sugar has been commercially developed since 1600. Prior to this, it was rare and more expensive than honey.

Nowadays most of us can find sugar within thirty seconds at any time of day. And sugar—and carbohydrates in general—have acquired something of an evil reputation in the past decade, as dieters turned their backs on carbs in an effort to shed pounds. But when it comes to your brain, the right amount of sugar is *vital* for peak performance.

We need *energy* to build our bodies and heal our brains—and another word for energy is calories. If a patient is in the hospital recovering from trauma, surgery, or an infection, what is the most important nutritional need? If you said protein, that's not the right answer. The most important nutrient is energy, in the form of calories. It takes lots of energy to heal. A woman who's just had a baby via C-section would be wise to eat the breakfast that the staff brings her, even if it contains sweetened, carb-heavy options like biscuits, grits, a Danish, coffee with sugar, and orange juice. This is also true for people going through detox or someone with an eating disorder who needs to regain weight.

This need for the right amount of carbs is especially true for an individual whose brain is healing. Studies have shown that when people eat a breakfast that increases their blood sugar, their memory improves. Conversely, people who fasted had less ability to recall a word list and a story read aloud.

When we are exposed to new information, our brain will store it in a holding tank called the hippocampus. During a night of sleep, the information will be filed into our long-term memory in the portion of our brain called the cortex. If we are eventually tested or need to retrieve that information, it will be made available to our working memory. The key ingredient that assures we will be able to effectively store the information and retrieve it later is the sugar that's available to our brain.

The message here is that learning is dependent on carbohydrates. The brain is especially sensitive to short-term nutrient deficiencies, and skipping breakfast affects your cognitive function, especially the speed and accuracy of your thinking processes.

Unfortunately, people with addictions and eating disorders often struggle with difficulties thinking clearly and being in control of their actions at all times. And people who eat sugary junk food throughout the day can send their blood sugar soaring and crashing—and they might not always have brain fuel available when they need it. It's important for them (and the rest of us, too) to keep our brains properly fueled and ready to handle the complexities of modern life.

This need for carbohydrate was a basic element of human design, and it supported the brainpower that mankind needed to outwit, outrun, and outlast its protein-eating adversaries. But nowadays our relationship to sugar is far different. We don't have to hunt and gather food for hours or days at a time before we can eat. Our supermarkets, restaurants, and convenience stores offer a vast array of heavily sweetened items at very cheap prices.

As a result, plenty of Americans are choosing to get too many carbohydrates—also known as "carbs"—every day in the form of sugar. In fact, it's quite easy at this point in mankind's development to eat so much that we *damage* our bodies and minds with sugar and other carbs. On the other hand, many people are choosing to go on low-carb diets that keep them from getting the sugar and other carbs that their brains need for proper functioning. For good brain health, the *optimal* relationship to sugar is somewhere between these two extremes.

Sugar, Sugar Everywhere

It's easy to become confused about the various terms that are used to describe sweet substances. So let's start with some of the more common ones that we put into our bodies:

Glucose

Carbohydrates are a category of nutrients found in starches (such as bread and pasta), vegetables, fruits, milk, and sweets. Sugar is a type of carbohydrate, and the basic unit of *all* carbohydrates is a sugar known as glucose. The carbohydrates are made of numerous single molecules of glucose that are strung together in various configurations. Enzymes in our digestive tract break down carbohydrates into glucose, where it is absorbed and used by cells in the body for energy. *All* carbohydrates and sweets eventually break down or are converted into glucose.

Glucose is critical for optimal brain function. The nervous system prefers glucose as its sole source of energy. The brain is unlike many other tissues that can use other fuels such as fat and protein. Not surprisingly, when your blood sugar (which is glucose) falls too low, the initial effect is reduced functioning of the brain. This gives rise to dizziness, disorientation, and even loss of consciousness.

When your blood sugar falls too far, your brain may also send out other signals that are quite irritating (and attention getting): headaches, shakes and jitters, irritability, difficulty concentrating, fatigue, weakness, nausea, and sweating. These signals are necessary to make you seek food, or to get your body to free up its stored sugar and transport it through arteries to your brain.

This condition is commonly known as *hypoglycemia* or *low blood sugar*. In severe cases, it can put you into a coma. Most cases of hypoglycemia occur when people with diabetes give themselves too much insulin, eat too little carbohydrate, or exercise too much. But these symptoms can also be familiar to people without diabetes, including many veterans of low-carbohydrate diets.

Fructose

The stuff you know as table sugar—the white granules you sprinkle into your coffee—is known scientifically as *sucrose.* It's chemically made up of glucose and fructose attached to each other. The American food industry has taught us a lot about fructose, for good and bad.

Corn refiners produce a product called "high fructose corn syrup" by first converting cornstarch to syrup that is nearly all sugar. They then use enzymes to alter the sugar to produce syrup that's high in fructose. This high fructose corn syrup—or HFCS—has a chemical structure similar to sucrose (table sugar). However, in sucrose, the fructose and glucose are bound together, and after you eat it they're split apart in the intestine and absorbed individually. In HFCS, they're already free of each other.

Food manufacturers are enthusiastic about HFCS for a lot of reasons. It enhances flavors. It improves foods' stability, texture, color, and consistency compared to sucrose. It protects frozen foods from freezer burn, keeps foods fresh in vending machines, and makes bakery products look more natural. It's also cheap. In the United States, production of HFCS increased from 2.2 million tons in 1980 to 9.4 million tons in 1999 as the stuff replaced sugar in a variety of food-processing uses.

As a result, consumption of HFCS rose by more than 1,000 percent during the two-decade period between 1970 and 1990! The increased consumption of HFCS far exceeds the growth in intake of any other food in America.

This has had a big effect on the way we fuel our bodies and brains. When manufacturers lower their costs, the savings don't always get passed along to the consumer, unfortunately. But in this case, we *did* see a cost benefit: using HFCS in processed foods made those products less expensive. For a similar price, we could get a much bigger amount of food and drink. An all-you-can-drink fountain beverage is now available at the same price as a 12-ounce soft drink. As a result, the economic incentive prompted people to drink a lot more HFCS-sweetened beverages.

Along the same timeline, Americans grew bigger, a change that affects not just the waistline but also our brain health. A number of studies have linked sugary sodas with obesity and poor health:

- Mice that drink water containing HFCS have been found to eat less food, but gain more weight and put on 90 percent more fat than mice that drink only water.
- Women who drink more than one sugary soda a day have been found to be 85 percent more likely to get type 2 diabetes.
- A 2011 study from the journal *Hypertension* found that blood pressure was directly related to drinking sugar-sweetened beverages. Each additional serving of these drinks per day was linked to a 1.1-point rise in systolic blood pressure.

The body does not process fructose the same way it handles glucose (nor does the body benefit from all this cheap fructose like our wallets do). High fructose inhibits the appetite hormone leptin—which plays an important role in telling us we're no longer hungry—by blocking its entry into the brain. However, it *doesn't* suppress the increase of another hormone called ghrelin, which sends signals that increase our appetite. This suggests that fructose in our diet may play a role in increased calorie intake and weight gain.

Once it's absorbed in the intestine and taken to the liver, fructose becomes converted to glucose or fat. Dietary fructose is readily converted into fat, which can encourage body fat to build up around the organs in the abdomen. Extra fat in the midsection can lower your sensitivity to your body's insulin, setting the stage for diabetes. Pure fructose or large amounts of HFCS can increase levels of "bad" LDL cholesterol and triglycerides and may even contribute to heart disease. All of these complications can have a major impact on your brain health.

Many people are preaching the evils of HFCS to consumers using outlets on the Internet. Indeed, we *are* eating a lot of the stuff. But to focus *too* heavily on HFCS in your eating habits probably isn't the best use of your time. The current consensus among diet experts is that we don't have enough evidence to support banning or restricting the use of HFCS.

As is often the case, much more research is needed to fully understand the effects of fructose in humans. More factors than just HFCS-laden sodas explain our epidemic of obesity and diabetes in this country. From 1970 to 2005, calorie intake in the United States rose by 24 percent from *all* types of food, not just sodas brimming with HFCS. HFCS makes up about half of the sweetener use in America. But worldwide, it only accounts for about 8 percent. Nevertheless, rates of obesity are also rising in countries that don't use much HFCS.

The fact remains that we should limit the consumption of *all* added sweeteners and foods that pack a lot of calories but few nutrients. That's because too much sugar (or calories in general) can affect tissues and hormones upstream from your brain, which then alters the balanced environment that your brain requires to function properly. Excess sugar can also directly affect the chemicals that bathe your brain.

Too Much Insulin Equals Bad News for Body and Brain

We already talked about the grogginess that can occur when our blood sugar goes too low. *High* blood sugar can wreck your concentration, too! When sugar levels are too high, we can experience fuzzy thinking, difficulty concentrating, and sleepiness. This confusion and lethargy may be due to too much serotonin, a neurotransmitter, in the brain. How?

High-carbohydrate meals and simple sugars can help more tryptophan—which is one of twenty amino acids that serve as building blocks for creating protein—get delivered to the brain. That's because carbohydrates stimulate your pancreas to release the hormone insulin. This helps drive away *other* amino acids that compete with tryptophan for entry into your brain. This allows more tryptophan to get in.

Once in the brain, tryptophan is converted to serotonin, which produces a calming effect. Serotonin also helps reduce cravings for carbs and sweets, and it triggers a desire to seek out protein. However, too *much* serotonin can cause drowsiness, fatigue, clumsiness, poor performance, apathy, and mental slowing.

That's a look at how excess sugar in your diet can harm your mental sharpness *now*. We should also be concerned with the long-term effect of high blood sugar. It can harm your brain through blood vessel disease and Alzheimer's disease.

To understand the effects of sugar in the body and brain, we have to better understand insulin, which goes hand in hand with our blood sugar. In body tissues *outside* the brain, insulin stimulates cells to gobble up sugar from the blood. The insulin acts like a key that unlocks a door, allowing the glucose to enter the cell.

When you eat a meal that's heavy in carbs or sugar, your pancreas will produce more insulin to help you file away the resulting surge of blood sugar in your cells. However, over time, your cells may begin to ignore the insulin, which allows your blood sugar to rise. As a result, your pancreas pumps out even more insulin in an effort to get your cells to pay attention. This is called insulin resistance. The insulin resistance and high insulin levels are responsible for prediabetes and diabetes.

An excessive outpouring of insulin may also contribute to heart disease and high blood pressure. That's because insulin promotes damage in the arteries that carry oxygenated blood to your body, including your brain.

However, inside your brain the management of blood sugar and insulin is different than in the rest of your body. It's so critical for your brain to maintain a healthy level of glucose that brain cells do not need insulin from your pancreas to absorb sugar from your blood. Your brain is capable of making its own insulin. However, circulating insulin from the pancreas has other functions in your brain, such as regulating satiation and satiety. Since brain cells don't require pancreatic insulin to absorb glucose, one may consider that excess insulin can actually *destroy* brain tissue.

But the view that insulin isn't important for the brain has been challenged. The hypothalamus in your brain (responsible for appetite, blood sugar, and mood control) and the hippocampus and cortex (responsible for memory and learning) have large numbers of receptors that pick up insulin.

If insulin becomes depleted in the brain, a person will have a larger likelihood of developing Alzheimer's disease. The complex processes involving insulin within the brain affect energy metabolism, inhibition of oxidative stress (which, as we learned earlier, is similar to rusting), and cell growth. Eventually the cells that require insulin to function and survive break down if they don't have enough insulin, creating the plaques and tangles in the brain that mark Alzheimer's disease.

However, *excessive* amounts of insulin can contribute to Alzheimer's too. These days, millions of people are suffering from the health effects of chronically high sugar and insulin levels. When insulin resistance leads to diabetes, the diabetes in turn can cause blood-vessel damage. Arteries carrying fresh blood become clogged, reducing the delivery of nutrients and oxygen. In the brain, this can cause damage that often shows up in the hippocampus, which handles short-term memory.

People with diabetes who don't properly control their blood sugar using diet and medications have been found to develop memory loss ten to fifteen years earlier. They may also have a 65 percent higher risk of Alzheimer's disease. Treating insulin resistance may even offer benefits for people who already have Alzheimer's.

Therefore, if you want to maintain proper physical and mental health, it's important that you control your blood sugar and insulin so that they're neither too *high* nor too *low*.

Blood Sugar Control: Keep Your Energy Stores Full Enough to Support Healing

To understand the brain's response to low blood sugar is to understand the physical symptoms that we perceive as "hunger." When asked what physical symptoms people experience that let them know they're hungry, dieters will typically respond, "Headaches, shakes and jitters, irritability, difficulty concentrating, weakness, and fatigue." When you check any medical textbook on symptoms of low blood sugar, you will notice a striking similarity.

A headache is a perfect example of how your body generates symptoms to get you to take action (and survive). *All* headaches are vascular in nature, meaning they involve blood vessels. When the supply of blood sugar to the brain is limited, your brain's blood vessels respond by dilating, which means they expand. This makes sense: the expansion allows more glucose-bearing blood to flow into your brain. However, it also causes sensitive nerves in the blood vessel walls to stretch, which gives off pain signals. This alerts you to go find sugar.

Again, the brain prefers to live off carbohydrates. Although you don't want so much that your insulin stays too high, you do need enough to help your brain heal and thrive. If you do not supply the needed fuel in your diet, your body will draw from its emergency store of glycogen in your liver (glycogen is glucose converted into a storage form). We hold enough glycogen to last us for three to four hours. When it's gone, your brain starts sending out those uncomfortable physical symptoms that let you know to replenish the stores.

Unless we are purposely trying to cut back on carbs, we often give in to our urges with the most concentrated form of carbohydrate we can get our hands on—often sweets or baked goods containing white flour. (In that regard, we're not all that different from our caveman ancestor, who wouldn't likely sample a bit of honey once he found a prized honeycomb, then move on. He'd gorge himself on the sweet stuff.)

We have a thermostat-like structure in the center of our brain—just behind our nose—called the hypothalamus. A thermostat on your home's wall measures the temperature of the surrounding air, then turns on your heater or air conditioner if the temperature is above or below a comfortable setting. In much the same way, your hypothalamus measures blood sugar and calls for adjustments if the level deviates too far from the norm. When we arise in the morning, our blood sugar is usually at its lowest. This is because we haven't eaten since the previous evening.

When we eat our first meal—which ideally is breakfast—our blood sugar begins to rise. After about twenty minutes, it reaches an acceptable level for the brain. At this time, if we *did* have symptoms of low blood sugar before breakfast, they would disappear. It takes twenty minutes, because food in the mouth does not go directly up to the brain, even though the brain and the mouth are just inches from each other. Instead, like a Delta flight, it goes to Chicago by way of Atlanta. That is to say, it goes in the opposite direction through the digestive tract, into the blood, and then "up" to the brain.

Your blood sugar will continue to rise until your pancreas releases insulin. When sugar exits the bloodstream into your cells, your blood sugar gradually begins to fall. Just about the time it reaches a critical low point, we redose ourselves with food (e.g., lunch). Our blood sugar will gradually rise and fall again until we replenish ourselves with dinner. Over the following hours it will drop again to its morning low.

This process normally serves us well—as long as we don't go without food too long and then gorge ourselves like our caveman ancestors. If we skip meals or eat poorly, we *still* may not face the consequences of low blood sugar. That's because our liver reserves kick in at the first hint of carbohydrate deficiency. Problems arise, however, when we follow an unhealthy eating plan and deplete our emergency stores. The scenario often goes something like this:

- We eat a small breakfast and our blood sugar rises, but we don't have enough carbs to keep it elevated until lunch.
- At lunchtime, our blood sugar is lower but not so low that we feel bad, and we eat a light lunch or just grab a snack because we're so busy.

- Around 3:00 or 4:00 PM, our blood sugar has plummeted, and without any stores, our brain screams for sugar. We walk—no, run!—to the snack machine and give in to the urge with a candy bar.
- Now our blood sugar skyrockets, and instead of putting out a merely sufficient amount of insulin, the pancreas dumps way too much of the hormone into the system. Our blood sugar then crashes to an even lower level due to the effects of all this insulin.
- Now the brain is riled up and shouts, "I THOUGHT I TOLD YOU I WANTED SOMETHING SWEET!" Convinced that you need to satisfy this urge, you continue to overindulge with sweets, even to the point where it's more accurately called a binge.

These urges *do* keep you from starving to death, but over the long term, this way of starving and gorging isn't good for your brain. It also helps set you up for extra body fat, diabetes, and heart and blood-vessel disease. Again, all of these are very bad for a healthy brain.

You're better off being a thinking man or woman who wisely uses your prefrontal cortex (which gives you the power of complex planning) to come up with a day-to-day solution to avoid hunger without gaining weight and developing chronic medical problems.

Since you know that a hungry body and brain need carbohydrate, we'll start there. Let's take three different forms of carbohydrate that you often encounter: candy, orange juice, and an apple. For the sake of consistency, let's presume that each is a 100-calorie portion (though in real life the candy and juice are far more likely to provide you with more than 100 calories before you're finished).

As carbohydrates, they will all break down to glucose, which is the form of sugar that *all* carbohydrates are in when they pass by the thermostat-like hypothalamus. One might conclude that all three carbohydrate foods would produce the same result since they are all 100 calories and pass through the brain as glucose.

They don't.

The candy goes to your stomach, which breaks the candy into small pieces, then moves it into your small intestine. Here your bloodstream absorbs it, where it moves up to your brain and heads past the hypothalamus. Your blood sugar is now higher. But at about the same time, your blood is also passing your pancreas, which puts out insulin that brings your blood sugar down. This 100 calories of candy—pure glucose—keeps your blood sugar elevated for only about ten to fifteen minutes!

Next, we try the orange juice, which has glucose, which makes your blood sugar go up and come down over a brief period. But unlike the candy, the OJ also has fructose. Fructose also causes the pancreas to produce insulin. This is because the pancreas has receptors that "taste" sweet fructose, much like your tongue does. When you eat fructose and glucose together, you get even more of an insulin release.

Remember, though, we said that *all* carbohydrates eventually turn to glucose. To do this, fructose must journey to the liver, where it is eventually converted to glucose and produces a *second* rise in blood sugar that is elevated for fifteen to thirty minutes. This is sort of like a time-released effect: first the glucose and fructose cause blood sugar to go up and then down, then the fructose is changed to glucose, and *it* causes blood sugar to go up and then down. As a result, you're getting more mileage (in the form of sustained blood sugar) for the same amount of gas.

But a better choice to keep your blood sugar elevated is to have the apple, because it contains glucose, fructose, *and* fiber. Think of the fiber as a piece of fabric that is tightly woven together. Trapped between the weave of the fabric are glucose and fructose, which are gradually released down your twenty-five feet of small intestine. In essence, the slow release of glucose and fructose leads to a *third* peak that keeps your blood sugar up thirty minutes to an hour.

Once all the sugar from your foods is used up, if you have also had any protein in your meal, it too will be converted into sugar. The protein component will keep your blood sugar up an additional one to two hours. If you ate any fat, it will help, too. However, the fat does not turn into sugar. Instead, it contributes by making your stomach empty itself more slowly into your small intestine. By controlling the "gateway" between your stomach and small intestine, it essentially produces a fifth peak and keeps your blood sugar elevated a third hour.

So now we know how to construct meals and snacks that provide the brain with a healing, sustaining flow of blood sugar that keeps it happy:

- Limit candy and refined white-flour carbohydrates that turn into a quick jolt of glucose.
- Eat fruits and vegetables that contain fructose and fiber that take longer to cause your blood sugar to rise.
- Also include a source of protein and fat with your meals and snacks to further spread out the rise in blood sugar.
- Get a middle-of-the-road amount of carbs. A low-carbohydrate diet, with just 15 to 40 grams per day, isn't good for your brain health (see the sidebar on ketosis below for the reason why). On the other hand, the average person takes in upward of 200 to 300 grams of carbohydrate per day. That may be too much for you. The minimum daily amount required by the brain is 120 to 150 grams, and it should be distributed evenly throughout the day, along with fiber, fat, and protein.

Avoid the Temptation of Ketosis

When your carbohydrate stores are depleted, your body reverts to a type of "safety mechanism" for fuel called ketones. It's in your brain's best interest to not switch to this fuel.

Ketones are a breakdown product of fat. This emergency fuel source is rather inefficient, but in a pinch (like when you aren't eating enough carbs and you draw down your liver's supply of glycogen), your brain and nervous tissue can keep running on them. This is called *ketosis*.

However, in theory, ketones can be neurotoxic or damaging to your nervous system. Ketones are alcohol-like derivatives and can produce hallucinations that impair your driving skills and even mimic the effect of driving under the influence. Obviously, a brain operating on ketones isn't performing at its optimal level, which is probably your goal if you're reading this book. (Also, ketones can even trigger a false positive on a Breathalyzer test that traffic officers give!)

Temporarily, ketones decrease hunger and speed up fat breakdown. Following a low-carb, high-protein diet can cause you to produce ketones for energy. But these types of diets can be bad for your health in the long term. Not only can the ketones reduce your brain's cognitive ability, they may also lead to kidney problems. Ketones produce a marked loss of water and electrolytes, and therefore are dangerously dehydrating. One sign that you're in ketosis is a fruity smell on your breath.

Switching to ketones for fuel isn't a long-term solution for weight loss success, either. Low-carb diets may restrict nutritious foods like fruits, vegetables, and beans, which means you'll miss out on the natural anti-oxidants and other phytonutrients they contain. And once you start eating carbs again, as you inevitably will at some point, you'll probably have out-of-control cravings for carbohydrates. When you make your return to carbs, you'll have substantial water retention, weight gain, and bloating.

So make sure you get enough carbohydrates during the day. If you want to limit your carbs, just make sure to stick with carbohydrate-rich foods that also provide a lot of vitamins, minerals, and phytonutrients. Feel free to cut out the "empty" carbs that don't also offer these benefits, like sodas and candy bars.

Let's talk about a few more sample foods here in addition to the orange juice and apple. Let's say you started off the day with a glazed Danish. You would feel good initially, but it would only keep your blood sugar elevated a mere fifteen minutes. Have some whole-grain cereal instead, and it will add fiber that helps your blood sugar stay up for an hour. Add skim milk to your cereal, and it will sustain your blood sugar for two hours. Add 1 percent milk instead, and the extra fat helps you go three hours.

Now it's lunchtime and you have a vegetable salad—which con-tains *above-ground* vegetables that basked in the sun while they grew. (A brief aside here: plants hit by the sun get all the carbon dioxide, water, and sunlight they require to grow. They do not need to store energy. Plants that weren't hit by the sun while they grew—like potatoes, winter squash, peas, legumes, and corn—must store energy. They tuck away energy in the form of starch.)

Without any carbohydrate, your sugar stays grounded, even though vegetables are very good for you. But add a few crackers containing fiber like Triscuits, have some lean turkey, and put a dab of salad dressing on your salad, and your blood sugar can be fueling your brain for hours.

Usually if you have lunch at noon, you are not planning dinner until about six. That is too long to go without food, since your healthy lunchtime formula only elevates your blood sugar for three to four hours. You will need to have a snack of complex carbohydrate, protein, and fat in the afternoon. And if you don't hit the sack until 11:00 PM or midnight, you'll probably need to redose your brain with a reasonably sized snack about two hours before going to bed.

Snack Time *Doesn't* Require Buffet Sizes

Just how big of a snack do you need? You might be amazed to learn just how little it takes to get your blood sugar to a healthy level. Even when people are in a *coma* and unconscious from low blood sugar, just two drops of honey under their tongue can bring them out of it quickly. The honey contains glucose that the bee has already digested. So the tongue can absorb it and allow it to enter the blood flow directly to the brain. If it takes just two drops of honey to raise the *lowest* blood sugar high enough, you don't need a candy bar to raise yours.

But often by the time we get around to a snack during our busy day, we're not thinking clearly. It's a bit like how a drowning person behaves. Picture yourself underwater, so the usual flow of oxygen isn't getting to your brain. You're about to faint when you break the surface of the water. Desperate, the first thing that you will do is gasp for oxygen. But your lungs are already filled with carbon dioxide and will not allow in additional air. What you have to do is breathe *out* first to make room for the oxygen.

Panic will make us perform self-defeating behaviors, whether we're drowning or just hungry. If you allow your blood sugar to get too low, when the symptoms occur you will likely find yourself "panicking" and consuming far more carbohydrates—and calories—than the smidgen you actually need. Your blood sugar will swing wildly more often. And you'll gain weight over time.

So don't wait until your brain is in panic mode and conjuring up unpleasant symptoms to get you to move quickly. Instead, plan ahead, and be sure you have nutritious snacks and meals on hand when you need them.

Fruits make a good snack choice. They're loaded with phytonutrients—which are terrific for your body and brain, as we discussed earlier in the book. And you'll rarely see someone pick up an apple and go on to gobble down ten, as we're more likely to do with cookies. Snacks that easily address our need to combine carbohydrate with protein and fat include trail mix containing nuts, raisins, dates, seeds, and cereal; yogurt with fruit; popcorn with Parmesan cheese; whole-wheat crackers with cheese or peanut butter; or cottage cheese and fruit.

A diet that fixes your brain is fairly straightforward. Unfortunately, some people can make a very simple and useful eating plan too complicated by worrying about the glycemic index. Please don't make this mistake.

A Few Simple Rules Keep Sweets in Their Proper Place

Is it okay to have an occasional sweet? Absolutely. However, you should learn to treat sweets as something to be consumed during special occasions—*not* as something that's mandatory at the end of a meal, or as a crucial part of your life that you can enjoy at any time. Nor should you gorge on sweets as a way to deal with mood swings or depression.

Always be sure to eat sweets with a meal or other nutrient-dense foods that contain a healthy amount of fiber, fat, and protein. In other words, if you're going to have a few cookies, eat them with a healthy food, *not* alone. This is especially important for people who have had an eating disorder or those who give in to cravings easily.

Here are a few other ways to ensure that you don't overindulge in candy, cake, pie, and other sweets:

- Eat sweets only when you're with other people.
- Aim to only eat *half* of the normal serving (this improves your chances of not going over).
- Don't eat sweets every day.
- Don't eat sweets within three hours before going to bed.
- Don't eat the same kind of sweet treat more than once in a week.

Glycemic Index: Better Off Ignored

In 1980, David Jenkins of the University of Toronto created a scale to compare how carbohydrates affect blood sugar compared to pure glucose.

Pure glucose is set at 100. If a food has a glycemic index of 56, it means the food creates 56 percent of the response of pure glucose. Generally, a food is considered to have a high glycemic index if it is greater than 70. This means that the food is digested and absorbed into the bloodstream quickly, which quickly raises blood sugar and quickly leads to a crash. A low glycemic index is considered to be below 50, so the food is digested and absorbed slowly and raises the blood sugar slowly. Low glycemic index diets provide the best blood sugar control. As a result, a low glycemic index food is preferred—but spending too much time worrying about the glycemic index *isn't* a good use of your time.

This is because a lot of factors affect a food's glycemic index. A boiled potato is 50, a baked potato is 75, and a microwaved potato is 90. Different heating methods produce the variation. In addition, we seldom eat just one kind of food alone. To accurately calculate the glycemic index of a food or meal you're about to consume, you'd need to consider all of the following (and more):

- How much you're going to eat
- When you ate your previous meal
- How slowly your stomach empties
- The amount of fiber, protein, and fat in the meal
- The ripeness of any plant foods you'll eat
- How you cooked the food
- And your age

Who wants to do all that? In addition, the glycemic index of foods is very hard to predict by just the perception we have that the food is natural and "healthy." For example, cherries are 22, watermelon is 72, and Lifesavers candy is 70. That analysis would have been hard to predict.

This is all a big strain on the brain that we're trying to heal and keep happy. So instead of living your life by a hard-to-remember number system, just keep in mind the importance of:

- Eating plenty of fruits, vegetables (especially nonstarchy kinds), legumes, and whole grains
- Limiting candy and sugary baked goods
- Not eating until you're uncomfortable. Stick to reasonable portion sizes.

THE BRAIN FIX TOOLBOX

When it comes to sugar and carbs, remember that:

Slower is better. Sugar and other forms of carbohydrate cause your blood sugar and insulin to rise. You want enough blood sugar and insulin, but having big crests and crashes of these substances is harmful for your concentration today—and they can lead to serious brain-harming diseases over time.

As a result, eat carbohydrates in a way that they slowly cause your blood sugar to go up and settle back down. This means eating carbs with fiber (such as fruit, whole grains, and beans) and combining them with a source of fat and protein.

Moderation is key. You don't have to exclude sweets and sodas completely from your life, but these need to be occasional treats, *not* a significant source of your daily calories.

Don't get distracted. It's easy to become afraid of processed food ingredients, such as high fructose corn syrup. You could spend an hour a day checking every food and drink to make sure it doesn't contain HFCS. People can get swept up in checking the glycemic index of foods and drinks and spend a lot of time that would be more useful for healing their body and brain in other ways. Just remember that your carb-heavy foods and drinks should provide a lot of fiber, vitamins, and phytonutrients. Does a soda provide your brain with valuable nutrients? Does a cellophane-wrapped cupcake from a box? Of course not.

Limit these in your diet for *that* reason. The HFCS these probably contain is a secondary concern. And if you eat a steady supply of nutritious foods in reasonable portions throughout the day, taking into account their glycemic index is probably not going to add a lot of value for your blood sugar.

Avoid satisfying your sweet tooth with the "fake stuff." Later in the book (in Chapter 12), we'll learn about the importance of staying hydrated with brain-supporting fluids, and we'll learn about artificial sweeteners. You can find plenty of dire warnings that these are dangerous poisons that you shouldn't allow in your body in *any* amount, but in truth, artificial sweeteners do appear to be safe for most people when used in reasonable amounts. But that doesn't mean they don't have an unwanted effect on your brain. In general, stick with foods that are sweetened with actual sugar. Just don't have too much of them.

5

A Healthy Brain Is a Fat Brain

IF YOUR SKULL HAD AN ingredient label on it like a can of food, you might be surprised to see what's in your brain. About 78 percent of the average three-pound brain is water. Let's take that away. Protein accounts for another 8 percent. Let's set it aside, too. Another 3 percent of your brain is made up of a variety of organic and inorganic compounds. Maybe 1 percent is carbohydrate. The remaining amount—accounting for more than half of the brain's nonwater weight—is fat. Some of this is cholesterol, some is polyunsaturated fat, and some is omega-3 fatty acids.

The importance of fat to brain development and function dates back to the beginning of mankind. The ancient *Australopithecine afarensis* had no access to fish oil on the savannah of Africa and as a result were stuck with a brain that did not increase in capacity over time (it was not much larger than a chimpanzee's brain at 0.85 pounds).

But in the East African Rift Valley, the *Australopithecine africanus* lived near water sources that provided the opportunity to eat seafood, scavenge for shellfish, and harvest algae. As a result, their frontal cortex— where thinking and reasoning take place—steadily increased in size. The larger brain made them capable of thinking more rapidly and rationally. The *Au. africanus* could adapt more easily to new environments and conditions. These changes enabled them to migrate widely and provided advantages over other species.

Today, our genes are very similar to those of our ancestors who lived during the Paleolithic period forty thousand years ago. Our genetic profile was established *thousands* of years ago, and there has been very little change since that time. However, we live in a vastly different nutritional environment that isn't providing what our genetic constitution was originally designed to work with. Hunters and gatherers consumed only two to three times as much omega-6 fatty acids compared to omega-3s (omega-3s are found in fish). Today, Western cultures consume *fifteen to twenty* times the amount of omega-6s (found in foods like corn oil) compared to the low intake of omega-3s. As a result, the ratio of omega-6s to omega-3s is much higher, and experts think this is contributing to all manner of diseases. It also sets the stage for an unhealthy brain.

When it comes to your brain, not all fats are equal. As we'll discuss in this chapter, *un*saturated fats are crucial for maintaining brain health. Both omega-3s and omega-6s are types of unsaturated fat. They are called *essential fatty acids* (EFAs) because you have to get them through your diet since your body can't make them. These days it's very easy to get omega-6s, since the corn oil they're found in permeates many processed foods. It's easy to get saturated fat and a similar kind of fat called *trans fat*, too. But omega-3s—the stuff that's so crucial to brain health—is not as easy to get. Like our prehistoric ancestors knew, you pretty much have to go fishing to find it.

Omega-3s Course Through Your Brain Your Entire Life

Even before you were born, elements found in fish oil were building your brain. When babies are developing in the uterus, omega-3s help promote blood flow through the placenta, which assists in delivering nutrients to the growing fetus.

Essential fatty acids, such as docosohexanoic acid (DHA), are transported across the placenta into the bloodstream of the fetus, with maximum impact on brain development. DHA is an omega-3 fatty acid that is extremely important to the development of neural tissue in the fetus and the growing newborn.

DHA is found in the membranes—or outer walls—of cells in your brain's gray matter. Thus, it helps you think. DHA is also the major polyunsaturated fatty acid found in the membranes of photoreceptors in the retina. Thus, it helps you see. Essential fatty acids stimulate the growth of nerve cells and regulate neural communication, which is the back-and-forth messaging between neurons. When DHA gets too low, it leads to changes in the membranes of neuron cells, which can lead to physical impairments.

British researchers reported that mothers who ate less than 340 grams of fish per week—which is three servings of four ounces each—gave birth to babies who had less-than-optimal neural growth. On intelligence exams, these children scored up to 25 percent lower than children born to mothers who consumed fish regularly.

DHA levels in mothers during pregnancy have long-term consequences for their kids' later behaviors. This is particularly true during the five months before birth and one month after. IQ scores of children whose mothers took DHA supplements during pregnancy and while nursing have been shown to be higher than those of children of mothers who did not take DHA. DHA consumption during pregnancy and breast-feeding has also been linked to improved problem-solving skills when the children are nine months old and greater intelligence at age four.

Also, omega-3s prevent early labor and delivery by blocking chemicals known as prostaglandins, which are responsible for setting off uterine contractions. Once you're out in the world, omega-3 fatty acids continue to hold an important role in your brain health, even though most of your brain growth is completed by the age of five or six.

When DHA was added to infant formula, the babies' visual acuity and IQ maturation was similar to that of breast-fed babies when researchers checked on them at age four. In another study, when mothers ate fish during pregnancy, their children showed a lower risk of cognitive impairment and scored higher on IQ tests.

Government food agencies appear to be convinced of the importance of the omega-3s DHA and EPA, as demonstrated by the many infant formulas and baby foods that are fortified with them. As for supplementing fish oils during pregnancy and nursing, it has been found safe for the fetus and infant.

Omega-3s keep showing benefits past early childhood. When DHA was given to young teens, 40 percent showed some improvement in intelligence. It seems that the late teen years are a critical period when the brain reorganizes its connections in response to experiences like learning new skills. (This is the plasticity we learned about earlier in the book.) The plasticity is critical for gaining intelligence and picking up appropriate social and emotional behaviors in adolescence.

In yet another study—this one involving four children between the ages of eight and thirteen—the kids were given a supplement combining the omega-3 fatty acid EPA and omega-6 fats. They were also asked to cut down on fatty snacks and soft drinks. Three months later, the children reportedly displayed improvement in reading, concentration, problem solving, and memory. Researchers also found that their reading age increased by a year, their handwriting became more legible and accurate, and they were more attentive in class.

A brain scan revealed that their levels of N-acetylaspartate (NAA) dramatically increased. This is a brain chemical linked to the growth of new nerve cell fibers. However, questions remain regarding the credibility of these results due to the small number involved, lack of peer review, and the fact that the research was supported by the maker of a nutraceutical product.

The essential fatty acids are among the most crucial molecules that determine your brain's ability to perform. EFAs don't just make up 20 percent of your nerve cell membranes but also continue to be involved in the creation and function of neurotransmitters throughout your life. The synapses—which are the spaces between nerve cells where cells communicate with others—contain especially high concentrations of essential fatty acids. Sixty percent of this is DHA.

DHA is a very long molecule, and it's very flexible. When it's incorporated into the membrane of your nerve cells, it helps make the membrane elastic, which allows signals to pass through it efficiently. If the *wrong* kind of fatty acid—such as an omega-6, saturated fat, or trans fat—is substituted for DHA and incorporated into the membrane, the neurotransmitters that one cell sends out can't connect with the next one properly. Thus, the brain loses some of its ability to send messages around, which is its essential job.

In order to pass signals down their length, nerve cells need channels—which are like tunnels—that penetrate their membrane. These allow ions to pass through, such as sodium, calcium, and potassium. This passage of ions back and forth sends an electrical signal down the nerve cell, which then releases neurotransmitter, which then affects the next cell. These channels need to be able to change shape to allow the ions to flow through. DHA makes these channels more elastic and easier to change shape. Trans-fatty acids and omega-6 fatty acids make the channels *less* flexible and harder to change shape.

A way to envision this activity is to picture a pitcher throwing a baseball to a catcher. If the catcher remains in the same position and does not reach out or move to meet the ball, he's not going to make many catches. The pitcher will be worthless unless his pitches are perfectly accurate, which is unlikely. But if the catcher is mobile and flexible, then he can move to meet the ball and make more catches. The first neuron (which is the pitcher) throws the neurotransmitter (which is the baseball) to the second neuron (the catcher). If receptors within the membrane of the second neuron are able to move in a fluid manner and configure themselves properly, there is a greater possibility that the neurotransmitter will be caught and that it will work properly.

Neurotransmitter systems that don't efficiently exchange information between cells can result in a host of problems, such as depression, anxiety, dyslexia, attention deficit hyperactivity disorder (ADHD), bipolar disorder, and violent behavior.

> The flexibility that comes from fish oil helps the fish, too! Fish are able to change direction rapidly in the water. That's because their high levels of omega-3 allow them to stay limber and make sharp turns. If fish were inflexible, like an iron ship, they would need to make a long, slow arc to complete a turn. Omega-3s also benefit the fish by helping them stay warm in chilly waters. The oil in their flesh remains fluid at very cold temperatures, allowing them to maintain their flexibility even when their surroundings get chilly.

The Perils of Getting Too Little Omega-3s

Since the American diet provides an abundance of omega-6s and trans fats compared to omega-3 fatty acids, your neurons will happily pick up the more rigid options to incorporate into their cell membranes, which, as noted earlier, do not work as well.

Remember our nerve cells, sending neurotransmitters between one another like a well-operating baseball team? Maintaining a good mood requires the neurotransmitter serotonin to dock correctly in receptors on nerve cell membranes. Research has found a correlation between omega-3s and the risk of depression or depression-related outcomes. So as we learn about the importance of omega-3s in brain health, depression makes a sensible starting point:

- In people with depression, levels of omega-3 have been found to be low in contrast to higher levels of omega-6s. The higher the ratio of omega-6s to omega-3s, the more likely we are to suffer from symptoms of depression. Countries with higher consumption of fish have lower rates of depression. For example, Greenland Eskimos are virtually free of depression. They also have little heart disease, even though they eat a lot of fat (and Eskimos in general eat little fiber from plant foods).

- Low DHA points to a higher risk of suicide in people with depression, too. The majority of data from placebo-controlled studies suggests that eating more omega-3s enhances mood and reduces depression. Eating seafood during pregnancy has a beneficial effect on mothers' mental well-being, whereas low omega-3 intake is linked to high levels of depressive symptoms.

- When EPA was taken together with the antidepressant fluoxetine (also known as Prozac), researchers found better improvement in depressive symptoms in people with major depressive disorder compared to using fluoxetine alone.

- Rats given omega-3 fatty acids stopped acting helpless after thirty days. The therapeutic effect of omega-3s on depression takes thirty days to kick in, which is also how long it typically takes to get relief from antidepressant medication. Therefore, it is reasonable to conclude that omega-3 supplementation would be a helpful approach to add to antidepressant therapy to treat major depressive disorders.

The Mediterranean diet—which is rich in fish, as well as plant foods like fruits, vegetables, whole grains, and nuts, which we've already established are important—may help lower the risk of depression by 40 to 50 percent. This diet improves the function of the delicate inner lining of blood vessels. This lining is involved in producing a substance called brain-derived neurotrophic factor (BDNF), which is responsible for the growth and function of nerve cells.

When problems affect your BDNF, depression may result. The omega-3 fatty acids in some fish might help improve your brain's function by activating BDNF. Greater BDNF production may help you become more resilient and better face the frustrations of daily stressors. The traditional Mediterranean diet, which includes several servings of fish each week, might be ideal for preventing depression, especially when combined with proper treatment from a mental health professional.

Omega-3s or fish oils have also been linked to brain-related benefits other than just relief from depression:

Hyperactivity and dyslexia. Researchers have found that DHA may be lower in children with attention deficit hyperactivity disorder. Higher omega-3 levels are associated with better attention, less hyperactivity, fewer behavioral problems, and improved social skills.

Oils rich in omega-3s have been found to boost concentration and brainpower in kids with ADHD symptoms better than the prescription drug Ritalin (and without the side effects of the drug). In another study, omega-3s did not improve reading difficulties in children with ADHD, but did in those who had dyslexia.

Substance abuse and anxiety. It's no secret that marijuana affects people's mood. Tetrahydrocannabinol, the active ingredient in marijuana, attaches to receptors in the brain to create a favorable mood. However, these receptors also respond to your body's natural endocannabinoids. Researchers have noticed that mice show impaired emotional behaviors when they are low on omega-3s. The absence of omega-3s appear to have kept their receptors from responding to their natural endocannabinoids, which play a role in mood control.

Anxiety disorders and substance abuse disorders often go hand in hand. Studies have shown that supplements containing polyunsaturated fatty acids help reduce anxiety in people with substance abuse issues and people who were taking tests. Omega-3 fatty acids have been shown to help improve anxiety symptoms such as insomnia, lack of concentration, appetite changes, and low mood.

Dangerous Behaviors. Low levels of omega-3s may be related to an increased risk of homicide and suicide. Making sure that people get enough omega-3s during their early development and adulthood appears to hold considerable promise in preventing aggression and hostility. In prisoners, supplementation of fish oils in the diet was linked to less violence and was shown to reduce a substance called corticotropin-releasing hormone, which is toxic to brain cells. People with aggressive tendencies and antisocial behavior, such as rule-breaking, might be helped by taking essential fatty acids to prevent the behavioral problems that our mental health providers, social service programs, and correctional institutions are designed to treat.

Schizophrenia and psychosis. Normally the prefrontal cortex of the brain, which controls higher thinking, decision-making, and impulse management, controls the limbic system of the brain—which handles emotions—through neurons that communicate using dopamine.

In people with schizophrenia, the activity of the prefrontal dopamine system is reduced. This in turn reduces the suppressive effect on the limbic system, which leaves the limbic dopamine system more active. The results are cognitive disorders and the symptoms associated with schizophrenia. Experts have long known that omega-3 fatty acid concentrations are lower in people with schizophrenia. It's also possible that people struggling with schizophrenia may not process fatty acids correctly, which leads to damaged brain cells.

Experts have hypothesized that giving omega-3 supplements might be an effective treatment for schizophrenia. And there is limited evidence that supplements of omega-3s can reduce schizophrenia symptoms.

In addition, some studies have reported that a high intake of fish or omega-3s may lead to a lower rate of psychotic-like symptoms. Due to the low risk of harm, people with psychoses may want to add omega-3 supplements to their current drug regimens in hopes of better controlling their symptoms.

Dementia. Older adults who regularly eat fish may have a lower risk of the subtle brain damage that contributes to stroke and dementia. People who eat more fish show fewer silent brain infarcts, which are tiny areas of tissue that have died because of insufficient blood supply. Researchers have reported that DHA lowers the risk of dementia, protects nerve cells, limits inflammation, and prevents the buildup of Alzheimer's-related plaques in the brain.

Alzheimer's disease is associated with loss of memory and mental function, usually in older people. Though it is progressive and has no cure, some researchers feel that the disease's progression may be slowed by using nutritional interventions such as antioxidants and supplements of omega-3s. Researchers have discovered that people with Alzheimer's have significantly less polyunsaturated fatty acids, such as DHA, in their cells.

Epidemiological studies, which look at a large number of people over an extended period of time, suggest that greater intake of DHA is linked to a lower risk of Alzheimer's. In addition, studies on aged mice—which were serving as a model for Alzheimer's disease—found that those that were given a DHA-enriched diet had less amyloid buildup in the brain, which is a marker for the disease.

Fish oil may help prevent Alzheimer's by increasing the production of a protein called LR11. This protein is decreased in people with the disease. Researchers believe the low levels found in people with Alzheimer's may be a contributing factor in the disease.

LR11 is known to destroy the protein that forms the plaques that build up in the brain during Alzheimer's. Higher levels of LR11 also prevent these toxic proteins from being manufactured. When these plaques form, levels of nitric oxide in the brain dwindle. Nitric oxide can protect neurons from degenerating and dying. Nitric oxide also helps regulate blood flow and strengthens immunity. However, it too has been found to be low in the brains of people with Alzheimer's disease. DHA may increase nitric oxide production and stimulate blood flow so that there is an adequate amount reaching the brain.

Treating damage that can result from our choices. Throughout childhood and adulthood, numerous mechanisms can destroy brain tissue. Addictive drugs can be toxic to nerve cells and damage the brain. Nutritional deficiencies and starvation—including from eating disorders—can cause cell death, too. The destruction can occur within months.

Stress, especially the chronic kind that can manifest itself as worry, can produce chemicals such as cortisol and corticotropin-releasing factor, which deplete nerve tissue. Fortunately, the destructive process ends once the addictive substance is eliminated, weight goes up to an acceptable range, or chronic stress is reduced. The process of reversing the damage depends on many factors, and consuming sufficient omega-3s may be uniquely beneficial.

Omega-3s have many other positive effects in your body that encourage brain health in a more *indirect* manner, too. Let's now turn our attention to some of these other benefits.

Omega-3s Can Help Your Brain in a Roundabout Way

Earlier in the book we discussed the importance of reducing inflammation in your body, since inflammatory chemicals are damaging to the brain. Though we've talked about the importance of antioxidants for keeping a lid on inflammation, getting the right fatty acids is *crucial* for limiting inflammation, too.

The role of fatty acids in inflammation is immense. Every cell in your body is covered by a membrane that consists of a double layer of fats. When a cell is injured, it releases this fat into its surroundings, where it is acted upon by an enzyme called cyclooxygenase (COX-2). The COX-2 enzymes will either convert the fat to an inflammatory agent or an anti-inflammatory agent. Inflammatory agents help heal the site of injury as part of the body's inflammatory response. This leads to pain, redness, swelling, invasion of white blood cells, scarring, and regeneration. This is helpful as long as the process does not persist continuously and become chronic. The body turns off chronic inflammation by manufacturing anti-inflammatory agents.

When our diet is high in omega-6s, the COX-2 enzyme converts them to inflammatory agents. The *opposite* occurs when COX-2 acts on omega-3s. When this happens, we get *anti*-inflammatory agents.

If our ratio of omega-6s to omega-3s is in the range of 1:1 to 3:1, this struggle between inflammation and anti-inflammation might be balanced.

However, people who eat a modern Western diet—which offers an abundance of omega-6-rich vegetable oils—have a ratio of about 20:1. That ratio is *way* out of balance if you want to keep your brain healthy.

Since omega-3s play a significant role in creating substances that counter inflammatory processes, the list of positive attributes that are associated with fish oil, DHA, or EPA is practically endless:

- Reducing atherosclerosis—the buildup of plaque in arteries that feed nutrients to your heart and brain
- Increasing good HDL cholesterol, which helps slow down plaque development
- Lowering bad LDL cholesterol, which contributes to plaque
- Reducing triglycerides, a type of blood fat
- Thinning the blood and making it less likely to clot
- Regulating heart rhythms
- Preventing strokes

Almost *every* chronic and autoimmune disease is in some way influenced by inflammation. It's reasonable to expect that the injured brain is undergoing a great deal of inflammation and could benefit from the anti-inflammatory contribution of omega-3s.

Weight loss. Abdominal obesity is a big supplier of inflammatory chemicals (more than twenty have been identified that come from fat cells in the abdomen). As a result, *any* attempts to reduce fat around your midsection would assist in brain healing.

Omega-3s might help reduce weight by:

- Stimulating the secretion of the appetite-suppressing hormone leptin. When you have enough leptin, you're less likely to overeat.
- Helping you burn dietary fat by moving fatty acids into your cells to convert to energy
- Dampening inflammation, which is known to promote weight gain
- Increasing blood flow to the muscles during exercise, which enhances fat burning

Not all studies have found that omega-3s help in weight loss when added to exercise and diet. But some research has found that getting more omega-3s could be a useful addition to exercise programs that are aimed at reducing body fat.

Insulin regulation. If you develop insulin resistance, in which insulin cannot attach to cells and open them up so they let in glucose, it leads to excess accumulation of insulin in your bloodstream. The extra insulin turns on critical enzymes that produce inflammatory substances. Omega-3s, however, can improve insulin sensitivity.

Heart health. Omega-3 supplementation may possibly reduce the risk of coronary heart disease. Japanese men have been shown to have a particularly high level of heart-healthy omega-3 fatty acids in their blood, which may help explain their low rate of heart disease. However, the average Japanese diet is not only rich in omega-3s but also relatively low in saturated fat. Saturated fat encourages coronary artery disease.

As always, it's important to remember that the heart and brain don't exist in isolation from each other. When your heart isn't pumping out blood like it should, your brain will surely suffer.

So How Do I Feed My Brain the Omega-3s It Needs?

The main source of omega-3s is cold-water fatty fish. That being said, fish don't actually make omega-3s very well. That job falls to algae and plankton, which *are* efficient at producing the stuff. Fish living in the ocean make omega-3s after gobbling this algae and plankton. They digest the fats from this free-floating food and then convert them into DHA and EPA. Wild Alaskan salmon (Chinook) also get their coloring from the plankton they eat. When you're shopping for this fish, remember that the deeper the color, the more omega-3 it contains.

In days gone by, farm-raised fish were fed corn or soy meal, which are high in omega-6 fatty acids. Fish cannot convert corn oil to omega-3s. Later, fish farmers began feeding them fishmeal, which is ground-up fish containing omega-3s.

Wild salmon has proportionally higher levels of omega-3s than farm-bred varieties. Farm-bred fish that are high in omega-3 fatty acids may pose other causes for concern. When they're fed fishmeal made from fish that were already exposed to pollution in the water—including

PCBs, dioxins, and methylmercury—they have a greater potential for contamination.

It takes approximately two to five pounds of ocean fish to produce one pound of farm-raised fish, which is occurring at a time when experts are worried about overfishing around the world. Some consumers also feel that farmed fish is inferior in taste and color (coloring agents or dyes are added to food pellets).

Not *all* fish you find in the store are good sources of omega-3s (neither are all farmed fish). The fish that we are most likely to consume that are high in these essential fatty acids are:

- Salmon
- Tuna
- Anchovies
- Sardines

Other seafood sources of omega-3s include mackerel, herring, halibut, whitefish, bluefish, black cod (sablefish), and swordfish.

Reel in Omega-3s with These Fish

If you're planning to use fish in your diet as a tool for repairing and protecting your brain, you might as well get as much benefit from your effort as possible. Here's how much DHA and EPA—which are types of omega-3s—you'll find in common types of seafood.

Fish	Grams per 3 ounces
Atlantic salmon, farmed, cooked in dry heat	1.8
Pacific herring, cooked in dry heat	1.8
Atlantic kippered herring	1.7
Atlantic salmon, wild, cooked in dry heat	1.6
Sablefish, smoked	1.6
Salmon, Chinook, cooked in dry heat	1.5
Tuna, bluefin, cooked in dry heat	1.3
Oysters, Pacific, cooked in moist heat	1.2

Tilapia is the fastest-growing fish in terms of popularity in the United States—and the most intensively farmed fish. High amounts of omega-6s from vegetable oils are used in their feed, and as a lean fish, they contain very little omega-3 fatty acids.

Health experts recommend that you eat two to three servings of cold-water fatty fish per week. However, if you're not a fan of fish—or don't have room in your grocery budget for it—you can also use fish oil supplements. These are one of the fastest-growing types of supplements on the market. Studies have reported that there is little—if any—difference in the activity from the oil in capsules compared to fish sources.

If you've ever tasted straight fish oil, you might wonder how you could swallow the stuff every day (or find people who could tolerate your breath afterward). That's why supplement makers put the oil in capsules, which reduces the bad taste. However, you can still summon up a fishy aftertaste. To avoid this, you may want to keep the capsules frozen until you swallow them. The oil itself doesn't freeze (remember those flexible fish swimming in the icy waters?). However, freezing delays the breakdown of the capsule until it passes through your stomach, which keeps the oil from returning the offensive taste back into your mouth.

Some people find that the oil can create bloating and diarrhea. If this happens, you may want to take the capsules with meals. Since fish oil is not a drug, the recommended amounts you may want to take vary. There is no standard or fixed therapeutic dosage that represents the optimal amount needed to keep your brain healthy.

The American Heart Association suggests a maintenance amount of 2.5 grams (2,500 milligrams) per day. This is the equivalent of about two to three servings of cold-water fatty fish per week. The use of fish oil supplements is not part of their recommendation.

> The first fish oil product, cod-liver oil, was promoted in 1775 as a miracle cure for arthritis. However, the oil was extracted from fish livers, and, unfortunately, the high concentration of vitamin A it contained could cause life-threatening toxicity. Not a good choice for fixing your brain! Manufacturers now extract oil from the body of the fish to reduce the threat of vitamin A overdose.

What About the Toxins in All This Fish I Need to Be Eating?

In recent years, the public has heard many warnings about potential contamination in fish, such as methylmercury, PCBs, and dioxins. Mercury is emitted into the atmosphere in substantial amounts by coal-fired power plants, as well as other man-made and natural sources. The pollution in the air finds its way into streams, rivers, lakes, and eventually the ocean. The mercury is converted to methylmercury by bacteria in the water and sediments of wetlands. Fish eat the bacteria, and larger fish eat smaller fish, and thus the methylmercury can accumulate in older and larger fish.

It reaches its highest concentration in large predatory marine animals such as marlin, shark, swordfish, tuna, and whales, and freshwater fish such as bass and pike. Contaminated smaller wild fish are used as feed at fish farms. Therefore, farm-raised fish can become concentrated with toxins, too.

The fatty tissue that contains omega-3s also collects toxins. The fattier the fish, the more omega-3s it contains, but also potentially more toxins. Methylmercury is hard to eliminate from the body, and it builds up in the nervous tissue. It may harm the fetal nervous system and the developing brains of children, resulting in delays in neurological development and learning disabilities. In adults, high levels can cause depression, trouble concentrating, and headaches.

Experts sometimes recommend these fish as safer choices:

- Wild Alaskan salmon
- Canned sockeye salmon
- Canned albacore light tuna

U.S. health officials recommended that pregnant women eat no more than 12 ounces of fish per week. Women should continue to eat fish during pregnancy, but choose varieties with lower mercury contamination.

The maximum amount is set at about 3 grams (3,000 milligrams) daily, though Greenland Eskimos are reported to consume from 7 to 10 grams a day. The side effects of fish oil capsules can include diarrhea, flatulence, halitosis (fish breath), flushing, increased risk of bleeding, and (when you take them in very high levels) elevated blood sugar.

As with antioxidant supplements, more is not necessarily better. The Fred Hutchinson Cancer Research Center found that men with the highest blood levels of DHA were more than twice as likely to come down with aggressive, high-grade prostate cancer versus the men who had the lowest levels. There is probably no cause for alarm, but it does point out the need for moderation and the complexity of understanding nutrients' relationship to cancer risk.

Other Sources of Omega-3s Besides Fish

For those who are allergic to fish or who cannot take fish oil supplements because of negative side effects, other good sources of omega-3s can be found in foods that have nothing to do with fish or fish oil. Historically, grass-fed beef was a good source, but modern animal husbandry has switched to grain-raised beef, which is omega-3 deficient. However, many foods are now available with added omega-3s, such as enriched eggs. These are certainly reasonable ways to add brain-healthy omega-3s to your diet.

Humans are also capable of making omega-3s from sources such as flaxseed, walnuts, canola oil, and purslane. These plants contain the precursor of omega-3s called alpha-linolenic acid (ALA). In fact, most of the oil in flaxseed is ALA. Flaxseeds also contain lignin, which has antioxidant properties. Almonds and walnuts are also excellent sources of ALA (and almonds also inhibit an enzyme called cholinesterase, which forms beta-amyloid plaques in the brain during Alzheimer's disease).

Though our bodies can make omega-3, the conversion is often inefficient, especially if the enzymes that handle the process are overwhelmed by excess omega-6 fatty acids. It takes about 10 grams of ALA to produce one gram of DHA/EPA.

If you go the flaxseed route, be sure to buy flaxseeds that have already been ground so your body can absorb the nutrients, since the body cannot digest whole flaxseeds. And remember, since not everyone can readily turn ALA into EPA and DHA, try to not count solely on these foods to cover your omega-3 needs.

The Other Fats You Should Get—or Avoid—for Brain Health

This chapter started with omega-3 fats and discussed them at some length because they're clearly so good for repairing and maintaining brain health. However, the foods you encounter every day provide *other* kinds of fat, too. Some of these are good additions to your diet, but some you should limit if you want to keep your brain supplied with a steady stream of nutrients and fuel.

The fats (and fat-containing foods) to add to your Brain Fix Toolbox are:

Olive Oil and Nuts

Olive oil is a good source of oleic acid. This monounsaturated fat is an omega-9 fatty acid. Oleic acid makes up a large part of the fatty myelin sheaths that surround nerves and improve cell-to-cell communication. Oleic acid may also help you keep your weight down. This could help protect your brain health, since obesity is related to your risk of heart disease and inflammation.

Oleic acid produces earlier and increased levels of hormones in the digestive system that suppress appetite and induce a general feeling of fullness and satisfaction. Olive oil, almonds, pecans, peanuts, and avocados are high in oleic acid.

Olive oil may help serotonin bind better to serotonin receptors in the brain, which may help reduce depression. Fatty acids in olive oil may also reduce your risk of coronary artery disease.

Extra-virgin olive oil in the diet has also been found to be effective in preventing LDL cholesterol from becoming oxidized (which means damaged by free radicals). White blood cells are thought to pick up only oxidized LDL and deposit it into artery linings. As a result, extra-virgin olive oil may slow the formation of atherosclerotic plaque that can impede blood flow to your brain. Olive oil also contains a compound called oleocanthal, which blocks COX enzymes (thus mimicking the pain-relieving and anti-inflammatory action of ibuprofen).

However, there are also fats that you'll encounter in common foods that you should *limit* if you want a well-oiled brain: saturated fat and trans fat. Remember that an important quality of the brain-healthy omega-3s is their flexibility. When they become incorporated into the membranes surrounding the neurons in your brain, they help these cells function properly.

Saturated fat and trans fat are more *inflexible* types of fat. Saturated fat (like in lard, animal fat, and butter) is solid at room temperature. Trans fat (which is found in many processed foods) is rigid. Trans fat is used in processed foods because it is chemically more like animal fat, which means it's more solid and less likely to go rancid. That makes it perfect for frying and industrial baking. From the food manufacturers' perspective, this is a good thing because it adds to a longer shelf life, better mouth feel, easier spreadability, and improved baking quality at higher temperatures.

Common sources of trans fat include vegetable shortening, margarine, crackers, cookies, doughnuts, microwave popcorn, salad dressing, peanut butter, fast foods, biscuits, taco shells, and cakes. Food manufacturers create trans fat through a process called *hydrogenating* vegetable oil. So if you see "hydrogenated" or "partially hydrogenated" on a food label, that's your clue that the food provides trans fat that you don't want.

Saturated fat and trans fat shouldn't be limited in your diet just because they lead to less flexible brain cells. They are also harmful to the blood vessels feeding your heart and brain, since both contribute to the buildup of plaque in the arteries. Because of this, less than 10 percent of your total calories should come from saturated fat. If you're eating 2,000 calories a day, that means no more than 200 calories should come from saturated fat, which equals 22 grams of the stuff.

Experts recommend that you should keep your consumption of trans fat as low as possible. To cut down on trans fat easily, just minimize your intake of fast foods, processed foods, and store-bought baked goods and snacks.

THE BRAIN FIX TOOLBOX

- For a healthy brain, you should hold yourself to an upper limit of about 50 grams of total fat if you're a woman or 65 grams if you're a man. You don't want to go *too* low, however, since your body needs enough fat on board to help you absorb certain vitamins and carry nutrients. An extremely low-fat diet can also increase your risk of depression.

- Get 2 grams of omega-3 fatty acids daily by eating cold-water fish or taking pharmaceutical-grade fish oil supplements. If you're a vegetarian, eat plenty of nuts and flaxseed.

- Reduce the saturated fat in your diet to less than 10 percent of your total daily calories. You can do this by cutting back on red meat and choosing low-fat dairy foods.

- Limit your consumption of processed foods that are high in hydrogenated and trans fat.

- Use olive oil for cooking and find ways to incorporate it into other foods, such as dressing for salads.

- Minimize oils that are high in omega-6s, since you want to keep your ratio of omega-6s to omega-3s lower than the typical Western diet provides. When you use oil in cooking, go for canola (which has an omega-6 to omega-3 ratio of 2:1) or olive oil (3:1 ratio). Limit corn oil (46:1), soybean oil (7:1), and sunflower, cottonseed, and peanut oils (which contain no omega-3s).

6

The Cholesterol Dilemma: Your Brain Needs to Get Enough of the Stuff

FOR SEVERAL DIET EXPERTS who gained national prominence, cholesterol and its effects in the body were a major concern. Nathan Pritikin was the creator of the Pritikin Longevity Center and author of the bestselling book *The Pritikin Program for Diet and Exercise*. His primary approach to promoting well-being was a low-cholesterol and low-fat diet that provided fewer than 10 percent of total calories as fat. After a long battle with leukemia, the sixty-nine-year-old took his own life in 1985, feeling that his life wasn't worth continuing. An autopsy found that his heart showed no sign of disease, and his blood vessels were free of the plaque buildup known as atherosclerosis.

Later, another diet that gained worldwide acclaim was the high-protein, low-carbohydrate Atkins Diet. Though it was popular, some of the tenets of this diet attracted controversy, such as its tolerance of fatty foods. Its creator, Robert Atkins, also met an untimely end. In 2003, at the age of seventy-two, he reportedly fell on ice and suffered head injuries while walking to his office in New York City.

Several months earlier, he had been hospitalized for a heart problem, which sources close to him asserted was not related to blockage in his arteries. He reportedly had only minimal signs of coronary artery disease. However, unanswered questions remain as to what may have caused his death: the head injury, a massive stroke (he never sought to brace himself to break the fall), or some other unknown cause.

These two figures contributed greatly to the dietary practices of millions of Americans who sought to improve their health and well-being. Their legacies stand out as a reflection of the ongoing effort to understand

and thereby prevent the leading cause of death in this country: cardio-vascular disease. Roughly 16.3 million American adults have coronary artery disease, which impairs the flow of blood to the heart. Another similar problem that's tied into the cardiovascular system is stroke. These strike an American every 40 seconds.

The point of bringing up Pritikin and Atkins is not to focus on their premature deaths, but rather to draw attention to the fact that despite the contrast in their dietary philosophy, the condition of their blood vessels was similar when they died. One man wanted to limit cholesterol in his followers' diets and the other was less concerned with the effects of cholesterol.

Nowadays, the medical establishment—armed with a variety of medications—is putting a high priority on lowering people's cholesterol levels. But getting your cholesterol as low as possible doesn't necessarily support optimal *brain* health!

Heart disease isn't a new concern for mankind. For proof, just look to Lady Rai, a nursemaid to Queen Ahmose-Nefertari of Egypt. She died in her thirties sometime between 1530 and 1570 BC. Though the cause of her death is unknown, she showed evidence of the same plaque and heart disease that are often regarded as the scourge of modern man. She is the most ancient person on record to have suffered from heart disease—and her demise occurred 3,500 years before the advent of issues often linked to heart disease in modern times, such as fast food, a sedentary lifestyle propelled by television, and cigarette smoking.

Cholesterol appears to be a key player in the buildup of plaque, which can choke your brain of oxygen and nutrients, leaving it starved and injured. Studies on cholesterol may have begun as far back as 1769 when a French chemist named Polutier de la Salle analyzed the soapy-looking substance. In 1913, a Russian scientist, Nikolai Anichkov, fed rabbits massive amounts of cholesterol. They subsequently died of heart disease. The damage in their blood vessels was similar to that seen in cases of human atherosclerosis. These studies are considered the first proof that dietary cholesterol causes heart disease.

However, several major studies, including the Seven Countries Study, the Framingham Study, and the Japanese Migrants Study, showed that dietary cholesterol appears to be *correlated* with vascular disease—in other words, they often travel together—but they didn't show that cholesterol causes the problem.

In 1990, researchers looked at 194 autopsies of people with severe vascular disease. These postmortem exams showed that the eighty cases with the most severe atherosclerosis had no evidence of elevated cholesterol, diabetes, or hypertension. Only 8 percent of the individuals autopsied had cholesterol levels above 240 mg/dL, which is regarded as high. In addition, studies such as the Nurses' Health Study showed only a weak link between the amount of cholesterol a person consumes and his or her blood cholesterol levels.

Numerous experts have attacked the idea that animal fats and cholesterol cause heart disease as flimsy, fraudulent, and wishful thinking. Several other causes of cardiovascular disease that are connected to diet habits may be just as critical to address as an individual's cholesterol levels, including high ratios of omega-6s to omega-3s, high blood sugar, low magnesium, trans-fatty acids, high saturated fats, and low antioxidants.

In addition, a substance called homocysteine has been shown by numerous studies to be an independent risk factor for atherosclerosis. Several other risk factors can make people more vulnerable to cardiovascular disease, including inflammation, older age, family history of heart disease, obesity, physical inactivity, insulin resistance, race, smoking, high blood pressure, stress, and sleep apnea.

There seems to be no consensus for what is the best predictor or leading cause of a heart attack. Along with other studies, the long-running Framingham Heart Study concluded that the best predictors for heart attack were smoking and hypertension, with high cholesterol being among the *least* predictive. In other words, if you want to figure out who's going to have a heart attack, focusing too much on cholesterol may not be a very fruitful use of your time. The leading candidate may very well be inflammation in the body instead—or homocysteine. Even the issue of hostility and anger enters into the controversy as to what provides the best prediction for a heart attack.

As a result, even though society presently puts a major priority on using cholesterol-lowering drugs and lifestyle approaches for preventing heart disease, this strategy may be overrated. And as you'll soon see, your brain's health is very reliant on having sufficient cholesterol.

Why Do We Even Have Cholesterol in the First Place?

Most people don't realize the *good* things that cholesterol does for us. Cholesterol helps us create bile (a fluid that's necessary for digestion); vitamin D; sex-related hormones like estrogen, progesterone, and testosterone; and stress hormones like cortisol. More important, cholesterol is found in every cell membrane, which is the soft "shell" that covers each cell.

Used-up cholesterol must be replaced on a continual basis. Approximately 20 percent of the cholesterol in your blood comes directly from the foods you eat. The majority, however, is manufactured in your liver and other tissues, such as your adrenal glands and intestines.

The fact that the majority of cholesterol is made by your body helps explain why a low-cholesterol diet will not necessarily lower the cholesterol present in your blood. A normal, healthy adult manufactures about 1,000 milligrams of cholesterol per day to maintain a relatively constant level in the blood. The body depends on cholesterol so much that it can actually manufacture as much as 3,000 milligrams per day! This is about ten times the amount that the American Heart Association recommends you get from your food each day.

When a cell needs cholesterol, it extracts it from your blood, creates its own, or—as usually is the case—does both. If it wants to draw cholesterol out of the bloodstream, it creates a protein that will serve as a receptor for cholesterol that's passing by in the blood. This protein is called the LDL-cholesterol receptor (LDL-r). The cell sends it to the surface membrane, where it binds to LDL cholesterol that's passing by. The LDL cholesterol is then transported into the cell, where it is used.

Because blood is water-based and cholesterol is fat-based and can't dissolve in water, the cholesterol must be carried through the bloodstream inside water-soluble particles called lipoproteins. HDL and LDL are both lipoproteins (these stand for high-density lipoprotein and low-density lipoprotein). LDL doesn't hold cholesterol tightly, and it will drop off its cargo at cells readily. HDL, however, *does* keep a tight hold on cholesterol, and it can remove it from cells and transport it back to the liver for removal.

When cells have an abundance of cholesterol, they make fewer LDL receptors to keep from taking in more cholesterol. Then excessive amounts of LDL cholesterol molecules build up in the blood. When you go on a weight-loss diet, cells create more LDL receptors. As a result, weight loss and dieting are useful techniques for lowering cholesterol. When you eat a high-cholesterol diet, your body creates less of its own cholesterol and makes fewer LDL receptors to clear cholesterol from the blood.

Failure to remove the cholesterol from the blood *should* be countered by the creation of less cholesterol from cells. In cholesterol-sensitive individuals (about 30 percent of the population), this internal monitoring mechanism does not work right, and their cholesterol level goes up when they eat high-cholesterol foods. Some experts theorize that these individuals were meant to be vegetarians, since their bodies are not genetically equipped to handle excess cholesterol. Plant cell walls are composed of fiber, not cholesterol, and do not contribute cholesterol to the diet.

LDL—which is considered the "bad" form of cholesterol—can cause problems for your blood vessels when it becomes altered, such as when it's damaged by free radicals. Cholesterol is not harmful if it is not oxidized, however. Over time, science has revealed that the true culprit in plaque buildup in blood vessels is not LDL cholesterol, but rather an *oxidized version* of LDL cholesterol.

The oxidized LDL cholesterol is gobbled up by white blood cells, which then turn into fatty foam cells. These can infiltrate the walls of blood vessels and contribute to the formation of atherosclerotic plaque. Over time, these faulty LDL particles that are attracted to the vessel wall eventually trigger inflammation, a series of events that occurs when the body attempts to heal itself.

HDL, on the other hand, is much like a vacuum in that it removes cholesterol from cells and carries it away to the liver for removal. It also has the capacity to remove cholesterol that has built up in the lining of blood vessels, and therefore it is referred to as the "good" cholesterol. We need a healthy balance of HDL and LDL, since both are important.

Your ratio of LDL to HDL should range from 3:1 up to 4:1. If your LDL cholesterol is 150 milligrams per deciliter (mg/dL) and your HDL cholesterol is 50 mg/dL, your ratio would be 3:1.

Once HDL cholesterol carries cholesterol to your liver, your body gets rid of it in feces or sends it to other tissues that use cholesterol for creating hormones. At the liver, the recycled cholesterol is used for creating bile. Bile acids digest food and make vitamin D. Bile also helps your body absorb vitamins A, D, E, and K. Your liver excretes bile into your digestive tract, which is how it sends it out of your body. Typically, half of the excreted bile is reabsorbed by the small intestine back into the bloodstream. Fiber from your diet keeps some of this cholesterol from being reabsorbed.

Cholesterol is important to your brain for many reasons, but one crucial role it plays is in creating your cells' membranes. Cholesterol is an important component of all cell membranes. This outer perimeter provides a protective wall that only allows certain substances to pass into and out of the cell. Substances must pass through two layers of fat in the cell membrane, and the makeup of these fats determines the ease with which molecules pass through. The best gatekeeper is a membrane that has a balance of fluidity and stiffness. Unsaturated fatty acids such as omega-3s contribute to the fluidity, as we learned in the last chapter. Cholesterol is sandwiched between the two layers of fat, which reduces movement and thereby contributes to stiffness.

Cholesterol: Crucial for Brain Function and Mood

The human brain weighs approximately three pounds, and water accounts for most of the weight. However, a considerable 12 percent of its weight is made up of fat and cholesterol. This makes cholesterol and fat the most abundant molecules in the brain aside from water. However, the cholesterol in your blood does *not* contribute to your brain's supply of cholesterol.

The system called the blood-brain barrier controls what is and what is not allowed to enter the brain. The cholesterol carried in the blood is too large to cross this barrier. As a result, your brain must depend on its own source of cholesterol. Glial cells, which make up 90 percent of the cells in the brain, create cholesterol. Glial cells—which include astrocytes, oligodendrocytes, and microglia—aren't neurons. Thus, they don't move your muscles or do the tasks that you regard as thinking. Instead, they support the development, function, and structure of the brain.

The cholesterol they make is mandatory for good brain function. Cholesterol is the primary compound in the substance called myelin, which surrounds each nerve cell like a sheath. Myelin is an electrical insulating material that forms a layer around the axon of neurons. Myelin serves to increase the speed at which nerve signals fly down the axon fiber. The coating is protective and can be damaged by disease or injury. Loss of myelin is the hallmark of autoimmune diseases such as multiple sclerosis and Guillain-Barré syndrome. Interruptions or gaps within the myelin sheath may cause nerve impulses to become disrupted, similar to a short in a wire.

Specialized glial cells migrate to the damaged site and activate a cascade of reactions that includes the creation of cholesterol. Cholesterol is an *indispensable* component of myelin, and the glial cells' ability to make it helps determine how well the brain is developed.

Your brain's need for cholesterol goes back to your earliest days in the womb. A fetus grows at a rate unparalleled by any other stage of life. To maintain its rapid growth rate, it requires a significant amount of cholesterol and fatty acids. Cholesterol plays a critical role in embryonic development by interacting with signaling proteins that control the early development of the brain.

Cholesterol is also required as a building block for various hormones that are critical to normal development. Cholesterol is so important to fetal development that pregnant women who don't have high enough cholesterol levels are at increased risk of having babies with developmental problems. Women who take the cholesterol-lowering drugs known as statins during pregnancy have been found to have a greater risk of giving birth to babies with developmental problems.

Later in life, if your cholesterol supply grows short, the deficit could cause difficulty with focusing or maintaining a positive mood. Three feel-good neurotransmitters—those chemicals that carry messages in your brain—are serotonin, dopamine, and oxytocin. When you have a lack of cholesterol in the membranes of your brain cells, they may not be able to pick up serotonin that other cells have released in order to send a signal. Dopamine-producing nerve cells are created during brain development, and they contain receptors for picking up brain chemicals, which must be activated by cholesterol. In addition, cholesterol may help the receptor for the hormone oxytocin to work properly.

In adult women and men, low cholesterol has been associated with depression and anxiety. This may be partially due to the failure of serotonin to bind properly at its receptor on nerve cells that pick it up when it's released between the cells.

Research has found that cholesterol levels were correlated with the severity of depressive symptoms in people with anorexia and bulimia. Numerous studies confirm an association between low cholesterol and suicidal behavior in women and men. People who reported previous suicide attempts, impulsive self-injuries, or thinking about suicide have been shown to have significantly lower cholesterol levels than people without suicidal thoughts. Lower cholesterol levels are also linked to a small but significant increased risk of completing suicide.

A significant association has also been found between low cholesterol levels and violence, aggression, and impulsive behavior. Human and animal research suggests that low cholesterol levels may reduce the activity of serotonin in the brain, which in turn may cause violent behaviors. More than 163 scientific papers have linked low cholesterol with a greater risk of accidents, aggressive and violent behavior, prison confinement among young males, borderline personality disorder, mood disturbances, drug addiction, addiction relapse, impulsivity, memory impairment, and premature death. Low cholesterol levels in adults are also associated with worse scores on cognitive tests that require abstract reasoning, attention and concentration, word fluency, and other skills.

A long-term Japanese study has also indicated that people with extremely low blood cholesterol levels may have an increased risk of intracerebral hemorrhage, which is a type of stroke marked by bleeding into the brain. A low level of cholesterol in the blood may reduce the blood's ability to clot. The National Research Council, after reviewing the data, concluded that the risk of cerebral hemorrhages seems to be seen only in people with a combination of very low cholesterol and high blood pressure.

It seems evident that cholesterol plays a crucial role in keeping our mood and behaviors stable. And we must maintain a steady level of cholesterol in our brains to assist in healing and regeneration.

Although our bodies get cholesterol from our diet, and to a larger extent the cholesterol made by our liver, as previously noted, the brain relies on glial cells to create its cholesterol. We should now give some thought to how statins—which are very common cholesterol-lowering drugs—may affect our brain function.

Is Lower Cholesterol from Statins a Good Thing for Your Brain?

Statins are considered to be among the most successful drugs of all time and have been credited with preventing millions of heart attacks and cases of disability from strokes. The statin drugs include Lipitor, Mevacor, Zocor, Pravachol, and Lescol—many of which have become household names.

The basic way that statins function is to decrease the formation of cholesterol in your liver. The production of cholesterol requires a long series of twenty-two steps. This cholesterol-making process requires an enzyme called HMG-CoA reductase. This is the link in the chain that statin drugs target.

The process that creates cholesterol also makes a substance called coenzyme Q_{10} (CoQ_{10}), which is the body's number one natural antioxidant for heart health. As a result, statins interrupt the production of CoQ_{10}. Drug manufacturers are aware of this and often combine CoQ_{10} with statins, and physicians frequently recommend supplementation of CoQ_{10} when they prescribe statins. CoQ_{10} plays several other important roles in maintaining a healthy body and brain, such as nerve conduction and neutralizing free radicals.

More than 25 percent of Americans age forty-five and older are taking statins, which are typically prescribed for the rest of their lives. Forty-two percent of Americans age sixty-five to seventy-four are taking them. It's likely that the number of Americans taking these drugs will continue to rise, as our experts (and drug companies) urge us to get our cholesterol lower.

The National Cholesterol Education Program has promoted lowering LDL cholesterol for those at risk of heart disease to less than 100 mg/dL, and for those with very high cardiovascular risk to less than 70 mg/dL. Statins have been clinically proven to lower "bad" LDL cholesterol levels by 40 to 60 percent when diet and exercise aren't lowering them enough.

The Scandinavian Simvastatin Survival Study showed that statins reduced total mortality in patients with coronary heart disease. However, there is evidence that patients who use statins are consistently more health-seeking than patients who don't stick to their statin regimens. As a result, we need to be wary sometimes about research that links preventive medicines to protective effects.

Some experts are skeptical that using statin therapy in people without symptoms is beneficial and safe. Studies that combined earlier research have found scant evidence that statins saved lives in the short term in people who didn't have heart disease. And the absolute safety of statins has not been demonstrated for people who have low risk of coronary heart disease.

Statins can be a lifesaver for people who have survived heart attacks by lowering the likelihood of another one. But the benefits of statin use haven't been proven in people older than sixty-five, and there is evidence that people older than seventy with somewhat higher cholesterol levels live longer.

In addition, side effects are common in pharmaceuticals, and statins are no exception. Cerivastatin (Baycol) was a statin that was taken off the market in 2001 due to a risk of rhabdomyolysis, in which muscles break down and block structures in the kidneys. The FDA issued a warning in 2011 that doctors should no longer prescribe simvastatin (Zocor) at the highest approved dosage of 80 milligrams, as it was related to a higher risk of muscle damage at this dose.

People on statins are also more likely to develop nerve problems that lead to pins-and- needles sensations, burning, weakness, and numbness. Other side effects include chronic muscle pain and injury, liver injury, psychological changes, cognitive impairment, amnesia, and cataracts.

Statins *have* been reported to protect nerve cells. They've also reportedly been able to reduce the risk of ischemic stroke (caused by blockages in the brain's arteries) and the progression of Alzheimer's disease when used preventatively. On the negative side, researchers have linked a small increase in the incidence of hemorrhagic stroke to statins.

Another way statins may impact one's mental health is via testosterone. Cholesterol is a building block for numerous hormones, including the male sex hormone testosterone. Some men have reported that their sexual performance declined after starting statins. There is some degree of concern that men taking statin drugs might have difficulty with erectile dysfunction as a result of lower levels of testosterone. Several studies also found lower libido in men taking statins. Other signs of testosterone deficiency include poorer athletic performance and grumpy mood.

Researchers have reported that they found lower levels of testosterone in men taking statins. This change is reversible, however, once the statin drugs are stopped. (It is important to note, however, that some studies have shown that statins do *not* have an effect on testosterone or other reproductive hormones. The lower level of testosterone in men taking statins could possibly be explained by other factors such as obesity and diabetes.) Men on statins may also relieve testosterone deficiency by taking the hormone in medication form.

In addition, cortisol—a hormone that is chronically produced in response to unresolved physiological and/or emotional stress or worry —is also made from cholesterol. Disturbing the balance of this hormone may trigger changes in behavior and mood.

Some types of statins can cross the blood-brain barrier, which means the brain is exposed to their effects, one of which is the reduction of the creation of cholesterol by glial cells. Since certain statins can cross this barrier, it would behoove researchers to investigate what effect these could have on sufficient cholesterol levels in the brain. Since statins have the potential to reduce cholesterol production in the brain, they might underlie depression, anger, and impulsivity, and they may increase suicidal tendencies. Researchers have also found signs that statins may inhibit the placement of new myelin on nerves as well.

Given the impact that low cholesterol can have on a properly functioning brain, it gives us a reason to be cautious in driving our cholesterol *too* low.

Finding a Brain-Healthy Balance Between High Cholesterol and Low Cholesterol

How do you find the path toward a healthy level of cholesterol that's neither too high nor too low? For most of us, moderation via a prudent diet will get us there. Unless your physician recommends a low-cholesterol diet (less than 250 milligrams daily), just be sensible when it comes to consuming high-cholesterol foods like eggs, mayonnaise, red meat, and dairy. Enjoy them occasionally, but don't make them the main items on your plate.

It's also helpful to ensure that fat accounts for less than 30 percent of your total calories. No more than 10 percent of your calories should come from saturated fat, which is found in foods like whole-fat dairy, red meat, and butter. Keeping your saturated fat low will help keep your cholesterol in check.

When it comes to statin drugs, knowing when to use them or not requires a good rapport with your doctor. Discuss whether you could manage your cholesterol with lifestyle changes such as a high-fiber, low-fat diet, aerobic exercise, and keeping your stress under control. Before this conversation, be sure your doctor is familiar with your family history of heart disease and (if possible) how your cholesterol has changed over time.

There is no simple recommendation for maintaining healthy cholesterol for your brain, other than making healthy lifestyle changes that will allow you—if at all possible—to regulate your cholesterol in a drug-free manner.

Though they are linked to concerns, statin drugs *can* be valuable in protecting our health. High total cholesterol is considered to be levels of 240 milligrams per deciliter or higher. The optimal level is less than 200. However, people's chance of reducing their number below 200 using diet, exercise, stress reduction, and weight loss is not great. An all-out effort may lower the number by 5 to 10 percent, but when it's not possible to bring it down further, statins can potentially lower the level by a remarkable 40 to 50 percent.

Nevertheless, people should make a greater effort to lower their cholesterol through lifestyle management. Doctors should be more insistent that patients comply with these recommendations of exercise, diet, stress reduction, and weight management. Like every drug, statins have side effects, and every effort must be made to minimize the need to be on a drug, no matter how safe it is reported to be.

It's still controversial whether lowering cholesterol in every healthy adult to below 190 is a good idea. Low cholesterol levels may tell us that the body is not healthy enough to produce cholesterol, and we need to know more about how low is *too* low for each person. As a result, if your doctor recommends statins, it's important to have a conversation about the benefits of the drugs versus their risks. If you haven't already had a heart attack or other problem related to coronary heart disease, it's a good idea for your doctor to first calculate your absolute risk of developing coronary heart disease in the near future before putting you on statin treatment.

 ## THE BRAIN FIX TOOLBOX
Tools for Launching a Healthy Outlook

- Unless your healthcare provider has recommended sticking to a low-cholesterol diet, simply eat in a way that puts a reasonable limit on the foods that make your cholesterol rise (such as eggs, red meat, and whole-fat dairy). You don't want to go overboard on these foods, but most of us don't want to completely rule them out of our diet either.

- Keep a good line of communication open with your doctor. If your doctor recommends statins, be sure you discuss whether they're truly necessary for your heart health. You may very well need them, but also have a discussion on other steps you can take to lower your cholesterol that will have other benefits for your body and brain.

7

Protein: Don't Overlook
Its Impact in Brain Healing

THE WORD PROTEIN comes from the Greek *proteios*, which roughly means "of first importance." Though we haven't gotten to protein until Chapter 7 in this book, the protein you eat is without a doubt very important for maintaining and repairing your brain.

Proteins are the building blocks of life, necessary for building all your cells. Antibodies, hormones, the hemoglobin in your blood, and roughly two thousand enzymes in your body contain protein.

If proteins are the building blocks of cells, amino acids are the building blocks of protein. The many proteins in your body are made of just twenty amino acids combined into sometimes complicated structures. Your body can create some of these amino acids on its own, but it has to take in others through foods. When you eat protein foods—which for most of us includes meat and dairy products—your digestive system breaks down the protein into its component amino acids. Then your body reassembles these raw materials into *new* proteins that your body needs.

Proteins, Amino Acids, and Your Brain

In your brain, proteins are needed for regenerating nerve tissue. They also help replenish neurotransmitters after they become depleted. These all-important chemicals are the major source of communication between brain circuits. Many of your neurotransmitters are called *monoamines* because they are composed of a single (mono) amino acid (amine).

Neurons secrete these monoamines into synapses—the spaces between neurons—throughout the brain. Monoamines become used up in people with depression. Medications can help you maintain a higher level of these neurotransmitters and a better mood, such as the so-called monoamine oxidase (MAO) inhibitor drugs that keep monoamines from breaking down.

One of the important monoamine neurotransmitters is serotonin. This chemical often has a calming effect on the mind, and many associate it with sleep (which is when we're the calmest). An amino acid called tryptophan acts as a precursor for serotonin.

Sweets May Calm You in a Complicated Way

When you consume simple sugars, or any carbohydrate that is high on the glycemic index, you have an increase in insulin secretion. The insulin blocks large amino acids from entering into competition with tryptophan to cross the blood-brain barrier. This allows easy passage for tryptophan, which is immediately converted to serotonin. The higher concentration of serotonin acts as an antidepressant or sedative. Since sugar produces this calm and centered state, some people may unconsciously eat sweets to correct any serotonin deficiency.

Another amino acid important for proper brain functioning is phenylalanine. It's used in creating both dopamine and norepinephrine. Amino acids take various shapes that affect their function in the brain. Phenylalanine in the so-called L form is associated with elevating mood, boosting memory, reducing stress, decreasing pain, and suppressing appetite. The D form, by contrast, may play a role in depression, sleep disturbances, anxiety, and agitation. Normally, the average diet contains about 1,000 milligrams a day of a mixture of the two forms.

Other chemicals that are important in the brain are related to proteins. One fairly large group is the opioid derivatives called endorphins. These are your body's natural pain-relieving chemicals. Endorphins are *peptides*, meaning they are made from several amino acids, particularly methionine. In addition, several other chemicals involved in neural communication involve amino acids, such as acetylcholine, nitric oxide, and phosphatidylserine.

One protein-related substance that's especially interesting when discussing brain health is the amino acid taurine. It was first isolated from ox blood in 1827 (thus its bull-sounding name). Taurine is especially important and abundant in the nervous system, particularly the brain. Researchers have found that taurine may increase concentration, mental alertness, endurance, and reaction speed. It may also improve one's overall sense of well-being. Research on rats led to findings that taurine improves insulin sensitivity. It also decreases the production of cholesterol and increases the excretion of cholesterol by converting it to bile acid. These actions of taurine may serve to prevent abdominal fat accumulation, hyperglycemia, and insulin resistance (which in turn could help improve blood sugar control).

Probably the most novel use for taurine is in reducing some of the effects of alcoholism. This amino acid may help maintain abstinence in alcohol-dependent patients who have completed detoxification. That's because taurine can repress the rewarding effect in the brain that's associated with alcohol. There is also scientific support that taurine protects against some of the harmful effects of chronic alcohol use.

Around 1997, a trendy carbonated beverage called Red Bull hit the shelves in the United States, ushering in a flood of other so-called energy drinks. Its ingredients include caffeine and taurine. The popularity of Red Bull stems from its legendary energy-boosting ability. However, no one can say for sure if taurine is responsible for the purported energy-raising effect, as it could be due to the sugar or caffeine.

Even though this benefit goes against the claim of being an energy enhancer and mood booster, taurine also has the potential to be effective in reducing excitable brain states. It may have some ability to inhibit adrenaline, which is associated with anxiety, and it may protect tissues from oxidative stress. These mechanisms of action may explain why taurine has been found to be useful in cases of insomnia, agitation, restlessness, irritability, obsession, anxiety, epilepsy, headaches, and depression.

So how much protein do we need in our daily diet? It may not be as much as you'd think, and it's not hard for most Americans to get enough. However, some of the foods that are high in protein aren't so great for your brain health. So picking your protein-rich foods carefully is wise.

Time to Shoot Down the Turkey Myth

Urban legend holds that foods with a high amount of tryptophan—which is used in the creation of serotonin—will make you sleepy. Turkey and milk are two foods that contain higher levels of tryptophan, so it would follow they would be associated with sleep. However, nutrition is not quite that simple. Tryptophan has to compete with other amino acids in those foods to enter the brain, and it doesn't simply flood the brain after you eat a tryptophan-rich food.

Turkey probably has the reputation of stimulating drowsiness because people typically eat turkey and other foods on holidays until they are stuffed. An overloaded gut will draw blood to the digestive tract and away from the brain. This makes less oxygen available to the brain, and likely explains that post-Thanksgiving lunch sense of sleepiness.

How Much Protein You Need (and Where to Get It)

It is fairly easy to determine exactly how much protein we require by calculating how much we lose on a daily basis. Your body breaks down its own proteins every day, which must be replaced daily since we do not store it.

Protein is the sole source of nitrogen, which we continuously get rid of in our urine. Free nitrogen needs to be packaged in urine and shipped off through the kidneys or it's toxic, especially to brain cells.

Most women lose about 42 grams of protein per day. Since an ounce of meat or dairy contains about 7 grams of protein, this implies that women should consume about 6 ounces of these protein foods per day. Men need to consume at least 63 grams of protein per day, which comes out to 9 ounces of protein-rich food. Most of us have little worry of developing protein deficiency since most women consume 13 ounces of protein-rich foods and most men get 17 ounces per day.

The 42 to 63 grams of protein per day mentioned above mark the *least* amount of protein a person needs. If you take in less than the minimal requirement, then your body will draw from its existing sources of protein to keep running. If you're starving for protein long enough, eventually your body will break down lean tissue in muscles and organs to ensure that enough protein is available for critical life-supporting organs such as the brain and heart.

Fortunately, very few people who eat a varied diet fail to take in adequate protein. However, if you have significant restrictions in your diet (as in vegetarianism or veganism, very low calorie diets, or eating disorders) you can develop a deficiency.

As a result, it may be more important for us to remember to not eat excessively *large* amounts of protein at one time. Too much protein is simply unnecessary. Getting too much protein won't hurt us; it simply is wasted. The body typically can only use about 2 to 3 ounces during a three-hour period. If our intake is more than we can use, our bodies will convert the excess to energy or store it as fat (which, of course, most of us *don't* need). Protein is the least efficient of the energy sources, behind carbohydrate and fat, so we really shouldn't look to it as a source of energy.

What if, rather than following the typical sedentary patterns of many Americans, you are physically active? Muscle makes up about 40 percent of the body's weight, and every day, you break down and replace 1 to 2 percent of your muscle mass. When you make more muscle mass than you break down, your muscles get bigger.

Hard training produces small injuries to the muscles that trigger growth. The muscles will continue to build new protein for more than forty-eight hours after a training session. If you do not eat anything after an intense workout, muscle breakdown will exceed muscle growth. Only later, after a meal, will protein production catch up and build muscle. The best plan for people who are building or maintaining muscle is to eat protein—mixed with carbohydrates—within four hours before exercising. This ensures that you have plenty of amino acids on hand for muscle growth.

Does this mean you have to have a plateful of chicken breasts, raw-egg milkshakes, or bins of protein powder to meet your needs? Not at all. The active person simply needs to add a mere 1 to 2 ounces of extra protein-rich foods per day. To gain a pound of muscle per week, you'd need just 7 to 14 extra grams of protein daily.

For athletes who eat optimal diets, there is no solid evidence that protein powders build muscle mass. Furthermore, to date there is no scientific evidence that megadoses of individual amino acids as supplements have a bodybuilding effect.

However, protein combined with carbohydrates does a better job of refueling muscles. Protein and carbohydrates reduce soreness and promote recovery when you take them in shortly after aerobics or working out with weights. Immediately after you exercise, your muscles are very sensitive to nutrients. Eating within thirty minutes of a hard, prolonged workout is very helpful for recovery. But taking in carbs and protein within ten minutes produces almost *twice* the benefit for replacing depleted stores of these nutrients and muscle-builders.

For vegans and vegetarians, the quality of protein can make a difference in its usefulness. Twenty amino acids make up proteins. They are put together in various combinations and amounts, but what dictates how much new protein your body can make from them is the availability of the "essential amino acids."

Nine amino acids are called *essential* because the body cannot make them from other nutrients (these are isoleucine, leucine, valine, lysine, tryptophan, phenylalanine, methionine, threonine, and histidine, in case you're ever on *Jeopardy* and need to know).

The amount of any given protein—let's say a digestive enzyme—that you can make depends on how much of each of its essential amino acids are available. This is of critical concern for vegetarians because nonanimal sources of protein may be missing a single essential amino acid completely. Legumes such as soy are missing methionine, and grains don't have lysine, for example. But if you have them together in a combination such as black beans and rice, they'll complement each other.

Soy will also need to be a staple in vegetarians' diets. Variety shouldn't be a problem, since soy comes in a wide range of nutritious foods such as tofu, soy milk, soy beans, soy powder, edamame, soy nuts, soy yogurt, soy sour cream, miso, tempeh, soy flour, textured soy protein, and so forth.

Another excellent source of protein is nuts of all kinds, as well as peanuts and the ever-popular peanut butter. To make sure you're complementing proteins, it would be wise to include at least seven to nine servings of grains per day. The only nutrient that you will additionally need to monitor is vitamin B_{12} (taking it via supplement will do). If you opt to be a quasi-vegetarian (consuming dairy and/or eggs), the challenge is easier because dairy and eggs are not only complete but high-quality proteins.

Less concern is necessary for meat, fish, and dairy eaters, since these foods all contain the complete array of amino acids. In general, when choosing animal sources of protein, it's wise to rely most heavily on those with less saturated fat. The lower fat selections include:

- Shrimp
- Turkey
- Fish
- Skinless chicken
- Lean pork
- Lean beef
- Eggs (egg whites are better)
- Low-fat dairy

Obviously these should be cooked using minimal oils, so preferable cooking methods include baking, broiling, grilling, roasting, or stir-frying. Other good protein sources include nuts, peanut butter, seeds, legumes, and soy products (like tofu). It's not that you can *never* have cheese, ribs, hot dogs, hamburgers, sausage, deli meats, bacon, or pot roast, but you should always eat these in moderation.The saturated fat in fatty red meat and dairy foods bumps up your bad LDL cholesterol and can set the stage for cardiovascular disease.

THE BRAIN FIX TOOLBOX

- Be sure to get an adequate supply of protein every day. For most people, this is not hard to do. However, if you're a vegetarian or vegan, it's more important to pay attention to your protein intake. In this case, you can help ensure that you're meeting your protein needs by mixing sources of incomplete proteins and eating soy foods regularly.

- Don't bother going overboard on protein. Excessive amounts get burned for energy or stored as fat. Many bodybuilders and other physically active people don't really need the chicken breasts and jugs of expensive protein powder that they pack into their bodies daily.

- As much as possible, when meeting your protein needs with animal-based foods, stick with those that are low in saturated fat. That means more fish and poultry and less full-fat dairy products and red meat.

8

Who Would Have Thought Fiber Was Good for the Brain?

YOU CAN ENCOUNTER A LOT OF FIBER during the day without realizing it. You know the stringy parts of a stick of celery? That's fiber. The crunchiness of a carrot comes from fiber, too. Sometimes fiber doesn't alert your teeth or mouth that it exists in a food. For example, bananas contain fiber.

Fiber is technically a carbohydrate, and it's found in plant foods. Your digestive system is powerful at processing the food you put into it, but it *can't* absorb fiber. Because of that, fiber helps protect your brain.

All carbohydrates are made up of molecules of glucose that are strung together. In order to digest a carbohydrate, you must have enzymes in your digestive system that will break the attachments between each glucose molecule. Man is not equipped with the enzyme to perform this task with fiber, so it enters one end of your digestive system and exits the other end without being absorbed.

Fiber: Helping Your Brain via Your Waistline

One of the best-kept secrets for losing weight is to include lots of fiber in your diet. By keeping your weight at a reasonable level, you'll help your brain in many ways:

- You're less likely to build up stores of body fat that increase inflammation.
- You're less likely to develop the high insulin that occurs during prediabetes or diabetes. High insulin, as you may remember from earlier in the book, can damage neurons in your brain.

- You're less likely to develop cardiovascular disease, which can interrupt the healthy flow of blood to your brain.

There are several mechanisms by which a high-fiber diet can help you lose weight. When you eat more fiber, it helps reduce the amount of calories that you absorb from the rest of your food. It also fills you up so you feel less hungry, and thus you're apt to eat fewer calories. And fiber can reduce carbohydrate cravings.

The greater the amount of fiber you consume, the fewer calories you absorb. When you eat fat along with fiber, the fat becomes partially trapped by the fiber. Since the fiber is not absorbed, the fat that clings within the fiber is not absorbed, either. For example, if you eat just a greasy hamburger on its own, you'll absorb 95 percent of the fat. But eat a high-fiber salad with salad dressing, and one third of the fat calories in the dressing are carried out of your body before they can be absorbed. That's right—fiber may prevent as much as one-third of the fat in a meal to be flushed out of your body without being absorbed.

Fiber can help you keep a trim waistline—which is friendly to your brain—in other ways, too. Most dieters search for ways to speed up their metabolism (in other words, the amount of calories their bodies burn handling natural processes day and night). You won't find a more natural way to do this than increasing your fiber intake. Your twenty-five feet of small intestine contain muscles that mechanically try to break the bonds in fiber and move it toward your colon. This requires more calorie expenditure and results in a rise in metabolism. No one can say for sure how many calories you'll expend by eating more fiber, but there have been estimates (not scientifically backed) that predict you may burn 200 calories (that's the equivalent of a two-mile brisk walk) by consuming 35 grams of fiber a day.

In addition, the type of fiber known as soluble fiber—found in oatmeal, beans, rice, and fruits—expands when water hits it. This can produce a filling effect on the stomach's pressure receptors, which makes you feel fuller. Your stomach also empties more slowly, which allows you to feel full longer following a meal that contains soluble fiber.

Adding fiber to a meal increases its volume and gives you the sense that you're eating more food. Think about it: a large salad or big bowl of vegetable soup will trick you into thinking you've eaten a lot of food, even if it may not contain a lot of calories. Compare this to unwrapping a high-calorie candy bar, which you can easily gobble in four bites long before any "fullness" signals hit the hunger center of your brain. Many times we still feel hungry after a snack or meal if we think we have not eaten enough. However, if our stomachs are stretched by the amount we've put into them, we *will* feel full because we perceive we have eaten so much.

Fiber also helps keep your blood sugar steady, which as we've learned earlier in the book is crucial for brain health. Fiber slows down the release of sugar into your bloodstream and thereby supports a steady release of insulin. Fiber works a bit like a fabric that traps other elements in food, including sugar. This produces a time-released effect over the entire length of the large intestine. When the gut slowly absorbs sugar after a meal, your pancreas doesn't need to release as much insulin at any one time. With steadier blood sugar levels, you feel less hungry between meals. This process might decrease your urge to eat in excess or to binge. The steadier blood glucose can also reduce your craving for sweets.

The ability of high-fiber foods to keep blood sugar steady can help ensure that your pancreas preserves its ability to create insulin. Maintaining this insulin is necessary to prevent the onset of diabetes.

Also, the addition of fiber to a meal often means you have to chew more. The satisfaction that comes from chewing creates a greater sense of fullness than you get from drinking fluids. Obviously you get more fullness and satisfaction from, say, eating four oranges than by drinking a 12-ounce glass of orange juice. Chewing may help reduce your appetite by stimulating your brain's medulla.

More Brain-Fixing Benefits from Fiber

Cardiovascular disease and stroke are the leading cause of death in America—and they're a big source of brain injury in our society. Upping our intake of fiber-containing foods can go a long way when it comes to preventing these diseases. This includes preventing the risk factors that go along with cardiovascular disease, such as high blood pressure and elevations in bad LDL cholesterol and triglycerides (a type of blood fat). For example, pectin is a fiber that directly keeps your body from absorbing cholesterol from your food. But preventing the absorption of dietary cholesterol is not the only way that fiber helps lower cholesterol. In a similar manner to which fiber binds fat, it also grabs up bile, a fluid that your liver creates from cholesterol. This keeps your body from reabsorbing the bile and adding it to your total cholesterol pool. By bumping up the amount of bile salts and acids that you excrete, your cholesterol level should drop. Your liver will have to create fresh bile by pulling more cholesterol from your bloodstream.

This is why makers of fiber-rich foods like certain cereals can make cholesterol-lowering claims on their food packaging. In one study, about 2 ounces of oat bran were added to a low-fat, low-cholesterol diet, and the participants had a 5 percent drop in cholesterol. Keep in mind that a 1 percent drop in cholesterol reduces your risk of heart disease by 2 percent. That means these people lowered their risk by 10 percent! By keeping your heart and blood vessels healthy, you help ensure that they keep sending plenty of life-sustaining blood to your brain.

However, the benefits of fiber continue even further. The bacterial population in your colon is capable of turning undigested fiber into short-chain fatty acids. When these are absorbed in the colon, they travel to the liver and prevent cholesterol from forming. These byproducts also serve as antioxidants!

Fiber may bring down inflammation, which is harmful to the blood vessels and your brain. Inflammation helps set the stage for heart disease by contributing to plaque buildup that narrows arteries, which can eventually lead to a heart attack. One marker of inflammation, called highly sensitive C-reactive protein, was reduced by 14 percent in people who were following diets that provided an average of 30 grams of fiber per day. Fiber may contribute to a lowering of inflammation by keeping glucose steadier, or by encouraging the intestinal bacteria that produce anti-inflammatory chemicals. Another study from 2004—which pooled the results of several other studies—found that every 10 grams of fiber added to the diet decreased the risk of dying from heart disease by 27 percent.

Considering the fact that fiber is found in fruits, vegetables, whole grains, and other brain-healthy foods, it just makes good sense for all of us to add more fiber to our diets. Experts recommend that we include 25 to 35 grams of dietary fiber from food sources spaced throughout the day. This practice will help ensure that you're getting an optimal diet that will pay long-term dividends for your brain.

It's not hard to get at least 25 grams of fiber each day. Many fiber-rich foods offer other brain-protecting nutrients, like the antioxidants in fruits and vegetables, so hopefully you've already found plenty of reasons to eat an abundance of foods containing fiber. And many foods containing fiber are pretty tasty, giving you yet another good cause to put them on your plate.

Check out this list and see how quickly you can hit 25 grams using foods that appeal to you:

Prunes, two	9 grams
Beans, half-cup	8 grams
Raisin Bran, one cup	7 grams
Whole wheat pasta, one cup	7 grams
Shredded Wheat, one cup	5 grams
Baked potato with skin	4 grams
Brown rice, one cup	4 grams
Popcorn, three cups	4 grams
100 percent whole wheat bread, one slice	2 grams
Ry Krisp, Finn Crisp, Wasa crackers, 10 count	6 grams
Triscuits, seven	4 grams

However, bumping up the fiber in your diet *too* quickly can lead to gas, bloating, and diarrhea. If you aren't currently getting much fiber—and you probably aren't, since the average American gets just 10 grams daily—slowly add more fiber-rich foods to your diet. Also, be sure to drink plenty of fluid each day and exercise frequently, which can help prevent the constipation that can result from fiber.

THE BRAIN FIX TOOLBOX

When it comes to fixing your brain with fiber, remember to:

- Get at least 25 grams of fiber daily.
- Slowly increase the amount of fiber in your diet if you aren't getting much now, in order to prevent side effects such as bloating and diarrhea.
- Get your fiber from foods as much as possible, rather than supplements. Many fiber-rich foods also contain other brain-healthy benefits, such as antioxidants.

9

Working the Salt Minds:
Mixed Messages About Salt

SALT HAS HAD AN IMPORTANT position in world history. For thousands of years it held a high value as currency . . . and a reason for waging war.

In the past century, this common seasoning has become an additive in all sorts of processed foods. Now it's the center of scientific research, as investigators try to figure out how salt could be affecting our health. Most of the focus on salt involves its role in hypertension—also known as high blood pressure—which is an issue fraught with controversy.

In the 1940s, a Duke University researcher named Walter Kempner, who was especially interested in high blood pressure, suggested that one approach for treating hypertension and the heart disease resulting from it was to severely restrict salt and fat in the diet. In the early 1960s, a special strain of rats that were highly sensitive to salt was bred in Lewis Dahl's laboratory at the Brookhaven National Laboratory. When he fed a high-salt diet to the sensitive rats, they became hypertensive. Having two strains of rats that differed in sensitivity to salt, Dahl provided evidence that hypertension related to salt had a genetic background.

There is very strong evidence that consuming a lot of sodium—or salt, which contains sodium—can increase your risk of hypertension. High blood pressure, in turn, raises the risk of heart disease and stroke, which are two of the top causes of death and disability in the United States. Hypertension alone accounts for 326,000 annual deaths and nearly $77 billion in healthcare costs. If everyone reduced their blood pressure by just 3 points, the nation could see its stroke mortality fall by 8 percent. This makes salt "the single most harmful element in the food supply," according to Michael Jacobson, the executive director of the Washington, D.C.–based Center for Science in the Public Interest.

Just cutting 1 gram of salt from meals each day could have a major impact on diseases that are harmful to brain health: 20,000 fewer cases of coronary artery disease, 18,000 fewer heart attacks, and 11,000 fewer strokes each year.

If salt is so bad for us, why is it in our food supply in the first place? Well, sodium actually has a valuable place in our bodies. The goal is to find the right amount that's not too high or too low.

Sodium: Necessary for Survival and Brain Health

In 1888, F. Newberry & Sons marketed a "miracle elixir" that claimed to cure headaches, brain troubles, nervous debility, sleeplessness, mania, indigestion, and a host of other maladies. The makers sold it with the compelling name of Effervescent Brain Salt. But the product was simply sodium chloride—which we know simply as "salt."

Salt is a critical nutrient because it is necessary for the function of *every cell* in your body. As sodium moves in and out of cells (which it does constantly), it can draw water into tissues, help the digestive system absorb nutrients, help maintain the crucial acid-base balance (pH) in the body, and regulate fluid in the bloodstream, which affects blood pressure. Low levels of sodium in the blood causes blood volume to decrease, and the sympathetic nervous system becomes more active in order to compensate. This can cause people to wake up more often and have difficulty going back to sleep. Salt may also be helpful in maintaining sexuality and libido.

Sodium also helps create the electrical signals that neurons use to send messages between each other. Also, the brain floats in a salty fluid called cerebrospinal fluid. For the brain to maintain an optimal sodium balance, it relies on cells that sense sodium levels. Specialized glial cells pick up on changes in sodium concentration. They spur you to crave salt to increase your sodium levels if necessary, or your kidneys to get rid of any excess.

Though developing low sodium levels in the blood doesn't happen often (a condition called hyponatremia), when it does occur, excess water enters cells and they become swollen. If this happens in the brain (a condition called cerebral edema), it is especially dangerous since the brain is confined in the skull. Thus, it's unable to expand except downward through the base of the skull into the spinal canal. This is a life-threatening medical emergency. Hyponatremia can lead to seizures, coma, and lack of breathing. Hyponatremia can occur if people drink too much water or lose too much salt, both of which can happen in long-distance running races.

As you can see, salt is necessary for survival much like food and water. And our brains are set up to ensure that we get enough of it. Salt craving has effects in the brain that are similar to those seen in cocaine, heroin, opiate, and nicotine addictions. Sodium-deprived rats are not motivated to scamper across a cage to push a bar that releases a dose of sugar water, which provides pleasure. This may be similar to how low levels of sodium can induce depression in humans. When sodium is restored, it makes us happier.

It's possible that people can develop an *addiction* to salt. Individuals have a marked difference in salt consumption, which could signify that some people develop a tolerance. When a person suddenly abstains from salt, symptoms such as loss of appetite and nausea can result—which we could see as a form of withdrawal. Some people won't cut back on salt despite the negative consequences such as high blood pressure, kidney disease, and congestive heart failure, which could point to loss of control.

The way that salt increases the pressure of blood in your arteries is not fully understood. However, the body has natural mechanisms to maintain the amount of sodium in the system. You have a complicated network of hormones that adjusts how much sodium you retain or lose in urine, which also helps maintain the proper fluid balance in your body. This means that your body should constantly keep your sodium level within a certain range at all times, much like a thermostat keeps the heat in your home at a reasonable setting.

Sodium, however, is just *one* factor in a complex interplay of mechanisms that influence hypertension. Obesity can be another significant contributor. An international collaboration of more than forty-two countries concluded that higher intakes of salt caused higher rates of heart disease, but the elevated rates of death were seen only in obese individuals.

As part of the National Health and Nutrition Examination Survey, researchers tracked 20,279 individuals starting in 1971, and in 1999 they reported an 89 percent greater number of stroke deaths, 44 percent more heart attack deaths, and 34 percent more deaths from all causes. Reevaluation of the data showed no difference between people with higher salt intakes and anyone else, once weight was factored in.

One issue that researchers are looking at these days is not sodium by itself, but the ratio of sodium to the mineral potassium. Higher sodium-to-potassium ratios (meaning more sodium versus little potassium) are associated with a higher risk of cardiovascular disease and death from all causes. The risk of death has been found to double when the ratio of sodium to potassium doubles. And research from 2011 found that the death rate increased 20 percent with every 1,000 milligram increase in sodium, and it *decreased* 20 percent for every 1,000 milligram increase in potassium.

The salt intake in Japan may be two to three times greater than in America, but the Japanese life expectancy is longer. It is possible that their high intake of potassium through diets plentiful in fish and vegetables, which are high-potassium foods, may offset this difference and reduce their risk of hypertension and cardiovascular disease.

One Nation, Under Less Sodium

Over the past few decades, many voices have joined in calling Americans to eat less sodium and salt. From an evolutionary perspective, humans adapted over time to operate on less than one gram of salt per day, which is 1,000 milligrams. This is *much* less than the average that people in industrialized and urbanized countries consume today. The average sodium intake in the typical American diet is now 3,400 milligrams.

In 1979, the First Surgeon General's Report encouraged Americans to lower their salt intake. By the 1990s, several research reviews reported that people with hypertension who cut their sodium intake reduced their blood pressure. Five large randomized trials confirmed that reducing dietary sodium also had modest effects on blood pressure in people with prehypertension, which means having somewhat higher than normal blood pressure.

The major DASH study demonstrated the short-term effects of diet on blood pressure. In addition to maintaining a low-sodium diet with 2,300 milligrams or less per day, the project asked participants to make other changes to their diet. They reduced red meat, fats, sweets, and sugary beverages, but increased whole grains, poultry, fish, nuts, and low-fat dairy. The program, which ran from 1992 to 1997, reduced the risk of heart disease by as much as 20 percent.

In the Multiple Risk Factor Intervention Trial (MRFIT), researchers studied a variety of dietary factors to see how they influence blood pressure. Potassium, protein, and polyunsaturated fat reduced blood pressure, whereas sodium, cholesterol, saturated fats, starches, and alcohol increased blood pressure.

However, the issue of sodium is not without controversy. A question that remains is: does a low-sodium diet keep people alive longer? In one study, low sodium intake was actually found to be associated with an *increased* risk of cardiovascular death. A low-sodium group that was being treated aggressively with antihypertensive drugs had a 37 percent higher risk of death from cardiovascular reasons and a 28 percent higher risk of dying from all causes.

The data that are available on the effect of sodium intake on people's life span are still inconclusive. The findings thus far highlight the need for more studies on dietary sodium and risk of death. However, the majority of studies *do* provide a strong link between high salt intake and high blood pressure. Given that high blood pressure can increase your risk of heart disease and strokes—which definitely have a major impact on brain health—it's wise to create the proper place for sodium while you're putting Brain Fix principles into place in your life.

How to Finally Kick a Salt Habit for Your Brain's Benefit

Health experts recommend that all Americans stick to less than 2,300 milligrams of sodium per day. But many of us should aim for even less.

Americans older than fifty-one, African Americans, and those struggling with elevated blood pressure, heart disease, stroke, diabetes, or chronic kidney disease should get no more than 1,500 milligrams daily. Surveys have found that the lower sodium recommendation of 1,500 milligrams applies to 69 percent of American adults.

Some experts argue that only people whose blood pressure is sensitive to the effect of sodium should be concerned about cutting back. Salt sensitivity is defined as having more than a 10 percent increase in blood pressure following a high-salt meal. Some 50 million Americans are thought to have salt sensitivity. Since one's salt sensitivity can change, adults begin to see a difference in their response to salt around the age of forty to fifty. Given that many people are indeed salt sensitive, it's probably wise to just cut back on your salt and sodium whether or not you fall within this group.

However, cutting down on the sodium in your diet takes more work than just throwing your salt shaker into the trashcan. Only about 6 percent of your sodium comes from adding it at the table, and another 5 percent from adding it while cooking.

Most of the sodium in the American diet comes from places other than the salt shaker. Much comes from processed, store-bought foods or items you buy in restaurants or fast-food joints. Salt acts as a preservative, and it's found in baking soda, baking powder, and the flavor enhancer monosodium glutamate (MSG).

Reducing sodium isn't especially simple. Our taste buds have grown accustomed to the salty taste of processed foods, and unlike sugar, there are few convincing substitutes for salty flavor. (However, the good news is that as you consume less salt, you begin to lose your taste for it.)

The food industry could cut the sodium it puts in foods, of course. And some makers do offer lower-sodium versions of foods. But efforts to lower the salt have fallen short partly because companies are afraid of losing customers who switch to competing products.

A good start is to cut back on highly processed foods and salty snacks. Making fruits, vegetables, whole grains, beans, lean sources of protein, and (unsalted) nuts the basis of your diet can slash your sodium intake considerably. This, by the way, is the Mediterranean diet that can do wonders for your brain health, as we've already discussed. The oft-promoted DASH diet for lowering blood pressure also emphasizes fruits and vegetables, as well as low-fat dairy foods.

Try to get enough calories in your diet that you're properly nourished, but not so many that you gain weight. In a study from the January 2012 issue of the *Lancet Neurology*, a stroke expert summarized the type of eating style that may protect you from strokes. Being undernourished bumps up your risk of strokes later in life, though the explanation isn't clear. Eating *too* much also increases your risk, probably by speeding up obesity, diabetes, high blood pressure, and high cholesterol. Eating a diet that lines up with the DASH diet or the Mediterranean diet may help, too, the study points out. Not only should your foods be low in salt and added sugars, they should offer plenty of potassium (which multiple servings of fruits and vegetables each day will cover).

Here are some other hints for cutting sodium and salt:

- Thoroughly rinse canned vegetables, as food packagers often add sodium to these. Even better is to use fresh or frozen vegetables.
- Go easy on condiments such as ketchup, mustard, and soy sauce, which tend to contain sodium. Instead, use herbs or salt-free seasoning blends.
- Minimize salty snack foods like crackers, salted popcorn, chips, and pickles.
- Be aware that processed meats like bacon, luncheon or deli meats, and ham can be packed with sodium.
- Eat at home more often. Restaurant foods, especially fast foods, tend to hold a lot of sodium.
- If you're taking in more calories than you need, simply eating less food is going to reduce your total sodium intake.

However, if you exercise to the point that you sweat a lot, you may need to replace sodium and other electrolytes with sports drinks.

While you're changing your diet to cut down on salt, be sure to get plenty of physical activity, because exercise helps counteract the negative impact of a high-salt diet on blood pressure. Researchers have reported that people who were the most physically active had a 38 percent lower risk of becoming highly salt sensitive. One explanation may be that blood vessels become more flexible to changes in blood volume and pressure when you exercise. Also, exercise causes you to excrete more salt through sweating.

Iodine Disappearing from Many People's Bodies

Iodine is a very important substance that's often been added to table salt since 1924. Iodine is a trace mineral that's critical for the production of thyroid hormone, and it's necessary during infancy for brain development.

Iodine deficiency can lead to cretinism (a form of mental retardation) and poor brain development. One study has shown that children with mild iodine deficiencies scored lower on IQ tests. Even a moderate deficiency can lower intelligence by 10 to 15 IQ points. An alarming study in Great Britain has claimed that 70 percent of teenage girls are iodine deficient, and as many as 100,000 babies are born every year with brain damage that could have been prevented if the mothers had used iodized salt.

The normal iodine requirement is 150 micrograms per day for most adults, though pregnant and lactating moms should be getting at least 200 to 300 micrograms. Yogurt, milk, fruits, vegetables, and enriched flour products contain small amounts of iodine. Iodized salt contains potassium iodide, so that 2,000 milligrams of salt offer approximately the recommended intake of 150 micrograms.

Americans are getting one-third less iodine than they once did, possibly due to eating less salt. This creates problems for all women, especially for pregnant or lactating adolescent females who may be facing borderline deficiencies that can influence their production of thyroid hormone.

To address this, be sure to:

- Eat plenty of fresh or locally grown fruits and vegetables. Avoid overcooking them, or save and consume the broth in which they're cooked.
- When you do use salt, choose iodized salt.
- Take a multivitamin/mineral supplement that contains iodine.

 THE BRAIN FIX TOOLBOX

- Keep your salt intake below 2,300 milligrams. You'll likely get more benefit from keeping it below 1,500 milligrams.
- The quickest way to slash your sodium intake is to shift to a diet that's mostly composed of fruits, vegetables, whole grains, beans, unsalted nuts, lean meat, and low-fat dairy and move *away* from foods that come in cans, boxes, and bags.
- Spend time reading labels when you *do* buy foods in those cans, boxes, and bags. The nutrition information will tell you how much sodium the food contains.
- Remember that your brain needs a certain amount of sodium every day, and going *too* low can leave you feeling bad. Once you get under 1,500 milligrams, lower is not necessarily better.
- Also, while you're pursuing a lower-sodium life, remember to also pay attention to not overdoing it on cholesterol, saturated fat, and calories (but the same diet—such as the DASH diet or Mediterranean diet—can cover all these bases at once).

10

Vitamins and Minerals: Nature's Wonder Drugs

VITAMINS AND MINERALS have gained a lot of recognition and credibility in our society during the past few decades. Although people don't often think of them in terms of brain health, nutrient supplements can offer many benefits for your brain. However, most of us could use a better understanding of what these supplements actually are.

Picture the inner workings of your body as a busy intersection with cars shooting past in every direction. The cars are carbohydrates, fats, and protein that your body uses for energy and repair.

Vitamins and minerals are the traffic cops standing in the middle of all this activity. They direct the traffic flow, which also includes the chemical reactions that involve these sources of energy and building materials. Vitamins and minerals don't provide energy any more than a traffic officer creates traffic. But they *do* help determine the rate at which the body carries out its crucial functions.

Mankind's Long Fascination with Vitamins

The world's interest in vitamins goes back more than a hundred years. Three compounds that were believed to belong to the amine family were found to prevent or cure the diseases beriberi, pellagra, and scurvy. In the early 1900s, these were classified as *vitamins*, with the "vita" coming from the Latin word for life and added to "amine."

Historically, people had little knowledge of the chemical composition of these compounds, so they were designated by letters (A, B, C, etc). Sometimes a single vitamin turned out to be many, so numbers were added (like B_1, B_2, and B_3). Vitamins were described as being essential molecules—meaning that the body can't make them—that are needed in very small amounts for normal growth and activity. Over time, certain compounds labeled as vitamins were shown to not be necessary for growth, maintenance, and repair, so we now have gaps in the numbers (for example, there's no B_4, B_7, B_8, or B_{11}). Certain entries were found to actually be the same vitamins (vitamins H, M, S, W, and X all turned out to be biotin, and G and Y became B_2 and B_6). Today there are thirteen known essential vitamins, and if any are missing from your diet, their absence will eventually result in disease.

The debate is ongoing as to whether we need to be supplementing our diets with vitamins and minerals, and if so, with how much. During my years in grad school, I often encountered an elderly gentleman who looked and acted half his age. He was always singing, dancing, and enjoying the company of younger women. One day, I built up the courage to ask him, "How do you stay so young?" He shouted, "Pills, my boy! Pills!" I further inquired, "Do you take them?" He answered, "No, my boy, I *sell* them!"

Such is the attitude of many when it comes to taking a supplement: the people selling them tend to sing their praises the loudest. There is a great profit potential and yet little evidence that supplements actually improve our health, longevity, and well-being. Still, many of us take them out of some perceived sense of need. When I was working on my doctorate, one of my professors was a leading nutrition expert. He constantly preached, "All the vitamins and minerals you will ever need are supplied by eating a variety of healthy foods. In science, we operate on the premise that nothing is true until it has been proven. Without hard data, if you take supplements, you are volunteering to be a guinea pig in an uncontrolled study."

One day, I observed him swallowing a multivitamin and mineral tablet. I asked him why he was taking a supplement if he was so convinced they're worthless. "In case I'm wrong," he replied.

Perhaps these two stories explain why an estimated 115 million Americans take multivitamin and mineral supplements periodically, while 87 million take them regularly. Proponents often argue that:

- Very few people eat properly.
- Foods are grown on depleted soils.
- Processing and cooking diminishes important micronutrients.
- We are constantly exposed to stress, pollution, contaminants, toxins, and illnesses.
- People have individual nutritional differences that are not accounted for in the Recommended Dietary Intake (RDI).

Surveys *do* tell us that few people in this country eat properly. And since there is little evidence that taking a vitamin and mineral supplement is harmful, people may take them just to hedge their bets on having a long, disease-free life span.

Even the government agencies that establish dietary guidelines admit that segments of the population might benefit from taking a daily multivitamin and mineral supplement. I agree. As a nutritionist, I choose to think of supplements as "adaptogens." If human cells were properly nourished and protected from mechanisms of cellular damage or death, then they might survive in perfect condition without any sign of aging or disease. If the entire body were kept in optimal condition, then we could expect to live a long and healthy life. Ideally, we'll get the nutrients we need from foods, but for many people, this likely isn't happening.

Using the proper levels of supplements could hopefully bring us closer to such a state—with an emphasis on *proper*. Since they are readily available and inexpensive, many people see fit to take vitamin and mineral supplements in megadoses to try to speed their benefits or enhance their potential. This can waste your money, and the practice may be harmful to your health, too. Human nature often makes us believe that if something is good, more of it must be better, right? When it comes to nutrients, this is *not* always true.

We know that too little of an essential nutrient can make us sick. A good historical example of this is from the days when sailors would get scurvy because citrus fruits (which contain vitamin C) were unavailable on their long voyages. However, *too much* can make us sick. For example, various clinical studies have suggested that in certain circumstances, antioxidant vitamins may actually have a pro-oxidant or harmful effect.

Vitamins in megadoses may cause injury that is confused with symptoms of disease. High vitamin intake is more hazardous to organs other than the nervous system, because vitamins' entry into the central nervous system is restricted.

That being said:

- High doses of B_6—more than 100 milligrams—over time may result in nerve damage that may eventually be irreversible. Too much B_6 can also interfere with medications that affect dopamine and interact with hormones, such as estrogen, that affect behavior.
- People who take too much vitamin D and calcium have been found to be more likely to show brain lesions, perhaps due to calcification in blood vessels.
- Megadoses of vitamin C can affect the activity of antidepressants and anti-inflammatory medications.
- Some speculate that excessive amounts of vitamin A can trigger changes in neurons and lead to neurotoxicity.
- Iron toxicity may be associated with irritability and stubbornness. Iron also gathers in the amygdala, which is associated with anger and hostility. Excess iron also may change levels of histamine in the blood and serotonin in the brain.

Therefore, it is imperative that you not follow the "more is better" dogma.

Some people reading this book should pay extra attention to getting enough nutrients. Vitamins, as a rule, are low in people with addictions and eating disorders, and these people have a dire need to fix the deficiencies. They also seem to be valuable in fighting depression and anxiety, which are major triggers for people struggling with recovery.

In this chapter, we'll address which nutrients are especially helpful for brain health, how much you need, and how you should get them into your body.

Vitamin A

Beta-carotene is a precursor of vitamin A. Research has found that supplements of beta-carotene, when taken for lengthy periods, could help preserve your memory and your thinking skills. It might also reduce the risk of dementia. Beta-carotene has also been shown to possibly lower the risk of cognitive decline in people who are at greater risk of Alzheimer's.

Vitamin A—also known as retinol—is toxic when taken in too large amounts. Since it's fat-soluble, your body stores it up. However, you can get vitamin A in a safe manner from foods that are rich in carotenoids. These provide orange and yellow pigments in fruits such as cantaloupes, apricots, peaches, and carrots. They are very similar in structure to vitamin A, in that they resemble two molecules of vitamin A linked together in a mirror image. Enzymes in your intestinal walls can split this structure in the middle to form molecules with vitamin A activity. These carotenoids are thus considered precursors of vitamin A, or provitamin A.

Your body isn't highly efficient at absorbing carotenoids such as beta-carotene and converting it to vitamin A. However, beta-carotene is completely safe if taken in moderate amounts, and your liver will convert it to vitamin A when needed. Other naturally occurring carotenoids are: alpha-carotene, lutein, cryptoxanthin, zeaxanthin, and lycopene. Carotenoids were originally thought to have no upper limit for intake, since there were no known harmful side effects. However, overloading a diet with beta-carotene to the exclusion of other important plant pigments and carotenes may be detrimental.

You can help meet your needs with any fruit or vegetable that contains orange or yellow pigment, including carrots, butternut squash, pumpkin, apricots, and cantaloupe. Dark leafy greens are also a source (the chlorophyll green masks the yellow color), as are liver and fish. Eating too many carrots can turn your skin yellow, which is not advisable.

For this and all the other nutrients, taking a multivitamin/mineral is a simple way to get these into your body.

B Vitamins

This large family of vitamins plays many important roles in brain health.

B_1. Vitamin B_1—also called thiamin—is essential for nerve stimulation and seems to be involved in the release of a neurochemical called acetylcholine, which regulates nerve function and cognition. Vitamin B_1 may also be a stress reliever, as it has the ability to encourage normal levels of the stress hormone cortisol. B_1 deficiency may lead to mood disorders, anxiety, insomnia, restlessness, mental confusion, muscle weakness, and nightmares.

B_2. Vitamin B_2—also known as riboflavin—is associated with enzymes that process carbohydrates. It may help alleviate aggressive personality and emotional states.

B_3. Getting too little vitamin B_3—also known as niacin—has been associated with depression, anxiety, irritability, and mental disturbances. When used in megadoses of 1,000 to 2,000 milligrams three times a day under medical supervision, it can help reduce cholesterol (though this recommendation has recently been challenged).

B_5. This one, which is technically called pantothenic acid, is found in virtually every food (thus the "pan" in its name, like panorama or panacea). Therefore, you're very unlikely to have a deficiency of this one, which is a good thing. B_5 is important for keeping your adrenal glands working, and it buffers against increases in the stress hormone cortisol. Pantothenic acid also serves as a cofactor in converting choline into acetylcholine, which increases stamina, including mental stamina.

Other B vitamins. Elevated levels of an amino acid called homocysteine, which goes hand in hand with low concentrations of the B vitamins folate, vitamin B_{12}, and B_6, are a possible risk factor for both Alzheimer's disease and another type of dementia called vascular dementia. High homocysteine levels have also been linked to a higher risk of brain damage, cognitive impairment, and memory decline. High levels are associated with poorer cognitive performance even in people who don't have dementia.

In addition, high homocysteine also has a negative impact on blood vessels in the brain that supply the organ with nutrients and oxygen. As a result, getting enough B vitamins is crucial for brain health. But there's even more to this story.

Low B_{12} and folate levels can also lead to a deficiency of S-adenosyl-methionine (SAM). This is the only source of a chemical called methyl, which performs many important reactions in the nervous system that involve serotonin, dopamine, and neural membranes.

To put it simply, you want your brain to think clearly. To do this, it needs to have enough "smart chemical"—in other words, dopamine—to plug into the "start thinking" sockets (found on the membrane of neurons in your brain). The smart chemical needs a special adapter—methyl—to fit into the sockets. If you do not have enough B_{12} or folic acid in your body, you can't attach the adapter to the smart chemical, and thus you have a poor connection to the brain cell. This poor connection leads to damage and destruction of the socket. You might then have poor mood stability and problems with memory.

SAM levels in the cerebrospinal fluid that bathes the brain have been found to be significantly lower in people who are severely depressed. Since SAM is intimately linked to folate and B_{12}, any deficiency in these vitamins ultimately has an impact on cognition and mood.

B Vitamins and Depression

B vitamins may be useful in treating depression, which is quickly becoming one of the most common disabilities in the world. Up to 10 percent of people have depression, and those with lower levels of folate have a higher risk. Taking folate supplements has been found to be beneficial for depression.

In addition, in one study, B_6 levels were about 48 percent lower in people with depression compared to people without it. Most of the depressed patients—57 percent—were B_6-deficient. After taking B_6 supplements, all the depressed patients showed improvement.

Research in 2008 also found that people with the lowest B_{12} levels had a sixfold greater rate of brain volume loss compared with people who had the highest levels of the vitamin. None of the participants in this study were deficient in B_{12}, but they merely had low levels within the normal range.

B_6 also deserves individual attention. Your brain requires enzymes to convert single amino acids (monoamines) into neurotransmitters that control your moods. The enzymes typically consist of a protein, a coenzyme (typically vitamin B_6 or B_3), and a mineral (like iron, copper, or magnesium). As a result, vitamin B_6 is used as an ingredient in the following brain reactions:

- Converting tyrosine to norepinephrine (anxiety)
- Converting L-dopa to dopamine (pleasure)
- Turning glutamic acid to GABA (calming)
- Turning tryptophan to serotonin (calming)

Making sure that you have an adequate supply of B_6, B_{12}, and folic acid can't hurt, and it may be helpful in maintaining your brain, especially as you get older.

The B-complex vitamins are grouped together because they work as a unit, not because they have similar structure or function. You don't want to take a high dose of one without addressing the others. This is because taking too much of one can cause a deficiency of another if it is not equally increased. For example, B_6 comes in an inactive form that has to be converted to the active form in the body by an enzyme that requires B_2. Taking too much B_6 without an increase in B_2 would produce a B_2 deficiency.

Here are a few suggestions on getting enough of these vitamins:

- Beginning around the age of fifty, changes in the acidity of the stomach decrease people's ability to absorb B_{12}. The recommendation for people as they progress into their fifties is to supplement with about 50 micrograms of B_{12} per day.
- Folate comes from plants, but the synthetic form used in supplements and fortified foods is called folic acid. Folic acid found in multivitamins and fortified grains is actually better absorbed than the folate that naturally occurs in legumes, spinach, and orange juice. The dosage allowable in folic acid supplements is 400 mcg per day, because taking large amounts could conceal a vitamin B_{12} deficiency.

- You can get vitamins B_1 through B_3 from grains. B_6 is best supplied by meat, fish, and dairy, but nuts, legumes, and bananas are also a source. Vitamin B_{12} only comes from animal sources.

As usual, taking a multivitamin is a quick way of getting the B vitamins without having to invest a lot of brainpower.

Vitamin C

Also known as ascorbic acid, vitamin C is highly concentrated in the brain, where it plays an important role in the creation of neurotransmitters, which allow brain cells to "talk" to each other.

Vitamin C helps convert dopamine to norepinephrine and tryptophan into serotonin. When used with conventional antidepressants, ascorbic acid has been shown to have an antidepressant-like effect.

Its antioxidant action may also help prevent damage to neurons during stress. At high doses, it helps the adrenal glands adapt to stress by normalizing a hormone called ACTH, which comes from the pituitary and stimulates the release of the stress hormone cortisol.

Vitamin C is also said to have a protective effect in people who drink alcohol regularly, and it may inhibit the development of tolerance and dependence on morphine.

Vitamin C is best absorbed when you take 200 to 250 milligrams over a three- to four- hour period. Megadoses aren't beneficial. At high doses, the amount you absorb decreases. Taking 100 to 300 milligrams daily is enough to keep your blood saturated. As the amount in your body approaches saturation, more gets excreted in your urine. Since vitamin C is converted to oxalates, taking too much raises the potential that you'll form oxalate stones in your kidneys (which are painful).

Some of the highest plant sources of vitamin C are acerola, Camu camu, and rose hips. However, you can more easily find it in citrus fruits, green peppers, strawberries, broccoli, cantaloupe, papaya, kiwi, and pineapple.

Choline

This is an essential nutrient that is usually grouped with the B-complex vitamins. It deserves a lot of attention for brain health. You need it to produce acetylcholine, which plays a role in memory, concentration, focus, and high-order thought processes. By making this neurotransmitter more available in your brain, you may improve these functions.

Low levels of acetylcholine in the brain—or less brain transmission using choline—have been linked to diseases like early dementia, Parkinson's disease, and bipolar disorder. Research has found that choline is effective in slowing Alzheimer's and managing Parkinson's disease. It may also improve cognition and memory in both healthy people and those with mild memory impairment.

If choline gets too low, brain cells undergo degenerative changes. Much like B_{12} and folate, choline also assists in preventing the formation of homocysteine, which appears to be harmful for the cardiovascular system.

In addition, choline contributes to the formation of every cell membrane. In that role, it helps keep the cell membranes of your neurons flexible, which is important for communication between brain cells. Choline is also required for fats to be able to move in and out of your cells.

Your body can create choline from the amino acids methionine or serine. However, the Institute of Medicine, which helps set the policy on the nutrients that Americans need, has classified it as an essential dietary nutrient.

Since it is necessary for memory, and hence learning, choline supplementation could have an effect on IQ. Experts recommend that we get 450 to 550 milligrams per day. Choline can be found in meat, fish, soy lecithin, milk, and eggs. The standard recommended dose of supplementation is 350 milligrams three times daily with meals, but you can take about 3 grams daily. Higher doses may benefit people who have a memory loss or deficit.

Vitamin D

This is a fat-soluble vitamin that your body readily produces when sunlight hits your skin. Yet many people find that this vitamin can be in short supply. The National Center for Health Statistics has reported that 8 percent of Americans are deficient in vitamin D and 25 percent are at risk of inadequacy (but only 1 percent have dangerously high levels).

People who are most susceptible to deficiency include those who are obese; people of color, whose skin makes less vitamin D from sunlight; and senior citizens, who also tend to make less vitamin D.

People taking statin drugs to lower their cholesterol may also have lower vitamin D. One of cholesterol's many functions in the body is to act as a precursor to vitamin D. As a result, if you inhibit the production of cholesterol, you'll also inhibit the production of vitamin D.

Vitamin D plays a role in the formation of nervous tissue. It may also help clear away toxic amyloid (beta-amyloid plaques are found in Alzheimer's disease) from the brain. Older people with low levels of vitamin D appear more likely to have problems with memory, learning, and thinking. Research supports a relationship between low vitamin D levels and impaired cognition in people with Alzheimer's disease.

Vitamin D also helps you absorb the calcium in the foods you eat, which is required for nerve health. Low levels of vitamin D have been linked to high blood pressure, high cholesterol, and depression—all of which can impact your brain health.

A lack of vitamin D could lead to a greater risk of high blood pressure—and its cardiovascular complications—because it controls a protein called renin, which plays a role in regulating blood pressure. Low levels of vitamin D may also increase the risk of calcium buildup in the walls of arteries. Population studies suggest that people with low levels of vitamin D have a greater risk of developing cardiovascular disease, including heart attack, stroke, and heart failure, compared to people with higher levels of vitamin D.

This vitamin is also linked to obesity. Low levels of vitamin D are common in obese adolescents. One possible explanation is that their vitamin D is locked away in body fat (obese people who lose 15 percent of their body weight may see their blood levels of vitamin D go up). Low vitamin D levels associated with obesity may play a role in the higher risk of heart disease in overweight people. An additional link to brain health is that vitamin D may help regulate the body's sensitivity to insulin and possibly the pancreas's rate of insulin production.

The current recommendation for vitamin D is 600 IU daily up to the age of seventy, and for older adults, the amount increases to 800 IU.

Good food sources of vitamin D include eggs and fatty fish like salmon, herring, mackerel, tuna, and sardines. Many brands of milk and cereal are also fortified with vitamin D.

Sunlight can be a powerful source of vitamin D. You only need about fifteen minutes of sun exposure each day to get the recommended amount. One reason for the decline in vitamin D levels in Americans may be our concern over skin cancer from sun exposure. Staying out of the sun or slathering on a heavy coating of sunscreen keeps us from getting one of our major sources of vitamin D. It's a good idea to get a few minutes of sunlight on your skin each day, but if you're going to be out in the sun for any extended length of time, be sure to protect yourself with long clothing, a hat, and sunscreen to avoid skin cancer.

Of course, you can get *too* much vitamin D. The daily upper limit is set at 2,000 IU per day, and it's wise to remember that since vitamin D is fat soluble, it can be stored in your body for extended periods of time.

Vitamin E

Vitamin E has received a lot of attention over the years as a potential treatment for everything from impotency to cancer. One enterprising marketer coined the phrase, "Vitamin E is a cure looking for a disease." Regardless of promoters' many inflated claims, there is enough evidence to recommend 200 to 250 IU per day.

Vitamin E is actually a family of substances called tocopherols and tocotrienols. Beta-, gamma-, and delta-tocotrienols have the highest antioxidant activity. These protect the fatty sheath surrounding the axons of brain cells and also the cell membranes.

Inositol

Inositol is an unofficial B vitamin, sometimes called B_8. It's similar in structure to the sugar glucose. Your body primarily stores it in your brain, nerves, the fluid around your brain and spinal cord, and your muscles. Your body contains more inositol than any other vitamin except niacin!

Inositol increases serotonin in your brain, and it seems to help your neurons use the serotonin more efficiently. Cells can become depleted of inositol. If this happens in the brain, your serotonin system may become less responsive, leaving you with depression.

Since inositol has a calming effect on the brain, it may be helpful for people with insomnia. Inositol also appears to be effective and safe for treating panic disorder, depression, obsessive-compulsive disorder, bulimia, and binge eating. Inositol's helpfulness—combined with a lack of significant side effects—suggests that it may be used as an addition to other treatments.

Bacteria in your intestines free inositol from phytic acid, which is found in citrus fruits, nuts, seeds and legumes, wheat germ, brewer's yeast, bananas, liver, beef brains and heart, whole grains such as brown rice, oat flakes, unrefined molasses, raisins, and vegetables such as cabbage.

The recommended daily intake is 100 milligrams per day, but be aware that this dosage is the *minimum* that you require to keep from becoming deficient. It's also important to remember that caffeine can deplete your body's supply of inositol, so that's a good reason to limit your intake of caffeine.

If you are interested in taking inositol, take note that experts have offered little reliable information to guide you in your choice of dosage. Studies have used a wide range of dosages for treating panic disorder, obsessive-compulsive disorder, and depression. These have ranged from 6 to 18 grams daily. It's a good idea to follow healthy nutritional guidelines and look to a trained medical provider for supplementation recommendations.

Now for Something Completely Different: The Minerals

You have ninety-six times more minerals in your body than vitamins by weight. Like the vitamins, they are necessary for life. Only seventeen minerals have proven nutritional value, and eight more are *possibly* essential, though some experts question them.

To be considered essential, a dietary deficiency of a mineral must consistently lead to poorer functioning, which is preventable or reversible by getting enough of the mineral. Biochemical researchers have determined that a mineral of some kind is involved in *every* reaction that takes place within the billions of cells in our bodies. These include enzyme reactions, hormonal activities, and brain thought processes. Let's take a closer look at some key minerals for brain health.

Calcium

Calcium is crucial for bone building, so it gets a lot of attention for preventing and treating osteoporosis. However, getting enough is vital for your brain, too. When a chemical signal reaches a neuron in the brain, calcium ions have the job of sending the signal into the cell by bringing important proteins together. In this way calcium acts as a so-called *second messenger*. These proteins trigger certain changes in the cell, including having the cell activate genes.

More calcium ions are found outside of the cells compared to within the cell. Big changes occur in the cell's activity if these calcium levels fluctuate even a bit. Cells in the brain are able to tell when calcium rises too high inside the cells. When this happens, calcium is pumped out of the cell. The cell dies if this process stops working and allows the calcium to build up.

Dairy foods—such as milk, cheese, and yogurt—are probably the most common calcium-rich foods in the American diet. Canned sardines and salmon with bones, turnip greens, and kale also naturally provide calcium. It's also added to brands of orange juice and soy and rice milk.

Calcium is also widely available in several types of supplements. One of the forms of calcium that your body can absorb and use most readily is the citrate form. It can be taken on an empty stomach. However, calcium citrate is only 9 percent calcium, and you may have to take many pills to meet the recommended dosage of 1,000 to 1,500 milligrams. Calcium carbonate, which is 40 percent calcium, is also easily absorbed if you take it with food that triggers your stomach to make acid.

Adults need 1,000 milligrams daily. Women need to bump up their calcium intake to 1,200 milligrams daily at the age of fifty-one, and men need to do so at age seventy-one. Dividing your supplemental calcium into two or more doses per day (with no more than 500 milligrams at a time) will maximize the amount your body absorbs. If you're counting on fortified drinks to help you meet your calcium needs, be aware that calcium can settle out of the liquid, forming a sludge at the bottom of the container, which makes the drinks as much as 85 percent lower in calcium than advertised. Be sure to shake them before drinking.

Magnesium

A survey of Americans found that magnesium is one of the lowest essential nutrients in our diet. That does not mean we have to take lots of magnesium, but it gives credence to the need for supplementation.

Magnesium improves neuroplasticity, which has been discussed throughout the book as an important factor for improving brain health. Magnesium also helps protect brain tissue from damage, such as from head trauma. Magnesium also lowers blood pressure, which can have a protecting effect on the brain. Since the brain operates on a balance between excitatory and inhibitory activity, when the excitatory neurotransmitter glutamate is activated, calcium ions rush in. If the excitation is not kept under control, neurons and other brain tissue can be damaged. Magnesium plays a key role in not allowing this to get out of hand.

Though the recommended intake is 400 milligrams per day, taking more than 350 milligrams at a time may cause diarrhea. Legumes, nuts, whole grains, vegetables (especially dark, leafy green choices), soybeans, halibut, nuts, cereal, oatmeal, and potatoes are all sources of magnesium. Relying on a multivitamin/mineral to supplement your magnesium is also a reasonable way to get it.

Potassium

Potassium plays many important roles in bodily processes. One such function involving potassium is nerve signal transmission. Depletion of potassium from the body decreases the amount of electrical signaling in the brain. This can lead to lethargy. Low potassium in the blood is a medical condition called hypokalemia. Symptoms include weakness, muscle cramps, fatigue, constipation, a rise in blood pressure, and abnormal heart rhythms.

Indirectly, potassium is responsible for many brain functions by maintaining a proper acid-base balance and regulating enzymes and hormone production, energy storage, and fluid levels. The electrolyte also helps oxygenate the brain and regulate the transfer of nutrients to cells, allowing clear thinking and stress reduction.

Diets that are high in foods that are good sources of potassium and low in sodium may reduce the risk of high blood pressure. Fruits (bananas, dried fruits, and citrus) and vegetables (especially potatoes and bitter-tasting options) are the best source of potassium. I would not supplement unless under a doctor's recommendation.

Zinc

As a supplement zinc is a classic example of the need for moderation and balance. Too little (less than 15 milligrams per day) or too much (more than 25 milligrams) can weaken the immune system. In addition, the amount of zinc you take in must stay balanced in relation to other minerals, especially copper.

Zinc functions as an antioxidant. It is second only after iron in terms of total brain concentration of minerals. Deficiencies have been linked to nervous system disorders, mental disturbances, loss of sensory ability, and impaired cognitive function. Oxidative stress, as we have covered previously, is associated with the development of problems including Alzheimer's and Parkinson's. When the blood-brain barrier is oxidized, it compromises what is allowed to enter the brain and can lead to brain tissue damage and a host of diseases.

Research has found that zinc may improve your thinking power and memory. The mineral works in conjunction with vitamin B_6 to encourage the proper function of neurotransmitters. The brain's hippocampus, which handles thought and memory, contains high levels of zinc. Maintaining sufficient zinc can be especially helpful for protecting people's thinking ability after an injury, since the body uses its zinc supply to help heal bodily damage, making less available for the brain. Good sources of zinc include protein foods (like pork, chicken, beef, cheese, milk, and yogurt), whole grains and legumes, nuts, and shellfish.

Some Vitamins Are Especially Important in Alcoholism

Research has found that in blood samples from people who abuse alcohol, hardly *any* essential vitamin or mineral is present in adequate amounts. The fat-soluble vitamins—A, D, E, and K—are particularly at risk of running low. Of particular note,

- Individuals who are alcoholic and have anxiety have been found to have lower levels of potassium.
- Zinc deficiency in alcoholism can keep enzymes from working properly, disturb cell membrane function, and compromise the immune system.
- The mineral selenium is a potent antioxidant that is reduced in patients with alcoholic cirrhosis. Those with the lowest levels have the most liver damage.
- B_6 deficiency is common in people with alcoholic cirrhosis, a type of liver disease.
- Wernicke Korsakoff syndrome, a neurological problem that is caused by a thiamine deficiency, is seen mainly in alcoholics and might be prevented by supplementation with thiamine. Eventually, this deficiency causes brain damage.

A healthcare provider who specializes in addictions should be able to identify and correct deficiencies caused by drug and alcohol abuse. Often this will require large doses administered under a doctor's care. The critical concern for patients throughout recovery and for the rest of their lives should be to eat a healthy diet, which should include a multiple vitamin and mineral supplement.

11

Healing with Herbs and Nutraceuticals

DRUGS OR SUPPLEMENTS that are thought to improve our cognitive abilities are called "nootropics." The term is derived from the Greek words *noos*, or "mind," and *tropein*, meaning "to bend or turn." Nootropics seem to usually work by changing the availability of the brain's supply of neurotransmitters, enzymes, and hormones.

These "smart" drugs and supplements may also help by improving the brain's oxygen supply or stimulating growth. Do these work? The jury is still out, since the effectiveness of these products has not been conclusively proven. However, nootropics could theoretically be helpful for boosting mental function in healthy people. Let's take a closer look at the nootropics that are available to consumers.

Ginkgo Biloba

The ginkgo is the oldest living species of tree, with geological records suggesting that it's been growing on Earth for 200 million years. Ginkgo has been used for centuries as part of ancient Chinese medicine for treating respiratory ailments, cognitive problems, and circulatory disorders. It was first brought to Europe in the 1700s. In recent years, ginkgo has gained worldwide popularity for treating the cognitive decline in dementia, type 2 diabetes, atherosclerosis, hypertension, anxiety, and sexual dysfunction caused by antidepressants.

In Europe, gingko extract is a leading over-the-counter drug for promoting good circulation and improving memory. It is one of the most well-researched herbs in the world, and annual sales of ginkgo have reached nearly $350 million in the United States. Thus, it could potentially hold a place for brain improvement.

Ginkgo has three main effects in the body. It:

- Improves blood flow, primarily in small capillaries that supply tissues and organs
- Protects against oxidative damage and free radicals by acting as an antioxidant, which leads to improved circulation, memory, and concentration
- Inhibits blood clotting by acting as an anti-inflammatory and by blocking a substance called platelet-activating factor

The improved blood flow is a boon to your brain. Your brain requires 20 percent of the oxygen carried in your blood if it's to work at its best. If your brain doesn't get enough oxygen, your ability to think clearly declines. Gingko, however, *increases* your brain's ability to use available oxygen.

Ginkgo leaf also seems to modestly improve symptoms of Alzheimer's disease and a form of dementia called vascular dementia, which is marked by interruptions in blood flow to the brain. Many controlled trials looking at ginkgo extract for treating dementia found significant improvement in cognitive ability, short-term memory loss, concentration, anxiety, and depressed mood.

Since no medications are currently approved for preventing dementia or Alzheimer's disease, scientists are interested in finding ways to protect people from these brain-damaging conditions. Will ginkgo help? It might.

Research has found few side effects in people who use ginkgo for a long period of time. However, people taking anticoagulants or anti-platelet drugs such as aspirin or warfarin should use caution when taking ginkgo, or avoid it all together. In addition, people taking monoamine oxidase inhibitor or selective serotonin reuptake inhibitor antidepressants and pregnant women should not take ginkgo without talking to a doctor first. Ginkgo's possible minimal side effects include increased risk of bleeding, digestive discomfort, vomiting, nausea, diarrhea, constipation, headaches, heart palpitations, dizziness, and restlessness. Stop taking ginkgo immediately if you have any side effects.

Ginkgo extract comes in the form of capsules and tablets. The standardized extract contains 24 percent ginkgo heterosides. Experts recommend anywhere from 120 to 240 milligrams daily taken by mouth in two to three equal doses for brain conditions. However, talk to a healthcare provider before using ginkgo, especially if you use more than 120 milligrams daily.

Golden Root (Rhodiola rosea)

This is an arctic root that the Vikings used for improving their strength and endurance. Native Americans also used it as an herbal medicine and a dye for clothing. Later, a Russian botanist began investigating this herb's possible use as an adaptogen (a substance that helps you cope with stressors in general). Over time, researchers have conducted more than 189 scientific studies to try to better understand its potential for healing.

Folk medicine practitioners use *Rhodiola rosea* to treat a wide range of conditions or to improve function, including impotence, fertility, asthma, nervous system disorders, physical endurance, and headache. However, this herb is reported to be most useful for treating a condition known in the past as "asthenia." Though this term has fallen out of favor in the medical jargon of the United States, others throughout the world commonly still regard it as a condition. Asthenia brings fatigue, less capacity for work, difficulty falling asleep, lack of appetite, headache, and irritability.

Rhodiola appears to treat these symptoms through its adaptogenic ability to bring the body into balance. Exactly how it does this is still unknown. However, it appears to have an effect on many of the major neurotransmitters, including serotonin and dopamine. It also affects your brain's amygdala, hippocampus, and hypothalamus, thus influencing your emotional state. *Rhodiola* may help you better manage stress by controlling how your adrenal glands release chemicals called catecholamines, such as norepinephrine.

Rhodiola may also help improve your memory. Researchers have linked it to changes in the brain's cerebral cortex in terms of improving thinking, analysis, calculating, and planning. These improvements may strengthen your ability to pay attention, increase your intelligence, and reduce your mental fatigue.

A number of clinical trials found that taking a *Rhodiola* extract had an antifatigue effect that improved people's mental performance, especially their ability to concentrate. In addition:

- One study looked at whether the herb could improve people's fatigue while they were working overnight shifts. The results showed that *Rhodiola* did reduce fatigue and improve people's short-term memory, ability to calculate, and concentration.
- In another study, students took golden root extract during an examination period. They showed a general state of well-being, improved coordination, less mental fatigue, and higher grades on their exams.
- Another study found that *Rhodiola* extract reduced depression in people with mild to moderate depression when they took it over a six-week period. In other research, people who took it with a tricyclic antidepressant had more improvement and fewer unwanted side effects from the antidepressant.

Since *Rhodiola rosea* is known to affect your response to stress, researchers have looked at it for treating binge eating (in which stress plays a major role). A component of the herb called salidroside, at doses found in an extract, was linked to a reduction in binge eating. The researchers concluded that extracts from the herb may be useful in treating binge-related eating disorders, and that salidroside appeared to be responsible for this effect.

Rhodiola may also be useful for people who are taking antipsychotic medications. These can lead to symptoms similar to those seen in Parkinson's disease, which include tremors, slow movement, and stiffness.

Overall, *Rhodiola rosea* has few side effects. Some people who are easily excitable may feel jittery and agitated, which you may be able to alleviate by lowering the dose. People with bipolar disorder shouldn't use this herb while they're in a manic state. It doesn't appear to interfere with medications aside from having an additive effect with stimulants. The recommended dosage is 100 to 300 milligrams per day, or for liquid forms, five to ten drops two to three times per day thirty minutes before eating. A *Rhodiola* formula standardized at 4:1 or an 8–12 percent alkaloid content should be used.

Guarana

Most of the world's supply of guarana comes from the Amazon rain forest. If you've ever encountered guarana, odds are good that it was in an energy drink.

Guarana—which produces small, bright red fruits—has one of the highest caffeine contents of any plant. The plant contains 7 percent caffeine, compared to the coffee bean, which has a comparatively low 1 to 2 percent. The plant uses its caffeine supply as a natural pesticide.

When guarana is consumed, the caffeine vanishes quickly and completely from your brain, and it has a short-lived effect. It doesn't negatively affect your concentration or higher brain function.

Caffeine interferes with the effects of adenosine, which is a leftover product from your body's use of a substance called ATP for energy. This causes your neurons to fire. Your body, thinking an emergency is going on, releases adrenaline and triggers a fight-or-flight response. Your liver then unloads extra sugar into your bloodstream. There is also an effect on dopamine, a chemical in the brain's pleasure center that pushes up blood flow to the muscles and inhibits blood flow to the skin and organs.

Caffeine also acts as a mood-altering agent, and it can have an antioxidant effect. It may improve blood flow through effects that inhibit blood clotting.

Research has found that guarana can improve cognitive performance and reduce mental fatigue. It also boosts memory and encourages feelings of alertness and well-being. People taking guarana have been found to have a faster reaction time and an improved ability to process information that they see. Guarana can also reduce fatigue and help people have better athletic performance. It also aids in suppressing the appetite, thus helping people lose weight.

However, the precaution for caffeine that we'll discuss in the next chapter about fluids also applies to the use of guarana. Though your body may be tired, caffeine prevents that message from getting through to your brain. Drinking caffeine to stay awake is like taking a painkiller to run on a sprained ankle. The painkiller does nothing to improve the healing of the ankle and ultimately could promote damage. Caffeine does nothing to help increase your energy and wakefulness, and ultimately it could lead to consequences on your ability to fall asleep.

The maximum safe dosage for guarana depends on several factors, including the caffeine content in your particular guarana product, how much caffeine you consume from other sources, and how you respond to caffeine, since some people can take more than others.

The key to using guarana appears to be to buy it from a trusted brand, use it sparingly, and see how it works for you before making it a regular part of your routine. While guarana seems to deliver the same pick-me-up that many coffee drinkers have come to rely on, if you are concerned about possible health risks, you might want to stick with a caffeine source that's more familiar to your body and better regulated, like tea, coffee, or even cola. Other compounds in guarana may slow down the rate at which caffeine gets into your system, so a single dose may last up to six hours, with its stimulatory effect more gradual and sustained.

Guarana is generally recognized as safe, as long as you don't combine it with other substances that act as stimulants. However, you should avoid it if you're allergic to it. Side effects from the caffeine in guarana can include irritability, insomnia, jitters, heart palpitations, anxiety, nervousness, increased urination, flushing in the face, cold feet, and digestive upset. Since guarana can keep the platelets in your blood from clumping together and clotting, you shouldn't take guarana if you're using the blood-thinning drug warfarin or platelet inhibitors such as Plavix or aspirin.

Also, use caution if you're taking analgesic medications, since guarana can increase their effectiveness by helping your body absorb them better. And if you're taking benzodiazepines to reduce anxiety, guarana counteracts this effect. Guarana may also make you more likely to have unwanted side effects when taking antipsychotics.

Jujube

Jujube is one of the world's oldest fruits. It's been used in Chinese medicine for more than two thousand years. Though rare in the United States, jujube trees are as popular in China as the apple tree is here. The name means "Christ's thorn," and the plant is mentioned seven times in the Bible. The fruit is about the size of a cherry to a plum and has a mahogany to red color when it's ripe. The flesh is crisp, white, and sweet, with a flavor that somewhat resembles an apple's.

Though it has been overlooked by the Western world, Asians recognize jujube as a valuable medicinal herb that makes an excellent general health tonic. Long before Western medicine developed, the Chinese herbalist Shennanong wrote about the healing properties of this fruit. He noted that the fruit had a calming effect and could treat fatigue.

It can also be an ideal food for healing and protecting the brain. Perhaps jujube's greatest contribution to the brain is its ability to calm the mind and reduce emotional upset. Here's how it works: communication between your cells relies on two messenger molecules called cGMP and cAMP (these are responsible for pretty much every process that takes place in the body). The jujube fruit has one of the highest concentrations of cAMP and cGMP of any plant known to man. A variety of interesting health benefits result from better intercellular communication.

Research suggests that cAMP affects higher-order thinking, planning, decision-making, learning, memory, and impulse control in the brain's prefrontal cortex. It causes ion channels to open, which can help regulate brain function and reduce cognitive and attention deficits. In addition, cGMP affects the hippocampus, amygdala, cerebellum, and other regions of the brain that play a role in learning, memory, motor adaptation, and other functions.

Jujube also acts as an adaptogen by encouraging normal functioning of the adrenal glands, allowing them to function optimally when you're under stress. The active ingredients in the plant that most likely produce these calming qualities are called saponins. Discussing antidepressant medications that work by either inhibiting the reuptake or breakdown of serotonin between nerve cells can help us better understand saponins. Experiments show that saponins have a similar action on serotonin and serotonin receptors as these medications.

Science also supports the belief that jujube may have the potential to protect neurons, particularly in certain regions of the brain. This could be due to the plant's ability to boost enzymes that prevent damage from lack of blood flow, combat damage from free radicals, and prevent the breakdown of fatty acids.

Phytonutrients contained in the jujube plant also support cardiovascular health. The plant boosts nitric oxide levels, which helps increase the diameter of blood vessels, which in turn promotes a healthy supply of oxygen to the tissues.

That's not all. The fruit is also known to suppress the release of many inflammatory chemicals, which in chronically high supply can lead to many diseases. And the jujube plant can significantly reduce pain and distress, much like aspirin.

You can often find dried jujubes in Asian markets and some health food stores. Powdered jujube is also available. When looking for jujubes, choose smaller ones with firm, wrinkled skin.

Usually, experts recommend taking 10 to 30 grams of dried jujube, either as a powder or boiled in water that you then drink. Jujube has no known drug interactions or reports of toxicity from overuse. However, avoid it if you have excessive phlegm, cramps and bloating, or intestinal parasites. As with any herb, be sure to talk to a qualified healthcare provider before using jujube.

L-theanine

Theanine was discovered in tea by a Japanese researcher in 1949. In fact, that's where you're most likely to find it, since aside from the basidiomycete mushroom, it's present almost exclusively in the tea plant. Accounting for up to 1 to 2 percent of tea's dry weight, L-theanine is an amino acid that gives tea its "savory" taste. ("Theanine" and "L-theanine" are interchangeable.)

L-theanine is able to cross the blood-brain barrier. Animal studies have shown that it increases the brain neurotransmitters serotonin, dopamine, and GABA. Increases in serotonin and dopamine are associated with calmness and pleasure. L-theanine's importance in creating the neurotransmitter GABA plays a key role in relaxation and sleep. GABA is the neurotransmitter that's activated by the popular sleep medications known as benzodiazepines.

Behavioral studies in animals suggest that L-theanine may lead to improvement in learning and memory, and thus better cognition. In humans, researchers have also linked L-theanine with improvement in learning performance, heightened mental acuity, and better concentration.

L-theanine has a relaxing affect that kicks in roughly thirty to forty minutes after you ingest it. It should be noted here that L-theanine counteracts the stimulating effect of caffeine, which is also found in tea.

Theanine could also be important for brain health by protecting neurons from excessive glutamate. Glutamate is an essential brain chemical that can be released in excessive amounts in some diseases, such as Lou Gehrig's disease and vascular dementia, and with brain injuries like strokes or head trauma. Theanine may protect against this damage by blocking glutamate from entering cells. It may also have an antistress effect and may serve as an antioxidant that protects LDL cholesterol from free-radical damage.

In supplement form, L-theanine is well tolerated, and it has no reported drug or nutrient interactions. Overall, it seems to have little or no harmful effects. For relaxation, the amount that has been used in research is 200 milligrams two to three times per day (400 to 800 milligrams can be used safely, and as little as 50 to 200 milligrams has been linked to a relaxation response). The FDA recommends a maximum dose of 1,200 milligrams daily.

A cup of tea contains approximately 15 to 30 milligrams. You can find potentially beneficial amounts of this substance in green, black, white, and oolong teas. Talk to your healthcare provider before you use theanine if you have any serious or chronic health problems.

Phosphatidylserine

Phosphatidylserine (PS) is a phospholipid that makes up the structural component of cell membranes. It's found in all cells, and your body makes it—which may give you a clue about how important it is. It's composed of the amino acid serine in combination with arachidonic acid, alpha-linoleic acid, and linoleic acid.

PS works in the brain—where it is one of the most plentiful fats— in assisting cell-to-cell communication. Without PS, nerve cells can't produce or conduct the electrical impulses required to communicate! Furthermore, PS influences the fluidity of the cell membrane (remember from earlier chapters that you don't want the membranes surrounding your brain's cells to be too rigid). When neuron cell membranes are more flexible, nutrients can enter easily and proper glucose metabolism for energy can be maintained. PS can also increase the number of receptor sites on brain cells, giving us more docking points for neural communication. Additionally, it strengthens the cell membranes of neurons and protects their contents from possible damage from the stress hormone cortisol.

About one to four hours after you eat it or take it, PS crosses your blood-brain barrier, where it's particularly attracted to your hypothalamus. PS may benefit cognitive functioning, especially mental processes that diminish with aging such as memory, learning, and concentration. Elderly people with cognitive decline who took PS had improved socialization, memory, learning, concentration, and recall. Several researchers found it may be helpful for ADHD and depression.

Based on the available scientific evidence, the FDA found a lack of agreement that a relationship exists between PS and reduced risk of dementia or cognitive dysfunction. However, the FDA did extend a "qualified health claim" status to PS, stating that "consumption of phosphatidylserine may reduce the risk of cognitive dysfunction in the elderly." PS increases brain energy and improves mood. It also improves coordination between the brain and adrenal glands, which in turn can help you cope better with stress.

Dietary sources include meat, fish, liver, and kidneys, and it's also found in lecithin, an additive in many foods, including chocolate and baked goods. Eating foods the body needs to build its own phosphatidylserine may also be a wise idea. These include foods high in the amino acid methionine (found in nuts, seeds, corn, rice, and other grains), folic acid (leafy green vegetables), essential fatty acids (fish and flaxseed oil), and vitamin B12 (eggs, dairy, fish, and meat). Including these foods will ensure that your body will produce sufficient amounts of PS.

PS supplementation has no reported side effects for healthy people. However, PS may cause blood thinning and should be used with caution among people taking Coumadin or other prescription antico-agulant (blood-thinning) drugs. Therapeutic doses range from 200 to 800 milligrams (taken in doses of 100 to 200 milligrams twice a day). PS is susceptible to free-radical damage, so one should take it with antioxidants such as vitamin E, vitamin C, and selenium.

Vinpocetine

This is extracted from the leaves of periwinkle plants (*Vinca minor*) and is widely used in Japan. It's also popular in Europe, where many doctors feel it's more effective than supplements such as ginkgo for improving memory and brain function. Vinpocetine may have a similar effect on the brain as ginkgo, but it may work more quickly.

It might be useful in treating strokes and transient ischemic attacks, which are also called "ministrokes." Vinpocetine crosses the blood-brain barrier and makes its way into brain tissue, especially in particular areas. This treatment works as an antioxidant and can protect neurons in the brain. It also improves blood circulation in the brain, relaxes blood vessels, and decreases blood clotting.

Studies that involved the use of doses up to 20 milligrams three times daily found no major adverse reactions. However, side effects may include dizziness, anxiety, nausea, indigestion, flushing, sleeping problems, headache, drowsiness, and dry mouth. It may also cause a temporary drop in blood pressure.

Vinpocetine appears safe to take with other drugs. However, because it decreases blood clotting, avoid using it if you're taking blood-thinning medications. It's also not for people with kidney damage, seizures, low blood pressure, or heart-rhythm problems. It's unknown whether it's safe in pregnant and lactating women.

Most people take about 10 milligrams three times per day. First-time users should only take 2 to 5 milligrams with meals to ensure that they're not overly sensitive to it. You may then increase the dosage to 10 to 40 milligrams daily. You'll absorb this herbal treatment better on an empty stomach.

Ginseng

This herb has a long history in North America. A French Jesuit priest thought that the climate in Canada was similar to that of Manchuria—where ginseng had long been used—so he embarked on a trip to seek ginseng roots. In 1716, he discovered *Panax quinquefolius*, or American ginseng, and returned to Paris with a sample.

Soon Canada was shipping tons of the herb to China, and American ginseng became an extremely profitable export. In 1784, George Washington wrote in his diary that he passed a packhorse carrying ginseng. Daniel Boone made a fortune selling ginseng at a time when the root was more profitable than furs. However, in 1788 he lost tons of his precious commodity when his boat overturned in a river.

American ginseng is now an endangered species, in part because it grows slowly, requiring at least six years before its root can be sold. As a result, American ginseng is now grown heavily in China.

Ginseng is another one of the herbs that brings about health improvements by acting as an adaptogen, bringing the body into a state of balance. Ginseng is often credited for boosting energy; improving sexual vigor; improving your body's endocrine function; delaying senility; improving memory; reducing stress; slowing atherosclerosis in the arteries; reducing cholesterol, triglycerides, and blood sugar; and inhibiting inflammation.

Ginseng comes in several types, which may be important when determining its benefit. Ginseng refers to the root of several species in the plant genus *Panax*. This comes from Greek, in which *pan* means "all" and *axos* means "cure." Common types include:

- Korean/Asian ginseng (*Panax ginseng*)
- American ginseng (*Panax quinquefolius*)
- Siberian ginseng (*Eleutherococcus senticosus*)
- Japanese ginseng (*Panax japonicus*)
- Brazilian ginseng (*Pfaffia paniculata*)

Panax is the most commonly used, but some experts believe that Siberian ginseng is the most potent type for improving brain function. Some have concluded that eleuthero ginseng is not really ginseng, but rather unique plants with different effects from the *Panax* forms. Its adaptogenic activity is brought about by other chemicals. Nonetheless, this type has some of the same stimulant and energy-improving effects, giving it a place among other commercially available ginseng preparations.

Panax ginseng may be able to boost brainpower. In one study, people who took 200 milligrams of the extract an hour before a test had higher scores. They also felt less mental fatigue. These results suggest that ginseng can improve performance and feelings of mental fatigue during times when you have to think for long periods. Ginseng may work in part by encouraging your brain cells to take up more blood glucose.

Since ginseng acts as a mild stimulant, it's sometimes recommended for people who are feeling lethargic or having trouble concentrating. It may work to counteract fatigue by stimulating the brain and increasing levels of adrenaline.

Ginseng may also be useful in controlling blood sugar, which has benefits for brain health. People with diabetes—as well as those without the condition—showed improvements in their long-term blood sugar control and less of a rise in blood sugar after a meal if they were taking ginseng. As a result, some researchers have felt that ginseng may be a useful addition to medication in treating people with non-insulin-dependent diabetes.

You can easily find a variety of ginseng types in health food stores. However, it's often hard to tell which type of plant you're getting. Finding an authentic product can be difficult, since good-quality roots cost a lot, and many products aren't authentic or they're adulterated with other ingredients. In addition, the herb varies so much in potency that it's hard to know how much to take of any brand, and some may not contain an effective amount.

As a result, it's important to check out your options and buy a brand from a company with a good reputation. To find brand-name products, check www.consumerlab.com or www.supplementreviews.com.

Ginseng may be most useful if you take it as an occasional pick-me-up rather than part of a regular regimen. Most experts recommend taking 100 to 200 milligrams daily for three to six weeks. Because you'll encounter a wide variation in the ginsenoside content of different products, look for products that supply a standardized level of ginsenosides. Products should be standardized to contain 4 to 6 percent ginsenosides or 0.5 to 1 percent eleutherosides.

People with high blood pressure may want to avoid using ginseng. Small doses have been shown to raise blood pressure (though in higher doses, ginseng may lower blood pressure). It may also lead to nervousness, confusion, restlessness, insomnia, poor appetite, and diarrhea. Experts also advise not to take ginseng with antidepressants or drugs that lower blood sugar.

 ## THE BRAIN FIX TOOLBOX

I included this chapter because people are always looking for "natural ways" to enhance their brain function. The information is therefore provided for people's edification, but I'm not necessarily recommending these supplements, since the message of this book is to achieve improvements by nutrition and lifestyle changes.

I often advise against supplementation because quality standards are often lacking for these products. The amount of active ingredient in pills and capsules often varies greatly from what's listed on the label. And some herbal supplements have been found to be contaminated with heavy metals or prescription drugs. Unfortunately, there is no way for the consumer to know exactly what is in supplements.

However, it's a good sign if a manufacturer abides by the rules of Good Manufacturing Practices (GMP) for drugs. Also look for the United States Pharmacopoeia (USP) seal, which means that a product has been independently tested, and it's been shown to contain the ingredients in the amounts listed on the label. Also, be sure to avoid treating conditions with supplements if they could improve with timely professional therapy or could result in serious health problems if neglected.

12

Keeping Your Brain Afloat Without Artificial Sweeteners and Caffeine

WATER IS NECESSARY FOR THE survival of both body and brain. You can live thirty to forty days without food, but most people won't survive beyond seventy-two hours without water.

As mentioned earlier, your brain's weight is largely composed of water. *All* your body's processes take place in fluid—in other words, water—which:

- Transports substances around your body
- Eliminates waste
- Lubricates moving parts
- Aids in digestion
- Regulates your temperature

Fluid plumps up your cells and keeps them working properly. When it's in short supply, a lack of water causes your cells to shrink and encourages them to fail.

But for all its importance, it's easy for us to run low on water. The thirst that signals us to drink tends to lag behind our bodies' need for water, thus, it's important to drink water even when you are not thirsty. A mere 2 percent drop in your body's water level can cause your brain to perform more poorly. Most people need to drink at least eight cups of water daily. Often people do not get a sufficient amount because they aren't thirsty, don't like the taste of water, don't make a habit of drinking, or simply prefer other beverages.

Staying well hydrated can also help prevent a common issue that hampers our mental and physical health: obesity. It costs your body 50 calories' worth of effort to absorb, circulate, metabolize, and excrete one quart of chilled water. If you drink two quarts, you'll burn 100 calories, which is the amount that many people would burn while jogging a mile. When you drink enough water, your liver is free to efficiently use stored fat as fuel. Water also helps fill your stomach, reducing hunger. Sometimes drinking water can eliminate food cravings, since often our desire for food is actually thirst that we confuse as hunger.

Unfortunately, the beverages that our society often guzzles to quench its thirst are the most common delivery systems for ingredients that might be harmful to brain health, namely, artificial sweeteners and caffeine. As a result, it's important to make sure that you generally keep your fluid levels topped off with drinks that *don't* contain these components.

Where Are You Getting Your Fluids?

Water is nearly free when it comes from your faucet. Twenty years ago, the notion of a billion-dollar bottled-water industry would have been challenged as a ludicrous idea by most of us. Now 70 percent of all beverages are consumed from containers. The United States has some of the best drinking water standards in the world, but many people prefer their water bottled.

There are those who prefer bottled water because it's portable and they think it tastes better. (Probably equally important is that somewhere in their subconscious they have an image of athletes drinking it at press conferences and supermodels carrying it on Paris walkways.)

Marketers may imply that bottled water is healthier, purer, and more wholesome, but it has never been proven healthier than what comes out of the faucet. In fact, some leading brands simply contain tap water that's been filtered! Plus, with bottled water, we have the additional concern of the environmental effect of all the plastic bottles that aren't recycled.

Still, drinking plenty of water is a good thing, whether bottled or from the tap. Even bottled water is better for your health than other alternatives that people often pour from bottles or cans.

According to some research, liquids make up 22 percent of the calories in the average American diet, and a big portion of these calories come from sugar-sweetened beverages. If you're interested in protecting your brain from the harmful effects of obesity, it's wise to limit sugary sodas and other sugar-sweetened drinks.

People often fail to compensate for calorie-laden drinks by consuming less food later. So they wind up taking in more calories than they need. We're better able to regulate our intake of solid food: if we eat more at one meal, we have a tendency to consume less food later in the day. Such is not the case for fluid consumption, since liquid calories do not satisfy as well. (Fluid calories simply don't register in the stomach and brain; when you chew food, it helps trigger internal signals of fullness.)

There is not a lot of awareness of the calories in beverages when we're drinking them. In fact, soft drinks may increase hunger, decrease fullness, or trigger cravings for more sweetness. And the larger the beverage, the more a person will drink.

Some experts are bent on proving that soda is a leading cause of obesity. A case can definitely be made supporting this notion. Soft drink consumption rose more than 60 percent among adults and more than doubled in kids and teenagers from 1977 to 1997. The prevalence of obesity roughly doubled during that same time.

Two cans of regular soda contain 20 teaspoons of sugar! Carbonated soft drinks are the single largest source of calories in the American diet, according to a 2005 report from the Center for Science in the Public Interest. Simply cutting out one sugary drink per day can result in 2.5 pounds of weight loss in eighteen months!

If you're directing a river of sodas, coffee, and other caffeinated drinks into your body to address your fluid needs, you could be nudging your brain's health further out of line with each cup, can, and bottle. But as you're about to see, switching from regular to diet soda may not markedly improve the situation either.

Artificial Sweeteners:
Chemicals Your Brain Really Doesn't Need

Sugar isn't *bad*, but we simply consume too much. As a result, it's reasonable for food developers and consumers to explore substances that taste like sugar without the calories and surge of insulin that accompany it. This way we could avoid the brain-harming consequences of excess sugar consumption, such as obesity and diabetes, yet still satisfy our sweet cravings.

However, artificial sweeteners don't offer an ideal solution. Let's take a quick look at some of the sugar substitutes you're likely to find around you.

Saccharin

As hard as it may be to believe, saccharin has been around since 1879. At Johns Hopkins University, a fellow named Constantin Fahlberg was trying to develop new chemical dyes from coal tar derivatives. He failed to wash his hands completely after a beaker boiled over and later noticed that the biscuits his wife cooked were particularly sweet.

During the sugar rationing that occurred during both world wars, this sugar substitute became familiar to many Americans. Though it was grandfathered in under the Federal Food and Drug Act of 1938 as generally recognized as safe, saccharin experienced a somewhat rocky journey in terms of its safety.

In 1977, researchers discovered that the compound caused bladder cancer in rats. Though the amounts given to the rats far exceeded human consumption, it became prohibited. There was a public outcry over its removal that inspired Congress (not the Food and Drug Administration) to allow its use, provided that a warning appear on all products containing saccharin.

A large number of studies supported the notion that the use of saccharin *didn't* result in bladder cancer in humans. As a result, the National Institutes of Health concluded that saccharin should not be listed among potential carcinogens. So in 2000, 123 years after its discovery, the warning was removed from saccharin-containing products.

No studies currently prove that saccharin is *not* safe for brain health, and until then we must assume that it's safe. I *do* question the use of saccharin and other artificial sweeteners over concerns that they may trigger cravings for sugar and contribute to obesity (as we'll see shortly).

Aspartame

Another common sugar substitute is aspartame, better known as Equal or NutraSweet. Its components (a mix of phenylalanine, aspartate, and methanol) are found in nearly every protein consumed by man. Because aspartame breaks down into amino acids, which are building blocks of protein, it naturally behaves like a protein.

Aspartame's opponents have had a heyday exposing and conjuring up arguments that support how this simple molecule is responsible for a host of neuropsychiatric and other disorders. The list of conditions is almost endless, including mood shifts, manic episodes, depression, nervousness, irritability, memory loss, nightmares, epilepsy, seizures, dizziness, slurred speech, fatigue, headaches, migraines, and fibromyalgia.

As we discussed in the protein section, the brain communicates by using neurotransmitters that are produced from monoamines and stored in nerve cells. A monoamine is a single amino acid, like the phenylalanine found in aspartame. Phenylalanine is an ingredient that turns into tyrosine, which eventually is converted into the neurotransmitters dopamine and norepinephrine. These are (presumably) responsible for the myriad of neurological conditions attributed to aspartame. It would be a stretch to assume that a reasonable amount of a sweetener could produce these changes in the brain, but because of this association, Equal had to be proven safe.

On a side note, phenylalanine and tyrosine have been reported to have antidepressant and stress-relieving benefits. These responses are probably due to the components that can become neurotransmitters that affect mood. However, one should be cautious about self-medicating with these, since studies have used high doses that have not been proven safe; plus, these reports are dated and limited.

Aspartate or aspartic acid, the second ingredient in aspartame, has also attracted attention from the sweetener's detractors. Aspartic acid works as a pesticide and is considered to be an *excitotoxin*. When insects are exposed to large amounts of this amino acid, it causes brain cells to become excessively excited to the point that they die. However, humans consume aspartate in much greater amounts in common proteins, and the body handles aspartame and foods like beans, eggs, fish, and meat the same way. In addition, aspartic acid is broken down quickly after ingestion.

Another concern is that the body metabolizes these amino acids into chemicals like methanol, formaldehyde, and a substance called DKP. Formaldehyde is the chemical used to embalm bodies and keep tissues preserved prior to burial. The thought of this foul-smelling chemical, which has been found in research to damage the central nervous system, would make many people understandably concerned.

The information that's often not discussed is that these breakdown chemicals exist only for a moment before they are broken down even further into safer compounds and eliminated from the body. Methanol content is higher in fruit juice, citrus fruits, and fermented beverages, which are natural products. As far as DKP goes, some scientists have expressed concern that the substance undergoes a nitrosation process in the stomach, which produces a type of chemical that could cause brain tumors. Others have argued that the nitrosation in the stomach would likely not produce a brain carcinogen, and if it did, it would only lead to a minuscule amount.

Aspartame has been researched longer and more rigorously than any other additive on the market to date, yet it continues to be criticized by health enthusiasts. More than two hundred scientific papers written during a thirty-year span support the FDA's stance that the amounts used by humans are too low to raise concern (except for people with the genetic condition PKU, who cannot safely consume phenylalanine). Nor does aspartame appear to cause headaches or produce changes in mood, behavior, or thought processes.

Again, when I was writing this book, in general there was no proof to support the notion that aspartame is not safe. We can conclude it is safe in moderate amounts. However, as with all artificial sweeteners, I am concerned about the issue of this product sustaining cravings for sugar.

Sucralose

In 1976, British scientists stumbled upon a sweet substance while seeking a new pesticide recipe. The resulting product became known as sucralose (Splenda), which consists of a sugar molecule with a portion of the chemical structure replaced by chloride. This configuration allows the consumer to experience a sweet taste sensation without all the calories. It has fewer than 5 calories per serving, which places it at the upper limit the FDA allows for a product to be considered calorie-free.

Of course, something made with chloride that was originally associated with a pesticide conjures up fears of major health problems. But just because something is made with chloride and can be absorbed into the bloodstream does not mean it's toxic, as more than 110 scientific studies have found. Splenda received approval in 1996, yet some still contend that there are not sufficient long-term studies on its possible side effects.

Again, this product may trigger cravings, so why bother with it? If you need to sweeten your food, just use small amounts of sugar, and then you know you are safe without introducing artificial sweeteners into your system.

Acesulfame-K

This sweetener, also known as Sunett, was also discovered accidently by someone licking fingers in the lab (this seems unwise, but it *has* led to a lot of interesting products). Though some reported that it may lead to headaches, depression, visual disturbances, and mental confusion, acesulfame-K is not metabolized or stored in the body. Critics point out the lack of long-term studies, but the FDA approved it for general use in 1988.

While it's probably safe, it has not been studied long enough and is not inexpensive. Again, you're better off going with small amounts of real sugar when you need a sweetener.

Sugar Alcohols

Many of you might be familiar with these ingredients in sugar-free gums. These alcohol derivatives do not trigger insulin production, but they do contain calories. A major drawback to using these frequently is the side effect profile, which can include diarrhea, bloating, and flatulence.

Stevia

One can hardly say that stevia is new, since it has been used for more than four hundred years in Paraguay, and more recently in Japan, without reports of ill effects. It is a natural derivative from the leaves of the plant *Stevia rebaudiana*. In 2000, it was approved as a food additive. Usually suppliers offer various mixtures of *Stevia* plus table sugar in order to cover up *Stevia*'s bitter taste and reduce its cost. *Stevia* doesn't cause blood sugar to rise, which is an additional benefit for people who like it because it's a natural sweetener.

It is clear from this discussion that the use of artificial sweeteners, for most individuals, doesn't come with the dire health risks that often get trumpeted online. When used in moderation, the choice of which one to use is completely a personal decision. With that said, it is wise to consider that very high doses (far above those in an ordinary diet) may cause a myriad of problems. And there will always be some people who are sensitive or allergic to some of these natural or synthetic products.

Still, for other reasons, drinking diet sodas isn't the best method for keeping your brain hydrated. People who drink more than one diet soda per day may develop the same risks for heart disease as those who toss back regular sugary sodas. Studies have found that artificial sweeteners can stimulate your appetite, increase carbohydrate cravings, encourage fat storage, and trigger weight gain.

A paper published in the journal *Circulation* points out that consuming diet sodas has been linked to a 31 percent higher risk of obesity, a 30 percent higher risk of increased waist circumference, a 25 percent higher risk of excess triglycerides and high fasting blood sugar, a 32 percent greater risk of low HDL levels, and a trend toward developing high blood pressure. None of these factors bodes well for optimal brain health.

Since diet sodas are 99 percent water, there are few possible explanations why this would occur. One is that people who drink diet sodas might also practice unhealthy habits like eating fried foods, smoking, overeating, and exercising sparingly. Another possible explanation is that artificial sweeteners may cause people to eat *more* at the next meal. A person who drinks a diet soda may feel it is acceptable to make up for those calories with a high-calorie food. Since the taste sensors of the tongue detect sugar, but the caloric increase is never verified by the brain, the body continues to search for calories until it is satisfied.

When you're thirsty, the most sensible choice is to drink a fluid that contains substances that support your health—or at the very least, *doesn't* contain substances that your body doesn't really need. Diet drinks probably aren't going to improve your health in any way, and some of them could have at least some theoretical chance of being harmful.

Avoiding these drinks can also help you sidestep another chemical in our food supply that most people regard as innocuous, but that can have a real impact on your mental health: caffeine.

Time to Slow Down on Your Caffeine Habit

As legend has it, people started drinking caffeine when a coffee-bean branch fell into a pot of boiling water in ancient China, and we haven't stopped since. The Aztecs were drinking coffee in the 1500s when Spanish conquistadors arrived. Soft drinks have been a popular caffeine-delivery system in America since the late 1800s when Coca-Cola appeared on the map in Atlanta, Georgia. As Americans shifted from agricultural jobs—which were governed by the availability of sunlight—to indoor manufacturing jobs on the clock, caffeine helped them make the change (and kept them from falling asleep while operating machinery).

Genes Help Determine the Body's Reaction to Caffeine

Researchers at Harvard University have found that a craving for coffee may be encoded in our genes. One such gene is linked to the process by which coffee is metabolized, and a second gene regulates the first one. Whether people carry a high- or a low-consumption variant may help determine how much coffee they crave.

One variant causes people to metabolize it faster, and the other leads to slower metabolism. The slow variant may affect the heart because it allows caffeine to linger. Research has found that high consumers drank an extra 40 milligrams of caffeine compared to low consumers. This study confirms that everyone handles caffeine differently, and this is to a degree determined by the genetic hand you were dealt. In other words, what may be healthy for *some* may not be healthy for *others*.

The FDA recognized caffeine as safe in 1958, which it reconfirmed in 1989. Nowadays, caffeine is regarded as the world's most popular drug, with 90 percent of the world's population consuming it. It's available in sodas, coffee, tea, chocolate, and—as a walk through a convenience store will show you—a variety of brightly packaged energy drinks.

Given that it's a legal substance that saturates many of our popular beverages, you may not have given caffeine much thought recently. However, it *is* a drug that affects your brain. In excess, it doesn't support optimal brain function. And some people should avoid it completely.

Here's what caffeine does in your brain. Remember that not every chemical you ingest can cross the barrier between your bloodstream and your brain. Caffeine, however, is invited to enter. When caffeine crosses the blood-brain barrier, it stimulates the release of dopamine in your brain's reward center in much the same way as addictive substances.

Caffeine also triggers dopamine release in the anterior cingulate gyrus and the prefrontal centers, which are the decision-making and impulse areas of the cerebral cortex. This puts the brain on high alert and ramps up your concentration and attention. Your blood sugar, pulse, respiration, and muscle tension also increase.

Caffeine also improves wakefulness through its effect on the chemical adenosine. As more caffeine crosses the blood-brain barrier, less adenosine can enter into the brain. Adenosine is a neurotransmitter that locks onto a receptor involved in regulating your brain's arousal level. Adenosine is the body's natural tool for calming down before sleep. (And sleep is necessary for recovery, restoration, and healing for your body and brain.)

Caffeine knocks out adenosine for several hours, which keeps your brain from quieting down. As a result, caffeine can lead to:

- Inability to fall asleep
- Poor quality of sleep
- Sleeping fewer hours
- Chronic insomnia
- Sleep deprivation

As a result, caffeine, though it has a pick-me-up effect, is a major cause of daytime sleepiness, fatigue, and trouble concentrating across the country.

But it's doing other things in the brain, too. A neurotransmitter called GABA makes cells in the brain's sleep center less likely to fire. As a result, GABA makes people more prone to sleeping because it calms, quiets, and sedates the brain. Caffeine can negate GABA's effects, which tips the scales toward arousal and inability to fall asleep. This can also lead to higher alertness and anxiety.

Caffeine content of common food items:

- Brewed instant coffee, 8 ounces: 100 to 250 milligrams
- 98-percent caffeine-free coffee, 8 ounces: 2 milligrams
- Energy drinks, 8 ounces: 50 to 500 milligrams
- Tea, 8 ounces: 50 milligrams
- Green tea, 8 ounces: 30 to 60 milligrams
- Mountain Dew, 12 ounces: 55 milligrams
- Diet cola, 12 ounces: 50 milligrams
- Cola, 12 ounces: 35 milligrams
- Chocolate, 1.5 ounces: 5 milligrams

Health Issues Linked to Caffeine

You could make good arguments for *and* against drinking caffeine. However, let's first dispel some common concerns that are unfounded. For example:

- Children and adults process caffeine the same way, and caffeine doesn't affect hyperactivity or kids' attention span, according to the National Institutes of Health.
- Caffeinated beverages don't negatively affect reproduction during pregnancy, nor do they reduce the chances of becoming pregnant.
- The American Cancer Society claims that caffeine doesn't lead to an increased risk of cancer.

- Modest caffeine use was found to not be associated with increases in blood pressure and risk of heart disease. Caffeine's effect on raising blood pressure is short-lived. However, evidence hasn't *proven* that guzzling lots of coffee won't increase the risk of high blood pressure. People with different genetic backgrounds may handle coffee differently.

It's true that a number of positive effects have been associated with caffeine (or coffee and tea). For example:

- Caffeine can improve mental functioning and mood, with benefits including alertness, vigilance, cheerfulness, better concentration, faster reaction times, and better accuracy on memory tests.
- Coffee may lower your risk of gallstones. Caffeine causes the gallbladder to contract more quickly and repeatedly. This keeps excess cholesterol from building up in the gallbladder and forming crystals.
- Combined with aspirin, it can dampen headaches better than aspirin alone.
- Caffeine's phosphodiesterase-inhibiting property also frees stored fatty acids from body fat, thereby aiding in weight reduction. Caffeinated beverages are often served hot, which by itself suppresses appetite.
- Caffeine can help make asthma attacks and symptoms less severe. Caffeine—which is found in cold medications—opens up bronchial passages and works as a decongestant.
- Caffeine's positive effect on mood could prevent the onset of depression in healthy people.
- Its effects on alertness can decrease car accidents due to fatigue.

In addition, coffee may reduce the risk of stroke. For example, drinking three cups of coffee daily over the long term was associated with a 21 percent lower risk of stroke in nonsmoking women. In another study, only 2.9 percent of men and women who drank at least six cups daily had a stroke, compared to 5 percent of those who drank only one or two cups. Ingredients aside from caffeine in coffee might reduce inflammation and oxidative stress while improving insulin resistance. This could lead to a lower risk of stroke.

Tea and coffee consumption has also been shown to reduce cardiovascular-related deaths. And research has found that drinking coffee daily—whether regular or decaf—is linked to a lower risk of diabetes. In one study, drinking three to four cups of coffee daily reduced the risk of type 2 diabetes by 29 percent. The lower risk of diabetes may be due to the effect of chlorogenic acid and magnesium on carbohydrate metabolism. Chlorogenic acid (a combination of caffeic acid and quinic acid) is the most abundant polyphenol—an antioxidant—in coffee. It slows the absorption of sugar into cells.

Caffeinated and decaffeinated types of coffee have similar antioxidant levels. The USDA has found that the average adult consumes 1,229 milligrams of antioxidants daily from coffee, with other major entries including tea (294 milligrams), bananas (76 milligrams), and dry beans (72 milligrams).

However, just as caffeinated drinks may offer potential health benefits, they can have negative effects, too. These include:

- Lowering the production of DHEA, which is a hormonelike substance made from cholesterol. This affects the immune, cardiovascular, and nervous systems.
- Stomach upset, reflux disease, and ulcers.
- Higher cholesterol. The cholesterol-raising substances kahweol and cafestol are found in some types of coffee. These are present in boiled coffee, but in lesser amounts in filtered coffee.
- Worsening vision in people with glaucoma or ocular hypertension
- An increase in serum homocysteine from coffee. Homocysteine is associated with cardiovascular disease.
- Menstrual irregularities and worsening PMS symptoms.

Weighed on the whole, we can't make a strong case for abstaining from coffee in general based on its physical effects. Still, people with a background of addiction should read on, since for them being a caffeine teetotaler *does* seem to be a wise decision.

The Role of Caffeine when Addictions Have Hurt Your Brain

The issue of whether or not caffeine is addictive is controversial. The DSM-IV (the American Psychiatric Association's publication that sets the criteria for psychological problems) doesn't hold that caffeine or coffee is addictive. Nor does the World Health Organization recognize caffeine as addictive.

Though caffeine dependence isn't an official diagnosis, some people need increasing amounts to feel the wanted effects, they feel withdrawal symptoms when they try to quit caffeine, and they find themselves unable to quit. Those symptoms are surely recognizable to people who've experienced an addiction to other substances.

Caffeine Gives a Jolt to Many Medicines

Think that coffee shops, supermarkets, and convenience stores are the only places to get caffeine? Guess again. Caffeine has an impressive number of uses in pharmaceuticals. For example, it's found in medications for:

- Stimulating the nervous system
- Shedding water as a diuretic
- Mild laxative properties
- Opening airways as a decongestant/bronchodilator
- Pain relief
- Weight loss

And there is still an ongoing debate over giving caffeine the "addictive" title. It stimulates the output of the feel-good chemical dopamine in the brain's reward center much the same way as the established addictive substances. And though not fitting entirely into the category of addictive substances, it is possible that caffeine may be considered a type of "gateway drug" that leads to more harmful drugs.

Caffeine use has been found to be common in people with psychiatric disorders. Coffee drinkers have been found to use more nicotine, tranquilizers, sleeping pills, and sugar than people who avoid caffeine.

Teenaged girls are four times more likely to smoke and start drinking alcohol at an early age if they have a history of drinking coffee. Of course, since 80 percent of the U.S. population uses caffeine, most coffee drinkers *don't* develop substance use problems.

The issue of caffeine and addiction is clouded, but there are reasons for why it would be highly recommended for people to completely avoid caffeine if they're vulnerable to addictions. There are even more convincing arguments for why people in recovery should refrain from coffee and caffeine. For starters, the goal in drug treatment is to balance the chemicals in the brain and reduce the likelihood of anxiety and depression, which could trigger drug-seeking behaviors.

Stress is something that people with addictions don't need. They certainly do not want to trigger anxiety by consuming caffeinated beverages. Both stress and caffeine cause epinephrine levels to rise, and both create the classic fight-or-flight response. Caffeine chemically creates this state by acting like the hormone ACTH, which tells the adrenal glands to put out more adrenalin (epinephrine). This may lead to nervousness, jitters, trembling, and irritability. While recovery programs present a plan to calm the brain down, staying constantly on edge due to caffeine negates this effort.

Furthermore, since many recovering addicts are placed on antidepressants, it makes no sense to take a drug that can counteract them. But this, too, is a controversial issue. Caffeine stimulates the central nervous system and acts as an antidepressant by elevating serotonin and dopamine. However, as mentioned earlier, caffeine also inhibits the calming effect of adenosine and speeds people up. Since caffeine is known to create anxious responses, some experts recommend that people using SSRIs should limit their caffeine intake or avoid it completely.

The bottom line would have to be that caffeine in *any* amount is not recommended for healing the brain in people recovering from drug addiction. In short:

- Though caffeine does not fit the classic criteria for an addictive drug, people who are vulnerable to addictive behaviors should not allow caffeine to prime their addiction-seeking behaviors.

- Caffeine can trigger anxiety, which is part of what these individuals should be striving to minimize.
- Good sleep architecture is critical for rewiring the brain, and caffeine makes it difficult (if not impossible) to achieve this.
- Caffeine may also interfere with drugs like antidepressants that are designed to make the recovery process easier.
- Impulse control and reasoning are more challenging when consuming caffeine. This is not ideal at a time when so many important decisions need to be made and relearning needs to take place.

The Role of Caffeine for Everyone Else Who Wants a Healthy Brain

For most of us, the decision about the role that caffeine should play in our lives comes down to fatigue and alertness. Most people drink caffeine for the sense of increased energy it provides. However, this energy is not real; it's actually a chemical stimulation that parallels fear! The signal we get is not designed to make one feel more awake, but rather it inhibits the body's natural drive to seek rest.

Caffeine is all too often used as a crutch to make up for inadequate sleep. Eventually it takes a toll on memory, learning, and cognitive functioning. Information crammed into the brain by pulling an all-nighter with the aid of coffee has less chance of sticking in the brain. One who drinks caffeinated beverages may be speedier at making decisions, but these aren't always the wisest decisions. A good night's sleep would be a better investment.

Some people choose to circumvent caffeine's negative impact on sleep by simply avoiding it after dinner. Unfortunately, the half-life of caffeine—or the length of time for half of the original amount to disappear—usually lasts from 7.5 to 12 hours after you drink it. So if you have a cup at 3:00 in the afternoon, chances are your sleep will still be affected if your bedtime is 11:00 PM. As a result, I'd recommend that *everyone* stick to moderate amounts of caffeine at most—about what you'd find in a cup or two of coffee a day.

If you realize that getting caffeine out of your life should be an aspect of your healing process, the key to caffeine abstinence is to gradually decrease your intake. You can do this by switching from a 12-ounce mug to a 5-ounce cup, blending regular coffee with decaf, simply diluting regular-strength coffee with water, and switching from coffee or sodas to tea (preferably green or English breakfast tea).

The whole process of weaning off caffeine may take anywhere from two to nine days. Making sure that you get plenty of exercise, a balanced diet, proper hydration, fresh air and sunlight, meditation, and appropriate sleep will help you feel better while you taper off caffeine. Also, *any* of these improvements will soon have you forgetting that you ever felt the need for caffeine in the first place! It is all about being master over caffeine rather than allowing it to be the master over you.

 ## THE BRAIN FIX TOOLBOX

- Be sure to get an adequate amount of fluid, day in and day out.
- Water, low-fat milk, and green tea are some of the best choices for meeting your body's fluid needs. Tap water is an inexpensive way to stay hydrated, but if you must have bottled water for some reason, it's a suitable choice.
- If you don't have a history of substance-use problems, caffeine in low to moderate amounts is okay, but you're better off getting it out of your life.
- If you need caffeine to help you stay awake, take time to explore why you're so sleepy during the day. Do you have poor sleeping habits at night? Is your diet causing you to become fatigued in the afternoon? Is anxiety or depression wearing you out? If any of these factors are hampering your energy, look for solutions rather than covering up the symptoms with caffeine.
- If you have had substance-use problems in the past, your best bet is to avoid caffeine. Since it has some qualities in common with drugs of abuse, keeping it out of your system is a good

idea. The same advice is even truer if you're currently in treatment for addiction.

- Artificial sweeteners may not pose the threat that some on the Internet claim, but they're still chemicals that your body doesn't really need. Heavy consumption of diet sodas may actually promote weight *gain*, as well. Avoiding them is a sensible idea.

13

MSG: An Additive You Might
Want to Subtract

THE TERM "CHINESE RESTAURANT SYNDROME" first showed up in medical literature in 1968. It involved a cluster of symptoms—including facial flushing and swelling, chest pain, headache, and burning mouth—that developed after eating Chinese food. Some people in the grips of it may think they're having a heart attack.

The syndrome, which can begin within minutes after eating the first dish, lasts about two hours. The ingredient in the food that's been implicated is monosodium glutamate, or MSG. The scientific consensus on MSG seems to be that it doesn't pose a threat to the brain. However, the unanswered questions that linger about MSG suggest that people should at least use it with caution under certain circumstances. Let's draw this food additive into the spotlight for a moment to better understand what it might do in your body (which in turn will give you an even better understanding of how your brain works).

Glutamine, Glutamate, and Your Brain

Glutamine is one of the few amino acids that directly cross the blood-brain barrier. Once there, it eventually turns into glutamate. This is the most abundant neurotransmitter found in the brain, where it's used in at least 90 percent of synapses.

One of glutamate's important functions is to help turn nerve signals into memories within the hippocampus, which is the brain's memory center. Glutamate is particularly important in one's ability to orient oneself in space, to follow a schedule, and to realize where you are, how you got there, and whether you've been there before.

To understand glutamate requires understanding the complementary neurotransmitter GABA, which is actually made *from* glutamate. Whereas glutamate is the most abundant neurotransmitter, GABA follows in second place. They function as opposites. If glutamate is excitatory, exhilarating, and arousing, GABA is calming, quieting, and tranquilizing. GABA dampens nerve transmission in the brain and reduces nervous activity. Glutamate tells nerve cells to "fire" and send out a nerve pulse, whereas GABA tells the cells *not* to fire.

Without GABA as an antagonist to glutamate, you'd have an inability to fall asleep, thus missing out on a crucial time for healing. Some popular sleep medications activate GABA circuits to promote sleep.

Problems can arise when glutamate is found in excess. This leads to an overreaction of receptors, which can cause an issue called "excitotoxicity." Glutamate, the excitotoxin, opens ion channels on the nerve cells, which act as doorways. High levels of calcium can flood the cells, resulting in overexcitement. This process in turn leads to a cascade of events, including inflammation and generation of free radicals. The excessive excitotoxin also causes destruction of membranes, structural proteins, enzymes, mitochondria, and DNA until the point of cell death. Nearby cleanup cells then devour these dead cells. This process can occur during brain injuries such as strokes, alcoholism or substance abuse, seizures, and Alzheimer's disease.

Why MSG Could Be Worrisome

There have been concerns that high glutamate intake could possibly set off the cascade of events that lead to neurotoxicity. MSG makes an obvious candidate. As this is the world's most widely used food additive, you don't have to venture into a Chinese restaurant to encounter it. MSG is also found in many processed foods. Glutamate is also found in proteins in cheese, soy, meat, fish, and dairy products. In 1957, a pair of ophthalmologists reported that MSG destroyed the retina of the eye. A decade later, a neurologist described lesions in the arcuate nucleus of the hypothalamus that appeared to be linked to MSG.

However, a 1995 report concluded that no studies indicated a link between MSG and neurodegenerative diseases. It is possible that MSG could aggravate certain conditions. However, several reasons point to why glutamate that you ingest orally would be inhibited from ever reaching the cells in your brain.

After you consume it, about 95 percent of glutamate is metabolized by cells in your intestines. Any remaining glutamate is unable to cross the blood-brain barrier. Within the brain, astrocytes soak up glutamate, at which time they can convert it back into glutamine to get rid of it from the brain. Glutamine is capable of both entering and leaving the brain through the blood-brain barrier.

However, though glutamate usually does not cross the barrier, this may not remain totally true if glutamate remains chronically elevated for extended periods of time. Also, some parts of the brain—including the hypothalamus and pineal gland—are not protected by the barrier and therefore are exposed to glutamate.

Then there are conditions that can cause glutamate receptors to become hyperactive. For example, lack of oxygen and low blood glucose puts neural cells into a low-energy state, and in these situations cells become more sensitive to even normal levels of glutamate. Having a magnesium deficiency can also make the receptors become hyperactive.

In addition, the barrier may become weakened and more permeable when a person has diabetes, hypertension, or a stroke, or is simply at an advanced age. Finally, glutamine can trigger a chain of events that sparks the generation and concentration of reactive oxygen species. These free radicals produce neural damage and also prevent glutamate uptake by astrocytes. This further increases glutamate around the cells.

As a result, consuming MSG in moderation—at most—is probably a wise idea just to stay on the safe side. Limiting your intake of this additive is smart for other reasons:

- MSG may increase your chances of becoming overweight. Obesity is not as common in China, which suggests that MSG is not a significant culprit for adding pounds. However, as a rule Chinese people are less sedentary than Americans. If it does affect weight, the mechanism might have to do with the hormone leptin, which regulates metabolism and appetite. People who consume MSG produce more leptin and can develop leptin resistance. Leptin resistance may damage the hypothalamus, which serves as the brain's appetite center. People consuming large amounts of MSG have been shown to gain weight without a change in calories because their bodies cannot appropriately process the food they consume.

- In addition, MSG is often found in foods that you'd do best to avoid for other reasons. MSG is found not only in soy sauce and other Asian cuisine but also in many processed foods such as chips, processed meats, and canned soups. Processed foods can be a major source of sodium, which can lead to high blood pressure that can put your brain's health in jeopardy.

 ## THE BRAIN FIX TOOLBOX

- Much like with the artificial sweeteners discussed in Chapter 12, strong evidence doesn't exist to suggest that everyone should completely ban MSG from their diet. However, clues *do* point to the wisdom of limiting MSG when possible.
- To cut back on MSG, start reading food labels. Consider limiting processed foods that contain the additive (which often contain other components that you'll want to minimize for optimal brain health, such as excessive sodium).

PART 3

Lifestyle Changes and Attitudes

14

Exercise: Crucial for Brain Healing

WHAT FACTOR MOST RELIABLY predicts how long you're going to live? Some research holds that it's your exercise capacity. With eight thousand Americans reaching their sixtieth birthday every day, many people are seeking ways to improve the quality of their lives, live longer, and protect their ability to think clearly as long as possible.

But most Americans aren't getting the physical activity that will help them reach these goals, whether they're young or old. If you look at how people's daily lives changed in the 1900s, you'd think that many Americans defined *progress* as "the elimination of any need for physical activity."

Our lives are now dedicated to convenience, so by the mere push of a button we can open the garage door, change the channel on the TV, or wash and dry a load of laundry. With the advent of electric toothbrushes, we don't even have to move our wrists back and forth to clean our teeth. Thanks to cars, buses, Segways, moving sidewalks at the airport, and mall escalators, we have no need to concern ourselves with walking very far or getting our heart rate elevated.

As a result, the majority of us have become sedentary. The 1996 Surgeon General's Report on Physical Activity and Health reported that barely 40 percent exercised the minimally recommended thirty minutes a day for five days a week. What is more startling is that one-quarter were *totally* inactive. Publishing this information did little good, since a subsequent surgeon general's report in 2001 claimed that those meeting the minimum requirement dropped 8 percent to a now-dismal 32 percent, and an astounding 40 percent participated in absolutely *no* leisure-time activity.

A few good role models have shown us the benefits of staying active, though their numbers may be shrinking. Just look at Jack LaLanne, who deep into his senior years was still pulling boats behind him as he swam and doing other memorable feats of strength and endurance.

Less well known, but just as impressive, is Norton Davey, who in his eighties had a very low 6 percent body fat measurement and was still competing in Ironman triathlons. If you visit 5K races and other amateur races in your area, you'll probably see plenty of people around you of all ages who are staying extremely active and mentally sharp.

Along with a host of physical improvements that we won't touch on here (such as stronger bones and muscles), research has shown that regular physical activity can go a long way toward keeping your mind sharp and your brain healthy.

Regular exercise can:

- Make you smarter
- Elevate your mood and attitude
- Improve your self-esteem
- Help you work through problems better
- Support creativity
- Relieve stress
- Produce a sense of well-being
- Help you keep a healthy weight
- Help control blood pressure and prevent heart disease
- Help prevent type 2 diabetes
- Counteract depression
- Help reduce anger and tension
- Promote better sleep
- Improve memory

Exercise may help delay aging in general, and you can even see these effects in your DNA. Telomeres are tiny pieces of DNA found at the ends of chromosomes that keep the chromosomes and genes stable. (Some have compared them to the little plastic tubes at the ends of shoelaces that keep them from fraying.) Over time and with added stress, such as drug abuse and eating disorders, these structures begin to unravel.

As a result, your decision-making ability may become poorer. You may become more impulsive. However, you can help keep telomeres from unraveling by getting short sessions of exercise daily.

How can exercise serve as this apparently universal healing pathway for almost every chronic ailment that can affect your brain? It's a rather simple explanation. Experts believe that stress is responsible for 90 percent of all primary care visits (it plays a role in conditions including high blood pressure, colds and flu, back pain, high cholesterol, and heart disease). But exercise is a great stress reliever.

It also addresses obesity, which is the second leading cause of preventable death. Diabetes, which is often linked to obesity, represents the nation's highest healthcare cost.

Chronic inflammation is the common link between stress, obesity, and diabetes. Cortisol (the stress hormone), excess fat, and sugar (found in higher levels during diabetes and prediabetes) stimulate receptors on most cells to free up a substance called NF-kB, allowing it to enter the nucleus of the cells and turn on the production of inflammatory chemicals known as cytokines. All of the various cytokines can be linked to pretty much *every* chronic disease state. So it follows that as exercise alleviates stress, reduces abdominal fat, and helps control blood sugar, we can see a clear pathway to its reduction of all chronic, debilitating diseases.

Exercise's Specific Effects on the Brain

Exercise also plays an important role in preventing or helping your brain heal from the physical, emotional, and lifestyle threats that many of us encounter in our daily lives.

Depression

Within the emotional center of the brain are nerve cells that communicate by releasing serotonin. The main function of serotonin is to regulate our emotions. Low levels may cause large mood swings and more impulsive behavior.

However, when the serotonin receptors on our neurons are full, we feel calm, centered, and in control. If the serotonin is depleted, which can happen during times of too much stress, the same neuron that originally released the chemical will suck it back up. This keeps the serotonin from filling the nerve receptors on the next neuron. This causes us to feel down or depressed. A solution is to keep the first neuron from taking the neurotransmitter back up, so it remains available to attach to the receptors on the next neuron. This is how serotonin reuptake inhibitor antidepressants are thought to operate.

Serotonin levels increase with exercise training. Exercise stimulates the release of serotonin and makes it attach to its receptor for a longer period of time, causing it to be more effective. Ultimately, exercise may have a similar action on your brain as what you get from antidepressant medications.

Also, exercise causes your body to break down fat, which liberates tryptophan—an ingredient used in making serotonin—that can potentially get into your brain. During exercise, serotonin levels rise, and this higher level lasts even after the exercise session.

Exercise is linked to more serotonin in the hippocampus and frontal cortex of the brain, which are critical for keeping your mood stable, as well as helping in learning and memory. Exercise boosts serotonin levels for up to an hour after the workout. However, this may not have a long-lasting effect on depression. Research from 2011 showed that months after an exercise program ended, participants were just as depressed as people who didn't join the program. This suggests that you must continue to be active—day after day, week after week, month after month— to enjoy the antidepressant effects of exercise.

Moving your feet also causes other changes in your brain. When doctors used high-tech imaging machines to create pictures of the brain, they found that depression causes the loss of neurons and the rewiring of circuits throughout the brain. The hippocampus and frontal cortex seem to be especially likely to break down during stress. Cortisol—our chronic stress hormone—contributes to cell death and remodeling of brain cells. Chronic stress and worry keep our brains continuously bathed in stress hormones. This puts a damper on the manufacturing of new neurons, and it causes dendrites—the branchlike extensions of neurons that pick up signals from other neurons—to retract. This limits the ability of circuits of neurons in the brain to send signals, which makes it harder for you to deal with stress.

Exercise, however, can *fix* the circuitry and *stimulate* the growth of neurons and their dendrite branches. Several studies have found that exercise can limit the changes in synapses (those gaps between neurons that they talk across) that occur when we're stressed.

Numerous studies have found that exercise might be considered a substitute for antidepressants in mild to moderate depression. The advantages of exercise are even more appealing given that antidepressants can carry side effects for some users.

In some studies, exercise was found to have an effect that was similar to the results from antidepressants. For example, 56 percent of people taking sertraline (also known as Zoloft) and 47 percent of those who were asked to do supervised exercise no longer had depressive symptoms after four months of treatment. All had a similar improvement in their depressive symptoms, whether they were exercising or taking antidepressants. However, you should talk to a doctor or mental health provider before you try to use exercise as a sole treatment for depression.

Even if you're taking an antidepressant or going to therapy, exercise may lead to more improvements. People who took tests of their depression severity before and after several weeks of exercise showed marked improvement. In some cases, people who exercised more intensely had more improvement. Research has also found that when they exercise more often or for longer periods of time, people with major depressive disorder have better rates of remission.

Fatigue

A lot of research finds that a major benefit of exercise is that it improves and increases restorative sleep. Getting regular aerobic exercise can increase the stage of sleep called "slow wave sleep," which is the most desirable type of sleep. During restorative sleep, your body releases growth hormone. This helps both your body and brain heal from injury. As a result, exercise can make you feel more alert and energized.

In addition, your body generates a substance called adenosine triphosphate (ATP) for energy by combusting carbohydrates, fat, and protein. However, throughout the day, this causes molecules of adenosine to accumulate, which signals the sleep center of your brain to let you know it's time to take it easy. If you're more active during the day, you'll produce more ATP. Doing this during the day helps you sleep better and longer at night.

Also, you burn lots of energy when you're physically active, and this energy produces heat. Your body needs hours to gradually cool down to the temperature you were at before you exercised. This cooling helps make you sleepy.

Finally, when we participate in an activity such as exercise, we have a tendency to ventilate our negative thoughts. It's like turning on a fan to rid the kitchen of old odors. This "letting go" during a conscious state allows us to create solutions to our problems and connect with pleasurable experiences.

When we instead *internalize* our problems instead of releasing them, they'll eventually pop up while we're asleep. This keeps us from getting enough restorative stages of sleep, when our body and brain rest and repair themselves. Those who free their minds during exercise have more energy and better control of their emotions because they accumulate more recuperative sleep at night.

Stress

For humans to avoid threats and survive the ones we encounter, we have to have an appropriate response to emotional stressors. When anxiety and chronic stress become uncontrollable, it's harmful to the brain. As mentioned earlier, studies have found very convincing evidence that the stress hormone cortisol can be toxic to neurons. High levels of cortisol can also lead fat to accumulate in the abdomen. When fat gathers here, it drives inflammation, which we've already talked about being harmful to brain function and repair.

Exercise has a complicated relationship with cortisol. Both emotional and physical stress (such as exercise) can lead the brain to release more cortisol. When you exercise at a low intensity, you cause circulating cortisol levels to *fall*, but moderate and vigorous activity may cause it to rise. However, exercising regularly helps your adrenal glands get used to the physical stress of exercise, so an intense bout may not lead to higher cortisol levels.

Addictions and Eating Disorders

Drugs and alcohol appeal to people who are addicted because they stimulate the brain's reward pathways, thus providing a pleasant experience. When people who are addicted try to quit or even just use less, they can have painful withdrawal symptoms and cravings, and they often relapse. Exercise may serve as a natural substitute for the substance, since it stimulates many of the same circuits in the brain.

In addition, exercise serves as an element of rehabilitation for addictions or eating disorders by giving people healthy, long-term distractions from the drugs or disordered eating. This distraction can help move you away from the cycle of negative thoughts that feed anxiety and depression when you are struggling with one of these issues. Participating in physical challenges improves your sense of self-control and the way you see yourself. Meeting goals or challenges—like getting in good enough shape to exercise for thirty minutes or enter a road race—can boost your self-confidence. As you gain more confidence and improve your self-esteem, depression may ease up.

Physical activity also improves your willpower and motivation. By feeling more accomplished when mastering physical activities, people who are in recovery from these problems may be better able to break away from them.

Sometimes this course of events is described as the "positive confidence cycle." Say I begin lifting weights, and within a short time I can lift more than when I started. It's almost *guaranteed* that I'll see improved strength if I work out enough and feed my muscles properly. This is going to make me feel good about my accomplishments. While working out, I'll probably also interact with others at the gym and share a mutual common interest. As a result, I'll feel more socially accepted than if I were just sitting at home. Now that I am lifting weights and feeling better, I also consider quitting smoking, eating better, and reducing my stress. After all, if I'm putting all this work into my body, why allow other factors to drag it down? This progressive domino effect of lifestyle change is often referred to as the "halo effect": exercise creates a glow that improves other parts of your life around it.

These aren't the only changes that exercise can trigger in the brains of people with drug addictions. Physical activity also has a beneficial effect on the brain's dopamine system. Studies that measure brain chemicals have found that exercise increases levels of dopamine and the number of dopamine receptors in the reward centers in rats' brains. In people, the dopamine system itself can reinforce a person's desire to keep exercising.

Also, beta-endorphins are substances that cells in your pituitary gland and spinal cord make that are similar to morphine. They have a pain-reducing effect. When beta-endorphin locks onto a certain kind of receptor in the brain, it triggers the release of dopamine. The dopamine can stimulate a sense of euphoria that runners often call the "runner's high." With their pain-reducing endorphins, the runners can go farther with less pain. (However, this intensity can put people's bodies in danger of physical harm.) It's possible that endorphins explain how exercise can reduce addiction cravings, though other neurotransmitters may be involved too.

When You Are Exercising *Too* Much

Exercise is beneficial in many ways for people who are recovering from addictions or eating disorders. However, it's important to not get *too* much exercise, which can actually become an addiction itself. Exercise turns on many neurotransmitter systems that are involved in the addictive process, such as dopamine, serotonin, and endorphins.

Experts have yet to reach agreement on how to define exercise dependence. However, common warning signs of exercise dependence include:

- Using exercise as a way to expend calories to compensate for eating, when taken to the extreme. This can actually be a form of purging.
- Exercising when you're ill or injured.
- Allowing yourself to eat only enough food to cover the calories you burned.
- Feeling panicked or guilty when you can't exercise.
- Missing social, family, and work activities in order to exercise.
- Getting too much of your self-worth from your exercise goals.
- Seeing exercise as work rather than something fun.

How to Get Your Body Moving for Your Brain's Sake

Many people will embark on an exercise program without giving a lot of thought or attention to how they are going to actually accomplish their goals. It is sort of like taking a trip and saying, "I don't know where I am going, but I am getting there quickly!"

As a result, too many people dive into purposeless motion and then give up quickly. Or they develop a sense of learned helplessness, in which they begin to believe that they'll *never* be able to stick with an enjoyable exercise routine. Often we perform certain tasks because we are conditioned to assume that if we get started, we will see results. But we may expect to enjoy benefits that are unreasonably big, or to see them unreasonably quickly.

Before starting an exercise program, first come up with *goals*. Your goals need to be:

- **Attainable.** For example, running a marathon is a great goal, but if you're new to exercise or are very out of shape, you're probably going to lose your motivation if this is all you have that's keeping you going. A better goal is a small one you can attain quickly—like being able to walk around the block. Remember—small improvements will go a long way toward improving your body and brain's health. You don't have to turn into a triathlete or bodybuilder to reap these rewards.

- **Easy to measure.** Simply saying "I want to exercise regularly" isn't going to keep you motivated for long either. What if you miss a few days or scale back to once a week? Is that still regular? Who knows? Commit to goals that allow you to track your success, or lack thereof. Tell yourself you're going to exercise for thirty minutes five times a week. Or that you're going to get ready for a 5K race next summer. You'll easily know if you achieve these goals or not.

- **Important to you.** Your goals have to be meaningful to *you*, not someone else. If you feel like you already look good, but your spouse wants you to lose weight, you won't be as likely to stick with a program as you would if you wanted to lose weight for *your* sake. You can make goals that are related to your brain health: perhaps you'd like to reduce your stress and depression naturally, avoid substance abuse or an eating disorder for another year, or lower your cholesterol and blood pressure by a certain amount to protect yourself from having a devastating stroke like a family member had.

Once you have goals in mind, it's time to devise a plan and define the amount of activity you want to do. You'll want to know the intensity, frequency, duration, and mode of exercise you'll use.

Intensity

Experts continue to debate the *intensity* of the exercise you need to get. The conversations have often settled on complicated formulas that include your VO_2max (how well your body uses oxygen during exercise) or your age-predicted maximum heart rate. You don't have to get that fancy, especially when you're starting out.

When you begin, it's important to not push yourself too hard. Thus, you'll want to stick to a moderate exercise level. A good way to monitor your intensity is by going at about a conversational pace. This means you're moving enough to feel your heart rate go up, but you're still able to carry on a conversation (though you shouldn't be able to belt out a song to your walking companion).

If you're at a moderate to intense pace, however, you might be able to carry on a conversation with difficulty. If you can't string six words together, you are exercising too rapidly and you've trotted right into the anaerobic zone. Anaerobic means "without oxygen," and when you're in this state, your body cannot burn fat. Stick to an easier pace.

Once you establish your exercise capacity range, you can remain in that zone by checking your pulse every once in a while. Experts strongly suggest that exercisers stick to a specific heart rate to avoid a cardiac episode by going too hard, but at the same time stressing the cardiovascular system enough that it gets stronger. That's easy if you are using a pulse meter that electronically checks your heart rate, but it's not so easy if you are trying to find your pulse with your fingers while exercising then computing your heart rate per minute. I can tell you from my years of working in cardiac rehabilitation that this is not easy. It's also often abandoned by frustrated exercisers who are fearful and overestimate their actual heart rates.

As a result, wearing a pulse meter or using an exercise machine that takes your pulse continually is a good idea. You can find relatively inexpensive heart rate monitors—which are often put on a strap worn around the chest, which then sends the information to a watchlike device on your wrist—at sporting goods stores and department stores.

Frequency

You'll want to exercise on a regular basis to accumulate the benefits of each exercise session. Remember, each session affects your body and brain's chemistry during the session and for only a limited time afterward. You'll want to string together a healthy number of these sessions to keep your system benefiting from these improvements as often as possible. Aim for exercising most days of the week.

Duration

Experts have come up with different recommendations for how much people need to exercise, and these often fall between thirty to sixty minutes (or more) per day, depending on whether you're using exercise for weight loss or to just keep your heart and muscles in shape.

In the fall of 2003, the Institute of Medicine concluded that everyone should exercise at least sixty minutes a day to maintain their weight. The American College of Sports Medicine modified this to thirty minutes most days of the week to achieve tangible health benefits. Since 75 percent of the U.S. population did not meet the institute's guidelines, those substantial recommendations might actually serve as an *impediment* to exercise. In 2005, the recommendations set forth by the national Dietary Guidelines recommended thirty minutes per day to prevent chronic ailments, sixty minutes per day to prevent weight gain, and sixty to ninety minutes per day to maintain weight loss.

How much should you do? Within limits, more is better. But if you're scared off by the thought of sixty minutes daily, remember that *some* is better than *none*. If you can't exercise for an extended block at a time, scatter several ten-minute sessions of walking or other types of exercise throughout your day.

Get Going

Always keep a set of clean workout clothes and shoes ready to go. We'll often look for any excuse to avoid a workout, and a lack of clothes and gear makes a great excuse! Keeping an extra set in the car or at work is a great idea, as you may find inspiration to go for a walk or duck into the gym when you least expect it.

Even people with hectic schedules can find time for physical activity by applying a little creativity. Most of us have little pockets of time embedded in the day if we just look for them. Every little bit helps. Consider the following suggestions:

- Go to work, school, the store, your church, and other regular destinations by foot or on a bicycle when possible.
- Park your vehicle farther away from your destination than usual and walk the rest of the way.
- Always climb the stairs instead of hopping on an escalator or elevator.
- Play with your kids.
- Get up and visit your coworkers in person instead of sending an e-mail or picking up the phone.
- Plant a huge garden and keep it going all summer. Or make a list of home-repair activities and knock off an item in your downtime.
- Avoid labor-saving devices. Turn off the self-driving mechanism on your lawn mower if possible.
- Exercise while watching television (for example, use hand weights or stationary exercise equipment such as a treadmill when you're in front of the tube).

- Better yet, vow to cut thirty minutes of television out of your daily schedule, which many of us could probably do without noticing the loss.
- Put on your favorite up-tempo music and start dancing.
- Buy a computer gaming system that requires you to wave your arms and move your body to control the activity on the screen. These offer games specifically to improve your fitness.

Mode

What's the best type of exercise? The one you'll do regularly! How many calories do I burn, how much exercise does it take to become aerobically fit, what is the most efficient exercise, and how intensely should I exercise are all moot points if you're not doing *something*. Just joining a health club will not help you. You have to show up and get moving. As the old Nike slogan implies: do something . . . anything . . . just do it!

One thing I've asked of my patients, after several weeks of repeatedly failed promises to join a gym or walk the track, is to make a contract that they'll complete just three minutes of exercise three times a week. I don't care if they choose to walk to their neighbor's mailbox and back, do dance videos, work out in a pool, climb the stairs, or jump on a pogo stick. However, the effort can't be something you would be doing anyway, like shopping, gardening, or playing with your child.

None of these three-minute activities burn enough calories to contribute to weight loss anyway. However, once people get started and agree to put in the time, it not only becomes a planned and regular habit, but they find themselves continuing the activity for *more* than three minutes. The excuse of not having time is totally eliminated, because all that is requested is a mere three minutes of movement anytime, anywhere, and at any pace. If you're ever feeling uninspired to get some physical activity, just make yourself put on your shoes and go for three minutes. You'll probably feel like continuing for longer once your three minutes are up.

One exercise approach that has gained popularity in recent years is to wear a pedometer (you can find these for less than twenty dollars) that counts your daily steps. The idea is to add an additional 200 to 300 daily steps each week as a way of progressively increasing your exercise. Most people start out at 2,000 to 3,000 steps per day. For good heart health, the usual recommendation is 5,000 steps per day. For weight loss, you'd need about 10,000 steps a day. This would amount to about five miles daily.

Think you'll have trouble walking that far? Get a dog. Walking a dog is often an ideal way to get Americans on the move. Research has found that dog walkers averaging a mile a day for a year lost 11 to 14 pounds. Having an obligation and dedication to their canine friends made them stick to a walking program, it doubled their speed, and it got them up and out when they would otherwise have remained sedentary.

Don't have a dog? Then involve your family in your fitness. Go on a family bike ride. Or play Frisbee golf. Or devise your own family Olympics or pedometer challenge.

Whatever you do, find an activity you like and stick with it. An even better idea is to find *multiple* activities so you don't get burned-out with any particular one. Find something you like to do outside so you can enjoy the great outdoors (like running or biking) when the weather's nice. Find something you can do indoors when the weather's bad, like work out to a video. Have something in mind to do alone—like walking on an elliptical trainer at the gym—or with a group, like walking around the perimeter inside a mall. This way you'll be familiar with an activity that suits your need that day, no matter what it is.

To Keep Your Body Balanced, Get All the Forms of Exercise You Require

It's important to avoid injury and discomfort when you're exercising, since these are major deterrents that make people lose interest in their fitness program. Before beginning each session, you should appropriately warm up by moving your arms and legs through their range of motion at each joint by slow walking or stepping in place and moving your arms for two to three minutes.

This gets blood circulating to the body parts that will be involved in the ensuing activity. It helps to transition your cardiovascular system to a higher work capacity, much like shifting car gears from park to third gear. Additionally, these rhythmic range-of-motion exercises help to lubricate your joints and tendons, allowing for less pain, strains, and sprains.

Once you have warmed up (and *only* after you have warmed up), you should consider stretching. There is an ongoing controversy that stretching beforehand may not eliminate muscle soreness or prevent overuse or acute sports injuries. It may even *cause* injuries and reduce muscle effectiveness. This means that the best time to stretch is just *after* your activity session to avoid injuries such as cramping and tearing.

After you finish your exercise session, it's necessary to cool down. This helps keep your blood from pooling in your lower extremities, which could result in dizziness or even fainting. Continuing to move after your workout at a significantly slower speed will help return the blood in the veins in your legs back to your heart.

Your muscles, tendons, and ligaments are best stretched when they are warm. Stretching should be slow and controlled, and you should hold each stretch for ten to thirty seconds. Take each stretch to the point of slight discomfort but not sharp pain. Again, it's important to remember that to avoid injuries in future exercise sessions, the very best time to stretch is during the cooldown stage when your muscles are warmest but also the tightest following activity.

Okay, so we've talked about aerobic exercises, which require large amounts of oxygen, use large muscle groups, are rhythmic in nature, and can be maintained over time at moderate intensity. And we've talked about flexibility exercises too. However, a healthy body that supports a healthy brain also needs to be *strong*. Strength or resistance training, which people often do with weights, contributes to your health and to weight loss. And it can boost your mood and self-esteem. That's because it is exciting to see how rapidly you can enjoy a 40 to 50 percent increase in strength within just the first two to four weeks.

A good starting point for each lift is to determine the maximum you can lift for one repetition. Then design the program to start lifting about 60 percent of that maximum eight to twelve times. Working with a personal trainer is a good way to learn how to lift correctly, and a trainer can help you decide on the appropriate amount of weight to lift.

Gradually, as it becomes easy to do each exercise twelve times, increase the weight slightly. Professional trainers often recommend performing eight to ten types of exercises (with one working each body part) per session. The entire workout session should take less than forty minutes.

Below are some basic principles of resistance exercise training that will help you achieve the best results for the effort you put into it:

- Make sure that whatever exercises you choose, you perform the lift using a full range of motion. If you're doing a barbell curl to work your biceps, you'd lower the dumbbell all the way down until your arm is almost fully extended, then curl it all the way back to your shoulder so your elbow is bent.
- Try to take two seconds to do the move, then four seconds to return to the starting position. At this slow pace, a curl would take six seconds per repetition.
- Exhale during the hardest part of the exercise—like pushing the bar off your chest during a bench press—and inhale during the easier phase.
- Rest between sets for about thirty to sixty seconds.
- Increase the weight you're lifting about 2 to 5 percent a week and expect a similar strength gain over time.
- Strive for muscle balance. That means if you work the biceps (at the front of your upper arms), work the triceps (which are on the back side of the upper arms) too.

Know When It's Time to Bump It Up

When you were a kid, you didn't stop working on your math once you conquered addition and subtraction. You moved on to multiplication, division, fractions, decimals, algebra, and perhaps even beyond. You asked more of your brain and pushed it further than you had before.

You'll need to do the same if you're trying to lose weight and your body reaches a set point. The set point theory states that the body is designed to regulate weight within a 10 percent heavier or lighter range. If you lower your body weight below the range or increase it above the range, your body will compensate in an attempt to keep your weight and body fat levels within the range. Although it is not rigid, this effort to maintain body fat storage is unconscious and automatic. For example, when you lower your body fat beyond a certain point, it triggers a "starvation reaction" that causes your metabolism and overall activity level to decrease and your appetite to increase. Think of it as your body counting calories without your awareness. The human body is highly adapted to change and is programmed for survival—not dieting!

Although it is an amazing survival mechanism, this process can make our weight loss efforts extremely difficult. As you reduce calories and lose weight, your metabolism decreases. It becomes harder and harder to lose more weight, and often your weight hits a plateau at the low end of your set point range. What's a person to do? The only logical approach in this situation is to increase your metabolism. How? Exercise harder.

When you need to break a set point (or enjoy a higher level of fitness or embrace your competitive spirit, for that matter), it's time to bump up your intensity level. Now is when your breathing moves up to the huff-and-puff level during your exercise sessions, and you move like you are late for an important meeting. You may also try more difficult activities like interval training (interspersing brief periods of fast movement and rest during your session), spinning (a type of stationary cycling that's renowned for pushing people hard), rowing, or cross-country skiing. It is critical to get your doctor's okay before taking on a heightened challenge. And be sure to stretch, warm up, cool down, and pace yourself.

Tips for bumping up your intensity include:

- Exercise at a pace that would require any conversation to be labored—not so hard that you cannot string three words together, but intense enough that it would be difficult or uncomfortable to hold a conversation or sing.
- Increase the frequency of your sessions or their length. Alternate longer, moderate intensity workouts with shorter, more intense workouts.
- Alternate upper-body strength-training workouts with lower-body workouts.
- Try circuit training, in which you go from one strength exercise (like lifting weights or strength-training machines) to the next with

very little rest in between, keeping your heart rate up. This allows you to get an aerobic workout and strength-training workout at one time.

 THE BRAIN FIX TOOLBOX

- Start seeing exercise as a crucial tool for fixing your brain and maintaining good brain health (since it can help prevent or treat obesity, diabetes, high blood pressure, strokes, depression, stress, eating disorders, and addictions).
- Exercise will only help your brain's health if you do it—*not* if you just think about it. Work your way up to at least thirty minutes of exercise most days of the week.
- If you can't go for thirty minutes at a time, aim for several sessions of ten minutes apiece throughout the day.
- Find a variety of physical activities that appeal to you and motivate you.
- Set fitness goals that inspire you to keep active. Goals should be attainable, measurable, and important to you.
- Be sure to regularly do activities that improve your cardiovascular system, increase your strength, and enhance your flexibility. Don't throw all your effort into just one of these.
- Consider working with a personal trainer to devise a fitness plan that best motivates you and suits your needs.
- Gradually bump up your workout length or intensity. This will help you see continual improvements and break through a weight set point if you're trying to lose weight.

15

Sleep: To a Healthy Brain, It's Not Just Wasted Time

AMERICA IS BECOMING the country that never sleeps.

Sixty percent of Americans report having persistent problems falling asleep or staying asleep. The number of Americans who say they get eight hours of sleep per night has dropped from 39 percent in 2001 to 28 percent in 2009.

Some people don't *want* to sleep more, or at least they don't want it badly enough to close their laptop computer, turn off the TV, set aside their cell phone, or stop playing a video game. Others look to their doctors for help in drifting off at night. Ten to 25 percent of the U.S. population uses sleeping pills, resulting in physicians writing more than 42 million prescriptions per year. This number is up 60 percent from 2000.

For more than a decade, the National Sleep Foundation has released its Sleep in America poll as part of its annual National Sleep Awareness Week. In 2009, four out of ten people agreed that sleep is at least as important as proper diet and exercise. Yet Americans claimed in the survey they were getting less than seven hours a night on weekdays and felt that they needed at least an additional hour.

This corresponds closely with the amount of sleep that researchers say adults are getting—about 6.9 hours on weeknights and 7.5 hours on weekends, for an average of seven hours. The average American in 1900, by contrast, slept two hours more per night.

Some experts consider lack of sleep to be America's largest, deadliest, and costliest problem. An estimated $150 billion is lost in productivity and mishaps due to lack of sleep, which is also responsible for more than 10 million outpatient doctor visits per year.

For good brain health, proper sleep—night after night—is a must. Just like a cleaning crew may come into an office building or factory in the dead of night so the routine business doesn't interfere with their job, your brain repairs itself while you're sleeping. Stress, eating disorders, addictive chemicals, and everyday life ravage the brain, and if you want it to heal and thrive, you must eliminate sleep disorders, get more uninterrupted sleep, and improve your ability to spend time in the right stages of sleep.

What's Happening While We're Asleep, Anyway?

Much of what goes on while we're asleep remains a mystery to us. You may look at the clock at 11:00 PM, and the next thing you know it's 6:30 AM, with perhaps a few dreams and a trip to the bathroom representing your only awareness of this period of time.

Nevertheless, your brain isn't turned off like an unplugged computer while you're asleep. Chemical reactions in the brain create electrical activity that can be picked up on the surface of the scalp by sensitive electrodes. This was known as far back as 1930, when researchers demonstrated that an EEG device could detect and record this electrical activity.

The brain waves that are created during this activity have been compared to throwing stones into a pond. Toss in a single stone, and a ripple of waves spreads out, becoming increasingly larger. In much the same way, activity from a single center in the brain would be captured as a distinct wave. Now throw a handful of pebbles into the water, and what you observe is a jumbled mess. It's impossible to discern any pattern in the waves. The same thing happens when your brain is very active, with numerous sites processing information and firing. The resulting waves are small, irregular, and chaotic.

When we are awake and active, the waves that are produced—called beta waves—have a high frequency and no constant pattern. We can be involved in deep concentration or logical thinking, or be exposed to sensory input or just sitting quietly. Or we can pick up the pace by engaging in conversation, performing work, or walking. This is a state of mind in which we are alert and completely aware of our circumstances. The more excited we become, the higher the number of cycles of brain waves we produce per second.

If we transition to a more relaxed state, like the period of grogginess immediately preceding sleep, we may become drowsy and yet still be awake. Our wave pattern—called alpha waves—now decreases in frequency. Once we close our eyes, we no longer have visual input, and the waves slow down further (and are interspersed with so-called theta waves). You enter phase I sleep. This stage lasts about five minutes and is a state of peacefulness, rest, and reflection. Your body temperature drops, muscles relax, and you begin to lose awareness of your surroundings. But you can be easily jarred into wakefulness, and it may be hard to distinguish if you were "just drowsy" or actually asleep.

As the number of theta waves increases, you begin the first stage of established sleep or phase II sleep. We spend about half of our cumulative sleep time in this phase. Your pattern of brain waves gets more uniform; however, the pattern is interspersed with irregular, brief bursts of fast activity called sleep spindles, which are sudden increases in wave frequency. About every two minutes, k-complexes—which are sudden increases in amplitude—occur. This is a part of our built-in security system that keeps us ready to be awakened if necessary.

As you transition in and out of this state, your mind enters a level of deeper meditation. Eventually you enter into phase III sleep, also known as slow wave sleep. Delta brain waves appear as very slow, coordinated waves. As the proportion of delta waves exceeds 50 percent, you enter into phase IV sleep. Breathing becomes slow and regular. Blood pressure and pulse fall 20 percent below waking levels. In stages I and II, you can easily awaken, but in stages III and IV, you arouse with more difficulty. It is very difficult to wake people who are in deep sleep, and if they do wake up, they're going to be disoriented or very groggy. Stage IV sleep, along with stage III, is also called "restorative" sleep.

Most of our deep sleep occurs in the first half of the night. For young people, this important restorative phase lasts for thirty-minute stretches and accounts for approximately 20 percent of total sleep. Unfortunately, by age sixty-five, this amount greatly declines and may account for no more than a total of twenty minutes a night after age seventy-five.

Finally, we enter rapid eye movement sleep, also called REM sleep or dream sleep. This also accounts for about 20 percent of our sleep. Though the brain is very active, with waves often approaching the beta waves of wakefulness, your body is paralyzed. Your heart and respiration rate rise, as do your blood pressure and body temperature, which are often at the same level as when you're awake.

It is only in this phase that we experience storylike dreams. Because the body is paralyzed except for occasional twitches, we are protected from acting out these dreams. The dream segments of sleep occur about three to five times a night, or about every ninety minutes. The time in REM increases progressively over the course of the night, and the final period may last half an hour. This phase of sleep restores your mind, supports memory and learning, and helps your brain clear out irrelevant information.

Ideally our "sleep architecture"—or the structure of our sleep—is composed of approximately four to six ninety-minute cycles. It takes about eight hours to get those four to six cycles. As your brain moves through these stages, it's processing old information and getting itself ready to deal with the challenges that the next day holds. Our goal should be to maintain as much slow wave and REM sleep as possible to allow for alertness, maximum performance, memory, concentration, creativity, optimal health, energy, and positive mood.

Better Sleep, Smarter Brain?

Most all of us—if given the choice—would want to be more intelligent, which requires good problem-solving skills, decision-making capabilities, reasoning, and judgment. Sleep can actually help improve all these qualities. The act of learning involves a highly efficient ability to remember information. It begins when we take information that we captured with our eyes and ears, then temporarily store it in our brain's memory-holding tank called the hippocampus.

Processing this information requires us to transfer it to the portion of the brain known as the cortex. The cortex proceeds to consolidate (choose what is important and discard what is not); edit (rearrange and restructure); and file what we've learned into long-term memory until we need to retrieve certain facts. This same process also takes place in the development of new skills.

During sleep stages III and IV, your brain is actively carrying out the task of converting fresh experiences into long-term memory. If you are sleep-deprived, you greatly diminish your ability to capture, store, and retrieve information. Quite simply, you cannot think effectively. Several studies have shown that if you are exposed to information in the morning and tested on it in the late afternoon, you'll perform better if you take a nap in between.

An area called the associative cortex is very active during REM sleep. This allows you to come up with new and useful ideas, link ideas and thoughts in novel ways, or simply tap into your creative process. Your brain continues to work on problems that baffle you, and it may come up with the right answer only after you have rested. Only the REM phase of sleep is capable of enhancing this process.

Your brain temporarily stores information that evokes emotion in a structure called the amygdala. Often these events are threatening and negative. If they're linked to overwhelming stress, they may infringe on your sleep, and the information may be filed inappropriately. If this happens, your brain cannot routinely sift and process through the information properly, and you have no control over how or when the events will resurface.

Lack of sleep may also cause your brain's prefrontal cortex (which normally functions to keep your emotional responses in check) to shut down. This can cause you to overreact to negative experiences. Instead of facing your problems like a well-reasoned adult, you'll be more apt to act moody, impatient, or irritable.

It's clear to see that many people aren't getting enough sleep, or their sleep is too often punctuated by wakefulness. Over time, lack of quality sleep can lead to chronic health problems or cause chronic problems to worsen.

The Ills that Result from Sleepless Nights

You're probably familiar with many of the consequences of lost sleep: You may feel groggy and irritable. Your focus is probably off. You don't perform at your best, and you're likely to dump sugary foods and caffeine into your system for an energy boost. But the effects of poor sleep go way beyond these concerns.

Because of the close association that sleep has to stress, depression, obesity, blood sugar control, hormonal fluctuations, and inflammation, a broad array of connections can be made between sleep deprivation and poor health. The influence of poor sleep on memory and brain function has implications for diseases such as Alzheimer's and Parkinson's. Too little sleep has also been associated with breast and colon cancer, which is suspected to be due to a combination of hormone levels, immune functioning, and body weight.

In addition, chronic poor sleep can actually boost your risk of dying prematurely in general. Let's take a look at other complications of poor sleep.

Poorer Heart Health

Lack of sleep has been found to contribute to high blood pressure in women by keeping the nervous system in a state of hyperactivity. High blood pressure, in turn, affects the heart and blood vessels throughout the body. In one study, each hour of lost sleep was associated with 37 percent higher odds of developing hypertension.

Merely shutting one's eyes, turning out the lights, and lying face up can produce a sizable drop in blood pressure. Women with insomnia have been found to have more inflammation and fibrinogen—which is a blood-clotting factor—as well as faster heart rates. The inflammation and resulting plaque buildup in arteries may be due to the large amount of the stress hormone cortisol that is released when sleep is poor. All told, people with sleep deprivation are more than twice as likely to die of heart disease. People who have trouble falling asleep may be 70 percent more likely to have coronary events.

Obesity

People who sleep less than six hours a night are more likely to have weight gain, increased body fat, and a bigger waist circumference. Research has found that those who sleep less than four hours nightly have a 73 percent chance of being obese, and those who sleep six hours have a 23 percent chance of obesity.

According to the National Sleep Foundation, 77 percent of obese adults report some kind of sleep problem. This may help explain why college students, shift workers, new parents, and worriers often put on extra pounds.

Though no one is certain why, some interesting chemical changes have been observed with sleep loss. For one, the levels of the appetite-suppressing hormone leptin fall while the appetite-*stimulating* hormone ghrelin rises. Bigger hormonal changes are associated with greater hunger and stronger cravings for carbohydrates.

There is a close association between stress, obesity, diabetes, and inflammation. Each has a significant influence over the others. Experts have noted that lack of sleep increases the risk of diabetes because it impairs the body's ability to regulate blood sugar. Getting less than four hours of sleep nightly for only one week was enough to disrupt the way people's bodies processed carbohydrates in one study. Metabolic issues like these are consistent with weight gain. Cortisol is another hormone closely associated with more abdominal fat. The abnormally high levels of cortisol recorded in those with poor sleep can trigger weight gain.

Conversely, people who are overweight tend to have less restful sleep due to heartburn, snoring, and sleep apnea, which can further exacerbate weight problems, and the process can take on a vicious cycle.

Some reports have also warned that too *much* sleep—more than nine hours per night—can lead to a greater risk of death, heart disease, and stroke; lower good HDL cholesterol; higher bad LDL cholesterol; and inflammation. It is not clear why, but it is possibly due to the fact that people who sleep longer are more likely to be depressed or chronically ill.

Pain

Chronic pain is one of the most pervasive medical conditions in the United States, affecting one in five Americans. The cost to the nation is $61 billion in lost productivity and much more in medical charges. According to the National Sleep Foundation, pain—such as from back pain, headaches, arthritis, cancer, and injuries—is a leading cause of insomnia. Approximately 20 percent of adults report pain that disrupts their sleep.

Areas of the brain involved in our perception of pain—including the frontal cortex, cingulate gyrus, and limbic system—are the same ones that are involved in falling asleep and staying asleep. Sleep and pain have a bidirectional relationship, in which experiencing pain causes sleeplessness, and poor-quality sleep makes pain worse. Pain and sleeplessness share a constellation of symptoms, including fatigue and depression. A vicious cycle can cause increasing pain and sleeplessness to amplify each other. For example, a person with lower back pain may become aroused from sleep several times per hour. Being sleep-deprived can leave him less able to cope with the pain the next day.

Fibromyalgia

This is a problem that affects 10 million Americans. It has no obvious bodily causes and does not show up on X-rays. Growing evidence now suggests that fibromyalgia is partly a brain disorder that sets the pain pathways into disarray so that the brain responds to imaginary wounds. The natural opioid system that regulates pain perception becomes dysfunctional. Disrupted sleep contributes to or worsens the chronic pain.

Fibromyalgia is associated with low levels of serotonin. This neurotransmitter is produced during stage IV sleep. The fact that women produce lower levels of serotonin may help explain why more than 90 percent of people with fibromyalgia are female.

Dysfunction of the serotonin pathway affects one's perception of pain. Serotonin influences the pain threshold by interacting with substance P. What's substance P? Acute pain begins with sensory neurons in the body that are constantly on alert for signs of injury. They are the mechanisms that alert us to one injury so we can take steps to avoid a *second* one. Substance P is generated peripherally in the body (in other words, on the outskirts farther away from the brain). It's a chemical that sends information about tissue damage from receptors in your body to your brain. Levels of substance P are higher in people with fibromyalgia. It builds up in the body's tissues and eventually transmits painful impulses to the spinal cord and brain, which lowers the threshold for pain.

An increase in pain can cause delta wave sleep—which is the restorative type of sleep—to become disrupted. Even young, healthy people who have consistent disruptions in stage IV sleep can have increases in muscle tenderness, which also occurs in fibromyalgia. When they go back to their normal sleep patterns, their discomfort goes away.

Problems for Addicts

Many people with substance abuse disorders have troubled sleep. One-third to three-quarters of alcoholics who are in the early stages of recovery have insomnia. However, having sleep problems makes it harder for people to recover from alcohol dependence.

People who use amphetamines or cocaine also often have insomnia while they're using, and feel excessively sleepy when they're in withdrawal. Opioid drugs usually make users sleepy in the short term, but people who use them longer become tolerant and may report insomnia. Smokers have more trouble falling asleep, and they spend less time in deep sleep.

Addicts in general have trouble sleeping even after they stop using, and their sleep problems may go on for years after they recover. Proper sleep is crucial while recovering from addiction. That's because when they're in an intense treatment program, it's paramount that individuals be prepared to accept new concepts, embrace a different lifestyle, and apply their creativity to this challenge.

This requires that they overcome their problematic mood swings like depression, as well as a sense of hopelessness and hostility they may have. To reap the most benefit from therapy, addicts need to restructure their problem-solving skills, decision-making capabilities, reasoning, and judgment. Fatigue can slow the therapeutic process, since it reduces alertness, attentiveness, responsiveness, and concentration. The effectiveness of treatment is most certainly compromised in people who aren't getting quality sleep and thus don't wake up feeling refreshed, responsive, positive, and committed to the hard work of recovery.

Eating Disorders

People with anorexia and bulimia often feel they have significant sleep problems. If people don't consume enough protein, the body will borrow proteins from itself. Often the chemicals or tissues that your body breaks down when it's deprived are not immediately crucial to survival. However, one of the first proteins to be broken down may actually promote your ability to stay alive.

From an evolutionary standpoint, if you can't get to food, your brain and body may assume that it's because predators are nearby, and thus it's not a good idea for you to be vulnerable to this threat. So your body breaks down serotonin, which normally calms you and may trigger sleep when it's released in your hypothalamus. Humans—and other animals—don't want to sleep in the presence of a threat such as a predator, and the absence of serotonin may allow you to be hypervigilant. People with anorexia often avoid fatty foods and the protein they contain, and this mechanism may be responsible for their insomnia.

Aging

If you sleep eight hours a day, that means you spend one-third of your life asleep. As a result, you might be inclined to stay awake longer so you're not "wasting" your life sawing logs. Actually, by starving your brain and body of the sleep they need, you may *accelerate* the aging process and shorten your life. How? It comes down to human growth hormone.

To understand how this works, let's first take a look at muscle growth. Intense weight lifting sends a signal to the muscles that they need to repair themselves and grow larger to defend themselves against future damage. This is how weight lifting triggers growth. The protein you eat will provide the raw materials to create additional muscle. A key step is the process that transports protein into the muscles. A brain hormone called human growth hormone (HGH) stimulates growth and repair by increasing the movement of protein into the muscles. This regenerates new cells, increases the size of existing cells, and fixes any damage.

It's not just your muscles that need repair in the face of the wear and tear that comes with aging, but all your internal organs and your skin. Energy is also a vital factor in this repair process. Growth hormone promotes the use of your body's stored fat as fuel. So when you secrete HGH, your body increases fat breakdown.

Growth hormone also causes you to create less of the stress hormone cortisol. This can be beneficial, since cortisol leads to a host of negative consequences, including abdominal fat, inflammation, and insulin resistance. Finally, growth hormone has been reported to stimulate the immune system, which could help ward off disease.

A small gland in your brain called the pituitary makes and stores growth hormone. Your pituitary doesn't allow HGH to seep out at a steady rate; instead, it releases it in six to twelve separate bursts each day. The largest output comes about an hour after you fall asleep. This critical period is during the deep phase III and IV sleep.

What is critical to understand is that if you want to reap the benefits of growth hormone for antiaging, maintaining a healthy weight, increasing muscle mass, improving energy and vigor, and enhancing your immunity, you will need plenty of quality sleep. Getting the maximum deep, restorative sleep is the surest way to increase growth hormone. On the contrary, fragmented sleep or sleep deprivation causes the output of growth hormone to dwindle.

Why Can't I Sleep More?

Many people find themselves at the end of the day with many more tasks that they need or want to do. Maybe they need to make their kids' lunches, spend precious time with their spouse, or finish the work they didn't attend to earlier in the day. Or maybe they're just too interested in watching TV, playing computer games, or talking on the phone. Other people *want* more sleep and head to bed at a reasonable hour, but their bodies just can't fall asleep or stay asleep for various reasons.

One common reason is insomnia. This term comes from the Latin meaning "no sleep." Failing to get *any* sleep at all is unlikely, since even people with extreme insomnia typically catch a few hours. Studies using twins suggest that insomnia might run in families. However, poor sleep might also be a learned behavior, in which parents with bad sleeping habits influence their children.

One type of insomnia is called "primary insomnia," which occurs on its own—and isn't due to other problems—and has an unknown cause.

Often it is described as a disease of hyperarousal, in which people have a tendency to be more revved-up. People with primary insomnia have been found to have up to 30 percent lower levels of GABA, a neurotransmitter that slows overall activity in many brain areas.

Secondary insomnia results from another cause, such as a disease, including bladder problems, chronic pain, or ADHD; a sleep disorder such as apnea or restless legs syndrome; or drugs such as medications, caffeine, or nicotine.

Obstructive sleep apnea is one of the most common sleep disorders. It affects roughly 18 million Americans. Though it's commonly associated with obesity, plenty of people with this problem are not obese. During sleep apnea, tissues in the upper airway relax, collapsing into the airway and blocking the flow of air into the lungs.

These individuals have brief periods of interrupted breathing, causing blood oxygen to fall. Eventually they awaken with a startle, gasping for air. This can happen hundreds of times per night. As a result, people with sleep apnea can have fragmented sleep, which doesn't provide the restorative time the body and brain require for repair. They feel fatigued during the day and may have depression and trouble thinking clearly. Untreated, sleep apnea can raise the risk of heart disease and stroke.

People with restless legs syndrome feel an uncomfortable tingling or crawling sensation in their legs. The problem is worse when they're lying down to rest, and moving the legs can provide temporary relief. The cause is unknown, but the roots may lie in a brain malfunction involving the control of muscle activity and movement.

"Chronic insomnia" is when a person has poor sleep that occurs despite having an adequate opportunity to sleep, which results in impairment, such as daytime fatigue or reduced cognitive performance.

Do I Really Need Eight Hours a Night?

The standard advice that people need eight hours of sleep nightly is a rough estimate. The optimal amount that people need varies from individual to individual. However, when you're getting enough sleep, it means that you're sleeping through the night, and you don't have excessive fatigue the next day.

To figure out how much sleep you need, when you're a few days into your next long vacation (after you've had time to catch up on any sleep that you normally miss), go to sleep without setting your alarm clock. How much sleep does it take for you to feel fully rested? "Fully rested" means you find it easy to get out of bed, you're not sleepy during the day, you don't have trouble concentrating, and you are generally in a good mood. That's how much you should be getting night after night for your brain to work at its best.

To Sleep, Perchance to Dream

Since we're talking about sleep, let's take a brief detour into those mysterious mental movies that have fascinated mankind throughout history: dreams. We attach a lot of significance to our dreams—in fact, it's the word that we also use when describing our fondest hopes and grandest aspirations.

The study of dreams is called *oneirology*. Man has studied this sleep phenomenon from the ancient Greeks and Egyptians to the current state-of-the-art brain imaging. Yet for all the effort we've put into it, we still know very little about the actual process of dreaming.

We do know that we spend about six years of our lives dreaming. Most people dream at least three to five times per night, with each period of dreams lasting from about five to twenty minutes. It is generally regarded that everyone has dreams, even if you cannot remember them. If you wake up immediately after the REM phase, you will remember 30 to 40 percent of the dream, but the ability to recall dreams rapidly drops over the next ten minutes. The best recall occurs if you wake up *during* the dream. Studies have found that that most dreams are in color—not black and white as once thought—and the majority of dreams are negative in nature.

Sigmund Freud thought that dreams represented a way to fulfill our wishes and that they were tied to events of the preceding day. Carl Jung felt that it was too simplistic to see dreams as a representation of our unfulfilled wishes. He was convinced that dreams meant more, reflecting the richness and complexity of the entire unconscious. To him, dreams give us a chance to reflect on our waking selves and solve problems.

In the 1960s, researcher William Dement theorized dreams to be a sort of safety valve that helped the brain let off steam that we couldn't release during the day. In the 1970s, Ann Faraday focused on the idea that dreams could apply to situations occurring in one's life; for example, a dream about failing a test may be a warning that we're unprepared for something.

There is an ongoing debate among neurologists and psychologists regarding the value and meaning of dreams. They could represent a random firing of the brain stem during REM sleep. The mind attempts to make sense out of the resulting haphazard chemical signals by fitting them into stories. The bizarre plots and rambling story lines leave you scrambling for an explanation. The brain's process of discarding irrelevant information would be like your computer trash bin collecting unwanted spam and then combining it into a strange, incomprehensible e-mail. For some scientists, analyzing dreams would fall into the same territory as interpreting cloud formations or doing palm reading.

But some credible experts in psychology would argue that dreams have practical functions. Dreams focus on thoughts, emotions, and immediate concerns that we are unable to handle during the course of our day. Dreams may spark our imagination and make us more creative. They give us a way to think outside the box and provide insight into new approaches to personal relationships and novel solutions to nagging problems. They may alert us to what we need to know, wake us up to challenges and opportunities, and guide us to the appropriate action to take.

Some experts go as far as to suggest that dreams are related to survival, warning us of challenges and dangers. This in turn allows us to rehearse how we'll avoid threats and focus on what we need to do to stay healthy. (These benefits may also arise from another state of consciousness that we will address later: meditation.)

Dreams Come in Many Flavors

Experts place dreams into different categories:

- **Daydreams:** A fantasy you have while awake, these come from your brain mulling over issues that are important, but not immediately relevant, when your surroundings don't offer any interesting or engaging stimuli. Idle daydreaming may be a form of arousal that keeps your brain ready to respond to the external world, kind of like how your car engine keeps running at intersections, and will zoom forward as soon as you take your foot off the brake.
- **Epic dreams:** These are very compelling dreams that stay with you for a long time. Even when it's been years since you had the dream, you may still remember it in detail. Epic dreams are often inspirational.
- **Recurring dreams:** These pop up repeatedly over a long period of time. They change very little, and they're the result of unresolved problems or conflicts. In some cases, addressing the conflict stops the recurring dream.
- **Lucid dreams:** These result from having the ability to know you are dreaming and have control over your dreams.
- **Healing dreams:** These bring a message to you about your health. These can tell you that something is wrong with your body even before physical symptoms develop.
- **Nightmares:** These are terrifying or deeply upsetting dreams that cause strong feelings of fear, horror, and distress. They can be related to high fever, trauma or stress, or stimulation from movies or books.

Dreams may have particular meaning for people with substance abuse issues. Being intoxicated can trigger vivid, intense dreams. Some studies have found that more than one-quarter of the dreams of recovering addicts and alcoholics involve seeking or using their drug of choice.

These dreams are often so vivid and feel so real that the addict or alcoholic wakes up momentarily convinced he has relapsed. These types of dreams are very common during the first year of recovery, and they may pop up even after years of sobriety.

Alcoholics Anonymous and the addiction community consider these dreams to be a positive sign of recovery, yet they also suggest that you need more support. People may interpret these dreams as a gift from their "higher power."And dreams about using drugs or drinking also serve as reminders that they are truly powerless. People who are addicted should be grateful for such dreams, as they further encourage them to strengthen their recovery. On the other hand, if you're having these dreams, they may indicate that you are missing drugs or alcohol and the benefits they once offered. To put a halt to them, you may need to replace the high from drugs or drinking with other good feelings.

Alcohol and Good Sleep Just Don't Mix

People often think of alcohol as an effective sleep aid. It isn't.

It's true that as a depressant, alcohol does have a sedative effect that makes you fall asleep faster. At low doses, alcohol enhances the effects of GABA, a neurotransmitter that stimulates sleep, and it may help adenosine work better, which also encourages sleep.

However, alcohol sharply reduces the deep-sleep stages and makes you more likely to wake up during the second half of the night. That's because later at night, your liver breaks down the alcohol so it no longer activates the neurotransmitters that stimulate sleep. The beneficial effect eventually wears off, producing "fragmented" sleep and making you more likely to wake up. After a brief period, often within three consecutive nights, you develop a tolerance to the sedative effect so alcohol doesn't even help you drop off to sleep.

Alcohol can inhibit sleep in other ways, too. It can trigger the release of adrenaline, putting your body on alert. Alcohol can also prevent tryptophan from being converted to the sleep-inducing neurotransmitter serotonin. As a diuretic, alcohol may also make you need to get up to go to the bathroom. Additionally, alcohol relaxes the throat muscles and interferes with brain mechanisms that lead to snoring and other breathing problems.

Drinking may cause other problems for alcoholics. In several studies, people with a history of drinking thought they were having more sleep problems than they actually were. They overestimated the time they needed to fall asleep, they couldn't accurately recall how well they were sleeping, and they thought they were spending more time awake at night than they really were.

The further they were off in these estimates, the more likely they were to relapse over the next three months. In other words, if sleep problems— or even perceived sleep problems—are not addressed, the risk of relapse is high.

Finding the Tools to Fix Your Sleep Problems

In the 1950s and 1960s, doctors prescribed barbiturates to help people sleep. But these had too many negative effects, including tolerance, dependence, withdrawal, and difficulty breathing.

Later, benzodiazepines such as Halcion, Valium, Atavan, and Xanax became popular for helping people fall asleep faster, wake up less often, and sleep longer overall. These work by making GABA receptors more attractive to molecules of GABA, which is a neurotransmitter that makes the cell less likely to react, thus leading to sedation. However, they were linked to a range of symptoms, including difficulty concentrating, trouble with coordination, confusion, memory impairment, irritability, and depression.

A new generation of drugs, sometimes referred to as the nonhypnotic benzodiazepines, began appearing in the early 1990s, with fewer side effects than some of the earlier benzodiazepines. These newer drugs also work on the GABA receptors but do not have a generalized effect on multiple brain receptors that also influence seizures, vigilance, thinking, memory, learning, eating, and anxiety. Ambien and Sonata begin acting within fifteen minutes and have a short half-life, thus they are less likely to cause next-day sleepiness. Sonata is approved for middle-of-the-night awakening. Lunesta and Ambien CR increase your total sleep time because they have longer half-lives of six hours.

These drugs still have side effects, including reduced slow wave sleep. However, for short-term use, the benefits of increased total sleep outweigh the drawbacks of decreased deep sleep. Still, it's important to remember that these are designed to only be used short-term—for two to four weeks—to prevent a rebound effect that leads to greater sleep problems.

Also, people with a history of substance abuse should avoid these newer sleep medications. Nonhypnotic benzodiazepines may be particularly appealing to people who use recreational drugs. "Fighting" the drug by trying to stay awake may lead to a "high" sensation, euphoria, or even hallucinations.Taking these medications for an extended period can also lead to dependence. They can also cause amnesia.

Doctors may also treat insomnia with antidepressants. Lower doses have fewer side effects than most approved sleep medications. How they work is not clear, though some experts claim the effect may result from reducing anxiety and depression. Typically, antidepressants reduce REM sleep, but have minimal impact on deep sleep.

Several over-the-counter sleep aids may also be helpful, the most popular of which is diphenhydramine (found in Benadryl, Tylenol PM, and Sominex). This is an antihistamine. Histamines in your system have a wakefulness-enhancing effect that can be blocked by antihistamines, thereby making you drowsy. Possible side effects include confusion, rapid heartbeat, daytime drowsiness, and decreased coordination.

Another action comes from diphenhydramine's suppression of acetylcholine. This is a brain-cell messenger, which when reduced (such as in Alzheimer's disease) affects memory and leads to muddled thinking. Because diphenhydramine is taken up by acetylcholine receptors, it can form a barrier to this neurotransmitter. Therefore, if you use diphenhydramine as a sleep aid, limit it to a short period of time.

Drug treatments for insomnia are like crutches for rehabilitation after you break your leg. Though you need crutches initially for support while your leg heals, eventually you have to put them away so you can strengthen your muscles to support you. The same is true for sleep problems. It's not wise to rely on medications of *any* kind for too long.

Fortunately, nonmedication approaches also offer ways to help you sleep better. These include the following:

Cognitive Behavioral Therapy

Numerous studies confirm that cognitive behavioral therapy is the best treatment for chronic insomnia. Once insomnia sets in, it may produce bad habits that prolong sleeplessness. The stress, frustration, and anxiety that come with being unable to fall asleep produce higher levels of cortisol. Worry fuels the sleeplessness, which soon becomes a chronic condition with apprehensions about the consequences (I will fail my test tomorrow) and performance anxiety (it will take me two hours to fall back asleep). One may attempt to combat the insomnia with misguided methods such as napping, drinking coffee, having a nightcap, or staying in bed longer in the morning. Instead of relaxing upon entering the bedroom, the person may feel anxious.

Cognitive behavioral therapy (CBT) helps people identify and change their thoughts and behaviors that are interfering with sleep. They then learn new ways to think about sleep and develop healthy strategies to sleep better. The benefits go beyond reducing insomnia; they also help with mood, pain, reasoning ability, problem solving, and health problems.

Herbal Remedies and Supplements

Herbal remedies are popular for all sorts of ailments, including sleep problems, because many people hold the view that they are natural and therefore free of risk. Of course, snake venom and poison ivy are also natural. If you're going to go with herbal remedies or other supplements—especially for long-term sleep problems—check with your doctor first. That being said, herbs that may offer some sleep-inducing benefits include valerian root, chamomile, and passion flower.

A supplement called melatonin is also popular for treating sleep problems. One of the mechanisms that is programmed into the human brain is a twenty-four-hour sleep-wake clock referred to as our circadian rhythm. When our surroundings grow darker, we secrete melatonin, a hormone that attaches to receptors in a part of the brain called the suprachiasmatic nucleus. This triggers the release of the neurotransmitter GABA, which suppresses wakefulness and promotes drowsiness. Melatonin peaks between 8:00 PM and midnight and drops at dawn as the world becomes lighter.

Some studies have shown that taking melatonin supplements about thirty minutes before bedtime increases people's sleep times. However, more recent research has found that synthetic melatonin has minimal to no benefit. When your body is producing its own melatonin, adding to the amount that's already available has no observable benefit.

Exercise

Moderate exercise may ease insomnia symptoms by helping you fall asleep faster, awaken less often, and have a greater percentage of deep sleep. Researchers have found that exercising about a half hour every other afternoon decreased the time that people with insomnia needed to fall asleep by half.

Exercise has been shown to stimulate the release of the calming neurotransmitter serotonin and keep it attached longer to receptors in the emotional area of the brain. Exercise can be a repetitive, lulling activity that allows you to "air out" negative thoughts. If you don't let these go, they can eventually surface during sleep, interfering with optimal sleep architecture. This shows up as diminished restorative sleep, which is when the body truly rests and repairs itself. People who exercise regularly have more energy and better control of their emotions because they accumulate more recuperative sleep at night.

Treatments for Sleep Disorders

If you think you have obstructive sleep apnea or restless legs syndrome, check with your doctor. A number of solutions are available for both problems. For example, treatments for apnea include:

- Weight loss
- Sleeping on your side
- Smoking cessation
- Wearing a pressurized mask that pushes air into your airways to hold them open
- And surgery to reduce the size of tissues that block your airways

Treatments for restless legs syndrome include:

- Cutting back on caffeine, alcohol, and tobacco
- Exercise
- Taking a warm bath before bed
- Medications

Improving Your Sleep Hygiene

The term "sleep hygiene" may seem odd if the first image that pops into your head when you hear the word "hygiene" is washing your hands. But just as washing your hands is a very simple, easy, and inexpensive way to keep from getting sick, sleep hygiene encompasses many straightforward methods that can help you sleep better without medications.

Here's a fairly comprehensive rundown of tips that are crucial for good sleep but that many people overlook or ignore in their day-to-day lives.

Pre-Bedtime Habits that Get You Ready for Sleeping

- Establish a relaxing bedtime routine, such as taking a warm bath or shower, or having your spouse or partner rub your back.
- Avoid reading anything stimulating, like action or horror novels, before bedtime.
- Avoid TV before bedtime, and keep the television out of your bedroom.
- Avoid busywork for two hours before bed, including housecleaning and paying bills.
- Avoid playing stimulating computer games during this time.
- Only use your bed for sleeping and sex. Don't eat in bed, watch TV in bed, or gather the family to hang out on the bed.
- Maintain a healthy relationship with your spouse. Arguments during the day or evening can lead to poor sleep quality, which can lead to further irritability. Resolve disputes before going to bed and postpone more difficult discussions until you have both had a good night's sleep.
- Be sure that your day's exercise is finished at least two to four hours before bedtime.

- Avoid meals and snacks that are high in carbohydrates, fat, or protein in the evening. However, don't go to bed hungry, either.
- Don't drink any fluids during the two hours before going to bed.
- Avoid caffeinated drinks and food—including sodas, coffee, tea, and chocolate—during the six hours before bed.
- Avoid foods that give you heartburn. Some people find that spicy foods, peppermint, onions, and fatty foods may encourage heartburn.
- Avoid smoking or other forms of tobacco for at least three to six hours before bed. It's best to quit entirely.
- Avoid alcohol at least three hours before going to bed.
- Avoid stewing over problems before bedtime. Stress, anxiety, and depression are common reasons for insomnia. Work on solutions to problems in your life, but do this during the day!

Create a Sleep-Inducing Environment

- Sleep in complete darkness. If necessary, use blackout drapes to keep out light from outside.
- Wear eyeshades to cover your eyes if you want things even darker.
- Avoid alarm clocks or other electronic devices with lighted displays that you can see from your bed.
- Wear earplugs if you can hear noises from outside your home.
- Use a white-noise maker. Choose a brand that makes different sounds.
- Avoid using loud alarm clocks. Consider using one that gently turns on the radio or makes other noises that gradually grow louder.
- Keep your bedroom cool and well-ventilated. Turn down the thermostat two hours before bedtime.
- Use a humidifier if you are congested or the air is especially dry.
- Don't watch the clock once you go to bed.
- Develop more realistic expectations about sleep. For example, it's not realistic to assume that everyone has to fall asleep as soon as their head hits the pillow, that you always have to get eight hours of uninterrupted sleep, that you should *never* wake up during the

night, or that you should *always* feel rested and energized the next day. Aiming for perfection can cause you to develop performance anxiety about sleep.

- As you're waiting to fall asleep, try one of these two exercises. *Progressive muscle relaxation:* Tighten the muscles in your feet, hold them tight for a few seconds, then relax them. Tighten the muscles in your lower legs, hold for a few seconds, then relax. Gradually work your way up your body, then tighten and relax the muscles in your hands and arms, and finish with your shoulders, neck, and face. *Guided imagery:* Picture yourself in the most relaxing environment you've ever visited or would like to visit (for many, this might be a beach or wooded surroundings). Imagine it in detail: how the sun feels on you, what the air smells like, and how the waves or the birds sound.

Keep a Sleep-Supporting Schedule

- Maintain a regular bedtime schedule. Go to bed and wake up at the same time every day, including weekends.
- Minimize napping during the day, and avoid any naps after 3:00 PM.
- Expose yourself to bright light as soon as you get up.

Falling Asleep Again After You Wake Up at Night

If you lie awake in bed after you stir in the middle of the night, you condition your body and mind that your bed is a place where you stay awake worrying rather than snoozing. So when you wake up during the night:

- Don't lie there tossing and turning. If you are unable to fall back to sleep quickly—within about twenty minutes—get up and go to another room.
- While you're there, do something nonstimulating, like reading a boring book or watching an infomercial on TV until you feel sleepy.
- But don't sit too close to the television, work on the computer, or turn on bright lights.
- Stay up until you are sleepy, and then return to bed.
- If you are hungry, eat a light snack (carbohydrates are best).

- Practice meditation and yoga techniques (which we'll cover in Chapter 16).
- If you often find yourself lying in bed with your mind racing, keep a journal and write down your worrisome thoughts before going to bed.

Try "Sleep Restructuring"

If your habits and thought processes have gotten to where you are anxious about whether you'll get to sleep, and then you stay awake after you wake up in the middle of the night, try this process to gradually get yourself back on track:

- During the reconditioning process, set your alarm and get up at the same time every morning, regardless of how little sleep you got during the night.
- Do not nap during the day.
- Start restricting the amount of time you spend in bed without sleeping. Start by estimating how much sleep you're getting. If you average five hours a night, but spend eight hours in bed, reduce your time in bed to about five and a half hours. This will decrease the unpleasant sense of lying awake, and it helps you more rapidly enter deeper sleep once you fall asleep. If you're cutting your time in bed to five and a half hours and you need to wake up by 7:00 AM, then on your first night of sleep restriction, you should go to bed at 1:30 AM, no matter how sleepy you are before then.
- Once you sleep well during the allotted time for several nights, you can add another fifteen or thirty minutes, making sure that you're remaining asleep for most of the night.
- Repeat the process until you are getting the amount of sleep you want.
- If your sleep becomes interrupted and fragmented again, take a step back by reducing your time in bed until your sleep becomes consolidated again.
- Be sure to not sleep at other times even if you feel sleepy. Taking naps reduces the drive that helps you become a more effective night sleeper.

- If you are still having trouble falling or staying asleep for five hours, something else may be going on, and you should check with your doctor.

THE BRAIN FIX TOOLBOX

- Be sure to get an adequate amount of sleep each night. Sufficient sleep isn't a luxury—it's mandatory for a properly working brain. Most people do best with at least seven hours nightly.
- Try to get enough sleep on a nightly basis, instead of trying to catch up on weekends.
- Avoid using sleeping medications for long periods of time. If you need medicine to help you fall asleep or stay asleep, it's better to look for the underlying cause and address that.
- Exercise and get physical activity regularly (as in at least a half hour on most days of the week). Be sure to wrap up your exercise during the day so your body has had several hours to cool off before bed.
- Several hours before bedtime, start setting the stage to help yourself fall asleep. That means avoiding exercise, heavy meals, alcohol, caffeine, and tobacco in the hours before going to bed.
- Also avoid arguments, paying bills, and stimulating books or computer games before bedtime.
- If you're having trouble staying asleep during the night, cut back the amount of time you spend in bed, so you're spending more of that time asleep. Gradually give yourself more time in bed as your time asleep improves.

16

Meditation and Yoga:
Listening to Yourself Think

THE WORDS *meditation* and *medication* are different by only one letter. That's no coincidence, since they share the same root, the Latin *meden*, which means "cure." Those who practice medicine know that medications have major limitations when it comes to curing most diseases. Yet people recover from illnesses and experience total and complete healing all the time!

The reason is quite simply that the body heals itself.

The background for this healing to take place is that the body needs to be brought into balance, with blood pressure that's not too high or low, a proper ratio between good HDL and bad LDL cholesterol, blood that's neither flowing too freely nor clotting, the proper level of inflammation that isn't harming the body, and a mental outlook that's not giddy and manic but not depressed and anxious.

Meditation can help bring both your body *and* your mind into this necessary balance.

The benefit of meditation lies where attention and concentration are focused in the present moment. The idea is to temporarily halt the stream of thoughts that normally occupy your mind, and to rise above reality by fully accepting it. This means letting your inner thoughts—which are *not* part of the real world—come and go naturally with an open attitude. As thoughts pop into your head, whether they're daydreams, fantasies, or worries about the future, you let them pass on through without thinking, analyzing, or challenging them.

Through this process, you can change how the emotions and thoughts in your mind affect you. And you can restore balance to an otherwise erratic and poorly working system of thoughts and behaviors, including anxiety, depression, addictions, and eating disorders.

One way of grasping this concept is to picture yourself composing a letter on your computer. Let's say you open up your word processing program and want to type your letter in the Arial font, with the text in 10-point type. However, when you begin typing, the program is set to make text in the Times New Roman font, size 12. So you pull down the appropriate menu prompts, change the font and type size, and proceed to complete your letter and log out of your computer.

An hour later, you fire up the computer so you can type another letter in 10-point Arial, but the program is reset to deliver 12-point Times New Roman. That's how it comes up every single time you launch the word processor. In order to *permanently* change the font and size, you need to enter into the program's settings and change the default mode.

The same thing may be occurring in your brain's hardwiring. After months—or more likely years—of dysfunctional thoughts and behaviors, your brain becomes set in a default mode. It's accustomed to feeling stressed, depressed, unfocused, or engaged in addiction or disordered eating. It may stay in this setting even if you want to change. Thus, it is not enough to just *want* to change, but you have to adjust your brain's default mode as well.

During the state of mind you can reach during meditation, you may be able to reset your brain's default setting.

Riding the Waves of Meditation

We learned about different types of brain waves during the chapter on sleep. Doctors can place electrodes on your scalp that pick up your brain's electrical activity, which registers as squiggly waves on sheets of printout paper.

When we are awake, we produce beta waves, which fire rapidly and inconsistently because we are aroused by movement, sensory input through our eyes and ears, communication, and concentration. It's like throwing a handful of pebbles and rocks into a pond, the movement of which creates waves rippling and crashing all over the place.

At bedtime, we quiet down, relax, and create slower alpha brain waves in a more uniform pattern. We continue to transition into an even more peaceful state with slower theta waves. If we're awakened at this point, we might claim that we have not been asleep. This is also the status of our brains when we are ruminating and making decisions, somewhere between wakefulness and sleep, alpha waves and theta waves, arousal and daydreaming. At this point, we are operating in a semiconscious zone in which we're unaware of how much time is elapsing or where exactly we are at the time.

Meditation gets you to the place you're in before you drop into deep sleep, but your brain's arousal is reduced and your brain wave activity is altered. You have a free flow of ideas drifting through your mind without censorship. This can lead to a positive mental state.

During meditation, the most common brain waves are alpha waves. However, gamma brain waves also increase. This type of wave action is usually weak when you're engaged in normal brain activity. These are the fastest of the brain-wave frequencies, and they're a sign that you're engaged in the highest state of focus, your top concentration, and the most optimal brain functioning.

When people are meditating, a lot of activity is occurring in the prefrontal area of the brain (the frontal lobe is the most highly developed part of the brain, which is responsible for reasoning, planning, and self-conscious awareness). As a result, they show increased levels of brainwaves linked to vigilance and attention.

This has led experts to suspect that the connections one makes while meditating can improve brain function. Meditation could help older people preserve their memory and ability to think about detailed information. Meditation could also help people who are sleep-deprived concentrate better, and it may help us maintain our focus and stay attentive during times of the day when we naturally become less sharp, such as the afternoon.

When researchers used functional MRI to study the brains of people who meditate daily, they found that these people had greater thickness in areas of the brain involved with memory and attention. Meditators have also been shown to have better blood flow and greater use of glucose in their brains.

Healing Your Brain and Body Through Meditation

Meditation has been linked to improvements in many measurements of health, including:

- Lowered blood pressure, cholesterol, and insulin resistance
- Improved immune system activity, as measured with higher levels of antibodies and anti-inflammatory chemicals
- Better sleep, as shown by an increase in brain waves that denote deep-sleep stages
- Improved tolerance of chronic pain
- A lower risk of dying in general, as seen in people who practiced Transcendental Meditation for twenty minutes twice a day. Research found that these people had a 23 percent lower rate of death from all causes compared to people who didn't meditate.
- Relief from stress. Many functions of our body aren't voluntary; in other words, they keep going day after day without us having to think about them. This involuntary system is the *autonomic nervous system*, which regulates our heartbeat, breathing rate, digestion, sweating, growth, maintenance, and repair. Part of its makeup is the *sympathetic nervous system*. This part of our nervous system mobilizes our bodies for fight or flight when we're threatened. During these episodes, our heart rate increases, we breathe heavily, blood vessels constrict, blood pressure rises, our blood becomes stickier, and our muscles grow tense. However, we also have an alternate *parasympathetic nervous system*, which encourages the "rest and digest" response. It kicks into action when our body needs to slow down to a peaceful rhythm, like when we're digesting food, relaxing, and healing. Meditation turns on the parasympathetic system and turns down its sympathetic counterpart.
- Reduced depression and improved mood. These benefits might come from a shift in the brain's activity in the prefrontal cortex from the right hemisphere to the left hemisphere. When the brain becomes rewired to the left side, one may feel enthusiasm, relaxation, mental calmness, and happiness. Reorienting from the stressful, fearful, and anxiety-filled moods of the right side of the

brain to a more peaceful, accepting state is helpful in psychologically balancing the brain to avoid addictive behaviors.

- Compassion. People who meditate may have improved feelings of compassion, which is a key element in the common twelve-step approach to recovery from addiction. In one study, graduate students and Tibetan monks were connected to an EEG device that measured brain waves while they watched videos of a painful medical procedure. In the students, the right prefrontal cortex (involved in anxiety and fear) lit up. But in the monks, the left prefrontal cortex was activated. This suggested that the students' thoughts were focused on how they would feel during this procedure, but the monks were more centered on compassion for the victims' feelings.

Meditation can have more special benefits for people who are recovering from addiction or trying to break unhealthy habits. People in recovery often decide to change their behavior or their thinking patterns, only to find themselves returning to their old ways. This can lead to a sense of hopelessness that they'll ever break free of their destructive behavior. However, the meditative state allows the brain to be reshaped or rewired.

While in therapy, people learn new ideas and beliefs that they're encouraged to genuinely accept. These linger in the brain's memory storage tanks in the hippocampus and amygdala until sleep—or meditation. During meditation, these new ideas and beliefs may be consolidated and reshaped in the brain to become a new default setting (like switching your word processor to automatically bring up a new font). Meditation is a vehicle to actively enhance the process of personal change. As a result, therapy can prime the pump for change, and meditation can drive these changes home.

In addition, the importance of getting in touch with one's spirituality and surrendering to a higher power are often cited as important steps for recovery from addiction. These are very difficult concepts for many people to grasp, especially when they are in the throes of addiction. An understanding of the neurological pathways involved in the meditative process may provide clues to how our mind, body, and spirit are linked.

During meditation, the right temporal lobe of the brain becomes highly active. Some researchers hold that this area may be the site where religious enlightenment occurs. (On a side note, experts have speculated that some people who are obsessed with religion or report communicating with the spiritual world—including Joan of Arc, Dostoyevsky, Proust, and Moses—may have had temporal lobe epilepsy. Seizures might cause the temporal lobe to become activated, leading to mystical experiences or finding God in "the moment." Other triggers of temporal lobe activation include fatigue, low blood sugar, and lack of oxygen.)

In addition, repetitive movements, prayers, and mantras (specific phrases) can focus our attention and exclude other sensory stimuli. These monotonous, repetitious actions or sayings can evoke a powerful emotional response that sends our arousal system into overdrive. The hippocampus, which is responsible for maintaining equilibrium, shuts off and inhibits additional neural input much like a traffic cop halts the flow of traffic during a wreck on the highway.

How to Meditate

More than 20 million Americans practice different forms of meditation. People can perform meditation while doing yoga or tai chi, or even while walking. However, practitioners typically meditate in a quiet place without distractions. They close their eyes to seal themselves away from the outside world while maintaining a comfortable posture, usually seated.

While meditating, people may focus on a word, phrase, or sound that is repeated silently over and over. This helps maintain one's focus. Or you can center your thoughts on your breath going in and out of your body. As distracting thoughts intrude, you allow them to go away naturally on their own, without censoring yourself or analyzing them further. Once you become aware of a wandering thought, redirect your focus to the special word or to your breathing, which brings your mind back to focusing on peaceful nothingness.

A type of meditation called *mindfulness meditation* has gained a foothold in American medicine and psychology. Mindfulness describes having a state of awareness and complete acceptance of the present moment.

The focus stays on whatever is being experienced in the moment without reacting to or judging that experience. Many of us spend much of our time dwelling on the past or fearing catastrophes that could come in the future. This leaves us unable to focus on the present moment, (which is our real life!) as opposed to the fantasy world in our minds.

Focusing on the present helps us better accept the thoughts and emotions we have in our everyday lives. We find a deeper awareness of our mind and finally have a chance to listen to ourselves think. For some this is like a spiritual awareness, in which meditation offers moments of listening to God. We practice being still and completely present in the moment. There is no reacting, no regret for the past, and no fear of the future. Since negative energy can suppress our thoughts, during meditation we are open to creativity, intuition, and forgiveness by letting go, not overreacting, and not challenging issues over which we struggle and cannot control.

In summary, meditation allows you to enter into a state that is void of the interferences that normally occupy your mind. It is the transition from wakefulness to sleep, where we get in touch with the flow of our emotions and thoughts so our brain can be rewired and healed, our immune system strengthened, and our sense of well-being enhanced. Stress is managed appropriately and released. The ego-driven self dissolves, fears of intimacy decrease, relationships improve, compassion emerges, and one develops a sense of thoughtfulness.

You can also achieve similar changes in your mind and body through yoga. Like meditation, yoga has its roots in Eastern traditions. Also like meditation, yoga has become well accepted by all types of Americans (in other words, you don't have to be a free-spirited vegetarian to realize its benefits). Yoga involves moving your body through specific movements while you focus on your breathing. You achieve a calm, peaceful, and almost trancelike state. Upon awakening from this self-described blissful experience, practitioners may rightly claim they are energized and have become one with the universe.

Yoga Equals Meditation with a Twist

Yoga is a 5,000-year-old practice from India and the Far East. More than 1,500 yoga poses were recorded in ancient text written in Sanskrit. Yoga is having a considerable impact in America these days, too. Approximately 20 million Americans practice yoga nowadays, spending an estimated $3 billion on yoga classes, mats, and other products annually.

The word *yoga* means "yoke." But it's not like yoking in the sense of strapping a beast of burden to a heavy load in order to pull it. Instead, yoga is intended to unite the body, mind, and spirit. You *want* these elements of yourself to be yoked together rather than operating separately. This allows your body—and mind—to find harmony and heal itself. Yoga calls for one to engage in slow, gentle, and painless stretches while the mind achieves a state of mental focus through deep, steady breathing and meditation.

Three elements—asana, pranayama, and dhyana—interact to allow you to reach a state of mind that directly affects the brain's healing ability.

- *Asana* describes the series of specific postures—which start simple and gradually become more complex—that the practitioner holds for a period of time.
- *Pranayama* refers to rhythmic and steady breathing, upon which the practitioner focuses his or her attention in order to calm the spirit.
- *Dhyana* is a mental state whereby one enters a state of mindfulness or awareness.

Research has confirmed that yoga has a real impact on the mind, as well as bodily issues that can affect your mind.

Pain

One study found that after taking twelve weeks of yoga classes, the number of participants who needed pain medication decreased from 60 to 21 percent. Yoga has also been shown to reduce the frequency and intensity of migraine headaches, possibly because it has a calming effect on the nervous system.

The field of physical therapy has long promoted flexibility training as an important component of pain management. The relaxation response that one has during yoga lessens tension, and the mindfulness during yoga can instill the confidence needed to effectively deal with the pain.

Back pain is a major problem that reduces Americans' quality of life. Treating spine problems in the United States costs $85.9 billion a year. Yoga stretching and relaxation techniques could go a long way in reducing this nationwide problem and the pain and suffering that goes along with it.

Muscle Tightness

When we are worried about a stressful situation, we're hardwired to fight it or run from it. This puts us in a state of hyperarousal, as our mouths get dry, our hearts beat rapidly, and our muscles grow tense. When you internalize stress, this state can produce a headache or neck, shoulder, or back pain due to muscle tightness. Tense and tight muscles produce pain, impede movement, and make joints, muscles, tendons, and ligaments more susceptible to injury.

Tight muscles also produce weakness and fatigue throughout the body. And muscle soreness escalates to stiffness and immobility. One soon becomes susceptible to further injury, weight gain, depression, and chronic pain. It naturally makes sense to relax and stretch the muscles to release tension, reduce fatigue, and feel better. Yoga is an effective way to accomplish this.

Obesity

Yoga can provide a form of aerobic exercise, since it improves your heart and lungs' ability to work efficiently. However, some types of yoga burn more calories than others:

- Hatha yoga: 175 calories per hour
- Ashtanga and power yoga: 330 calories per hour
- Vinyasa yoga: 445 calories per hour
- Bikram or hot yoga: 630 calories per hour

Weight management is a welcome benefit of yoga—and this doesn't come just from the aerobic exercise aspect. By relieving stress, you can reduce the chronic output of the stress hormone cortisol. This hormone often serves to increase your appetite, and it encourages fat deposits around the midsection. Finally, improving your mindfulness during yoga can help you learn to become more aware when your stomach is full while eating.

Better Oxygen Use

The secret to a long life is to keep breathing as long as you can: when you breathe in, you *in*spire . . . and when you don't breathe, you *ex*pire. Your brain craves oxygen. When you don't have it, you die in a very short time. So we can unequivocally state that your breath is a "life force." The critical element in breathing, of course, is oxygen. Your lung capacity helps determine how much you can inhale with each breath, but you have the ability to increase the amount of oxygen you take in by as much as five times! Getting the oxygen into your lungs is just the first step. Respiration is your ability to extract oxygen from your lungs, transport it to every cell in your body, and deliver it to structures within your cells that produce energy.

Say we observe someone breathing while under stress. With each breath, the stomach contracts inward and lifts the sheet of muscle between the abdomen and chest (the diaphragm) upward. This minimizes the lungs' capacity to expand and take in adequate oxygen. When the person exhales, his stomach expands outward, lowering the diaphragm so carbon dioxide isn't squeezed out of his lungs. This inefficient movement of air in and out of the lungs results in low oxygen— and anxiety that stems from that lack of sufficient oxygen.

Many of us breathe that way all the time, depriving our brains and bodies of the substantially larger quantities of oxygen we could be sucking in and circulating. Now let's examine a *better* way to breathe. As you inhale, your stomach should move *outward*, lowering your diaphragm and allowing your lungs to take in the maximum amount of oxygen-rich air.

After your lungs are comfortably expanded and full of oxygen, you pause for a moment. Then you slowly and gradually exhale, pulling in your belly. This efficiently squeezes out the carbon dioxide in your lungs to make room once again for oxygen. Not only are you getting the good stuff in and the bad stuff out, but your entire body relaxes, lowering your heart rate and blood pressure. This is good for your cardiovascular system, which feeds your brain.

Additionally, because this type of breathing involves concentration, your other distracting thoughts get pushed to the edges, since the mind can only focus intensely on one thought at a time.

Can we breathe this way thousands of times all day long? Probably not. But we can certainly breathe this way a lot more often than most of us do. Yoga—and meditation in general—teaches you to breathe deeply and steadily. You don't have to confine this healthy breathing style to the times that you're actually meditating or doing yoga. By taking breaks throughout the day to focus on your breathing, you can improve your oxygen uptake while recentering yourself in the present moment.

 ## THE BRAIN FIX TOOLBOX

- Explore a style of meditation that appeals to your lifestyle and interests. Meditation doesn't run counter to religious beliefs, and it may actually supplement and complement any beliefs you already have.

- Make a point to meditate on a daily basis. You may be able to find a class in your town or city. A good place to start looking would be your hospital or, if you have one nearby, a Buddhist center. You can also learn to meditate using books, CDs, or DVDs.

- Try to keep your brain focused on the present moment. If worrisome memories of the past or fears of the future intrude, let them pass on through your mind. Don't get pulled into them.

Gently redirect your thoughts toward your present surroundings.

- Try a yoga class, if one is available in your area. If you have musculoskeletal, back, or neck problems, or any chronic disease, talk to your doctor first. Ask about your instructor's credentials and background in working with any special needs you may have.

- Breathe deeply. People who smoke take cigarette breaks; why not take a breathing break? Several times a day, stop what you're doing and pay attention to your breathing patterns. Breathe deeply to the bottom of your lungs, so your stomach moves outward, and slowly and deliberately expel the air.

17

Get the Message About Massage

TOUCHING IS A FORM OF expression similar to language. It's not healthy for your mind to go long periods of time without conversation, and it's not ideal to go without touch either.

Newborn babies crave the skin-to-skin contact they get while nursing. As children, we get hugs that communicate caring and protection. Later as teens or young adults, we encounter an intimate and passionate world where an embrace can lead to other loving expressions of togetherness. Throughout our whole lives, we have a constant need to be hugged and comforted when we're sad, grieving, or hurting. We also like to be squeezed when we are elated over successes and achievements.

These touches have measurable effects in our bodies and minds. Research has found that married women feel instant relief from stressful situations when they hold their husbands' hands. Similarly, when people received painful shocks, holding hands with a loved one provided relief from their pain. Cuddling or holding hands for ten minutes can reduce signs of stress, such as elevated blood pressure, rising heart rate, and high levels of cortisol. This may help explain why married men tend to be healthier and happier, but people who are isolated and lonely tend to have poorer health.

Unfortunately, it's not always possible to satisfy the natural instinct to touch and be touched. Some people grow up in families where touching is discouraged or considered improper. Some people are abandoned as children or adults. People may feel ugly or unlovable if family members or partners avoid intimate contact. For many who have struggled with trauma, abuse, addictions, or eating disorders, it is necessary to overcome shame and negative thoughts about their bodies. For these people—or *anyone* who wants to benefit from this mind-relieving therapy—massage can cover this need.

Massage allows us to experience our bodies in a positive way through the power of healthy touch. It gives us an opportunity to accept our bodies the way they are and to reconnect our minds with our bodies. We shift our thinking away from our weight, shape, or elements, which we perceive as defects. Massage provides an opportunity to show kindness, nurturing, and attention toward a body that may not otherwise get this feedback.

What is massage? It's not simply touching or kneading body parts at random. Therapeutic massage involves systematically manipulating tissues to affect the nervous, muscular, and circulatory systems in a specific way. The contact stimulates receptors in the body that transmit messages to the spinal cord that go on into the brain. The motion and pressure can produce the sensation of pleasure, possibly by causing the release of dopamine in the brain. This in turn relaxes muscles and reduces tension.

As blood vessels contract and dilate, you feel a sense of warmth in the tissues that are being massaged. Just the monotonous and repetitive nature of the motion contributes to a sense of calmness, peace, and relaxation. Substances that contribute to pain—such as bradykinin, substance P, and prostaglandins—can be dispersed in your body so they don't accumulate and produce painful contractions and tightness. As a result, massage therapy can help improve pain management.

Massage therapy has popular appeal in the United States, with 8.7 percent of adults getting at least one massage per year. Numerous studies have demonstrated that therapeutic massage can provide other benefits, including:

- Reduced symptoms of depression
- Lower levels of the stress hormone cortisol after several weeks of massage therapy
- Less body dissatisfaction in people with eating disorders, as well as reduced anorexia and bulimia symptoms
- A reduction in attention deficit disorder or attention deficit hyperactivity disorder behaviors

- Potentially strengthened immune system, given that it can lower anxiety and depression

 ## THE BRAIN FIX TOOLBOX

- Give massage a try. If you've never had one, ask around for references for good massage therapists from your doctor, friends, a local gym, or a physical therapy practice.
- Be sure to ask your massage therapist about his or her qualifications or certifications. Discuss what type of massage you'll be getting beforehand.
- If you have a musculoskeletal problem, cancer, or other chronic disease, talk to your doctor before having a massage.

18

A Special Note of Encouragement
for Readers with Addictions
or Eating Disorders

WHEN IT COMES TO AN ADDICTION or eating disorder, the concept that these problems are "diseases" is more difficult to comprehend than it is for, say, heart disease. Heart disease develops due to a lack of blood flow through the arteries that feed the heart muscle. The underlying process behind an addiction or eating disorder has traditionally been harder for people to picture.

There is a premise in evidence-based medicine that if something can't be measured, it cannot be studied scientifically. Now, of course, we know that these behaviors aren't the result of a character defect, lack of willpower, or bad habits. Technology has helped change society's way of thinking about these problems.

The twenty-first century has introduced a host of brain-imaging techniques, such as PET, fMRI, SPECT, and EEG, which have expanded our ability to explore how emotional events and distorted perceptions can be generated by the brain. (For example, PET scans capture patterns of glucose use in the brain and fMRI techniques detect increases in blood flow.) However, brain imaging is a new frontier and researchers are not always sure what they are capturing.

Still, the future of neuroscience will provide insight that will greatly contribute to therapists' effectiveness in treating these diseases. Many of the concepts we're discovering now must be viewed as "footprints in the sand."

We know we are going in the right direction, but where the path will eventually take us is still a mystery. Taking a look into what's occurring in the brains of people with these problems helps establish the importance of the strategies needed for recovering from them.

Signs of Trouble

We begin with the simple notion that the brain is broken in cases of addiction and eating disorders. For example, there are clear indications that the appearance and function of the brain in a person with anorexia are different than in someone who is not anorectic. The brain has loss of gray and white matter, which shows up as tissue shrinkage. Imaging may show larger ventricles (natural fluid-filled spaces in the brain), widening of sulci (the indentations that give the brain its squiggly shape), thinning of the cortex, or loss of cell density.

The brain may have less blood flow, lower use of glucose, or changes in the frequency of brain waves. More cell death results from the starvation and malnutrition that accompanies the progression of an eating disorder.

Basically, the brain has holes in it, and it is not running properly on all cylinders. Some of these defects or susceptibility to damage undoubtedly exist from the person's very beginning due to genetics. Having other conditions such as autism spectrum disorder, ADD/ADHD, personality disorder, anxiety, or obsessive-compulsive disorder could further complicate the picture.

Substance abuse can break down nervous tissue and drain neurotransmitters. The addictive substances (such as nicotine, cocaine, opioids, and THC in marijuana) are neurotoxic and thereby damaging to the brain. Cortisol, the stress hormone, plays a significant role in destroying and changing neurons and circuitry. Though neural changes are triggered by stressful events, the degree of that damage is determined by one's resilience and ability to handle that stress.

These problems can also accelerate common neurodegenerative processes, such as aging, free-radical activity, and inflammation. The combined destructive potential from addiction, malnutrition, genetics, aging, stress, and other illnesses makes a case for a major brain reconstruction project. Repair involves generating new neurons and dendrites, replenishing and balancing neurotransmitters, rewiring neural circuits, and increasing the number and sensitivity of receptors.

In most cases, the body—including the brain—gets better and sees a return to health because the body heals itself, *not* because a drug fixes the problem. Drugs can play a role by acting as a catalyst for healing and making a cure more likely to occur, but all healing in essence is self-healing.

Nature tries to keep an organism internally stable and balanced despite changing external conditions. Disease is prevented or a cure is found when the body is brought into a state of homeostasis, or balance.

We want our good HDL and bad LDL cholesterol to stay balanced in a healthy ratio to ward off vascular disease. We want to avoid high blood pressure without creating too-low blood pressure. We want antioxidants to neutralize free radicals, but megadoses of supplements can result in the creation of *harmful* pro-oxidants.

The key message is that we want to establish balance and practice habits designed to bring the body into a state of equilibrium. The same goes with the brain. Changing the brain will additionally require the individual not only to play an active role but, most important, to *believe* in the possibility of healing.

Clearly, the plan for recovery requires that the person with the addiction or eating disorder be motivated to be an active participant in the brain's self-healing process, which ultimately results in neuropsychobiological balance (which means the neural foundation for our behaviors).

We will begin our investigation into the brain's healing process by breaking it into three basic divisions and describing how each one is designed to respond to stress. Why stress? Because ultimately addictions and eating disorder behaviors would not be an issue if people could self-regulate their actions. And if there were no stressors in our lives, or if we all learned appropriate skills for coping or self-soothing, we would have no need to seek out pleasures that cause harm. We are designed to seek pleasure and avoid pain. Since we can't completely avoid pain, our bodies innately seek out pleasure, sometimes in the form of drugs, alcohol, food, anorexia, gambling, and so forth.

The Hindbrain: Fight or Flight . . . or Freeze

Stress disturbs one's homeostasis—that crucial healthy balance—and alters the brain. The hindbrain, located between the brain stem and the midbrain, is the most primitive, least evolved part of the brain (it's often referred to as the *reptilian* brain).

The hindbrain's mechanism of coping with stress is through musculoskeletal contraction. Headaches, high blood pressure, spastic colon, and neck tension are a few of the physical symptoms we feel when we are exposed to fear or experience anxiety.

The source of headache discomfort is not from the brain itself, since it actually contains no pain receptors. Rather, the pain results from the stimulation of sensory nerves inside blood vessels at the base of the skull, causing them to change diameter. Smooth muscles in the colon can cramp when we are worried, eliciting pain. Our neck and back muscles tighten when we become tense and bothered. The body can tense, tighten, and become immobile, as if it were in "freeze mode."

At other times, our body switches to a hyperaroused state. Respiration quickens to supply oxygen, temperature rises and produces sweating, and heart rate increases to transport oxygen and nutrients to hardworking tissues.

This mode prepares us to either run and hide from danger or remain and defend ourselves. The sympathetic nervous system (SNS) governs this fight-or-flight circuitry. When the threat subsides and the body returns to its rest-and-relax state, it is under the influence of the parasympathetic nervous system (PNS). During this period, the heart rate drops, blood pressure lowers, and breathing slows. Both systems are necessary and useful for the appropriate situation. They balance each other such that when one is activated the other is suppressed.

On January 15, 2009, a U.S. Airways flight took off from LaGuardia Airport, but had to descend just three minutes later because a flock of geese had gotten sucked into the plane's engines. The captain, Chesley "Sully" Sullenberger, alerted the flight attendants to prepare the passengers for impact. He then calmly led the 155 occupants to a safe "emergency ditching" on the Hudson River.

An atmosphere of silence permeated the cabin as each person braced for an unknown fate. Three and a half minutes later, panicked passengers quickly exited onto the plane's wing, with seventeen jumping into the water without seat cushions. Some nervously listened for instructions for the best course of action amid smells of burning jet fuel in the 22-degree air. Others remained perfectly still and had to be assisted out of the plane while water rose above their shoulders.

In 155 passengers, the hindbrain was fully engaged and operating during this crisis. The initial shock over the crew preparing for an emergency landing incited a psychic numbing throughout the cabin. The freeze response continued for some who found themselves immobile despite imminent danger. Others were driven to overrespond when they leaped into the freezing cold water, subjecting themselves to hypothermia and shock. The crew remained task-oriented and maintained their integrity, which Captain Sullenberger described as "doing the right thing even when it is not convenient."

Basic bodily functions (involving smooth muscles, the heart, lungs, kidneys, intestines, circulatory system, and so on) are under control of the PNS and SNS systems. Collectively, these are called the autonomic nervous system (ANS). When the PNS is mobilized in response to threats, the rest of the nervous system typically locks up. Nature provides numerous examples of this freezing behavior: mice playing dead when caught by a cat, dogs falling totally submissive in the jaws of a dominant canine, or rabbits remaining perfectly still in an underground lair invaded by a snake. This behavior is a reflex or instinctive response that supports survival.

Functional brain imaging suggests that the brain's higher centers (the frontal cortex) have reduced activity when we are confronted with an imminent danger to survival. "Psychic numbing" is the term for when the brain shuts down against threats it cannot handle. With this startle response, the body freezes, time slows, and we have less sensation of pain. Most of the time we can let go of the event afterward. The memory of the stress is stored by the hippocampus in the proper perspective. However, occasionally the trauma lingers, even though the threat has passed, and the individual continues to respond as if under attack. The memory can invade the present and be relived as flashbacks. Although all 155 occupants of that U.S. Airways flight were rescued safely, for some the memories of this frightening event may persist for years.

Individuals with addiction or eating disorders may have a history of imminent threats to their existence or prolonged traumas that have disrupted the workings of their hindbrain. Feelings of hopelessness and powerlessness may saturate their being and interfere with their progress in the recovery process.

However, trauma resolution therapies (such as exposure to the stressful event, medications, eye movement desensitization and reprocessing [EMDR], and sensorimotor psychotherapy) are designed to help refile highly charged emotional experiences and introduce coping skills that turn down the volume on the autonomic nervous system. In so doing, the individual is capable of putting memories in perspective and regaining control over their lives. This, in turn, helps them gain control over their substance use or eating disorder.

The Midbrain:
Balancing Unpleasant from Pleasant

Within the midbrain, we find the limbic system, which is essentially the center of emotions and feelings. The limbic system allows one to balance out unpleasant experiences with pleasant ones. Monkeys cornered by a predator will initially scream, jump, and bare their teeth. But soon they revert to grooming their fur, which would seem useless when they're faced with possible death.

However, this response makes sense. Infant primates will run to their mother when they are frightened or afraid. Their mother will groom them in an attempt to create a sense of calm. Self-soothing or mutually soothing behavior by monkeys seems to calm them down and produce pleasure. Instinctively, primates fall back on grooming to distract themselves, patch things up after fighting, or show affection.

Humans do much the same thing. When we're stressed out—even over a situation that doesn't immediately threaten our survival, such as concern over cutbacks at work—some unconsciously bite their nails (a form of grooming). Some reach for ice cream. Some turn to illicit drugs.

Looking into the brain's limbic area can unravel what is happening in these situations. Nerves communicate using a neurotransmitter that travels across synapses to attach to receptors on the receiving nerves. In the case of the hypothalamus, the neurotransmitter is serotonin.

Today, not only do we have to deal with our personal stressors, but the media constantly inundates us with crises occurring around the world. As empathetic human beings, some people will begin to deplete the stores of serotonin in their hypothalamus. With serotonin reduced, their mood becomes low. Serotonin is what allows us to calm down so we can sleep. If we completely ran out, we'd suffer from sleep deprivation and die. So as a protective mechanism, when levels are low, the secreted serotonin is rapidly taken back up before it has a chance to attach to neighboring receptors. The individual now has full-fledged depression.

Medical researchers created selective serotonin reuptake inhibitors (SSRIs) that can keep serotonin from being taken back into the nerve. This allows the neurotransmitter to remain in the synapse and eventually attach to the appropriate receptor and calm the individual toward normal behavior. SSRIs that have become household names include Prozac, Paxil, Zoloft, and Lexapro. They will not *cure* depression in most cases because they do not create more serotonin. Medications merely allow what little serotonin you have left to work more efficiently. The *permanent* cure is that one needs to cope better with the problem that's bothering them so the body will continue to create more serotonin and not deplete its stores.

Therapeutic approaches such as dialectical behavioral therapy (DBT) and cognitive behavioral therapy (CBT) can help improve people's coping skills. However, therapy takes time and cooperation on the part of the patient. Plus, there is some inescapable stress in our lives for which we can't find solutions.

The depletion of serotonin in the hypothalamus triggers a cascade of events that eventually affects the nucleus accumbens (the reward center of the brain). Pleasurable sensations are created by the release of dopamine in the nucleus accumbens and caudate nucleus.

Much like serotonin, dopamine is secreted and crosses a synapse to attach to receptors across the way, thus producing pleasure. An unpleasant experience (linked to low serotonin) will be balanced with a pleasant experience (thus extra dopamine). Certain people tend to need more dopamine because they are born with fewer dopamine receptors. In some people, having a genetic cause of fewer receptors makes them more likely to seek more "rewarding" experiences to compensate for decreased serotonin. Experiences such as drugs or behaviors that "feel good" will be encoded in the hippocampus. When these people have a need to cope or feel good, their brain will crave those experiences to produce a state of normalcy.

If a person who coped by drinking alcohol went through a recovery program, they most likely would begin to use food to cope instead. After someone chooses to stop smoking cigarettes, they typically revert to eating. This swapping of behavior is analogous to changing seats on the *Titanic*. No matter where you're sitting, you'll eventually sink.

Yet another person who had been a compulsive eater but chose to stop coping with food might look to her willpower instead of relying on comfort foods. However, for most people, willpower is not a pleasure, and deprivation isn't a good substitute for the pleasure derived from eating.

In this situation, there is nothing available left for coping with the stress. As a result, the person has a void. Over time, the void keeps getting larger and larger until the dieter fills it back up with even more food than before. This feeling of loss of control produces guilt and the cycle continues: she might develop binge-eating behavior. Or control *itself* may become a pleasure and now she finds herself fighting anorexia, with refusing to eat reducing her anxiety.

The bottom line is that in order to overcome a vicious cycle, the question that people need to ask themselves is, *What am I going to use in the future to cope with stress now that I cannot use a drug (or binging, purging, or restriction)?*

It's not enough just to give up these things. Instead, full recovery calls for therapies designed to substitute *appropriate* activities that release dopamine.

The Neocortex: Happiness and Fear

Brain imaging has brought us a deeper understanding of the neurobiological map of emotions. Above the midbrain and extending forward, you'll find the brain's executive functioning portion, which is called the frontal cortex, or neocortex.

This is a highly developed network of circuits that gives us the capacity to think about the future and act accordingly. It allows us to make long-term goals based on foresight and reasoning. When activated, the neo-cortex also provides for learning, decision-making, impulse control, and emotional modulation.

We can divide the prefrontal cortex into two distinct parts. The left prefrontal cortex (LPFC) is linked to feelings of happiness and enthu-siasm. Research has found more activity in this area when people are smiling more, feeling optimistic, and showing positive emotions.

The right prefrontal cortex (RPFC) holds *negative* feelings such as fear, sadness, and anxiety. Fear helps alert us to danger, and the amygdala regulates how responsive we are to highly charged emotional events. If the RPFC is overactive and the LPFC is underactive, the amygdala can go into overdrive. Threatening thoughts can flood the brain with signals that lead to helplessness and despair.

About 40 to 50 percent of our happiness level is determined by genet-ics. This doesn't mean that our brain wiring is locked into place and that we are stuck obeying our genes' commands. The power of our own thoughts, the way we respond to stress, and our activities can move our "happiness meter" by as much as 40 percent.

The stress hormones cortisol and corticotropin-releasing factor (CRF) can damage neurons, leading to a decrease of cells in the LPFC. Chronic emotional stress is also toxic to neurons, which can lead to a decrease in total brain volume.

These changes hamper the brain's "positive outlook" portion, but allow the anxiety-driven RPFC to work harder. Therapies that involve forgiveness, letting go, and surrendering control can reduce the out-pouring of CRF that can reduce LPFC cell density and serotonin. Also, antidepressants may lower cortisol secretion.

If neurons have disappeared, one might suspect that bringing back happiness would not be possible. However, some research has suggested that SSRIs stimulate the growth of neural cells in both the hippocampus and prefrontal cortex. Brain-derived neurotrophic factor can stimulate dendrites between the cells to grow. These increase the flow of informa-tion between neurons and improve the brain's plasticity. Though it may take several weeks, antidepressants can also stimulate dendrite growth. Research has supported using cognitive behavioral therapy, exercise, and meditation to stimulate nerve cell and dendrite growth.

From the time we were conceived, "wires" in our brains were strung together to create a balance between fear and optimism. Along the way, due to life events and stressors, this wiring can be reconnected so it creates more caution, hypervigilance, and anxiety.

If networks in the brain's positive-outlook center of the LPFC become inhibited, the more primitive limbic system steps in as a backup. It's important to discover if, through therapy, the individual can harness his thoughts and behaviors to stimulate rewiring of the positive-outlook LPFC.

Making the prefrontal cortex the primary location of well-being once again frees the midbrain from seeking other sources of pleasure to improve one's mood. Factors that can improve our well-being and positive outlook include gratitude, self-confidence, compassion, forgiveness, hope (specifically belief or assurance of that hope), and healthy relationships.

Talk therapy is one way to learn how to put these factors to work in one's life. However, to support brain growth and plasticity, the individual with the addiction or eating disorder must *believe* in the process! Hope is a form of positive thinking about the future. Hope conquers our bonds of denial and resistance and brings us toward healing. A strong spiritual foundation and belief system improves our sense of hope. Without it, the final outcome relies on luck and chance.

Recovery from any addiction or eating disorder is often a very difficult, challenging, and drawn-out process. Long before any constructive ' therapy can begin, people must break through their denial and admit they have a problem.

Even after they accept that their behavior is inappropriate, many continue to resist getting the needed treatment. They may have a feeling that the addiction or disordered eating is not *that* severe, and it will go away if they just work harder to change their dysfunctional behavior.

If they do commit to treatment, too many times they only apply themselves to what they *think* recovery looks like. If the individual never connects with the final stage of recovery, which is emotional commitment and total surrender, the recovery will be fleeting. Too often people will either find themselves relapsing, switching disorders, or fighting their cravings tooth and nail for the rest of their lives.

If these issues are a problem for you, hopefully this chapter has given you a better sense of how events in your brain may be contributing to the addiction or eating disorder. Understanding the workings of your brain and its capacity for healing can give you a template for visualizing a healthy recovery, which can help you stick to a healthy new path.

 ## THE BRAIN FIX TOOLBOX

- If you have an addiction or eating disorder, it's important to realize that these problems can cause harmful changes in the brain that make recovery more difficult. Going through therapy or a treatment program—or taking medication such as antidepressants—can help rewire your brain to support a healthy new life.

- To shift your brain back to healthy thinking, it's crucial that you truly believe in the possibility that you can heal and change your behaviors. Believing in healing is mandatory.

- Be sure to find new ways to cope with stressors while you shed unhealthy old coping strategies such as disordered eating or a substance use. Many people who give these up simply switch to *other* unhealthy behaviors in an effort to cope with their stress.

19

Change Your Mind—and Behaviors—for Good

I ONCE HEARD A WELL-KNOWN sports nutritionist discuss the perfect diet to enhance athletic performance. After she described her inconvenient, expensive, and tasteless food plan, I asked how other dietitians could inspire any athlete to follow this boring and complex regimen. Her quick response was, "My job is to teach, theirs is to do."

I have worked in the field of nutrition, weight management, addictions, eating disorders, psychology, and exercise physiology for more than thirty years. After years of education, training, experience, and research, I feel confident in my ability to help anyone successfully lose weight, get fit, recover from an addiction, or conquer an eating disorder.

Though I acquired a lot of head knowledge through the years, my practice only took off and flourished when I owned up to the most important ingredient in making these changes: the process does not begin, continue, finish, or persist without a heavy dose of motivation.

Unlike the nutritionist above, my goal isn't just to preach my recommendations and consider my job finished. It's to show clients and readers *how* to make the changes that will keep their brain working at its peak. These aren't just onetime bursts of activity. These changes need to be lifelong. And since they require you to modify deeply held values like what you eat, how you spend your leisure time, and where you seek your sources of pleasure, sticking with these changes can be difficult.

Food does not become nutrition and start building health until it passes your lips. Muscles don't grow until you provide stress through resistance training. Recovery does not begin until you recognize you have a substance problem. The brain does not regenerate until you stimulate it through cognitive therapy. In other words, *nothing* happens without action. I always felt it was my job to encourage, motivate, and inspire others to stick to time-proven methods of achievement.

I've spent a great deal of my time working with individuals with eating disorders and drug addictions. Though these people have behaviors that are infamous for being difficult to change, in some sense, it's often *easy* to get them to take their lives in a new direction. That's because most of them have hit the proverbial "bottom."

At this point, they know they can't keep living the way they have been. They're tired of feeling sick and rudderless. They know that their death could be coming soon if they don't make permanent changes.

If you're merely unhealthy—say you have prediabetes or prehypertension—making these changes is harder. That's because many of the problems that raise your risk of brain-hurting conditions like diabetes, heart disease, and stroke don't make you feel bad! If you lower your cholesterol or blood pressure, odds are good that you're not going to feel better. You probably won't say to yourself, "Whew, I'm never inviting *that* crisis into my life again!" Your only immediate reward is that numbers on a blood pressure or cholesterol test will drop.

So when I talk to clients about making behavioral changes, I often focus on problems related to their behaviors that they can *see* and *feel*. I emphasize how good they'll look and feel if they shed extra weight. Their clothes will fit better, they'll get less winded while going on errands, and their joints will ache less.

This is how I developed an interest in discussing brain health. The threat of high blood pressure and cholesterol wasn't spurring older folks to grasp the importance of behavioral change. But when I talked to them about preserving their *brainpower*, they really sat up and took note. They wanted to preserve their memories and their ability to live on their own outside of a nursing home, which meant changing their diet and exercise habits.

So what will it take for *you* to make the permanent changes that will help you protect your brain?

Behavioral Change Step 1:
Modify Your Thinking to Change Your Health

After years of going to the same well, a peasant decided that she wanted wine instead. So she went to the well and lowered her bucket. No matter how many times she went to the well, no matter what time of day she went, no matter how many times she hauled up the bucket, all she found was water. Still, every time she set off to the well, she hoped that the bucket would bring up wine this time.

You've probably heard sayings or seen bumper stickers that point out the error of this kind of thinking:

- "Common sense dictates that when a lot of people try the same answer to the same problem and most of them fail, there is something wrong with their solution."
- "Keep doing what you have always done, and you will keep getting what you have always gotten."
- "Insanity is continually doing the same thing and expecting different results."

Many Americans follow a lifestyle that is specifically designed to deliver poor health! Smoking, getting minimal exercise, and eating a diet that's heavy on junk food and light on plant foods tends to lead to illness! If your activities and behaviors have led to poor health, sticking with these behaviors is going to provide more of the same results. *New* results require *new* choices.

You *cannot* enjoy lifelong brain health without making some or most of the changes in this book! Change is the defining moment when you decide to quit a bad habit or reach for a new goal. As one old joke teaches us, "How many psychologists does it take to change a lightbulb?" The answer is "One, but the lightbulb *must really want to change!*"

Change occurs when the pain of where you are—or probably someday will be—exceeds the pain to change. Many of the motivations that we think can bring about change are deceptive and fleeting. Criticism, threats, and warnings from other people might get you thinking about changing, but eventually this prodding falls on deaf ears.

Social or professional embarrassment may be motivating in the moment (like seeing yourself in swimwear for the first time at the beginning of the summer), but people easily forget and move on.

Other potential stimulators for change include someone paying you to reach a goal, having a desire for a new image, wanting to set an example for others, and joining a competition, but these are merely temporary diversions. Eventually you'll go back to your own ways.

Also, high blood sugar, high blood pressure, and high cholesterol *should* be enough reasons to take action. But the threat of diabetes, heart disease, and strokes often doesn't come to mind when people are choosing between a salad or a greasy hamburger. Even when people get a diagnosis of these problems, they often continue their lives as usual. Obesity, anxiety, depression, fatigue, and insomnia are uncomfortable states of being, but not so bad that people can't usually adapt to them and try to live their lives with them.

To reach perpetual change, one must incorporate elements that bring forth hope, companionship, and happiness, and that ultimately take care of your spiritual, relationship, and fulfillment needs, respectively. It all starts with changing your thinking.

Behavioral Change Step 2:
Turn the Dial Away from Denial

Here's a good acronym for DENIAL: Don't Even Notice I Am Lying.
People who tell themselves they don't need to change are
often lying to themselves without even realizing it.

Most people don't wake up and decide to quit smoking out of the blue. Or run a marathon. Experts on behavioral change know that people instead typically go through a series of stages that take them from *not* wanting to change to maintaining a change for years. This is called the Stages of Change model (also sometimes known as the transtheoretical model).

Here are the stages I've come to recognize in clients with substance issues (though this pattern applies to many of our behaviors):

- Sometimes we recognize there is a problem, but we simply do not want to do anything about it. We are in the *resistance* phase of change.
- When we recognize we have a problem and want to do something about it, but only want to change it *our* way, this is the *experimental* phase of change. Usually people employ quick, easy, magical, gimmicky techniques that have failed in the past and aren't evidence-based. This is akin to fad diets (or dropping the bucket into the well and hoping for wine this time!).
- Eventually we understand there is a tried-and-true method for making the change, and we decide to learn more about it. This is the *intellectual* phase of the change process. After a while we think we know everything there is to know about the problem and the solution. However, we're just talking the talk and still falling short of achievement.
- We stall because we are not practicing what we have learned. It is merely an act where we go through the motions, do what is expected of us, and become accountable. But we're not authentic. We fail to believe we can be successful or that we have to actually do what is asked of us. This is the *compliance* phase of change, and we will waver here until we develop self-efficacy and learn to walk the walk as well as just talk about change.
- Eventually we get to the stage of *emotional acceptance* and *commitment*. At this point we surrender and are finally willing to trust and believe in the method the experts are preaching and do what it takes to achieve it.

Behavioral Change Step 3:
Commit to Finding New Sources of Pleasure

*A pig and chicken were discussing how they could reward
the farmer who had cared for them so diligently over the past year.
The chicken suggested that they prepare a delicious breakfast
of bacon and eggs for him. To this the pig exclaimed, "That's fine
for you to suggest, because for you it is only participation.
For me, it would be total commitment."*

Finally making a decision to change is a big moment—but it is only the beginning. The hard work comes later. As a result, you need commitment to see this goal through. Doing so may require you to redefine how you see the things in your life that are pleasurable and painful.

The prime motivator of human behavior is to avoid pain and seek pleasure. It is that simple. It is how we are designed. Some people find pleasure in smoking. Some find it in television or snack cakes or illegal drugs. When it comes to pain, a big source of the pain that we try to avoid or cope with in our everyday lives is *stress*. We also tend to find that doing without those things that give us pleasure is painful.

Stress is a necessary and inevitable consequence of life. Unfortunately, we often fail to learn how to deal with stress in a healthy manner. Stress is not the big problem; it is how we *deal* with it that results in poor health and behavioral consequences.

For example, if I am filling out my taxes and discover I owe $2,000 instead of getting a return—which is stressful!—I reach into the freezer and grab a chocolate ice-cream bar. The unpleasant pain of funding the government is countered by the pleasure of a frozen treat.

The limbic system basically allows one to balance out unpleasant experiences with pleasant experiences. Take a group of a hundred monkeys and subject them to the same stressful situation of being cornered by a predator. Instinctively, all hundred monkeys will behave the same way. First they will scream, jump up and down, and show their teeth. Eventually they will become exhausted, and their next effort will be grooming. This behavior shows up as frantically removing tiny parasites from their bodies. To the primate, this is a pleasurable experience, which they revert to in times of stress. Even when they mate, though they initially appear to be attacking each other, eventually they start grooming each other, which equates into calming each other down.

We see this balance of pleasure and pain in people with eating disorders. Picture a young lady who's tightly restricting her food intake. She gets so hungry that she begins craving ice cream. She decides she will have just a small bite from the container, but it feels so good she wants to continue the pleasure. So she proceeds to have bowl after bowl, which is an example of bingeing. Soon her stomach hurts from the fullness and she feels guilt over having broken her resolve to strictly stick to her diet. She purges to relieve the pain, feels temporarily relieved, and promises to do a better job of sticking to her diet. It is only a matter of time before she experiences that same uncomfortable feeling that triggers her to repeat the binge-purge behavior.

Pain doesn't *have* to prompt you to seek immediate pleasure, though. We tend to regard pain as the ultimate enemy instead of seeing its value to us. Pain is a warning light telling you that you have an injury or other threat, and you need to deal with it. A system of receptors and memory banks are wired together to protect you from dangers that jeopardize your life.

We are also equipped with chemicals that work as natural painkillers to turn off the pain and trigger pleasure. Mankind has unfortunately discovered ways to artificially produce the same euphoria in the absence of pain, either through behaviors (like eating, gambling, or pornography) or drugs (like alcohol, cocaine, and opioids). No matter how hard we try to cultivate pleasure artificially and keep it coming our way, eventually the pleasure diminishes and the vexation returns.

The solution is to discover and harness ways to alleviate pain—or increase our pleasure—in a way that's healthy for our bodies.

- Start examining why you do the behaviors that aren't good for your health. If you smoke, why? Take a look at the moments when you light up. What prompted you to do so? Was it the pain of boredom? Stress? Similarly, take a moment to ask yourself, *Why am I reaching for this chocolate ice-cream bar because I'm agitated over my taxes? What else could I do to alleviate this stress?*
- Find ways to incorporate healthy elements into your life that you've avoided before—especially healthy eating and exercise. Make these as easy and appealing (in other words, not painful) as possible. Ease into exercise just a few minutes at a time. Go walking with friends so your conversation keeps you from thinking about the effort. Similarly, as you try to eat more fruits and vegetables, don't make yourself suffer through broccoli and Brussels sprouts if you don't really like them. Find alternatives that you enjoy. Use lots of herbs and spices to flavor your food and give it a kick.

Behavioral Change Step 4: Establish a Purpose

Henry Ford had accumulated a vast fortune,
but when someone asked him how much more he
wanted, he said, "Just a little bit more."

Abraham Maslow created a hierarchy of basic human needs; the lower levels had to be achieved before progressing further. The first tier is composed of the basic requirements for survival and safety such as air, food, water, clothing, and shelter.

Once these needs are met, the next groupings are love and social belonging, as we have an innate need to experience intimacy and long-lasting friendships. The top of the hierarchy is the need to do the things for which you are best suited and to recognize your personal strengths and virtues. This requires feeling self-worth, respect, and fulfillment.

Many of us act as though we could find fulfillment if we had enough money, beauty, intelligence, popularity, education, freedom, and youth. None of these possessions completely and permanently meet our needs because they are open-ended (we always want more) or eventually fade.

Instead, look around you and find the good things in your life that can bring you pleasure if you recognize them. What skills do you have that you aren't fully utilizing? How would you like to be spending your time differently? What issues are going on in your life that make you think less of yourself?

Appreciating the gifts you've been given can help quell stress, depression, and other sources of pain in your daily life and provide you with a source of pleasure you hadn't previously realized. If you need help recognizing these things, finding a spiritual outlet may be useful. So may getting out of your house and volunteering for a worthy cause or spending time with a mental health counselor or therapist.

Behavioral Change Step 5: Become Goal Oriented

Achieving fulfillment is a tall order that involves many smaller steps along the way. These are your *goals*. Your goals should be personal and relevant and agree with your values. All goals should be formulated to create *internal* satisfaction rather than *external* recognition. They should be something you achieve rather than conquer. They should have long-term importance for you, and they should make your spiritual and social life more meaningful.

It is a good idea to break up each goal into small, clear, and concise steps. Each step within those goals should be specific, and you should have a reasonable chance of attaining it. When people set their goals on material incentives alone (like making more money or buying a new car), they are likely to get used to this reward and want something more, something bigger, or something faster (as in Henry Ford's case).

Set your goals to accomplishments that give you hope, make you feel better about yourself, or give your life new meaning. Be sure to set goals that make you stretch, but offer a good chance of success, so you don't have to deal with the painful disappointment of failure.

In short, goals should be SMART:

- **Specific:** You know exactly what you hope to achieve and how to get there.
- **Measurable:** You can see when you've accomplished each goal or step within a goal.
- **Attainable:** Making the changes within the goal is within your grasp.
- **Realistic:** On a similar note, your goals shouldn't require resources that you don't have or can't obtain.
- **Timely:** Attach a reasonable deadline for achieving your goal.

While you're chasing your goals, also be sure to:

- Make changes gradually. It's not realistic to completely overturn your normal life in one fell swoop.
- Try the easiest changes first. This gets you used to change and gives you successful examples to prove to yourself that you can change.
- Accept lapses. The Stages of Change theory I mentioned earlier recognizes that people don't move smoothly to a successful change then stay there. Relapses do occur, and when they do, it's important that you steer yourself back to your goal behavior. Don't get stuck in a lapse.

- If you feel like you need help, seek it out. Find a mentor who's stopped smoking, gotten off drugs, or lost weight and kept it off. Ask your family and friends to support your effort.

Behavioral Change Step 6:
Take a Personal Inventory

A personal evaluation or inventory is necessary to identify your personal strengths and virtues. We must be absolutely honest with ourselves. When working with clients, I sometimes find it useful to tell them that I have a PhD in nutrition. This shows that I've spent years acquiring information. However, my clients have a PhD in *themselves*. They have the quintessential collection of information about what they can, can't, and would be willing to do to achieve their goals.

While taking a personal inventory of what you're all about, ask yourself these questions:

- Do you need to see results quickly? Or are you able to work for some time toward a goal without seeing immediate results?
- Are you optimistic that things will work out well, or do you usually fear the worst?
- Do you have a lot of energy to apply to goals, or are you already distracted and taxed by your other obligations?
- Can you tolerate risks, or do you need routines and security?

While you're taking this inventory of your personality, make a trip to your healthcare provider and ask for an assessment of your *body*. This should include tests, lab work, screenings, and various other measurements to establish a baseline for comparison. It is useful to have set of guidelines that clarify what is considered healthy and achievable for your age and gender.

Even if you aren't motivated by falling blood pressure and cholesterol numbers, seeing these change over time can help remind you that you're making health improvements and sticking with them.

Behavioral Change Step 7: Look on the Bright Side

Long ago, a shoe salesman was assigned to
a backwoods region of the world. After only a few days,
he wrote back to the company, demanding to return home
because no one in the remote villages wore shoes.
An upbeat fellow salesman was sent in his place.
He immediately wrote back, "Send all the shoes you
can spare. No one here wears shoes
and everyone needs them!"

It is amazing how the attitude of many in today's world is geared toward the negative. Traffic lights are called "stoplights," even though they are green an equal amount of the time and we could just as easily call them "go lights." Weather forecasters report precipitation as the percent chance of rain rather than the possibility of sunshine. We are made aware of every negative happenstance over and over again by the media.

Most of the time our perceptions and the way we evaluate our circumstances determine whether a given event will appear to be a positive or a negative to us. Midway through a race, if you look ahead, you may feel a sense of discouragement if you keep thinking of the people who are beating you. Take a moment to look behind you, and you may see an even *larger* number trying to catch up with you. Better yet, look to the right or left and see all the spectators who didn't even commit to run that distance! Climb a mountain and you may become fatigued looking ahead to see how far you need to climb. But look behind you and feel grateful for how far you have come!

Instead of dwelling on these common obstacles to change, seek out solutions to them, and focus on your creativity in getting them behind you!

- Lack of time
- Inconvenience
- Cost
- Pain and discomfort involved

- Boredom, monotony
- Too many restrictions
- Few immediate rewards

Few phenomena on Earth can waste your time and energy as efficiently as negativity can. See yourself getting better each day and use your mind to visualize where you want to be and how things will be when you get there.

Believe that your plan for change will be successful. Having an attitude of self-confidence is actually more important than knowing all there is to know about how to accomplish the goal! A sense of optimism can come from:

- Seeing reasons why you can instead of reasons you can't
- Looking at things not as what they are, but what they could be

Don't just tell it to yourself—proclaim it to the world around you, too! Sixty-five percent of what we say about ourselves is transmitted by our clothes and body language. Make sure your teeth are clean, your breath is fresh, and you practice good posture.

Elements of self-confidence include:

- Making eye contact
- Keeping a broad smile
- Speaking up
- Enunciating your words
- Having a firm handshake and a powerful vocabulary

Practice gratitude and enthusiasm at every opportunity: call people by their name, meet and speak to everyone in the room, broadcast good news, bury bad news, give a good word or none at all, and make others feel important. Whenever you leave a person, ask yourself, *Does that person feel better because I have entered their life?*

Say an acquaintance runs into you and asks, "How are you?" If you answer "Not so well," you make both you and the acquaintance feel down. When you respond, "I feel great!" you tend to pick yourself up and allow the acquaintance and anyone in listening range to feel your positive outpouring.

When you attract people with your positive outlook, they will be comfortable getting closer so they can learn more about you. It is more about your demeanor, charm, and self-confidence than your looks.

Behavioral Change Step 8:
Use Your Imagination as a Road Map

Buddhism is not a belief system or someone you pray to. The point of Buddhism is that it's a vehicle, much like a raft that takes you from one shore to the other. It is a method of enlightenment that shows us the way.

The twelve steps of addiction programs are also a road map composed of fundamental moral principles that provide insight into how to break the bonds of addiction. Self-help books, motivational speakers, the Plate Diet (in which you cover portions of your plate with certain types of food), and the laws of the major religions of the world are all templates to guide us on the path toward betterment.

Animals know how to survive without being taught how, but without a creative imagination, they cannot conceive of trying to better their way of life. Humans, however, are blessed with the gift of a creative imagination. With this imagination we are capable of achieving a great deal if we can crystallize our thinking and devise strategies to obtain our goals.

Envision yourself living a healthy life. If you want to break free from drug use, if you want to be fit, if you want to be mentally sharp deep into your senior years, just picture yourself doing it! Once you have this image in mind, start constructing a road map that will take you from where you are to where this goal awaits you.

Behavioral Change Step 9: Break Out of a Rut

A woman who was entertaining friends at a dinner party tells the story of how she prepared the most delicious roast. The hostess stated that she cooked the roast equally divided into two pans. She wasn't sure why this was so important, but her mother had always prepared it this way. Upon quizzing her mom about the reason for this practice, her mom replied she didn't know, but that is what her mother had always done. Finally, when Grandma

was asked to provide an explanation she exclaimed, "For heaven's
sake, I cooked the roast in two pans because I never had
a pan big enough to hold the whole thing!"

Allow yourself to see the world differently. The field of medicine wouldn't have achieved the successes we enjoy if doctors had clung to the old ways of doing things.

Bleeding and forced purging used to be common practices to relieve the body of various mysterious factors that triggered internal illness. These are now seen to be harmful in many cases. Long ago, mankind saw little need to separate its sewage from its drinking water. When sanitary disposal of human waste and safe drinking water were introduced, human longevity took a major upswing.

Surgeons used to see the tonsils and appendix as merely gathering places for unidentified pathogens, thus they lopped them out for little reason. Today we recognize the contribution of these glands as critical to our immune system. In the 1920s, Joseph Goldberger stepped away from treating pellagra as an infection and determined that it was really due to a niacin deficiency in the diet that was easily corrected by supplementing with vitamin B3. Even as recently as the 1990s, Australian physicians recognized that chronic ulcers were caused by the bacterium *H. pylori* and recommended treating it with antibiotics.

See what kind of changes you can enjoy in your own life by seeing new ways of fixing problems! Perhaps the concerns in your life aren't caused by the factors you'd always assumed. You may be able to make big changes by applying energy to the *true* causes of what's bothering you. If chronic stressors keep sending you to the familiar comforts of junk food, root them out and try creative new solutions to solve them.

Behavioral Change Step 10:
Recognize Stumbling Blocks

Tom Sawyer observed a cart in the open square containing
watermelons. He decided that when the proprietor was not looking,
he would sneak up and steal one. Without hesitating, he grabbed a
melon and ran behind a building so he could consume his prize.

But upon taking a bite, he immediately realized the error of his ways,
and quickly returned the melon to the owner and stole a riper one.

Of course, I don't want you to actually *steal* anything. But I do urge you to be flexible and capable of changing your plans. And don't get stuck in the stage of turning your problems over and over without making a move to solve them. I call this "analysis paralysis." At some point you will need to find the confidence to proceed. Sometimes we can get stuck in the information-accumulating process and never feel bold enough to strike out, take risks, and move forward.

All too often, we sit and wait to make a change because the timing just doesn't feel right. Perhaps we feel too busy or stressed right now to make a change. We'll just wait until later when we have more resources to apply to the change. This is often a cop-out. It's when we're at the most stressful points that we discover our strengths. When things feel impossible, we can find our best opportunities!

A few thoughts that I find inspiring along these lines are:

- Work harder, and it becomes harder to surrender.
- Push yourself beyond what you can do and something beautiful happens inside you.
- Good is not enough if better is possible.
- The price is worth the prize.

Behavioral Change Step 11: Persevere

Two frogs fell into a bowl of cream. One thought the chances of
escape were impossible, so he gave up the will to survive and drowned.
The other was determined to think of a way out. She swam and thought,
swam and thought, and swam and thought some more. Eventually the
cream was churned into butter and she stepped safely out of the bowl.

If you ever feel the urge to give up on your goal, review the consequences of what will happen if you quit. What kind of life will you be returning to? What progress will you lose if you give up on what you have already achieved?

To improve your odds of sticking to your target:

- Make yourself accountable. Tell others what you're hoping to accomplish (losing weight, being more socially active, going to counseling to learn to deal with anxiety, sticking to a support group). Ask them to encourage you to stick with it and not quit.
- Make sure your goals are measurable, and check regularly on your progress.
- Focus on the positive gains you've made.
- Display reminders of your successes (like photos of you at your new weight, finisher's ribbons from run/walks, or chips or medallions from AA marking your abstinence).
- Repeat your healthy decisions over and over and over. Doing the same thing repeatedly creates habits and instinctive behavior.
- Always allow yourself time to meet your goals. These need to be high on your list and they cannot take a backseat. Most of the strategies in this book are *not* a time drain, and with deliberate choice you can weave them seamlessly into your day. Until you get to this point, make the time for them. When it comes to the important things in life, are we ever really too busy? When you decided to have a baby, did you reserve time to raise him or her? When you fell in love, did you set your job obligations aside to make more time for your relationship? When you obtained a career opportunity, did you say no because it would spoil your schedule?

Behavioral Change Step 12:
Practice the Qualities of an Achiever

A young boy wanted desperately to go out on the family's boat. His mother told him that he must first be able to swim the width of their pool. He practiced and improved until he got the courage to attempt the distance in the deep end. With his entire family watching, he took off and swam until he got to the middle of the pool. Then he panicked. His choices were to return to his starting point and be left with the knowledge that he could not accomplish the task (a form of learned helplessness), or he could struggle the same distance to the

opposite side and gain the confidence that he could repeat
the journey if need be (a form of self-efficacy).

Here are the qualities of an achiever. When you incorporate these into your life, you can conquer the unhealthy habits that have been dragging down your physical and mental health:

1. An achiever has vision. Achievers dream of things that haven't been and believe they are possible.
2. An achiever has the courage to risk failure, knowing that setbacks are lessons to learn from.
3. An achiever understands his weaknesses and improves upon them.
4. An achiever relies on honest feedback and constant self-assessment.
5. An achiever adjusts her thought processes as well as her behaviors to produce a total approach to improve her self-confidence.
6. An achiever actively creates a life of balance, moderation, and simplicity; these values help improve health and lifestyle management.
7. An achiever views other achievers as partners who provide challenges and the chance to improve.
8. An achiever understands that adhering to a plan is like riding a roller coaster with its many ups and downs. You have to accept both the good and the bad.

Behavioral Change Step 13: See the Upside of Failures

It's important to have goals and the drive to attain them, but be sure to leave room for flexibility and adaptability. If you fail—and sometimes this is inevitable because there are so many challenges that are completely beyond our control—do not condemn yourself. These moments offer opportunities for healing. Sometimes we are made better, not bitter, by lack of success. Find some humor in your failure and do not take yourself so seriously. It is important to forge forward and tell yourself that it's better to lose the battle but win the war.

Figure out what caused the stumble and find a solution so it doesn't set you back again. One saying I like, which is credited to Karen Hendricks, is, "Successful people are so labeled because they have a string of accomplishments to their names. Interestingly, they also have a string of failures. The successful person has converted these setbacks to positive experiences that become springboards to their success."

Behavioral Change Step 14:
Be Ready to Hold Your Ground

You've probably been practicing unhealthy habits and behaviors for many years—probably even decades. Eventually you'll become accustomed to the new healthy habits you're adopting. But you may long hear the call to return to your previous ways. Remember that maintaining your new behaviors takes continual effort—though eventually the energy you must expend should decrease.

Imagine tying one end of a bungee cord around your waist and the other end to an immovable post. Then you start walking away from the post. Initially it is easy to put distance between yourself and the post, but eventually the tug backward is hard to overcome. If you lose your footing, the recoil will be quick and strong. But when you hold yourself in that position of greatest resistance for a long time, the elasticity in the bungee cord weakens to the point where it eventually loses its power over you. The same is true when you walk away from your old behaviors.

Behavioral Change Step 15:
Reflect on Your Success

Along your journey toward better physical and mental health, you may overcome the greatest pains and anguishes of your life. You may stand up to your personal demons that have always been apart of your existence and finally conquer them once and for all.

The finest, and hardest, thing we human beings can do is to become free of our own special enemy, the traitor within who wants to hold us back. Very few people ever do this. But you can, and you're well on your way to getting started. The strength and pride that now belong to you will always be there when you need them.

Sam Walton's Rules for Building a Business

You may not know who Sam Walton is, but you've surely been in one of his stores. Walmart is now a familiar part of the landscape in towns and cities across the country, and the stores stand as a testament to Sam's foresight, creativeness, and drive.

You can create a life that honors your inner values and strengths by following a few lessons from Sam Walton's rulebook:

- Commit: believe in your goals more than anything else.
- Share your profits with all your associates and treat them as partners. (In terms of the "profits" of improving your health, consider serving as a mentor to other people who are seeking to make healthy changes.)
- Motivate, challenge, and encourage your partners to set high goals.
- Appreciate everything your partners do for the business. (If your family and friends are supporting and encouraging you, show your gratitude.)
- Celebrate your success: show enthusiasm and have fun.
- Listen to your partners, figure out ways to get them talking, and force good ideas to bubble up within. (If your friends and loved ones want to help you, pay attention.)
- Make good on all your mistakes. Do not make excuses but apologize. Stand behind everything you do.

20

A Final Note:
Go Nuts and Heal Your Brain

YOU CAN LEARN A LOT about what your brain needs by examining the lowly walnut. At first glance, the raw tree nut looks like it's covered with a thin coating not unlike our skin. Once you peel back the outer layer and discover a hard shell, you'll see that it remarkably resembles the human skull.

If you keep digging further and split the shell in half, you will find a thin membrane surrounding the nut that is tightly attached to the shell. Our brain, coincidentally, is encased in a thin outer membrane that holds it in place within the cranial vault. With one half of the shell removed, you'll see that the edible portion of the nut itself is divided into two halves, with a noticeably undulating surface. Similarly, the human brain is divided into a left and right hemisphere, with alternating sulci (grooves) and gyri (raised areas between the grooves) creating a convoluted appearance.

But our brains have more than just their similar structure in common with the walnut. You can think of walnuts as a hard-shelled fruit that's *packed* with essential nutrients that support brain health.

You'll find:

- **Carbohydrates** to provide energy for the brain to heal. This energy is packaged with fiber (two grams of the stuff per ounce of walnuts) to maintain a slow and continuous release of energy. This time-released effect keeps our liver saturated with emergency stores of sugar for later use in the evening when our brain heals.

- **Fatty acids**—in the form of alpha-linolenic acid—that act as a precursor for the highly valued omega-3s that are important for brain signaling and structural composition. Walnuts also contain shorter-chain fatty acids that offer benefits for your thinking ability that are similar to omega 3s.
- **Protein.** The 12 to 20 percent protein content is extraordinary for supplying the precursors for neurotransmitters, which play a major role in communication and mood stabilization.
- **Vitamin E.** Walnuts contain a generous supply of vitamin E in both the tocopherol and the highly neuroprotective tocotrienol forms.
- **Minerals** such as calcium, potassium, boron, manganese, magnesium, copper, zinc, and iron. These enhance electrical conductivity in neurons.
- **Valuable B vitamins** (such as B_1, B_2, B_3, and B_6). These play a role in creating neurotransmitters and enzyme systems.
- **Antioxidant and anti-inflammatory phytonutrients** such as phenolic acids, flavonoids, and tannins.
- And finally, an *absence* **of not-so-healthy components** that you find in so many other foods today, such as saturated and trans fat, artificial ingredients, and caffeine.

One reason to want to heal your brain is to achieve a feeling of happiness. Walnuts can help here, too. They contain a chemical called pyrazine that triggers the pleasure center of the brain. When this chemical is roasted, an alkylpyrazine compound is formed, producing an aroma. This smell travels through the olfactory system to areas of the brain that detect pleasure.

We've also previously learned about the importance of good blood circulation for brain health. Walnuts can help improve blood vessel health by supporting the cells lining their surface, stabilizing blood sugar, and lowering bad LDL cholesterol.

The research on the benefits of walnuts has been so supportive that the FDA allows the nuts one of the few permitted health claims. A 1.5-ounce serving of walnuts each day—which is twenty halves—as part of a low-cholesterol and low-saturated fat diet without increasing your calorie intake can help reduce your risk of coronary heart disease.

The nutritional advice in this book was pieced together by assessing the current scientific literature that supports brain healing. There was no intention to promote any particular diet or philosophy. Yet on inspection, you might have observed that the Brain Fix's eating recommendations clearly resemble the Mediterranean diet.

Followers of this food plan enjoy generous amounts of fruits and vegetables, omega-3 and monounsaturated fatty acids found in olive oil and fish, and high-fiber whole grains and beans, while at the same time minimizing dairy products and red meat.

Studies support that following this guideline helps lower rates of depression. One reason is that olive oil is believed to improve binding of serotonin to receptors. Evidence also suggests that the Mediterranean diet relieves mild cognitive impairments.

The target audience for this book is anyone who has a brain. We can *all* benefit from brain-healing efforts. I often used examples derived from the addiction and eating-disorder populations to help explain the fundamentals. It is possible that people who struggle with these conditions will be especially likely to follow the recommendations if the pain of where they are is greater than the pain of changing.

For the *remainder* of you possessing brains, one obstacle facing you when making changes is that the results will not be immediate. However, the fundamental principle in engaging in change is to keep it simple, and the Brain Fix approach is very straightforward. In essence, you'll just:

- Make sure that complex carbohydrates such as fruits, vegetables, and whole grains account for about half of your calories.
- To get as many phytonutrients as possible, have a variety of at least three fruits and five servings of darkly pigmented vegetables daily.
- Get 25 to 35 grams of fiber per day.
- Eat four to five meals and snacks each day consisting of complex carbohydrates, protein, and a small amount of fat.
- Minimize simple sugars and reduce or eliminate artificial sweeteners.

- Have two 4- to 6-ounce servings of cold-water fatty fish such as salmon or tuna each week or 2 grams of fish-oil capsules daily to supply the daily amount of omega-3 fatty acids.
- Limit saturated and trans-fatty acids from foods such as red meat and commercially baked snacks.
- A multivitamin and mineral tablet, along with plenty of sunshine and 1,000 milligrams of calcium, will provide additional insurance that you're getting the needed micronutrients.
- Drink two quarts of water per day and work at keeping your caffeine consumption low.
- Get twenty to sixty minutes of exercise or physical activity daily, at least at a moderate level.
- Yoga will not only improve your flexibility and relaxation, it can also incorporate meditation. Practice it frequently.
- It is imperative that you make whatever adjustments, short of taking medication, that are necessary to ensure seven to nine hours of quality sleep.

Finally, even though scientists cannot trap spirituality under a microscope to prove its importance, I believe it to be the *most* crucial part of brain healing. Fostering a spirit of hope, belief, self-esteem, forgiveness, compassion, gratitude, altruism, and strong relationships is the essence of achieving true happiness.

Life is a journey filled with riveting ups and tumultuous downs. Navigating that journey is challenging. Having hope and healthy relationships provides you with a guiding mechanism for structure, direction, and the motivation to adhere to any new strategy that you design.

References

Chapter 2: Know Your Brain's Worst Enemies

Almeida, O. P., et al. 24-month effect of smoking cessation on cognitive function and brain structure in later life. *Neuroimage* (2011) 55: 1480–89.

Alzheimer's Association. Alzheimer's Disease Facts and Figures, 2011, http://www.alz.org/downloads/Facts_Figures_2011.pdf.

Alzheimer's Association. Common Types of Dementia, http://www.alz.org/alzheimers-disease_related_diseases.asp.

Amen, D. G. *Making a Good Brain Great*. New York: Three River Press, 2005, 24–31.

American Diabetes Association, Diabetes Statistics, http://www.diabetes.org/diabetes-basics/diabetes-statistics/.

Aubry, M., et al. Summary and agreement statement of the first international conference on concussion in sport: Vienna recommendations for the improvement of safety and health of athletes who may suffer concussive injuries. *British Journal of Sports Medicine* (2002) 36: 6–10.

Bartsch, A., et al. Manifestation of early brain recovery associated with abstinence from alcoholism. *Brain* (2007) 130: 36–47.

Beluche, I., Carrière, I., Ritchie, K., and Ancelin, M-L. A prospective study of diurnal cortisol and cognitive function in community-dwelling elderly people. *Psychological Medicine* (2010) 40: 1039–49.

Bowen, A. P. Second impact syndrome: A rare, catastrophic, preventable complication of concussion in young athletes. *Journal of Emergency Nursing* (2003) 29: 287–89.

Centers for Disease Control and Prevention. Concussion, http://www.cdc.gov/concussion/signs_symptoms.html.

Centers for Disease Control and Prevention. How many people have TBI? http://www.cdc.gov/traumaticbraininjury/statistics.html.

Centers for Disease Control and Prevention. Illegal drug use, http://www.cdc.gov/nchs/fastats/druguse.htm.

Chowdhury, U., and Lask, B. Clinical implications of brain imaging in eating disorders. *Psychiatric Clinics of North America* (2001) 24: 227–34.

Chowdhury, U., Gordon, I., and Lask, B. Neuroimaging and anorexia nervosa. *Journal of the American Academy of Child and Adolescent Psychiatry* (2001) 40: 738.

Crichton, G. E., et al. Metabolic syndrome, cognitive performance, and dementia. *Journal of Alzheimer's Disease* (October 4, 2011).

Ellison, A. R., et al. Eating disorders. In H. W. Hoak et al., eds., *Neurobiology in the Treatment of Eating Disorders.* New York: John Wiley and Sons, 1998, 255–69.

Epel, E. S., et al. Accelerated telomere shortening in response to life stress. *Proceedings of the National Academy of Sciences* (2004) 101: 17312–15.

Fried, P., Watkinson, B., James, D., and Gray, R. Current and former marijuana use: Preliminary findings of a longitudinal study of effects on IQ in young adults. *Canadian Medical Association Journal* (2002) 166: 887–91.

Gallinat, J., et al. Smoking and structural brain deficits: A volumetric MR investigation. *European Journal of Neuroscience* (2006) 24: 1744–50.

Ghosh, D., Mishra, M. K., Das, S., Kaushik, D. K., and Basu, A. Tobacco carcinogen induces microglial activation and subsequent neuronal damage. *Journal of Neurochemistry* (2009) 110: 1070–81.

Henneman, W. J., et al. Hippocampal atrophy rates in Alzheimer disease: Added value over whole brain volume measures. *Neurology* (2009) 72: 999–1007.

Holley, M. F. Meth and marijuana: Interaction between marijuana use and methamphetamine addiction. Mothers Against Methamphetamine, http://www.mamasite.net.

Iverson, G. L. Outcome from mild traumatic brain injury. *Current Opinion in Psychiatry* (2005) 1: 301–17.

Kaye, W., et al. New insights into symptoms and microcircuit function of anorexia nervosa. *Nature Reviews Neuroscience* (2009) 10: 573–84.

Kim, S. Y., Breslow, R. A., Ahn, J., and Salem, N., Jr. Alcohol consumption and fatty acid intakes in the 2001–2002 National Health and Nutrition Examination Survey. *Alcohol: Clinical and Experimental Research* (2007) 31: 1407–14.

Kuchibhotla, K. V., Lattarulo, C. R., Hyman, B. T., and Bacskai, B. J. Synchronous hyperactivity and intercellular calcium waves in astrocytes in Alzheimer mice. *Science* (2009) 323: 1211–15.

Kühn, S., Schubert, F., and Gallinat, J. Reduced thickness of medial orbitofrontal cortex in smokers. *Biological Psychiatry* (2010) 68: 1061–65.

Manev, H. Putative role of neuronal 5-lipoxygenases in an aging brain. *FASEB Journal* (2000) 14: 1464–69.

McEwen, B. S. Protective and damaging effects of stress mediators: Central role of the brain. *Dialogues in Clinical Neuroscience* (2006) 8: 367–81.

McGuire, P., and Atakan, A. Brain scans pinpoint cannabis mental health risk. International Cannabis and Mental Health Conference, April 2007.

Morrison, P. D., et al. Disruption of frontal theta coherence by Δ(9)-tetrahydrocannabinol is associated with positive psychotic symptoms. *Neuropsychopharmacology* (2011) 36:827–36.

Naqvil, N. H., Rudrauf, D., Damasio, H., and Bechara, A. Damage to the insula disrupts addiction to cigarette smoking. *Science* (2007) 315: 531–34.

Patton, G. C., et al. Cannabis use and mental health in young people: Cohort study. *BMJ* (2002) 235: 1195–98.

Paul, C. A. Drinking alcohol shrinks the brain: Even moderate consumption reduced brain volume, study found. American Academy of Neurology, Boston, May 2, 2007.

Pollice, C., Kaye, W. H., Greeno, C. G., and Weltzin, T. E. Relationship of depression, anxiety and obsessionality to state of illness in anorexia nervosa. *International Journal of Eating Disorders* (1997) 21: 367–76.

Salvemine, D. Blocking potent oxidant could prevent morphine tolerance. *Journal of Clinical Investigation*, November 2007.

Stranahan, A. M., et al. Diabetes impairs hippocampal function through glucocorticoid-mediated effects on new and mature neurons. *Nature Neuroscience* (2008) 11: 309–17.

Uz, T., et al. Glucocorticoids stimulate inflammatory 5-lipoxygenase gene expression and protein translocation in the brain. *Journal of Neurochemistry* (1999) 73: 694–99.

Walker, J. M., et al. Chronic opioid use is a risk factor for the development of central sleep apnea and ataxic breathing. *Journal of Clinical Sleep Medicine* (2007) 15: 455–61.

Whalley, L. J., Fox, H. C., Deary, I. J., and Starr, J. M. Childhood IQ, smoking and cognitive change from age 11 to 64 years. *Addictive Behaviors* (2005) 30: 77–88.

Whitmer, R. A., Gunderson, E. P., Barrett-Connor, E., Quesenberry, C. P., Jr., and Yaffe, K. Obesity in middle age and future risk of dementia: A 27-year longitudinal population-based study. *BMJ* (2005) 330: 1360.

Whitmer, R. A., Karter, A. J., Yaffe, K., Quesenberry, C. P., and Selby, J. V. Hypoglycemic episodes and risk of dementia in older patients with type 2 diabetes mellitus. *JAMA* (2009) 201: 1565–72.

Yucel, M., et al. Regional brain abnormalities associated with long-term heavy cannabis use. *Archives of General Psychiatry* (2008) 65: 694–701.

Zhao, L., et al. Insulin degrading enzymes a downstream target of insulin receptor signaling cascade: Implications for Alzheimer's disease intervention. *Neuroscience* (2004) 24: 11120–26.

Zipursky, R. B., Lambe, E. K., Kapur, S., and Mikulis, D. J. Cerebral gray matter and white matter volume deficits in adolescent girls with anorexia nervosa. *Journal of Pediatrics* (1996) 129: 794–803.

Chapter 3: Antioxidants

Albanes, D., et al. Alpha-tocopherol and beta-carotene supplements and lung cancer incidence in the alpha-tocopherol, beta-carotene cancer prevention study: Effects of baseline characteristics and study compliance. *Journal of the National Cancer Institute* (1996) 88: 1560–70.

American Cancer Society. Cancer Facts and Figures, 2011.

American Heart Association. Heart Disease and Stroke Statistics—2011 Update. *Circulation*, February 1, 2011.

Benjamin, J., et al. Double-blind placebo-controlled, crossover trial of inositol treatment for panic disorders. *American Journal of Psychiatry* (1995) 152: 1084–86.

Benzie, I. Evolutoin of dietary antioxidants. *Comparative Biochemistry and Physiology* (2003) 136: 113–26.

Carr, A., and Frei, B. Does vitamin C act as a pro-oxidant under physiological conditions? *FASEB Journal* 13:1007–24.

Cavazzoni, M., Barogi, S., Baracca, A., Parenti Castelli, G., and Lenaz, G. The effect of aging and an oxidative stress on peroxide levels and the mitochondrial membrane potential in isolated rat hepatocyte. *FEBS Letters* (1999) 449: 54–56.

Centers for Disease Control and Prevention. State-specific trends in fruit and vegetable consumption among adults: United States, 2000–2009. *Morbidity and Mortality Weekly Report*, September 10, 2010.

Colbert, L. H., et al. Physical activity, exercise, and inflammatory markers in older adults: Findings from the Health, Aging and Body Composition Study. *Journal of the American Geriatrics Society* (2004) 52: 1098–1104.

Crowe, F. L., et al. Fruit and vegetable intake and mortality from ischaemic heart disease: Results from the European Prospective Investigation into Cancer and Nutrition (EPIC)-Heart study. *European Heart Journal* (2011) 32 (10): 1235–43.

Cutler, R. G. Oxidative stress profiling: Part I; Its potential importance in the optimization of human health. *Annals of the New York Academy of Science* (2005) 1055: 93–136.

Dhawan, S., Kapil, R., and Singh, B. Formulation development and systemic optimization of solid lipid nanoparticles of quercetin for improved brain delivery. *Journal of Pharmacy and Pharmacology* (2011) 63: 342–51.

Empana, J. P., et al. Contributions of depressive mood and circulating inflammatory markers to coronary heart disease in healthy European men: The Prospective Epidemiological Study of Myocardial Infarction (PRIME). *Circulation* (2005) 111: 2299–305.

Fisher, A.E.O., and Naughton, D. P. Iron supplements: The quick fix with long-term consequences. *Nutrition Journal* (2004) 3: 2.

Fisher, A.E.O., and Naughton, D. P. Vitamin C contributes to inflammation via radical generating mechanisms: A cautionary note. *Medical Hypotheses* (2003) 61: 657–60.

Gregersen, G., et al. Oral supplementation of myoinositol: Effects on peripheral nerve function in human diabetics and on the concentration in plasma, erythrocytes, urine and muscle tissue in human diabetics and normals. *Acta Neurologica Scandinavica* (1983) 67: 164–71.

Guarente, L., et al. Cellular degeneration and disease. Thirty-ninth Annual Meeting of the American Society for Cell Biology, Washington, DC, December 11–15, 1999.

Han, Y. N., Ryu, S. Y., and Han, B. H. Antioxidant activity of resveratrol closely correlates with its monoamineoxidase-A inhibitory activity. *Archives of Pharmacal Research* 13: 132–35.

He, F. J., Nowson, C. A., and MacGregor, G. A. Fruit and vegetable consumption and stroke: Meta-analysis of cohort studies. *Lancet* (2006) 367: 320–26.

He, F. J., Nowson, C. A., Lucas M., and MacGregor, G. A. Increased consumption of fruit and vegetables is related to a reduced risk of coronary heart disease: Meta-analysis of cohort studies. *Journal of Human Hypertension* (2007) 21: 717–28.

Heo, H. J., and Lee, C. Y. Protective effects of quercetin and vitamin C against oxidative stress-induced neurodegeneration. *Journal of Agricultural and Food Chemistry* (2004) 52: 7514–17.

Hsuai, G., et al. A potent antioxidant, lycopene, affords neuroprotection against microglia activation and focal cerebral ischemia in rats. *In Vivo* (2004) 18: 351–56.

Hu, H. L., et al. Antioxidants may contribute in the fight against ageing: An in vitro model. *Mechanisms of Ageing and Development* (2000) 121 (1–3): 217–30.

Joseph, J. A., et al. Grape juice, berries and walnuts affect brain aging and behavior. *Journal of Nutrition* (2009) 139: 18135–75.

Joseph, J., and Nadeau, D. *The Color Code: A Revolutionary Eating Plan for Optimum Health.* New York: Hyperion, 2002.

Joshipura, K. J., et al. The effect of fruit and vegetable intake on risk for coronary heart disease. *Annals of Internal Medicine* (2001) 134: 1106–14.

Liu, S., et al. A prospective study of fruit and vegetable intake and the risk of type 2 diabetes in women. *Diabetes Care* 27: 2993–96

National Academy of Sciences, Institute of Medicine—Food and Nutrition Board. Dietary reference intake for vitamin C, vitamin E, selenium and carotenoids. *University of California Wellness Letter*, 2000.

Penland, J. G. Dietary boron, brain function, and cognitive performance. *Environmental Health Perspectives* (1994) 102 (Suppl.): 65–72.

Penland, J. G. The importance of boron nutrition for brain and psychological function. *Biological Trace Element Research* (1998) 66: 299–317.

Pocernich, C. B., Lange, M.L.B., Sultana, R., and Butterfield, D. A. Nutritional approaches to modulate oxidative stress in Alzheimer's Disease. *Current Alzheimer Research* (2011).

Rao, A. V., and Balachandran, B. Role of oxidative stress and antioxidants in neurodegenerative disease. *Nutritional Neuroscience* (2002) 5: 291–309.

Shukitt-Hale, B. The effects of aging and oxidative stress on psychomotor and cognitive behavior. *Age* (1999) 22: 9–17.

Shukitt-Hale, B., Carey, A. N., Jenkins, D., Rabin, B. M., and Joseph, J. A. Beneficial effects of fruit extracts on neuronal function and behavior in a rodent model of accelerated aging. *Neurobiology of Aging* (2007) 28: 1187–94.

Shukitt-Hale, B., Carey, A., Simon, L., Mark, D. A., and Joseph, J. A. The effects of Concord grape juice on cognitive and motor deficits in aging. *Nutrition* (2006) 22: 295–302.

Shukitt-Hale, B., Cheng, V., and Joseph, J. A. Effect of blackberries on motor and cognitive function in aged rats. *Nutritional Neuroscience* (2009) 12: 135–40.

Shukitt-Hale, B., Cheng, V., Bielinski, D., et al. Differential brain regional specificity to blueberry and strawberry polyphenols in improved motor and cognitive function in aged rats. Society for Neuroscience, October 14, 2006, Atlanta, Georgia.

Shukitt-Hale, B., Denisova, N. A., Strain, J. G., and Joseph, J. A. Psychomotor effects of dopamine infusion under decreased glutathione conditions. *Free Radical Biology and Medicine* (1997) 23: 412–18.

Shukitt-Hale, B., Erat, S. A., and Joseph, J. A. Spatial learning and memory deficits induced by dopamine administration with decreased glutathione. *Free Radical Biology and Medicine* (1998): 1149–58.

Shukitt-Hale, B., Lau, F. C., et al. Blueberry polyphenols prevent kainic acid-induced decrements incognition and alter inflammatory gene expression in rat hippocampus. *Nutritional Neuroscience* (2008) 11: 172–82.

Szabo, L. Plant foods to the rescue. *USA Today*, August 10, 2004.

Tredici, G., et al. Resveratrol, map kinases and neuronal cells: Might wine be a neuroprotectant? *Drugs under Experimental and Clinical Research* (1999) 25: 99–103.

Virgili, M., and Contestabile, A. Parital neuroprotection of in vivo excitotoxic brain damage by chronic administration of the red wine antioxidant agent, trans-resveratrol in rats. *Neuroscience Letters* (2000) 281: 123–26.

Voelker, R. Radical approaches: Is widespread testing and treatment for oxidative injuries coming soon? *JAMA* (1993) 270: 2024.

Wang, X. L., Rainwater, D. L., Mahaney, M. C., and Stocker, R. Cosupplementation with vitamin E and coenzyme Q_{10} reduces circulating markers of inflammation in baboons. *American Journal of Clinical Nutrition* (September 2004) 80 (3): 649–55.

Wang, Y., et al. Dietary supplementation with blueberries, spinach, or spirulina reduces ischemic brain damage. *Experimental Neurology* (2005) 193: 75–84.

Wersching, H., et al. Serum C-reactive protein is linked to cerebral microstructural integrity and cognitive function. *Neurology* (2010) 74: 1022–29.

Wolf, G. The discovery of the antioxidant function of vitamin E: The contribution of Henry A. Matill. *Journal of Nutrition* (2005) 135: 363–56.

Yorek, M. A., Dunlap, J. A., and Stefani, M. R. Restoration of Na(+)-K+ pump activity and resting membrane potential by myoinositol supplementation in neuroblastoma cells chronically exposed to glucose orgalactose. *Diabetes* (1991) 40: 240–48.

Zafra-Stone, S., et al. Berry anthocyanins as novel antioxidants in human health and disease prevention. *Molecular Nutrition & Food Research* (2007) 5: 675–83.

Zhuang, H., Kim, Y. S., Koehler, R. C., Doré, S. Potential mechanism by which resveratrol, a red wine constituent, protects neurons. *Annals of the New York Academy of Sciences* (2003) 993: 276–86.

Chapter 4: Sugar

Basciano, H., Federico, L., and Adeli, K. Fructose, insulin resistance, and metabolic dyslipidemia. *Nutrition & Metabolism* (London) (2005): 2, 5.

Benton, D., and Parker, P. Y. Breakfast, blood glucose and cognition. *American Journal of Clinical Nutrition* (1998) 67 (Suppl.): 772S.

Benton, D., Maconie, A., and Williams, C. The influence of the glycaemic load of breakfast on the behavior of children in school. *Physiology & Behavior* (2007) 92: 717–24.

Biessels, G. J., Bravenboer, B., and Gispen, W. H. Glucose, insulin and the brain: Modulation of cognition and synaptic plasticity in health and disease; A preface. *European Journal of Pharmacology* (2004) 19: 1–3.

Blake, T. M., Varnhagen, C. K., and Parent, M. B. Emotionally arousing pictures increase blood glucose levels and enhance recall. *Neurobiology of Learning and Memory* (2001) 75: 262–73.

Brand-Miller, J., and Foster-Powell, K. *The New Glucose Revolution: Pocket Guide to Sugar and Energy.* New York: Marlow and Co., 2004.

Bray, G. A., Nielsen, S. J., and Popkin, B. M. Consumption of high-fructose corn syrup in beverages may play a role in the epidemic of obesity. *American Journal of Clinical Nutrition* (2004) 79: 537–43.

Brown, I. J. Sugar-sweetened beverage, sugar intake of individuals, and their blood pressure: International study of macro/micronutrients and blood pressure. *Hypertension* (April 2011) 57 (4): 695–701. Epub. February 28, 2011.

Coulston, A. M., and Johnson, R. K. Sugar and sugars: Myths and realities. *Journal of the American Dietetic Association* (2002) 102: 352–54.

Cranston, I., et al. Regional differences in cerebral blood flow and glucose utilization in diabetic man: The effect of insulin. *Journal of Cerebral Blood Flow & Metabolism* (1998) 18: 130–40.

de la Monte, S. M., Tong, M., Lester-Coll, N., Plater, M., Jr., and Wands, J. R. Therapeutic rescue of neurodegeneration in experimental type 3 diabetes: Relevance to Alzheimer's. *Journal of Alzheimer's Disease* (2006) 10: 89–109.

Elliott, S. S., Keim, N. L., Stern, J. S., Teff, K., and Havel, P. J. Fructose, weight gain, and the insulin resistance syndrome. *American Journal of Clinical Nutrition* (2002) 76: 911–22.

FAO. Carbohydrates in human nutrition. Report of a Joint FAO/WHO Expert Consultation. *FAO Food and Nutrition Paper* (1998) 66: 1–140.

Foster, J. K., Lidder, P. G., Sünram, S. I. Glucose and memory: Fractionation of enhancement effects? *Psychopharmacology* (1997) 137: 259–70.

Hasselbalch, S. G., et al. No effect of insulin on glucose blood-brain barrier transport and cerebral metabolism in humans. *Diabetes* (1999) 48: 1915–21.

Havel, P. Dietary fructose: Implications for dysregulation of energy homeostasis and lipid/carbohydrate metabolism. *Nutrition Reviews* (2005) 63: 133–57.

Hopkins, D. F., and Williams, G. Insulin receptors are widely distributed in human brain and bind human and porcine insulin with equal affinity. *Diabetic Medicine* (1997) 14: 1044–50.

Jahren, A. H., and Kraft, R. A. Carbon and nitrogen stable isotopes in fast food: Signatures of corn and confinement. *Proceedings of the National Academy of Sciences* (2008) 105: 17855–60.

Kava, R. Avoid added sugars: Good dietary advice or another red herring? It is time to differentiate between good and bad diets rather than simply good or bad foods. American Council on Scientific Health, September 21, 2000.

Kleinman, R. E., et al. Diet, breakfast and academic performance in children. *Annals of Nutrition and Metabolism* (2002) 46 (Suppl. 1): 24–30.

Korol, D. L., and Gold, P. E. Glucose, memory and aging. *Proceedings of the National Academy of Sciences* (1998) 67 (Suppl.): 764S–71S.

Kyriazis, G. A., Soundarapandian, M. M., and Tyrberg, B. Sweet taste receptor signaling in beta cells mediates fructose-induced potentiation of glucose-stimulated insulin secretion. *Proceedings of the National Academy of Sciences,* February 6, 2012.

Laaksonen, D. E., Niskanen, L., Lakka, H. M., Lakka, T. A., and Uusitupa, M. Epidemiologyand treatment of metabolic syndrome. *Annals of Medicine* (2004) 36: 332–46.

Ma, Y., et al. Association between dietary carbohydrates and body weight. *American Journal of Epidemiology* (2005) 161: 359–67.

Mayes, P. A. Intermediary metabolism of fructose. *American Journal of Clinical Nutrition* (1993) 58: 754S–65S.

Murphy, J. M., et al. The relationship of school breakfast to psychosocial and academic functioning: Cross-sectional and longitudinal observations in an inner-city school sample. *Archives of Pediatrics & Adolescent Medicine* (1998) 152: 899–907.

Park, O. J., et al. Mechanisms of fructose-induced hypertriglyceridemia in the rat: Activation of hepatic pyruvate dehydrogenase through inhibition of pyruvate dehydrogenase kinase. *Biochemical Journal* (1992) 283: 753–57.

Politt, E. American Health Foundation's Fortifying Children's Foods for Optimal Growth and Development Symposium, New York, New York. *American Journal of Clinical Nutrition* (1998) 67 (Suppl.): 748S–804S.

Sato, Y., et al. Immunohistochemical localization of facilitated diffusion glucose transporters in rat pancreatic islets. *Tissue and Cell* (1996) 28: 637–43.

Schulze, M. B., et al. Sugar-sweetened beverages, weight gain, and incidence of type 2 diabetes in young and middle-aged women. *JAMA* (2004) 292: 927–34.

Shapiro, A., et al. Fructose-induced leptin resistance exacerbates weight gain in response to subsequent high fat feeding. *American Journal of Physiology: Regulatory, Integrative and Comparative Physiology* (2008) 295: R1370–75.

Sizer, F. S., and Whitney, E. N. *Nutrition: Concepts and Controversies.* Independence, KY: Cengage Learning, 2010, 549.

Stanhope, K. L., et al. Consuming fructose-sweetened, not glucose-sweetened, beverages increases visceral adiposity and lipids and decreases insulin sensitivity in overweight/obese human. *Journal of Clinical Investigation* (2009) 119: 1322–34.

Swarbrick, M. M., et al. Consumption of fructose-sweetened beverages for 10 weeks increases postprandial triacylglycerol and apolipoprotein-B concentrations in overweight and obese women. *British Journal of Nutrition* (2008) 100: 947–52.

Taghibiglou, C., et al. Mechanisms of hepatic very low density lipoprotein overproduction in insulin resistance: Evidence for enhanced lipoprotein assembly, reduced intercellular apoB degradation, and increased microsomal triglyceride transfer protein in a fructose-fed hamster model. *Journal of Biological Chemistry* (2000) 275: 8416–25.

Taquchi, A., Wartschow, L. M., and White, M. F. Brain IRS2 signaling coordinates life span and nutrient homeostasis. *Science* (2007) 20: 369–72.

Wesnes, K. A., Pincock, C., Richardson, D., Helm, G., and Hails, S. Breakfast reduces declines in attention and memory over the morning in schoolchildren. *Appetite* (2003) 41: 329–31.

Chapter 5: A Healthy Brain Is a Fat Brain

Adcock, G. J., et al. Mitochondrial DNA sequences in ancient Australians: Implications for modern human origins. *Proceedings of the National Academy of Sciences* (2001) 98: 537–42.

Akter, K., et al. A review of the possible role of essential fatty acids and fish oils in the aetiology, prevention or pharmacotherapy of schizophrenia. *Journal of Clinical Pharmacy and Therapeutics* (2011).

Albanese, E., et al. Dietary fish and meat intake and dementia in Latin America, China, and India: A 10/66 Dementia Research Group population-based study. *American Journal of Clinical Nutrition* (2009) 90: 392–400.

Amminger, G. P., et al. Long-chain omega-3 fatty acids for indicated prevention of psychotic disorders: A randomized, placebo-controlled study. *Archives of General Psychiatry* (2010) 67: 146–54.

Appleton, K. M., Rogers, P. J., and Ness, A. R. Updated systematic review and meta-analysis of the effects of n23 long-chain polyunsaturated fatty acids on depressed mood. *American Journal of Clinical Nutrition* (2010) 91: 757–70.

Beauchamp, G. K., et al. Phytochemistry: Ibuprofen-like activity in extra-virgin olive oil. *Nature* (2005) 437: 45–46.

Birch, E. E., et al. Visual acuity and cognitive outcomes at 4 years of age in a double-blind, randomized trial of long-chain polyunsaturated fatty acid–supplemented infant formula. *Human Early Development* (2007) 83: 279–84.

Booth, S., and Zeller, D. Mercury, food webs, and marine mammals: Implications of diet and climate change for human health. *Environmental Health Perspectives* (2005) 113: 521–26.

Browning, L. M. N-3 polyunsaturated fatty acids, inflammation and obesity-related disease. *Proceedings of the Nutrition Society* (2003) 62: 95–99.

Buydens-Branchey, L., and Branchey, M. Long-chain n-3 polyunsaturated fatty acids decrease feelings of anger in substance abusers. *Psychiatry Research* (2008) 157: 95–104.

Buydens-Branchey, L., and Branchey, M. N-3 polyunsaturated fatty acids decrease anxiety feelings in a population of substance abusers. *Journal of Clinical Psychopharmacology* (2006) 26: 661–65.

Chauhan, N. Walnut extract inhibits the fibrillization of amyloid beta-protein and also defibrillizes its preformed fibrils. *Current Alzheimer Research* (2004) 1: 183–88.

DeFin, L. F., Marcoux, L. G., Devers, S. M., Cleaver, J. P., and Willis, B. L. Effects of omega-3 supplementation in combination with diet and exercise on weight loss and body composition. *American Journal of Clinical Nutrition* (2011) 93: 455–62.

Feart, C., et al. Plasma eicosapentaenoic acid is inversely associated with severity of depressive symptomatology in the elderly: Data from the Bordeaux sample of the Three City Study. *American Journal of Clinical Nutrition* (2008) 87: 1156–62.

Freeman, M. P. Omega-3 fatty acids in major depressive disorder. *Journal of Clinical Psychiatry* (2009) 70 (Suppl.): 7–12.

Gale, C. R., et al. Breastfeeding, the use of docosahexaenoic acid fortified formulas in infancy and neuropsychological function in childhood. *Archives of Disease in Childhood* (2010) 95: 174–79.

Gesch, C. B., Hammond, S. M., Hampson, S. E., Eves, A., and Crowder, M. J. Influence of supplementary vitamins, minerals and essential fatty acids on theantisocial behavior of young adult prisoners. *British Journal of Psychiatry* (2002) 181: 22–28.

Giselle, P., et al. A diet enriched with the omega-3 fatty acid docosahexaenoic reduces amyloid burden in an aged Alzheimer mouse model. *Journal of Neuroscience* (2005) 25: 3032–40.

Golding, J., Steer, C., Emmett, P., Davis, J. M., Hibbeln, J. R. High levels of depressive symptoms in pregnancy with low omega-3 fatty acid intake from fish. *Epidemiology* (2009) 20: 598–603.

Harris, W. S., Pottala, J. V., Sands, S. A., and Jones, P. G. Comparison of the effects of fish and fish oil capsules on the n-3 fatty acid content of blood cells and plasma phospholipids. *American Journal of Clinical Nutrition* (2007) 86: 1621–25.

Hedelin, M., et al. Dietary intake of fish, omega-3, omega-6 polyunsaturated fatty acids and vitamin D and the prevalence of psychotic-like symptoms in a cohort of 33,000 women from the general population. *BMC Psychiatry* (2010) 26: 10–38.

Helland, I. B., Smith, L., Saarem, K., Saugstad, O. D., and Drevon, C. A. Maternal supplementation with very-long-chain n-3 fatty acids during pregnancy and lactation augments children's IQ at 4 years of age. *Pediatrics* (2003) 111: e39–e44.

Herdon, J. G. Brain weight throughout the life span of the chimpanzee. *Journal of Comparative Neurology* (1999) 409: 567–72.

Hibbeln, J. R. From homicide to happiness—A commentary on omega-3 fatty acids in human society. *Nutrition and Health* (2007) 19: 9–19.

Hibbeln, J. R. Omega-3 fatty acid deficiencies in neurodevelopment, aggression and autonomic dysregulation: Opportunities for intervention. *International Review of Psychiatry* (2006) 18: 1–12.

Hibbeln, J. R. Omega-3 status and cerebrospinal fluid corticotrophin releasing hormone in perpetrators of domestic violence. *Biological Psychiatry* (2004) 56: 895–97.

Hibbeln, J. R., and Salem, N. Dietary polyunsaturated acids in depression: When cholesterol does not satisfy. *American Journal of Clinical Nutrition* (1995) 62: 1–9.

Hibbeln, J. R., Davis, J. M., et al. Maternal seafood consumption in pregnancy and neurodevelopmental outcomes in childhood (ALSPAC study): An observational cohort study. *Lancet* (2007) 369: 578–85.

Hill, A. M., Buckley, J. D., Murphy, K. J., and Howe, P.R.C. Combining fish-oil supplements with regular aerobic exercise improves body composition and cardiovascular disease risk factors. *American Journal of Clinical Nutrition* (2007) 85: 1267–74.

Hirafuji, M., Machida, T., Tsunoda, M., Miyamoto, A., and Minami, M. Docosahexaenoic acid potentiates interleukin-1 beta induction of nitric oxidesynthase through mechanism involving MAPK activation in rat vascular smooth muscle cells. *British Journal of Pharmacology* (2002) 136: 613–19.

Horrocks, L. A., and Yeo, Y. K. Health benefits of docosahexaenoic acid (DHA). *Pharmacological Research* (1999) 40: 211–25.

Irribaren, C., et al. Dietary intake of n-3, n-6 fatty acids and fish: Relationship with hostility in young adults—The CARDIA study. *European Journal of Clinical Nutrition* (2004) 58: 24–31.

Jazayeri, S., et al. Comparison of therapeutic effects of omega-3 fatty acid eicosapentaenoic acid and fluoxetine, separately and in combination in major depressive disorder. *Australian and New Zealand Journal of Psychiatry* (2008) 42: 192–98.

Johnson, M., Östlund, S., Fransson, G., Kadesjö, B., and Gillberg, C. Omega-3/omega-6 fatty acids for attention deficit hyperactivity disorder: A randomized placebo-controlled trial in children and adolescents. *Journal of Attention Disorders* (2009) 12: 394–401.

Kim, J. L., et al. Fish consumption and school grades in Swedish adolescents: A study of the large general population. *Acta Paediatrica* (2010) 99: 72–77.

Kirby, A. Children's learning and behavior and the association with cheek cell polyunsaturated fatty acid levels. *Research in Developmental Disabilities* (2010) 31: 731–42.

Knoops, K.T.B., et al. Mediterranean diet, lifestyle factors, and 10-year mortality in elderly European men and women: The Hale Project. *JAMA* (2004) 292: 1433–39.

Krabbendam, L., Bakker, E., Hornstra, G., and van Os, J. Relationship between DHA status at birth and child problem behavior at 7 years of age. *Prostaglandins, Leukotrienes and Essential Fatty Acids* (2007) 76: 29–34.

Kulkarni, K. S., Kasture, S. B., and Mengi, S. A. Efficacy study of Prunusamygdalus (almond) nuts in scopolamine-induced amnesia in rats. *Indian Journal of Pharmacology* (2010) 42: 168–173.

Laasonen, M., Hokkanen, L., Leppämäki, S., Tani, P., and Erkkilä, A. T. Project DyAdd: Fatty acids in adult dyslexia, ADHD and their comorbid combination. *Prostaglandins, Leukotrienes and Essential Fatty Acids* (2009) 81: 89–96.

Lafourcade, M., et al. Nutritional omega-3 deficiency abolishes endocannabinoid-mediated neuronal functions. *Nature Neuroscience* (2011) 14: 345–50.

Lesperance, F., et al. The efficacy of omega-3 supplementation for major depression: A randomized controlled trial. *Journal of Clinical Psychiatry* (August 2011) 72 (8): 1054–62. Epub. June 15, 2010.

Logan, A. C. Omega-3 fatty acids and major depression: A primer for the mental health professional. *Lipids in Health and Disease* (2004) 3: 25.

Loonam, T. M., Noailles, P. A., Yu, J., Zhu, J. P., and Angulo, J. A. Substance P and chole-cystokinin regulate neurochemical response to cocaine and methamphetamine in the striatum. *Life Sciences* (2003) 73: 727–39.

Lucas, M., et al. Dietary intake of n-3 and n-6 fatty acids and the risk of clinical depression in women: A 10-y prospective follow-up study. *American Journal of Clinical Nutrition* (2011) 93: 1337–43.

Maes, M., et al. Fatty acid composition in major depression: Decreased omega-3 fractions in cholesteryl esters and increased C20: 4 omega 6/C20: 5 omega-3 ration in cholesteryl esters and phospholipids. *Journal of Affective Disorders* (1996) 38: 35–46.

Ma, Q. L., et al. Omega-3 fatty acid docosahexaenoic acid increases SorLA/LR11, a sorting protein with reduced expression in sporadic Alzheimer's disease (AD): Relevance to AD prevention. *Journal of Neuroscience* (2007) 27: 14299–307.

Marchioli, R., et al. Early protection against sudden death by n-3 polyunsaturated fatty acids after myocardial infarction: Time course analysis of the results of the Gruppo Italiano per lo Studiodella Sopravvivenza Nell'Infarto Miocardico (GISSI)—Prevenzione. *Circulation* (April 23, 2002) 105 (16): 1897–903.

Miller, T. W., Isenberg, J. S., Shih, H. B., Wang, Y., and Roberts, D. D. Amyloid-ꞵ inhibits No-cGMP signaling in a CD-36- and CD47-dependent manner. *PLoS ONE* (2010) 5: e15686.

Mischoulon, D. Docosahexanoic acid and omega-3 fatty acids in depression. *Psychiatric Clinics of North America* (2000) 23: 785–94.

Mori, T. A., Bao, D. Q., et al. Dietary fish as a major component of a weight-loss diet: Effect on serum lipids, glucose and insulin metabolism in overweight hypertensive subjects. *American Journal of Clinical Nutrition* (1999) 70: 817–25.

Mori, T. A., Burke, V., Puddey, I. B., Shaw, J. E., and Beilin, L. J. Effect of fish diets and weight loss on serum leptin concentration in overweight, treated hypertensive subjects. *Journal of Hypertension* (2004) 22: 1983–90.

Neuringer, M., Connor, W. E., Lin, D. S., Barstad, L., and Luck, S. Biochemical and functional effects of prenatal and postnatal omega-3 fatty acid deficiency on retina and brain in rhesus monkeys. *Proceedings of the National Academy of Sciences* (1986) 83: 4021–25.

Niu, S-L., et al. Reduced G protein coupled signaling efficiency in retinal rod outer segments in response to n-3 fatty acid deficiency. *Journal of Biological Chemistry* (2004) 279: 31098–104.

Ohara, K. The n-3 polyunsaturated fatty acid/dopamine hypothesis of schizophrenia. *Progress in Neuro-Psychopharmacology & Biological Psychiatry* 31, 2 (2007): 469–74.

Oken, E. Maternal fish consumption, hair mercury, and infant cognition in a US cohort. *Environmental Health Perspectives* (2005) 113: 1376–80.

Oken, E., Radesky, J. S., et al. Maternal fish intake during pregnancy, blood mercury levels and child cognition at age 3 years in a US cohort. *American Journal of Epidemiology* (2008) 167: 1171–81.

Power, G. W., and Newsholme, E. A. Dietary fatty acids influence the activity and metabolic control of mitochondrial carnitine palmitoyltransferase I in rat heart and skeletal muscle. *Journal of Nutrition* (1997) 127: 2142–50.

Prasad, M. R., Lovell, M. A., Yatin, M., Dhillon, H., and Markesbery, W. R. Regional membrane phospholipid alterations in Alzheimer's disease. *Neurochemical Research* (1998) 23: 81–88.

Puri, B. *Chronic Fatigue Syndrome: A Natural Way to Treat.* London: M. E. Hammersmith Press, 2004.

Puri, B. K., and Boyd, H. *The Natural Way to Beat Depression: The Groundbreaking Discovery of EPA to Change Your Life.* London: Harder, 2005.

Ramirez-Tortosa, M., et al. Extra virgin olive oil increases the resistance of LDL to oxidation more than refined olive oil in free-living men with peripheral vascular disease. *Journal of Nutrition* (1999) 129: 2177–83.

Richardson, A. J., and Montgomery, P. The Oxford-Durham Study: A randomized, controlled trial of dietary supplementation with fatty acids in children with developmental coordination disorder. *Pediatrics* (2005) 115: 1360–66.

Roberts, L. J., and Fessel, J. P. The biochemistry of the isoprostane, neuroprostane and isofuran pathways of lipid peroxidation. *Brain Pathology* (2005) 15: 143–48.

Sanchez-Villegas, A., et al. Association of the Mediterranean dietary pattern with the incidence of depression: The Seguimiento Universidad de Navarra/University of Navarra follow-up (SUN) cohort. *Archives of General Psychiatry* (2009) 66: 1090–98.

Schwartz, G. J., et al. The lipid messenger OEA links dietary fat intake to satiety. *Cell Metabolism* (2008) 8: 281–88.

Sears, B. *The Omega Rx Zone: The Miracle of the New High-dose Fish Oil.* New York: HarperTorch, 2002.

Simon, J. A., Fong, J., Bernert, J. T., Jr., and Browner, W. S. Serum fatty acids and the risk of stroke. *Stroke* (1995) 26: 778–82.

Simopoulos, A. P. Importance of the ratio of omega-6/omega-3 essential fatty acids: Evolutionary aspects. *World Review of Nutrition and Dietetics* (2003) 92: 1–174.

Sinn, N., and Bryan, J. Effect of supplementation with polyunsaturated fatty acid and micronutrients on learning and behavior problems associated with child ADHD. *Journal of Developmental & Behavioral Pediatrics* (2007) 28: 82–91.

Sublette, M. E., Hibbeln, J. R., Galfalvy, H., Oquendo, M. A., and Mann, J. J. Omega-3 polyunsaturated essential fatty acid status as a predictor of future suicide risk. *American Journal of Psychiatry* (2006) 163: 1100–1102.

Trinkaus, E. The Neanderthals and modern human origins. *Annual Review of Anthropology* (1987) 15: 193–218.

Von Schacky, C. N-3 fatty acids and the prevention of coronary atherosclerosis. *American Journal of Clinical Nutrition* (2000) 71 (Suppl.): 224S–27S.

Weaver, K. L., et al. The content of favorable and unfavorable polyunsaturated fatty acids found in commonly eaten fish. *Journal of American Dental Association* (2008) 108: 1178–85.

Yehuda, S., Rabinovitz, S., and Mostofsky, D. I. Mediation of cognitive function by high-fat diet following stress and inflammation. *Nutritional Neuroscience* (2005) 8: 309–15.

Zaalberg, A., Nijman, H., Bulten, E., Stroosma, L., and van der Staak, C. Effects of nutritional supplements on aggression, rule-breaking, and psychopathology among young adult prisoners. *Aggressive Behavior* (2010) 36: 117–26.

Zhou, Y. E., Kubow, S., Dewailly, E., Julien, P., and Egeland, G. M. Decreased activity of desaturase-5 in association with obesity and insulin resistance aggravates declining long-chain n-3 fatty acid status in Cree undergoing dietary transition. *British Journal of Nutrition* (2009) 102: 888–94.

Chapter 6: The Cholesterol Dilemma

Abramson, J., and Wright, J. M. Are lipid-lowering guidelines evidence based? *Lancet* (2007) 369: 168–69.

Allam, A. H., et al. Computed tomographic assessment of atherosclerosis in ancient Egyptian mummies. *JAMA* (2009) 302: 2091–94.

Amerenco, P., et al. High-dose atorvastatin after stroke or transient ischemic attack. *New England Journal of Medicine* (2006) 355: 549–59.

American Heart Association. Heart Disease and Stroke Statistics—2011 Update. *Circulation* (February 1, 2011).

Arvanitakis, Z., et al. Statins, incident Alzheimer disease, change in cognitive function and neuropathology. *Neurology* 70 (May 6, 2008) 19 (Part 2): 1795–1802.

Atkins, R. C. *Dr. Atkins' Diet Revolution.* New York: D. McKay Co./Bantam Books, 1972.

Atkins, R. C. *Dr. Atkins' New Diet Revolution.* New York: M. Evans and Company, 1992.

Castelli, W. P. Making practical sense of clinical trial data in decreasing cardiovascular risk. *American Journal of Cardiology* (2001) 88: 16F–20F.

Castelli, W. P. The new pathophysiology of coronary artery disease. *American Journal of Cardiology* (1998) 82: 60T–65T.

Centers for Disease Control and Prevention. Health, United States, 2010.

Chilton, F. H. *Inflammation Nation: The First Clinically Proven Eating Plan to End Our Nation's Secret Epidemic.* Whitby, ON: Fireside, 2005.

Coplo, A. *The Great Cholesterol Con: Why Everything You Have Been Told about Cholesterol, Diet and Heart Disease is Wrong.* London: John Blake, 2006.

Corona, G., Boddi, V., et al. The effect of statin therapy on testosterone levels in subjects consulting for erectile dysfunction. *Journal of Sexual Medicine* 7, 4 (Part 1, 2010): 1547–56.

Corona, G., Rastrelli, G., et al. Update in testosterone therapy for men. *Journal of Sexual Medicine* (2011) 8: 639–54.

de Graaf, L., Brouwers, A.H.P.M., and Diemont, W. L. Is decreased libido associated with the use of HMG-COA-reductase inhibitors? *British Journal of Clinical Pharmacology* (2004) 58: 326–28.

Dolga, A., et al. Lovastatin induces neuroprotection through tumor necrosis factor receptor 2 signaling pathways. *Journal of Alzheimer's Disease* (2008) 13: 111–22.

Dormuth, C. R., et al. Statin adherence and risk of accidents: A cautionary tale. *Circulation* (2009) 119: 2051–57.

Dursun, S. M., Burke, J. G., and Reveley, M. A. Low-serum cholesterol and depression. *BMJ* (1994) 309: 273–74.

Engleberg, H. Low-serum cholesterol and suicide. *Lancet* (1992) 339: 727–29.

Fackelmann, K. A. Japanese stroke clues: Are there risks to low cholesterol? *Science News*, April 22, 1989.

Favaro, A., Caregaro, L., Di Pascoli, L., Brambilla, F., and Santonastaso, P. Total serum cholesterol and suicidality in anorexia nervosa. *Psychosomatic Medicine* (2004) 66: 548–52.

FDA. FDA Drug Safety Communications: New restrictions, contraindications, and dose limitations for Zocor (simvastatin) to reduce the risk of muscle injury. June 6, 2011.

Fedder, D. O., Koro, C. E., and L'Italien, G. J. New National Cholesterol Education Program III guidelines for primary prevention lipid lowering drug therapy: Projected impact on the size, sex and age distribution of the treatment eligible population. *Circulation* (2002) 105: 152–56.

Folkers, K., et al. Lovastatin decreases coenzyme Q levels in humans. *Proceedings of the National Academy of Sciences* (1990) 887: 8931–40.

Gades, N. M., et al. Longitudinal evaluation of sexual function in a male cohort: The Olmsted County Study of Urinary Symptoms and Health Status among Men. *Journal of Sexual Medicine* 6, 9 (2009): 2455–66.

Gaist, D., et al. Statins and risk of polyneuropathy: A case-control study. *Neurology* (2002) 58: 1333–37.

Gillman, M. W., Cupples, L. A., Millen, B. E., Ellison, R. C., and Wolf, P. A. Inverse association of dietary fat with development of ischemic stroke in men. *JAMA* (1997) 278: 2145.

Golomb, B. A. Cholesterol and violence: Is there a connection? *Annals of Internal Medicine* (1998) 128: 478–87.

Graham, D. J., et al. Incidence of hospitalized rhabdomyolysis in patients treated with lipid-lowering drugs. *JAMA* (2004) 292: 2585–90.

Grundy, S. M. Executive summary of the third report of the National Cholesterol Education Program (NCEP) Expert Panel on Detection, Evaluation and Treatment of High Blood Cholesterol in Adults (Adult Treatment Panel III). *JAMA* (2001): 2486–97.

Guillem, E., Pélissolo, A., Notides, C., and Lépine, J. P. Relationship between attempted suicide, serum cholesterol level and novelty seeking in psychiatric in-patients. *Psychiatry Research* (2002) 112: 83–88.

Hall, S. A., et al. Do statins affect androgen levels in men? Results from the Boston Area Community Health Survey Cancer. *Epidemiology, Biomarkers & Prevention* (2007) 16: 1587–94.

Hayward, R. A., Hofer, T. P., and Vijan, S. Narrative Review: Lack of evidence for recommended low-density lipoprotein treatment targets; A solvable problem. *Annals of Internal Medicine* (2006) 145: 520–30.

Hoover, E. When his health deserted him, diet and fitness guru Nathan Pritikin turned to suicide. *People*, March 11, 1985.

Igna, C. V., Julkunen, J., Vanhanen, H., Keskivaara, P., and Verkasalo, M. Depressive symptoms and serum lipid fractions in middle-aged men: Physiologic and health behavior links. *Psychosomatic Medicine* (2008) 70: 960–66.

Kagan, A., McGee, D. L., Yano, K., Rhoads, G. G., and Nomura, A. Serum cholesterol and mortality in a Japanese-American population: The Honolulu heart program. *American Journal of Epidemiology* (1981) 114: 11.

Kannel, W. B., Castelli, W. P., and McNamara, P. M. The coronary profile: 12-year follow-up in the Framingham Study. *Journal of Occupational Medicine* (1967) 9: 611–19.

Kendrick, M. *The Great Cholesterol Con: The Truth about What Really Causes Heart Disease and How to Avoid It.* London: John Blake, 2008.

Keys, A. *Seven Countries: A Multivariate Analysis of Death and Coronary Heart Disease.* London: Harvard University Press, 1980.

Kratz, M. Dietary cholesterol, atherosclerosis and coronary heart disease. *Handbook of Experimental Pharmacology* (2005): 195–213.

Krumholz, H. M., et al. Lack of association between cholesterol and coronary heart disease mortality and morbidity and all-cause mortality in persons older than 70 years. *JAMA* (1994) 272: 1335–40.

Langsjoen, P. H., and Langsjoen, A. M. Overview of the use of CoQ$_{10}$ in cardiovascular disease. *Biofactors* (1999) 9: 273–84.

Langsjoen, P. H., and Langsjoen, A. M. The clinical use of HMG CoA-reductase inhibitors and the associated depletion of coenzyme Q$_{10}$: A review of animal and human publications. *Biofactors* (2003)18: 101–11.

Lester, D. Serum cholesterol levels and suicide: A meta-analysis. *Suicide and Life-Threatening Behavior* (2002) 32: 333–46.

Li, G., et al. Statin therapy is associated with reduced neuropathology changes of Alzheimererdisease. *Neurology* (2007) 69: 878–85.

Littarru, G. P., and Langsjoen, P. Coenzyme Q$_{10}$ and statins: Biochemical and clinical implications. *Mitochondrion* (2007 Suppl.): S168–S74.

Lowe, G.D.O. The association between elevated levels of inflammation biomarkers and coronary artery disease and death. *Canadian Medical Association Journal* (2006) 174: 479–80.

Martinez-Carpio, P. A. Relation between cholesterol levels and neuropsychiatric disorders. *Revista Neurologica* (2009) 48: 261–64.

Mauch, D. H., and Pfrieger, F. W. CNS synaptogenesis promoted by glia-derived cholesterol. *Science* (2001) 294: 1354–57.

McCully, K. S. Atherosclerosis, serum cholesterol and the homocysteine theory: A study of 194 consecutive autopsies. *American Journal of Medical Science* (1990) 299: 217–21.

McCully, K. *The Homocysteine Revolution: A Bold New Approach to the Prevention of Heart Disease.* Lincolnwood, IL: Keats, 1998.

McLaughlin, K., and Winslow, R. Report details Dr. Atkins's health problems. *Wall Street Journal,* February 10, 2004.

Meggs, W. J. *The Inflammation Cure.* Chicago: Contemporary Books, 2004.

Miron, V. E., et al. Statin therapy inhibits remyelination in the central nervous system. *American Journal of Pathology* (2009) 174: 1880–90.

Modai, I., Valevski, A., Dror, S., and Weizman, A. Serum cholesterol levels and suicidal tendencies in psychiatric inpatients. *Journal of Clinical Psychiatry* (1994) 55: 252–54.

Moride, Y., et al. Clinical and public health assessment of benefits and risks of statins in primary prevention of coronary events: Resolved and unresolved issues. *Canadian Journal of Cardiology* (2008) 24: 293–300.

New, A. S., et al. Serum cholesterol and impulsivity in personality disorders. *Psychiatry Research* (1999) 85: 145–50.

Niaura, J. F., et al. Hostility, the metabolic syndrome and incident coronary heart disease. *Health Psychology* (2002) 21: 588–93.

Ormiston, T., Wolkowitz, O. M., Reus, V. I., and Manfredi, F. Behavioral implications of lowering cholesterol levels: A double-blind pilot study. *Psychosomatics* (2003) 44: 412–14.

Ornish, D. *Dr. Dean Ornish's Program for Reversing Heart Disease: The Only System Scientifically Proven to Reverse Heart Disease without Drugs or Surgery.* New York: Ivy Books, 1990.

Ornish, D. *Eat More, Weigh Less: Dr. Dean Ornish's Life Choice Program for Losing Weight Safely While Eating Abundantly.* New York: HarperCollins, 1993.

Páramo, J. A., Rodríguez, J. A., and Orbe, J. Integrating soluble biomarkers and imaging technologies in the identification of vulnerable atherosclerotic patients. *Biomark Insights* (2006) 1: 165–73.

Partonon, T. Association of low-serum total cholesterol with major depression and suicide. *British Journal of Psychiatry* (1999) 175: 259–62.

Patalay, M., Lofgren, I. E., Freake, H. C., Koo, S. I., and Fernandez, M. L. The lowering of plasma lipids following a weight reduction program is related to increased expression of the LDL receptor and lipoprotein lipase. *Journal of Nutrition* (2005) 135: 735–39.

Pfrieger, F. W. Cholesterol homeostasis and function in neurons of the central nervous system. *Cellular and Molecular Life Sciences* (2003) 60: 1158–71.

Pfrieger, F. W. Outsourcing in the brain: Do neurons depend on cholesterol delivery by astrocytes? *BioEssays* (2003) 25: 72–78.

Pfrieger, F. W. Role of cholesterol in synapse formation. *Biochimica et Biophysica Acta* (2003) 1610: 271–80.

Pfrieger, F. W. Role of glia in synapse development. *Current Opinion in Neurobiology* (2002) 12: 486–90.

Pfrieger, F. W. Role of glial cells in the formation and maintenance of synapses. *Brain Research Reviews* (2010) 63: 39–46.

Pfrieger, F. W. Roles of glial cells in synapse development. *Cellular and Molecular Life Sciences* (2009) 66: 2037–47.

Pfrieger, F. W., and Ungerer, N. Cholesterol metabolism in neurons and astrocytes. *Progress in Lipid Research* (2011) 50: 357–71.

Pritikin, N. *The Pritikin Program for Diet and Exercise.* New York: Bantam, 1979.

Ratkowski, R. A. Radio interview on cholesterol. Natural Life Chiropractic. The facts about cholesterol and statin medications, by Dr. Lisa Orwich, D.C., July 27, 2011. Retrieved at http://www.naturallifechiropractic.com/facts_about_Cholesterol_and_statins.html.

Ravnskov, U. *Fat and Cholesterol Are Good for You.* Sweden: GB Publishing, 2009.

Ravnskov, U. *The Cholesterol Myths: Exposing the Fallacy that Cholesterol and Saturated Fat Cause Heart Disease.* UK: New Trade Publishers, 2000.

Ray, K. K., et al. Statins and all-cause mortality in high-risk primary prevention: A meta-analysis of 11 randomized controlled trials involving 65,229 participants. *Archives of Internal Medicine* (2010) 170: 1024–31.

Sacchetti, P., et al. Liver X receptors and oxysterols promote ventral midbrain neurogenesis in vivo and in human embryonic stem cells. *Cell Stem Cell* (2009) 5: 409–19.

Saher, G., et al. High cholesterol level is essential for myelin membrane growth. *Nature Neuroscience* (2005) 8: 465–75.

Scandinavian Simvastatin Survival Study Group randomized trial of cholesterol lowering in 444 patients with coronary heart disease: The Scandinavian Simvastatin Survival Study (4S). *Lancet* (1994): 439–46.

Schartz, I. J., et al. Cholesterol and all-cause mortality in elderly people from the Honolulu Heart Program: A cohort study. *Lancet* (2001) 358: 351–55.

Sears, B. *The Anti-Inflammation Zone.* New York: Reagan Books, 2005.

Sears, B. *The Omega Rx Zone: The Miracle of the New High-dose Fish Oil.* New York: Harper-Torch, 2002.

Shimamoto, T., et al. Trends for coronary heart disease and stroke and their risk factors in Japan. *Circulation* (1989) 79: 503–15.

Simons, K., and Ikonen, E. How cells handle cholesterol. *Science* (2000) 290: 1721–26.

Steinberg, D. *The Cholesterol Wars: The Skeptics vs. the Preponderance of the Evidence.* Waltham, MA: Academic Press, 2007.

Sternberg, S. Mummy's CT scans show heart disease came before fast food. *USA Today*, November 11, 2009.

Suarez, E. C. Relations of trait depression and anxiety to low lipid and lipoprotein concentrations in healthy young adult women. *Psychosomatic Medicine* (1999) 61: 273–79.

Tsugane, S. Human ecological and epidemiological studies of Japanese immigrants and their descendants in South America. *Nihon Eiseigaku Zasshi* (1992) 47: 775–84.

Wang, X., et al. Inverse association of plasma level of high-density lipoprotein cholesterol with intracerebral hemorrhage. Hypertension Division, Cardiovascular Institute and Fu Wai Hospital, Chinese Academy of Medical Sciences and Peking Union Medical College, Beijing, China, 2010.

Wolf, G. The function of cholesterol in embryogenesis. *Journal of Nutritional Biochemistry* (1999) 10: 188–92.

Woollett, L. A. Fetal lipid metabolism. *Frontiers in Bioscience* (2001) 6: D536–D45.

Zureik, M., et al. Serum cholesterol concentration and death from suicide in men: Paris prospective study I. *BMJ* (1996) 313: 14.

Chapter 7: Protein

Beckman, H., and Ludolph, E. DL-phenylalanine as an antidepressant: Open study. *Arzneittelforschung* (1978) 28: 1283.

Birdsall, T. C. Therapeutic applications of taurine. *Alternative Medicine Review* (1998) 3 (2): 128–36.

Brosnan, J., and Brosnan, M. E. The sulfur-containing amino acids: An overview. *Journal of Nutrition* 136, 6 (2006 Suppl.): 1636S–40S.

Bryant, C. X., Peterson, J. A., and Franklin, B. A. *101 Frequently Asked Questions about "Health and Fitness" and "Nutrition and Weight Control."* Urbana, IL: Sagamore Publishing, 1999.

Butchko, H. H., and Kotsonis, F. N. Aspartame: Review of recent research. *Comments on Toxicology* (1989) 3: 253.

Chen, S. W., et al. Possible anxiolytic effects of taurine in the mouse elevated plus-maze. *Life Sciences* (2004) 75: 1503–11.

Clark, N. *Sports Nutrition Guidebook.* 2nd ed. Champaign, IL: Human Kinetics, [1991] 1997.

Conolly-Schoonen, J. Dietary protein intake differences based on activity levels. *Diabetes & Endocrinology: Medscape* 3 (2001): 1.

Dawson, R., Jr., Biasetti, M., Messina, S., and Dominy, J. The cytoprotective role of taurine in exercise-induced muscle injury. *Amino Acids* (2002) 22: 309–24.

Drewnowski, A. Changes in mood after carbohydrate consumption. *American Journal of Clinical Nutrition* (1987) 46: 703. Letter.

Ericson, M., Molander, A., Stomberg, R., and Söderpalm, B. Taurine elevates dopamine levels in the rat nucleus accumbens: Antagonism by strychnine. *European Journal of Neuroscience* (2006) 23: 3225–29.

FAO. Protein requirements. *FAO Nutritional Studies*, 16 (1957).

Food and Nutrition Board. A Report of the Panel on Macronutrients, Subcommittees on Upper Reference Levels of Nutrients and Interpretation and Uses of Dietary Reference Intakes, and the Standing Committee on the Scientific Evaluation of Dietary Reference Intakes. Dietary Reference Intakes for Energy, Carbohydrate, Fiber, Fat, Fatty Acids, Cholesterol, Protein, and Amino Acids (Macronutrients). Washington, DC: National Academies Press, 2005.

Franconi, F., et al. Plasma and platelet taurine are reduced in subjects with insulin-dependent diabetes mellitus: Effects of taurine supplementation. *American Journal of Clinical Nutrition* (1995) 61: 1115–19.

Fujita, T., Ando, K., Noda, H., Ito, Y., and Sato, Y. Effects of increased adrenomedullary activity and taurine in young patients with borderline hypertension. *Circulation* (1987) 75: 535–32.

Genton, L., Melzer, K., and Pichard, C. Energy and macronutrient requirements for physical fitness in exercising subjects. *Clinical Nutrition* (2010) 29: 413–23.

Green, T. R., Fellman, J. H., Eicher, A. L., and Pratt, K. L. Antioxidant role and subcellular location of hypotaurine and taurine in human neutrophils. *Biochimica et Biophysica Acta* (1991) 1073: 91–97.

Geiß, K.-R., Jester, I., Falke, W., Hamm, M., and Waag, K.-L. The effect of a taurine-containing drink on performance in 10 endurance athletes. *Amino Acids* (1994) 7: 45–56.

Gürer, H., Ozgünes, H., Saygin, E., and Ercal, N. Antioxidant effect of taurine against lead-induced oxidative stress. *Archives of Environmental Contamination and Toxicology* (2001) 41: 397–402.

Hoffman, J. R. Protein: Which is best? *Journal of Sports Science and Medicine* (2004) 3: 118–30.

Huxtable, R. J. Physiological actions of taurine. *Physiological Reviews* (1992) 72: 101–63.

Kendler, B. S. Taurine: An overview of its role in preventive medicine. *Preventive Medicine* (1989) 18: 79–100.

Kerstetters, J. E. Low protein intake: The impact on calcium and bone homeostasis in humans. *Journal of Nutrition* (2003) 133: 8555–8615.

Kong, W. X., et al. Effects of taurine on rat behaviors in three anxiety models. *Pharmacology Biochemistry and Behavior* (2006) 83: 271–76.

Konig, P., et al. Orally administered taurine in therapy resistant epilepsy. *Wien Klin Worchenschr* (1977) 89: 111–13.

Lieberman, H. R. Nutrition, brain function and cognitive performance. *Appetite* (2003) 40: 245–54.

Lieberman, H. R., Wurtman, J. J., and Chew, B. Changes in mood after carbohydrate consumption among obese individuals. *American Journal of Clinical Nutrition* (1986) 44: 772.

Matsuzaki, Y., et al. Decreased taurine concentration in skeletal muscles after exercise of various durations. *Medicine & Science in Sports & Exercise* (2002) 34: 793–97.

Mizushima, S., Nara, Y., Sawamura, M., and Yamori, Y. Effects of oral taurine supplementation on lipids and sympathetic nerve tone. *Advances in Experimental Medicine and Biology* (1996) 403: 615–22.

Miyazaki, T., et al. Optimal and effective oral doses of taurine to prolong exercise performance in rats. *Amino Acids* (2004) 27: 291.

Nakaya, Y., et al. Taurine improves insulin sensitivity in the Otsuka Long-Evans Tokushima Fatty rat, a model of spontaneous type 2 diabetes. *American Journal of Clinical Nutrition* (2000) 71: 154–58.

Nandhini, A. T. Stimulation of glucose utilization and inhibition of protein glycation and AGE products of taurine. *Acta Physiological Scandinavica* (2004) 181: 297–303.

Paille, F. M., et al. Double-blind randomized multicentre trial of acamprosate in maintaining abstinence from alcohol. *Alcohol* (1995) 30: 239–47.

Panula-Lehto, E., et al. Effects of taurine, homotaurine and GABA on hypothalamic and striatal dopamine metabolism. *Naunyn-Schmiedeberg's Archives of Pharmacology* (1992) 346: 57–62.

Quertemont, E., Goffaux, V., Vlaminck, A. M., Wolf, C., and De Witte, P. Oral taurine supplementation modulates ethanol-conditioned stimulus preference. *Alcohol* (1998) 16: 201–6.

Rasmussen, B. B., and Phillips, S. M. Contractile and nutritional regulation of human muscle growth. *Exercise and Sport Sciences Reviews* (2003) 31: 127–31.

Schaafsma, G. The protein digestibility corrected amino acid score. *Journal of Nutrition* (2000) 130: 18655–75.

Seidl, R., Peyrl, A., Nicham, R., and Hauser, E. A taurine and caffeine-containing drink stimulates cognitive performance and well-being. *Amino Acids* (2000) 19 (3–4): 635–38.

Stegink, L. D. Plasma and erythrocyte concentrations of free amino acids in adult humans administered abuse doses of aspartame. *Journal of Toxicology and Environmental Health* (1981) 7: 291.

Timbrell, J. A., Seabra, V., and Waterfield, C. J. The in vivo and in vitro protective properties of taurine. *General Pharmacology* (1995) 26: 453–62.

Van Gelder, N. M. Neuronal discharge hypersynchrony and the intracranial water balance in relation to glutamic acid and taurine redistribution: Migraine and epilepsy. In H. Pasantes-Molales, D. L. Martin,W. Shain, et al., eds., *Taurine: Functional Neurochemistry, Physiology, and Cardiology.* New York: Wiley-Liss, 1990, 351.

van Hall, G., Saris, W. H., van de Schoor, P. A., and Wagenmakers, A. J. The effect of free glutamine and peptide ingestion on the rate of muscle glycogen. *International Journal of Sports Medicine* (January 2000) 21: 25–30.

Whitworth, A. B., et al. Comparison of acamprosate and placebo in long-term treatment of alcohol dependence. *Lancet* (1996) 347: 1438–42.

Zhang, C. G., and Kim, S. J. Taurine induces anti-anxiety by activation strychnine-sensitive glycine receptor in vivo. *Annals of Nutrition and Metabolism* (2007) 51: 379–86.

Zhang, M., et al. Beneficial effects of taurine on serum lipids in overweight or obese nondiabetic subjects. *Amino Acids* (2004) 26: 267–71.

Zhang, M., Izume, I., et al. Role of taurine supplementation to prevent exercise-induced stress in healthy young men. *Amino Acids* (2004) 26: 203–7.

Chapter 8: Who Would Have Thought?

Anderson, J. W. Dietary fiber and associated phytochemicals in prevention and reversal of diabetes. In V. K. Pasupleti and J. W. Anderson, eds., *Nutraceuticals, Glycemic Health and Type 2 Diabetes*. Ames, IA: Blackwell Publishing Professional, 2008, 111–42.

Anderson, J. W. Physiologic and metabolic effects of dietary fiber. *Federation Proceedings* (1985) 44: 2901–6.

Anderson, J. W., Randles, K. M., Kendall, C. W., and Jenkins, D. J. Carbohydrate and fiber recommendations for individuals with diabetes: A quantitative assessment and meta-analysis of the evidence. *Journal of the American College of Nutrition* (2004) 23: 5–17.

Anderson, J. W., Story, L., et al. Hypocholesterolemic effects of oat bran or bran intake on hypercholesterolemic men. *American Journal of Clinical Nutrition* (1984) 40: 1146–55.

Birketvedt, G. S., Shimshi, M., Erling, T., and Florholmen, J. Experiences with three different fiber supplements in weight reduction. *Medical Science Monitor* (2005) 11: 15–18.

Burton-Freeman, B. Dietary fiber and energy regulation. *Journal of Nutrition* (2000) 130: (Suppl.): 272S–75S.

Butcher, J. L., and Beckstrand, R. L. Fiber's impact on high-sensitivity C-reactive protein levels in cardiovascular disease. *Journal of the American Academy of Nurse Practitioners* (2010) 22: 566–72.

Cummings, J. H. The effect of dietary fiber on fecal weight and composition. In G. Spiller, ed., *Dietary Fiber in Human Nutrition*. Boca Raton, FL: CRC Press, 2001, 183–252.

Ebbeling, C. B., et al. Altering portion sizes and eating rate to attenuate gorging during a fast-food meal: Effects on energy intake. *Pediatrics* (2007) 119: 869–75.

Flood-Obbagy, J. E. The effect of fruit in different forms on energy intake and satiety at a meal. *Appetite* (2009) 52: 416–22.

Ford, H., and Frost, G. Glycemic index, appetite and body weight. *Proceedings of the Nutrition Society* (2010) 69: 199–203.

Gropper, S. S., and Acosta, P. B. The therapeutic effect of fiber in treating obesity. *Journal of the American College of Nutrition* (1987) 6: 533–35.

Haber, G. B., Heaton, K. W., Murphy, D., and Burroughs, L. F. Depletion and disruption of dietary fiber: Effects on satiety, plasma glucose and serum insulin. *Lancet* (1977): 679–82.

Judd, P. A., and Truswell, A. S. The effect of rolled oats as blood lipids and fecal steroid excretion in men. *American Journal of Clinical Nutrition* (1981) 34: 2061–67.

Keenan, J. M., Wenz, J. B., Myers, S., Ripsin, C., and Huang, Z. Q. A randomized controlled trial of oat bran cereal for hypercholesterolemia. *Circulation* (1991) 82: 1889.

King, D. E., et al. Effect of a high-fiber diet vs a fiber-supplemented diet on C-reactive protein level. *Archives of Internal Medicine* (2007) 167: 502–56.

Liukkonen, L. M., et al. Fiber in beverages can enhance perceived satiety. *European Journal of Nutrition* (2009) 48: 251–58.

Liu, S., et al. Whole-grain consumption and risk of coronary heart disease: Results from the Nurse's Health Study. *American Journal of Clinical Nutrition* (1999) 70: 412–19.

Mattes, R. D. Effects of a combination fiber system on appetite and energy intake in overweight humans. *Physiology & Behavior* (2007) 23: 705–11.

Pereira, M. A., et al. Dietary fiber and risk of coronary heart disease. *Archives of Internal Medicine* (2004) 164: 370–76.

Smeets, P. A., Erkner, A., and de Graaf, C. Cephalic phase response and appetite. *Nutrition Reviews* (2010) 68: 643–55.

Steffen, L. M., et al. Associations of whole-grain, refined grain, and fruit and vegetable consumption with risks of all-cause mortality and incident of coronary artery disease and ischemic stroke: The Atherosclerosis Risk in Communities (ARIC) Study. *American Journal of Clinical Nutrition* (2003) 78: 383–90.

Van Horn, L., Liu, K., et al. Serum lipid response to oat product intake with a fat-modified diet. *Journal of the American Dietetic Association* (1986) 86: 759–64.

Van Horn, L., Moag-Stahlberg, A., et al. Effects of lipids on adding instant oats to a usual American diet. *American Journal of Public Health* (1991) 81: 183–88.

Viskaal-van Dongen, M., Kok, F. J., and de Graaf, C. Eating rate of commonly consumed foods promotes food and energy intake. *Appetite* (2011) 56: 25–31.

Weickert, M. O., et al. Cereal fiber improves whole-body insulin sensitivity in overweight and obese women. *Diabetes Care* (2006) 29: 775–80.

Whelton, S. P., et al. Effect of dietary fiber on blood pressure: A meta-analysis of randomized, controlled clinical trial. *Journal of Hypertension* (2005) 23: 475–81.

Chapter 9: Working the Salt Minds

Alam, S., and Johnson, A. G. A meta-analysis of randomized controlled trials (RCT) among healthy normotensive and essential hypertensive elderly patients to determine the effect of high-salt (NaCL) diet on blood pressure. *Journal of Human Hypertension* (1999) 13: 367–74.

Alderman, M. H., Madhavan, S., Cohen, H., Sealey, J. E., and Laragh, J. H. Low urinary sodium is associated with greater risk of myocardial infarction among treated hypertensive men. *Hypertension* (1995) 25: 1144–52.

American Heart Association. Heart Disease and Stroke Statistics (2010 update), Dallas, Texas, American Heart Association, 2010.

Blackburn, H., and Prineas, R. Diet and hypertension: Anthropology, epidemiology, and public health implications. *Progress in Biochemical Pharmacology* (1983) 19: 31–79.

Caggiula, A. W., Milas, N. C., Kelsey, S., and Kuller, L. H. Potassium and blood pressure: The Hypertension Is Preventable study. In *Proceedings of the 2nd International Conference on Preventative Cardiology and the 29th Annual Meeting*. AHA Council on Epidemiology, Washington, DC, June 1989.

Centers for Disease Control and Preventon. Application of lower sodium intake recommendations to adults: United States, 1999–2006. *Morbidity and Mortality Weekly Report (MMWR)* (2009) 58: 281–83.

Centers for Disease Control and Prevention. Sodium intake among adults, United States, 2005–2006. *Morbidity and Mortality Weekly Report (MMWR)* (2010) 59: 746–49.

Chen, S. T., Maruthur, N. M., and Appel, L. J. The effect of dietary patterns on estimated coronary heart disease risk: Results from the dietary approaches to stop hypertension (DASH) trial. *Circulation: Cardiovascular Quality and Outcomes* (2010) 3: 484–89.

Cohen, H. W., Hailpern, S. M., Fang, J., and Alderman, M. H. Sodium intake and mortality in the NHANES II follow-up study. *American Journal of Medicine* (2006) 275: e7–e14.

Cutler, J. A., Follmann, D., and Allender, P. S. Randomized trials of sodium reduction: An overview. *American Journal of Clinical Nutrition* (1997) 65 (Suppl. 2): S643–S51.

Dahl, L. K. Effects of chronic excess salt feeding: Induction of self-sustaining hypertension in rats. *Journal of Experimental Medicine* (1961) 114: 231–36.

Dahl, L. K. Effects of chronic excess salt ingestion: Evidence that genetic factors play an important role in susceptibility to experimental hypertension. *Journal of Experimental Medicine* (1962) 114: 1173–1790.

Dahl, L. K. Possible role of chronic excess salt consumption in the pathogenesis of essential hypertension. *American Journal of Cardiology* (1961) 8: 571–75.

Dahl, L. K. Role of dietary sodium in essential hypertension. *Journal of American Dietetic Association* (1958) 34: 585–90.

Graudal, N. A., Galløe, A. M., and Garred, P. Effects of sodium restriction on blood pressure, renin, aldosterone, catecholamines, cholesterols and triglyceride: A meta-analysis. *JAMA* (1998) 279: 1383–91.

Hankey, G. J. Nutrition and the risk of stroke. *Lancet Neurology*, January 2012.

He, F. J., and MacGregor, G. A. Effects of longer-term modest salt reduction on blood pressure. *Cochrane Database of Systematic Reviews* (2004) 3: CD004937.

He, J. Study: More exercise cuts sodium levels. AHA Meeting on Nutrition, Physical Activity, and Health. Atlanta, March 23, 2011.

He, J., Ogden, L. G., et al. Dietary sodium intake and subsequent risk of cardiovascular disease in overweight adults. *JAMA* (1999) 282: 2027–34.

He, J., Whelton, P. K., Appel, L. J., Charleston, J., and Klag, M. J. Long-term effects of weight loss and dietary sodium reduction on incidence of hypertension. *Hypertension* (2000) 35: 544–49.

Hellmich, N. Experts to FDA: Regulate salt; Reports suggest gradual reduction so tastes can adjust. *USA Today*, April 21, 2010.

Hellmich, N. Keeping a lid on salt: Not so easy; known as a silent killer it is part of how we live. *USA Today*, April 28, 2010.

Hypertension Prevention Trial Research Groups. The hypertension prevention trial: Three-year effects of dietary changes on blood pressure. *Archives of Internal Medicine* (1990) 150: 153–62.

Institute of Medicine. Food and Nutrition Board. Dietary reference intakes for water, potassium, sodium, chloride, and sulfate, 2004, http://www.nap.edu/openbook.php?isbn=0309091691.

Kempner, W. Effect of salt restriction on experimental nephrosis. *JAMA* (1965) 191: 51.

Maberly, G. F., Haxton, D. P., and van der Haar, F. Iodine deficiency: Consequences and progress toward elimination. *Food and Nutrition Bulletin* (2003) 24 (Suppl.): S91–S98.

McCarron, D. A., Geerling, J. C., Kazaks, A. G., and Stern, J. S. Can dietary sodium be modified by public policy? *Clinical Journal of the American Society of Nephrology* (2009): 1878–82.

McCarron, D. A., Stern, J. S., and Graudal, N. Public policy and dietary sodium restriction. *JAMA* (2010) 303: 1917–18.

Midgley, J. P., Matthew, A. G., Greenwood, C. M., and Logan, A. G. Effect of reduced dietary sodium on blood pressure: A meta-analysis of randomized controlled trials. *JAMA* (1996) 275: 1590–97.

Mintel, G.N.P.D. Pass the salt? Mintel research (August 2009), http://www.mintel.com/press-centre/press-releases/381/pass-the-salt-mintel-research-shows-sodium-usage-starting-to-change-its-course. Santiago-Fernandez, P., et al. Intelligence quotient and iodine intake: A cross-sectional study in children. *Journal of Clinical Endocrinology & Metabolism* (2004) 89: 3851–57.

Stamler, J. The INTERSALT study background methods, findings, and indications. *American Journal of Clinical Nutrition* (1997) 65: 626S–42S.

Stamler, R., Stamler, J., et al. Primary prevention of hypertension by nutritional-hygienic means: Final report of a randomized controlled trial. *JAMA* (1989) 262: 1801–7.

Stamler, J., Wentworth, D., and Neaton, J. D. Is relationship between serum and risk of premature death from coronary heart disease continuous and graded? *JAMA* (1986) 256: 2823–28.

Trials of Hypertension Prevention Collaborative Research Group. Effects of weight loss and sodium reduction intervention on blood pressure and hypertension incidence in overweight people with high normal blood pressure: The trials of hypertension Phase II. *Archives of Internal Medicine* (1997) 157: 657–67.

Trials of Hypertension Prevention Collaborative Research Group. The effects of non-pharmacological interventions on blood pressure of persons with high normal levels: Results of the trials of hypertension prevention Phase I. *JAMA* (1992) 267: 1213–20.

USDA. HHS: Dietary Guidelines for Americans, 2005, http://www.health.gov/Dietary Guidelines.

USPHS. HHS: Health People—The Surgeon General's Report on Health Promotion and Disease Prevention, 1979, http://profiles.nlm.nih.gov/NN/B/B/G/K/_/nnbbgk.pdf.

Vanderpump, M.P.J., et al. Iodine status of UK schoolgirls: A cross-sectional survey. *Lancet* (2011) 377: 2007–12.

Yang, Q. Sodium and potassium intake and mortality among US adults: Prospective data from the third National Health and Nutrition Examination Survey. *Archives of Internal Medicine* (2011) 171: 1183–91.

Chapter 10: Vitamins and Minerals

Agnoli, A., Ruggieri, S., Denaro, A., and Bruno, G. New strategies in the management of Parkinson's disease: A biological approach using a phospholipid precursor (CDP-choline). *Neuropsychobiology* (1982) 8 (6): 289–96.

Allen, L. H. Calcium bioavailability and absorption: A review. *American Journal of Clinical Nutrition* (1982) 35: 783–808.

Alvarez, X. A., et al. Double-blind placebo-controlled study with citicoline in APOE geno-typed Alzheimer's disease patients: Effects on cognitive performance, brain bioelectrical activity and cerebral perfusion. *Methods & Findings in Experimental & Clinical Pharmacology* (1999) 21: 633–44.

Anderson, J. L., et al. Relation of vitamin D deficiency to cardiovascular risk factors, disease status and incident events in a general healthcare population. *American Journal of Cardiology* (2010) 106: 963–68.

Bell, H., et al. Reduced concentration of hepatic alpha-tocopherol in patients with alcoholic liver cirrhosis. *Alcohol and Alcoholism* (1992) 27: 39.

Binfaré, R. W., Rosa, A. O., Lobato, K. R., Santos, A. R., and Rodrigues, A. L. Ascorbic acid administration produces an antidepressant-like effect: Evidence of the involvement of monoaminergic neurotransmission. *Progress in Neuro-Psychopharmacology and Biological Psychiatry* (2009) 33: 530–40.

Bishai, D. M., and Bozzetti, L. P. Current progress toward the prevention of the Wernicke-Korsakoff syndrome. *Alcohol and Alcoholism* (1986) 21: 315.

Bishop, G. M., Dang, T. N., Dringen, R., and Robinson, S. R. Accumulation of non-trans-ferrin-bound iron by neurons, astrocytes, and microglia. *Neurotoxicity Research* (2011) 19: 443–51.

Bottiglieri, T., et al. Cerebrospinal fluid S-adenosylmethione in depression and dementia: Effects of treatment with parenteral and oral S-adenosylmethionine. *Journal of Neurology, Neurosurgery, and Psychiatry* (1990) 53: 1096–98.

Bowman, B. A., and Russell, R. M. *Present Knowledge in Nutrition.* 9th ed. Vols. 1 and 2. Washington, DC: International Life Sciences Institute, 2006.

Bressa, G. M. S-adenosyl-L-methionine (SAMe) as antidepressant: Meta-analysis of clinical studies. *Neurologica Scandinavica Supplement* (1994) 154: 7.

Chengappa, K. N., et al. Inositol as an add-on treatment for bipolar depression. *Bipolar Disorders* (2000) 2: 47–55.

Cheung, Y. T., et al. Effects of all-trans-retinoic acid on human SH-Sy5Y neuroblastoma as in vitro model in neurotoxicity research. *Neurotoxicology* (2009) 30: 127–35.

Clarke, R. B-vitamins and prevention of dementia. *Proceedings of the National Academy of Sciences* (2008) 67: 75–81.

Clarke, R. Homocysteine, B vitamins and the risk of dementia. *American Journal of Clinical Nutrition* (2007) 85: 329–30.

Clarke, R. Vitamin B$_{12}$, folic acid and the prevention of dementia. *New England Journal of Medicine* (2006) 354: 2817–19.

Clarke, R., Lewington, S., Sherliker, P., and Armitage, J. Effects of B-vitamins on plasma homocysteine concentrations and on risk of cardiovascular disease on dementia. *Current Opinion in Clinical Nutrition & Metabolic Care* (2007) 10: 32–39.

Cook, C. C., et al. Trace element and vitamin deficiency in alcoholic and control subjects. *Alcohol and Alcoholism* (1991) 12:77.

Dangour, A. D., et al. A randomized controlled trial investigating the effect of vitamin B$_{12}$ supplementation on neurological function in healthy older people: The older and enhanced neurological function (OPEN) study protocol. *Nutrition Journal* (2011) 10: 22.

Dickens, A. P., Lang, I. A., Langa, K. M., Kos, K., and Llewellyn, D. J. Vitamin D cognitive dysfunction in older adults. *CNS Drugs* (2011) 25: 629–39.

Dolske, M. C., Spollen, J., McKay, S., Lancashire, E., and Tolbert, L. A preliminary trial of ascorbic acid as a supplemental therapy for autism. *Progress in Neuro-Psychopharmacology and Biological Psychiatry* (1993) 17: 765–74.

Durga, J., van Boxtell, M. P., et al. Effect of 3-year folic acid supplementation on cognitive function in older adults in the FACIT trial: A randomized, double blind, controlled trial. *Lancet* (2007) 369: 208–16.

Durga, J., van Tits, L. J., Schouten, E. G., Kok, F. J., and Verhoef, P. Effect of lowering of homocysteine levels on inflammatory markers: A randomized controlled trial. *Archives of Internal Medicine* (2005) 165: 1388–94.

Elvehjem, C. A., Madden, E. J., Strong, F. M., and Woolley, D. W. The isolation and identification of the anti-black tongue factor 1937. *Journal of Biological Chemistry* (2002) 277: e22.

Elvehjem, C. A., Madden, E. J., Woolley, D. W., and Strong, F. M. Relation of nicotinic and nicotinic amide on canine black tongue (1937). *Journal of the American Chemical Society* (1937) 59: 1767.

Fava, M., Giannelli, A., Rapisarda, V., Patralia, A., and Guaraldi, G. P. Rapidity of onset of the antidepressant effect of parenteral S-adenosyl-L-methionine. *Psychiatry Research* (1995) 56: 295.

Fischer, L. M., da Costa, K. A., Kwock, L., Galanko, J., and Zeisel, S. H. Dietary choline requirements of women: Effects of estrogen and genetic variation. *American Journal of Clinical Nutrition* (2010) 92: 113–19.

Foiravanti, M., and Yanagi, M. Cytidinediphosphocholine (CDP-choline) for cognitive and behavioral disturbances associated with chronic cerebral disorders in the elderly. *Cochrane Reviews* (2002): 2.

Funk, C. The effect of a diet of polished rice on the nitrogen and phosphorus of the brain. *Journal of Physiology* (1912) 44: 50–53.

Funk, C. The preparation from yeast and certain foodstuffs of the substance the deficiency of which in diet occasions polyneuritis in birds. *Journal of Physiology* (1912) 45: 75–81.

Gilbody, S., Lightfoot, T., and Sheldon, T. Is low folate a risk factor for depression? A meta-analysis and exploration of heterogeneity. *Journal of Epidemiology & Community Health* (2007) 61: 631–37.

Goldstein, M. R., Mascitelli, L., and Pezzetta, F. Rosuvastatin and vitamin D: Might there be hypovitaminosis D on JUPITER? *International Journal of Cardiology* (2010) 145: 556–56.

Grodstein, F., Kang, J. H., Glynn, R. J., Cook, N. R., and Gaziano, J. M. A randomized trial of beta carotene supplementation and cognitive function in men: The Physicians' Health Study II. *Archives of International Medicine* (2007) 167: 2184–90.

Harel, Z., Flanagan, P., Forcier, M., and Harel, D. Low vitamin D status among obese adolescents: Prevalence and response to treatment. *Journal of Adolescent Health* (2011) 48: 448–52.

Hu, P., et al. Association between serum beta-carotene levels and decline of cognitive function in high-functioning older persons with or without apolipoprotein E 4 alleles: MacArthur studies of successful aging. *Journals of Gerontology Series A: Biological Sciences and Medical Sciences* (2006) 61: 616–20.

Johansson, U., Johnsson, F., Joelsson, B., Berglund, M., and Akesson, B. Selenium status in patients with liver cirrhosis and alcoholism. *British Journal of Nutrition* (1986) 55: 227.

Johnson, S. R. Premenstrual syndrome therapy. *Clinical Obstetrics and Gynecology* (1998) 41: 405–21.

Kagan, B. L., Sultzer, D. L., Rosenlicht, N., and Gerner, R. H. Oral S-adenosylmethionine in depression: A randomized, double-blind, placebo-controlled trial. *American Journal of Psychiatry* (1990) 147: 591–95.

Korpela, H., Kumpulainen, J., Luoma, P. V., Arranto, A. J., and Sotaniemi, E. A. Decreased serum selenium in alcoholics as related to liver structure and function. *American Journal of Clinical Nutrition* (1985) 42: 147.

Kulkarni, S. K., Deshpande, C., and Dhir, A. Ascorbic acid inhibits development of tolerance and dependence to opiates in mice: Possible glutamatergic dopaminergic modulation. *Indian Journal of Pharmaceutical Sciences* (2008) 70: 56–60.

Levine, M., Dhariwal, K. R., Welch, R. W., Wang, Y., and Park, J. B. Determination of optimal vitamin C requirements in humans. *American Journal of Clinical Nutrition* (1995) 62: 134S–35S.

Levine, M., Morita, K., Heldman, E., and Pollard, H. B. Ascorbic acid regulation of norepinephrine biosynthesis in isolated chromaffin granules from bovine adrenal medulla. *Journal of Biological Chemistry* (1985) 160: 15598–603.

Levine, M., Padayatty, S. J., and Espey, M. G. In situ kinetics: An approach to recommended intake of vitamin C. *Methods in Enzymology* (1997) 279: 43–54.

Levine, M., Rumsey, S., and Wang, Y. Principles involved in formulating recommendations for vitamin C intake: A paradigm for water-soluble vitamins. *Methods in Enzymology* (1997) 279: 43–54.

Lipinski, J. F., et al. Open trial of S-adenosylmethionine for treatment of depression. *American Journal of Psychiatry* (1994) 141: 448.

Llewellyn, D. J., et al. Vitamin D and risk of cognitive decline in elderly persons. *Archives of International Medicine* (2010) 170: 1135–41.

McCleane, G. J., and Watters, C. H. Pre-operative anxiety and serum potassium. *Anaesthesia* (1990) 45: 583.

Mitri, J., Muraru, M. D., and Pittas, A. G. Vitamin D and type 2 diabetes: A systemic review. *European Journal of Clinical Nutrition* (2011).

Morita, K., Levine, M., and Pollard, H. B. Stimulatory effect of ascorbic acid on norepinephrine biosynthesis in digitonin-permeabilized adrenal medullary chromaffin cells. *Journal of Neurochemistry* (1986) 46: 939–45.

Oudshoorn, C., Mattace-Raso, F. U., van der Velde, N., Colin, E. M., van der Cammen, T. J. Higher serum vitamin D_3 levels are associated with better cognitive test performance in patients with Alzheimer's disease. *Dementia and Geriatric Cognitive Disorders* (2008) 25: 539–43.

Payne, M. E. Meeting of the American Society for Nutrition, presentation at the Experimental Biology meeting, May 2007, in Washington, DC.

Piro, A., Tagarelli, G., Lagonia, P., Tagarelli, A., and Quattrone, A. Casimir Funk: His discovery of the vitamins and their deficiency disorders. *Annals of Nutrition and Metabolism* (2010) 57: 85–88.

Prasad, A. S. Discovery and importance of zinc in human nutrition. *Proceedings of the Federation of American Societies for Experimental Biology* (1984) 13: 2829.

Russ, C. S. Vitamin B_6 status of depressed and obsessive compulsive patients. *Nutrition Reports International* (1983) 27: 867–73.

Scott, K., Zeris, S., and Kothari, M. J. Elevated B_6 levels and peripheral neuropathies. *Electromyography and Clinical Neurophysiology* (2008) 48: 219–23.

Secades, J. J., and Frontera, G. CDP-choline: Pharmacological and clinical review. *Methods & Findings in Experimental & Clinical Pharmacology* 17 (1995) (Suppl. B): 1–54.

Sen, A. P., and Gulati, A. Use of magnesium in traumatic brain injury. *Neurotherapeutics* (2010) 7: 91–99.

Signore, C., Ueland, P. M., Troendle, J., and Mills, J. L. Choline concentrations in human maternal and cord blood and intelligence at 5 years of age. *American Journal of Clinical Nutrition* (2008) 887: 896–902.

Slutsky, I., Abumaria, N., et al. Enhancement of learning and memory by elevating brain magnesium. *Neuron* (2010) 65: 165–77.

Slutsky, I., Sadeghpour, S., et al. Enhancement of synaptic plasticity through chronically reduced Ca+2 flux during uncorrelated activity. *Neuron* (2004) 44: 835–49.

Smith, A. D. The worldwide challenge of dementia: A role for B vitamins and homocysteine. *Food Nutrition Bulletin* (2008) (Suppl. 2) 65: S143–S72.

Sullivan, L. M., et al. Homocysteine and cognitive performance in the Framingham offspring study: Age is important. *American Journal of Epidemiology* (2005) 162: 644–53.

Susick, R. L., Jr., Abrams, G. D., Zurawski, C. A., and Zannoni, V. G. Ascorbic acid chronic alcohol consumption in the guinea pig. *Applied Pharmacology* (1986) 84: 329.

Svirbely, J. L., and Szent-Gyorgyi, A. The chemical nature of vitamin C. *Biochemical Journal* (1932) 26: 865–70.

Szent-Gyorgyi, A. The identification of vitamin C. *Science* (1938) 87: 214–15.

Talbott, S. *The Cortisol Connection: Why Stress Makes You Fat and Ruins Your Health—and What You Can Do About It.* Alameda, CA: Hunter House, Inc., 2002.

Tang, J. Y., et al. High prevalence of vitamin D deficiency in patients with basal cell nevus syndrome. *Archives of Dermatology* (2010) 146: 1105–10.

Thompson, J. N., and Duval, S. Determination of vitamin A in milk and infant formula by HPLC. *Journal of Micronutrient Analysis* (1989) 6: 147–59.

Thompson, W. G. Vitamin B_{12} and geriatrics: Unanswered questions. *Acta Haematologica* (1989) 82: 169–74.

Townsend, A. M. Pellagra: Its history and symptomology. *Journal of the National Medical Association* (1900) 1: 88–91.

Ueland, P. M. Choline and betaine in health and disease. *Journal of Inherited Metabolic Disease* (2010) 34: 3–15.

Vogiatzoglou, A. Vitamin B_{12} status and rate of brain volume loss in community-dwelling elderly. *Neurology* (2008) 71: 826–32.

Wandzilak, T. R. Effect of high-dose vitamin C on urinary oxalate levels. *Journal of Urology* (1994) 151: 834–37.

Zeisel, S. H., and da Costa, K. A. Choline: An essential nutrient for public health. *Nutrition Reviews* (2009) 67: 615–23.

Chapter 11: Healing with Herbs and Nutraceuticals

Al-Reza, S. M., Yoon, J. I., Kim, H. J., Kim, J. S., and Kang, S. C. Anti-inflammatory activity of seed essential oil from Zizyphus jujube. *Food and Chemical Toxicology* (2010) 48: 639–43.

Amaducci, L. Phosphatidylserine in the treatment of Alzheimer's disease: Results of a multicenter study. *Psychopharmacology Bulletin* (1988) 24: 130–34.

Amaducci, L., Crook, T. H., et al. Use of phosphatidylserine in Alzheimer's disease. *Annals of the New York Academy of Sciences* (1991) 640: 245–49.

Amen, D. G. *Making a Good Brain Great.* New York: Three Rivers Press, 2005.

Baghkhani, L., and Jafari, M. Cardiovascular adverse reactions associated with Guarana: Is there a causal effect? *Journal of Herbal Pharmacotherapy* (2002) 2: 57–61.

Beavo, J. A. Cyclic nucleotide phosphodiesterases: Functional implications of multiple isoforms. *Physiological Reviews* (1995) 75: 725–48.

Bennett, A. W., and Bealer, B. K. *The World of Caffeine: The Science and Culture of the World's Most Popular Drug.* New York: Routledge, 2001, 192–93, 230, 259–60.

Berlin, D. Ginkgo: Keeping head and heart healthy. *Nutrition in Complementary Care* (1999) 2: 3.

Berube-Parent, S., *Pelletier, C., Doré, J., and Tremblay, A.* Effects of encapsulated green tea and guarana extracts containing a mixture of epigallocatechin-3-gallate and caffeine on 24h energy expenditure and fat oxidation in men. *British Journal of Nutrition* (2005) 94: 432–36.

Bonoczk, P., et al. Role of sodium channel inhibition in neuroprotection: Effect of vinpocetine. *Brain Research Bulletin* (2000) 53: 245–54.

Bourgain, R. H., Andries, R., and Braquet, P. Effect of ginkgolide PAF-acether antagonists on arterial thrombosis. *Advances in Prostaglandin Thromboxane Leukotriene Research* (1987) 17B: 815–17.

Brambilla, F., and Maggioni, M. Blood levels of cytokines in elderly patients with major depressive disorder. *Acta Psychiatrica Scandinavica* (1998) 97: 309–13.

Brambilla, F., Maggioni, M., Panerai, A. E., Sacerdote, P., and Cenacchi, T. Beta-endorphin concentration in peripheral blood mononuclear cells of elderly depressed patients— effects of phosphatidylserine therapy. *Neuropsychobiology* (1996) 34: 18–21.

Bush, T. M., et al. Adverse interactions between herbal and dietary substances and prescription medications: A clinical survey. *Alternative Therapies in Health and Medicine* (2007) 13:30–35.

Bydlowski, S. P., D'Amico, E. A., and Chamone, D. A. An aqueous extract of guarana (Paullinia cupana) decreases platelet thromboxane synthesis. *Brazilian Journal of Medical and Biological Research* (1991) 24: 421–24.

Caffarra, P. The effects of phosphatidylserine in patients with mild cognitive decline: An open trial. *Clinical Trials Journal* (1987) 24: 109–14.

Cao, J. X., et al. Hypnotic effect of jujubosides from Semen Ziziphi Spinosae. *Journal of Ethnopharmacology* (2010) 130: 163–66.

Cenacchi, T., Bertoldin, T., Farina, C., Fiori, M. G., Crepaldi, G. Cognitive decline in the elderly: A double-blind, placebo-controlled multicenter study on efficacy of phosphatidylserine administration. *Aging* (Milano) (1993) 5:123–33.

Cheraskin, E., and Ringsdorf, W. M. Blood glucose levels after caffeine. *Lancet* (1968) 2: 689.

Chiu, P. J., Tetzloff, G., Ahn H. S., and Sybertz, E. J. Comparative effects of vinpocetine and 8-Br-cyclic, GMP on the contraction and 45Ca-fluxes in the rabbit aorta. *American Journal of Hypertension* (1988) 1: 262–68.

Cifani, C., et al. Effect of salidroside, active principle of *Rhodiola rosea* extract, on binge eating. *Physiology & Behavior* (2010) 101: 565–62.

Cohen, A. J. Long-term safety and efficacy of Ginkgo biloba for antidepressant-induced sexual dysfunction. *PsychiatryOnline* (1998), www.priory.com/pharmol/gingko.htm.

Cohen, A. J., and Bartlik, B. Ginkgo biloba for antidepressant-induced sexual dysfunction. *Journal of Sex & Marital Therapy* (1998) 24: 139–43.

Cohen, A. J., and Bartlik, B. Treatment of antidepressant-induced sexual dysfunction with Gingko biloba extract. *Health Watch* 6, 1 (1996).

Crime Times. New research supports value of omega-3 supplements in reducing ADHD symptoms. *Crime Times* (2007) 13: 4, 5.

Crook, T., Petrie, W., Wells, C., and Massari, D. C. Effects of phosphatidylserine in Alzheimer's disease. *Psychopharmacology Bulletin* (1992) 28: 61–66.

Crook, T., Tinklenberg, J., et al. Effects of phosphatidylserine in age-associated memory impairment. *Neurology* (1991) 41: 644–49.

Darbinyan, V., Aslanyan, G., et al. Clinical trial of *Rhodiola rosea* L. extract SHR-5 in the treatment of mild to moderate depression. *Nordic Journal of Psychiatry* (2007) 61: 343–48.

Darbinyan, V., Kteyan, A., et al. *Rhodiola rosea* in stress-induced fatigue: A double-blind cross-over study of a standardized extract SHR-5 with a repeated low-dose regimen on the mental performance of healthy physicians during night duty. *Phytomedicine* (2000) 7: 365–71.

Delwaide, P. J., Gyselynck-Mambourg, A. M., Hurlet, A., and Ylieff, M. Double-blind randomized controlled study of phosphatidylserine in senile demented patients. *Acta Neurologica Scandinavica* (1986) 73: 1236–40.

Dézsi, L., Kis-Varga, I., Nagy, J., Komlódi, Z., and Kárpáti, E. Neuroprotective effects of vinpocetine in vivo and in vitro: Apovincaminic acid derivatives as potential therapeutic tools in ischemic stroke. *Acta Pharmaceutica Hungarica* (2002) 72: 84–91.

Diamond, B. J., et al. Ginkgo biloba extract: Mechanisms and clinical indications. *Archives of Physical Medicine and Rehabilitation* (2000) 81: 668–78.

Diboune, M., et al. Soybean oil, blackcurrant seed oil, medium-chain triglycerides, and plasma phospholipid fatty acids of stressed patients. *Nutrition* (1993) 9: 344.

Ellison, J., and DeLuca, P. Fluoxetine-induced genital anesthesia relieved by ginkgo biloba extract (letter). *Journal of Clinical Psychiatry* (1998) 59: 199–200.

Engel, R. R., et al. Double-blind cross-over study of phosphatidylserine vs. placebo in patients with early dementia of Alzheimer type. *European Neuropsychopharmacology* (1992) 2: 149–55.

Espinola, E. B., Dias, R. F., Mattei, R., and Carlini, E. A. Pharmacological activity of Guarana (Paullinia cupana) in laboratory animals. *Journal of Ethnopharmacology* (1997) 55: 223–29.

Fang, X. S., et al. Pharmacological studies on the sedative-hypnotic effect of Semen Ziziphi spinosae (Suanzaoren) and Radix et Rhizoma Salviae miltiorrhizae (Danshen) extracts and the synergistic effect of their combinations. *Phytomedicine* (2010) 17: 75–80.

Fredholm, B. B., Bättig, K., Holmén, J., Nehlig, A., and Zvartau, E. E. Actions of caffeine in the brain with special reference to factors that contribute to its widespread use. *Pharmacological Reviews* (1999) 51: 83–133.

Fuchs, N. K. Retrieving lost memories—naturally. *Women's Health Letter*, March 1, 2002.

Goyal, R. Possible attenuation of nitric oxide expression in anti-inflammatory effect of Ziziphus jujube in rat. *Journal of Natural Medicines* (2011) 65: 514–18.

Granata, Q., and DiMichele, J. D. Phosphatidylserine in elderly patients: An open trial. *Clinical Trials Journal* (1987) 24: 99–103.

Granger, A. S. *Ginkgo biloba* precipitating epileptic seizures. *Age and Ageing* (2001) 30: 523–25.

Gregory, P. J. Seizure associated with *Ginkgo biloba*? *Annals of Internal Medicine* (2001) 134: 344.

Gurley, B. J., Gardner S. F., and Hubbard, M. A. Clinical assessment of potential cytochrome P450-mediated herb-drug interactions. AAPS Annual Meeting & Expo, Indianapolis, Indiana, October 29–November 2, 2000, presentation #3460.

Hall, T., et al. Evaluation of consistency of the standardized Asian ginseng product in the ginseng evaluation program. *Herbalgram* (2001) 52: 31–45.

Halpern, G. *Ginkgo: A Practical Guide*. New York: Avery Publishing Group, 1998.

Haskell, C. F., Kennedy, D. O., Milne, A. L., Wesnes, K. A., and Scholey, A. B. The effects of L-theanine, caffeine and their combination on cognition and mood. *Biological Psychology* (2008) 77: 113–22.

Haskell, C. F., Kennedy, D. O., Wesnes, K. A., Milne, A. L., and Scholey, A. B. A double-blind, placebo-controlled, multidose evaluation of the acute behavioral effects of guarana in humans. *Journal of Psychopharmacology* (2007) 21: 65–70.

Heiss, W. D., Kessler, J., Mielke, R., Szelies, B., and Herholz, K. Long-term effects of phosphatidylserine, pyritinol, and cognitive training in Alzheimer's disease: A neuropsychological, EEG and PET investigation. *Dementia* (1994) 5: 88–98.

Heiss, W. D., Slansky, I., et al. Activation PET as an instrument to determine therapeutic efficacy in Alzheimer's disease. *Annals of the New York Academy of Sciences* (1993) 695: 327–31.

Heiss, W. D., Szelies, B., Kessler, J., and Herholz, K. Abnormalities of energy metabolism in Alzheimer's disease studied with PET. *Annals of the New York Academy of Sciences* (1991) 640: 65–71.

Hirayama, S., Masuda, Y., and Rabeler, R. Effects of phosphatidylserine administration on symptoms of attention-deficit/hyperactivity disorder in children. *Agro Food* (September/October 2006) 17: 32–36.

Hoppe, H. Drogen kunde Band 2, *Angiosperm* 8. Berlin, Germany: Walter de Gruyter, 1975, 986–87.

Hsu, H. Y. *Oriental Matria Medica: A Concise Guide*. New Canaan, CT: Keats, 1986.

Jiang, J. G., Huang, X. J., and Chen, J. Separation and purification of saponins from Semen Ziziphus jujube and their sedative and hypnotic effects. *Journal of Pharmacy and Pharmacology* (2007) 59: 1175–80.

Jiang, J. G., Huang, X. J., Chen, J., and Lin, Q. S. Comparison of the sedative and hypnotic effects of flavonoids, saponins, and polysaccharides extracted from Semen Ziziphus jujube. *Natural Product Research* (2007) 21: 310–20.

Higashiyama, A., Htay, H. H., Ozeki, M., Juneja, L. R., and Kapoor, M. P. Effects of L-theanine on attention and reaction time response (2011) 3: 171–78.

Kakuda, T., Nozawa, A., Unno, T., Okamura, N., and Okai, O. Inhibiting effects of theanine on caffeine stimulation evaluated by EEG in the rat. *Bioscience, Biotechnology, and Biochemistry* (2000) 64: 287–93.

Kakuda, T., Yanase, H., et al. Protective effect of gamma-glutamylethylamide (theanine) on ischemic delayed neuronal death in gerbils. *Neuroscience Letters* (2000) 289: 189–92.

Keheyan, G., Dunn, L. A., and Hall, W. L. Acute effects of Ginkgo biloba extract on vascular function and blood pressure. *Plant Foods for Human Nutrition* (2011).

Kennedy, D. O., et al. Improved cognitive performance and mental fatigue following a multi-vitamin supplement with added guarana (Paullinia cupana). *Appetite* (2008) 50: 506–13.

Kidd, P. M. Phosphatidylserine; membrane nutrient for memory: A clinical and mechanistic assessment. *Alternative Medicine Review* (1996) 1: 70–84.

Kidd, P. M. *PS (Phosphatidylserine) Nature's Brain Booster for Memory, Mood, and Stress.* St. George, UT: Total Health Communications, Inc., 2005.

Kimura, K. L-Theanine reduces psychological and physiological stress responses. *Biological Psychology* (2007) 74: 39–45.

Kleijnen, J., and Knipschild, P. Ginkgo biloba. *Lancet* (1993) 340: 1136–39.

Klinkhammer, P., Szelies, B., and Heiss, W.-D. Effect of phosphatidylserine on cerebral glucose metabolism in Alzheimer's disease. *Cognitive Deterioration* (1999) 1: 197–201.

Klotter, J. Phosphatidylserine, omega-3 and ADHD. *Townsend Letter*, April 1, 2008.

Krasik, E. D., Morozova, E. S., et al. Therapy of asthenic conditions: Clinical perspectives of application of *Rhodiola rosea* extract (golden root). In *Proceedings of Modern Problems in Psychopharmacology.* Kemerovo City, Russia: Siberian Branch of Russian Academy of Sciences, 1970, 298–330.

Krasik, E. D., Petrova, K., et al. New data on the therapy of asthenic conditions (clinical prospects for the use of *Rhodiola* extract). *Proceedings of All-Russia Conference: Urgent Problems in Psychopharmacology*, May 26–29, 1970. Sverdlovsk, Russia: Sverdlovsk Press, 1970, 215–17.

Kurkin, V. A., and Zapesochnaya, G. G. Chemical composition and pharmacological properties of *Rhodiola rosea. Chemical and Pharmaceutical Journal* (Moscow) (1986) 20: 1231–44.

Lamant, V., Mauco, G., Braquet, P., Chap, H., and Douste-Blazy, L. Inhibition of the metabolism of platelet-activating factor (PAF-acether) by three specific antagonists from ginkgo biloba. *Biochemical Pharmacology* (1987) 36: 2749–52.

Latorraca, S., et al. Effect of phosphatidylserine on free radical susceptibility in human diploid fibroblasts. *Journal of Neural Transmission Parkinson's Disease Dementia Section* (1993) 6: 73–77.

Lazarova, M. B., et al. Effects of meclofenoxate and extr *Rhodiola rosea* L on electroconvulsive shock impaired learning and memory in rats. *Methods & Findings in Experimental & Clinical Pharmacology* (1986) 8: 547–52.

Leung, A. Y. *Encyclopedia of Common Natural Ingredients Use in Food, Drugs and Cosmetics.* 2nd ed. New York: John Wiley & Sons, 1996, 186–89.

Li, B. L., et al. Sedative, hypnotic and antiseizure effects of compound gardenia oil and jujube seed oil in mice. *Nan Fang Yi Ke Da Xue Xue Bao* (2008) 28: 1636–39.

Lima, W. P., et al. Lipid metabolism in trained rats: Effect of guarana (*Paullinia cupan Mart.*) supplementation. *Clinical Nutrition* (2005) 24: 1019–28.

Lim, S., et al. EGb761, a Ginkgo biloba extract, is effective against atherosclerosis in vitro, and in a rat model of type 2 diabetes. *PLoS One* (2011) 6: e20301.

Lu, K., et al. The acute effects of L-theanine in comparison with alprazolam on anticipatory anxiety in humans. *Psychopharmacology* (2004) 74: 39–45.

Maggioni, M., et al. Effects of phosphatidylserine therapy in geriatric patients with depressive disorders. *Acta Psychiatrica Scandinavica* (1990) 81: 265–70.

Magnusson, B. *Fagringar: Vaxter som berar oss [Beauty: Herbs that Touch Us]* . . . stersund. Sweden: Berndtssons, 1992, 66–67.

Mahadevan, S., and Park, Y. Multifaceted therapeutic benefits of Ginkgo biloba L: Chemistry, efficacy, safety and uses. *Journal of Food Sciences* (2008) 1: 14–19.

Marina, T. F. Effect of *Rhodiola rosea* extract on bioelectrical activity of the cerebral cortex isolated to a different extent from the brain. In A. S. Saratikov, ed., *Stimulants of the Central Nervous System*. Tomsk, Russia: Tomsk State University Press, 1968, 27–31.

Marina, T. F., and Alekseeva, L. P. Effect of *Rhodiola rosea* extract on electroencephalograms in rabbit. In A. S. Saratikov, ed., *Stimulants of the Central Nervous System*. Tomsk, Russia: Tomsk State University Press, 1968, 22–26.

Mason, R. 200 mg of Zen: L-theanine boosts alpha waves and promotes alert relaxation. *Alternative and Complementary Therapies* (2001) 7: 91–95.

Massoni, G. Effects on microcirculation of Gingko biloba in elderly people. *G Gerontology* (1972) 20: 444–50.

Mindell, E. *Soy Miracle*. New York: Fireside, 1995.

Mishra, T., and Bhatia, A. Augmentation of expression of immunocytes' functions by seed extract of Ziziphus mauritiana (Lamk.). *Journal of Ethnopharmacology* (2010) 127: 341–45.

Monteleone, P. Effects of phosphatidylserine on the neuroendocrine response to physical stress in humans. *Neuroendocrinology* (1990) 52: 243.

Monteleone, P., Maj, M., Beinat, L., Natale, M., and Kemali, D. Blunting by chronic phosphatidylserine administration of the stress-induced activation of the hypothalamo-pituitary-adrenal axis in healthy men. *European Journal of Clinical Pharmacology* (1992) 42:385.

Nagy, Z., et al. Meta-analysis of Cavinton. *Praxis* (1998) 7: 63–68.

Narr, H. Phytochemical and pharmacological investigation of the adaptogens: Eutherococcus senticocus, Ocimum sanctum, Codonopsis pilosula, Rhodiola crenulata. Dissertation. Faculty of Chemistry and Pharmacy, Ludwig-Maximilians-Universität München, Munich, Germany, 1993.

Nathan, P. J., Lu, K., Gray, M., and Oliver, C. The neuropharmacology of L-theanine (N-ethyl-L-glutamine): A possible neuroprotective and cognitive enhancing agent.

Journal of Herbal Pharmacotherapy (2006) 6: 21–30. *Natural Health.* Guide to the smart nutrients. March–April 1998.

Nicolaou, K. C., et al. Synthesis and biological properties of pinane-thromboxane A2, a selective inhibitor of coronary artery constriction, platelet aggregation and thromboxane formation. *Proceedings of the National Academy of Sciences USA* (1979) 76: 2566–70.

Nunzi, M. G., et al. Behavioral and morph-functional correlates of brain aging: A preclinical study with phosphatidylserine. In N. G. Bazan, ed., *Neurobiology of Essential Fatty Acids.* New York: Plenum Press, 1992, 393–98.

Palmieri, G. Double-blind controlled trial of phosphatidylserine inpatients with senile mental deterioration. *Clinical Trials Journal* (1987) 24: 73–83.

Panossian, A., Wikman, G., and Sarris, J. Rosenroot (*Rhodiola rosea*): Traditional use, chemical composition, pharmacology and clinical efficacy. *Phytomedicine* (2010) 1: 481–93.

Pepeu, G., Pepeu, I. M., and Amaducci, L. A review of phosphatidylserine pharmacological and clinical effects: Is phosphatidylserine a drug for the ageing brain? *Pharmacological Research* (1996) 33: 73–80.

Petkov, V. D., Stancheva, S. L., Tocuschieva, L., and Petkov, V. V. Changes in brain biogenic monoamines induced by the nootropics drugs adafenoxate and meclofenoxate and by citicholine (experiments on rats). *General Pharmacology* (1990) 21: 71–75.

Petkov, V. D., Yonkov, D., et al. Effects of alcohol aqueous extract from *Rhodiola rosea* L. roots on learning and memory. *Acta Physiologica et Pharmacologica Bulgarica* (1986) 12: 3–16.

Prance, G., and Nesbitt, M. *Cultural History of Plants.* New York: Routledge, 2004, 179.

Reay, J. L., Kennedy, D. O., and Scholey, A. B. Single doses of Panax ginseng (G115) reduce blood glucose levels and improve cognitive performance during sustained mental activity. *Journal of Psychopharmacology* (2005) 19: 357–65.

Sadzuka, Y., Sugiyama, T., Suzuki, T., and Sonobe, T. Enhancement of the activity of doxorubicin by inhibition of glutamate transporter. *Toxicology Letters* (2001) 123: 159–67.

Saratikov, A., Marina, T. F., and Fisanova, L. L. Effect of golden root extract on processes of serotonin synthesis in CNS. *Journal of Biological Sciences* (1978) 6: 142.

Saratikov, A. S., and Krasnov, E. A. Clinical studies of *Rhodiola*. In A. S. Saratikov and E. A. Krasnov, eds., *Rhodiola Rosea Is a Valuable Medicinal Plant (Golden Root).* Tomsk, Russia: Tomsk State University Press, 1987, 216–27.

Saratikov, A. S., and Krasnov, E. A. *Rhodiola Rosea Is a Valuable Medicinal Plant (Golden Root).* Tomsk, Russia: Tomsk State University Press, 1987.

Schreiber, S. An open trial of plant-source derived phosphatidylserine for treatment of age-related cognitive decline. *Israel Journal of Psychiatry and Related Sciences* (2000) 37: 302–7.

Shibota, M., Kakihana, M., and Nagaoka, A. The effect of vinpocetine on brain glucose uptake in mice. *Nippon Yakurigaku Zasshi* (1982) 80: 221–24. [Article in Japanese.]

Shin, H. R., Kim, J. Y., Yun, T. K., Morgan, G., and Vainio, H. The cancer-preventive potential of Panax ginseng: A review of human and experimental evidence. *Cancer Causes and Control* (2000) 11: 565–76.

Shou, C., Feng, Z., Wang, J., and Zheng, X. The inhibitory effects of jujuboside A on rat hippocampus in vivo and in vitro. *Planta Medica* (2002) 68: 799–803.

Siegers, C. P. Cytotoxicity of alkylphenols from Ginkgo biloba. *Phytomedicine* (1999) 6: 281–83.

Siepina, V. S., Wollschlaeger, B., and Blumenthal, M. Ginkgo biloba. *American Family Physician* (2003) 68: 923–26.

Sinforiani, E., et al. Cognitive decline in ageing brain: Therapeutic approach with phosphatidylserine. *Clinical Trials Journal* (1987) 24: 115–24.

SMID Group. Phosphatidylserine in the treatment of clinically diagnosed Alzheimer's disease. *Journal of Neural Transmission Supplement* (1987) 24: 287–92.

Sohn, M., and Sikora, R. Ginkgo biloba extract in the therapy of erectile dysfunction. *Journal of Urology* (1989) 141: 188A.

Spasov, A. A., Mandrikov, V. B., and Mironova, I. A. The effect of the preparation rhodiosin on the psychophysiological and physical adaptation of students to an academic load. *Eksperimental'naia i klinicheskaia farmakologiia* (2000) 63: 76–78.

Spasov, A. A., Wikman, G. K., Mandrikov, V. B., Mironova, I. A., and Neumoin, V. V. A double-blind, placebo-controlled pilot study of the stimulating and adaptogenic effect of *Rhodiola rosea* SHR-5 extract on the fatigue of students caused by stress during an examination period with a repeated low-dose regimen. *Phytomedicine* (2000) 7: 85–89.

Starks, M. A., Starks, S. L., Kingsley, M., Purpura, M., and Jäger, R. The effects of phosphatidylserine on endocrine response to moderate intensity exercise. *Journal of the International Society of Sports Nutrition* (2008) 5: 11.

Stewart, D. E. Venlafaxine and sour date nut. *American Journal of Psychiatry* (2004) 161: 1129–30.

Stole, S. Indole derivatives as neuroprotectants. *Life Sciences* (1999) 65: 1943–50.

Sugiyama, T., and Sadzuka, Y. Combination of theanine with doxorubicin inhibits hepatic metastasis of M5076 ovarian sarcoma. *Clinical Cancer Research* (1999) 5: 413–16.

Sugiyama, T., and Sadzuka, Y. Theanine and glutamate transporter inhibitors enhance the antitumor efficacy of chemotherapeutic agents. *Biochim et Biophysica Acta* (2003) 1653: 47–59.

Sugiyama, T., and Sadzuka, Y. Theanine, a specific glutamate derivative in green tea, reduces the adverse reactions of doxorubicin by changing the glutathione level. *Cancer Letters* (2004) 212: 177–84.

Sugiyama, T., Sadzuka, Y., et al. Membrane transport and antitumor activity of pirarubicin, and comparison with those of doxorubicin. *Japanese Journal of Cancer Research* (1999) 90: 775–80.

Szakall, S., et al. Cerebral effects of a single dose of intravenous vinpocetine in chronic stroke patients: APET study. *Journal of Neuroimaging* (1998) 8: 197–204.

Talbott, S. *The Cortisol Connection.* Alameda, CA: Hunter House, 2002.

Tang Center for Herbal Medicine Research, University of Chicago.

Ginseng. August 9, 2011, http://tangcenter.uchicago.edu/herbal_resources/ginseng.shtml.

Taylor, C. L. Phosphatidylserine and cognitive dysfunction and dementia (Qualified Health Claim: Final Decision Letter). Office of Nutritional Products, Labeling and Dietary Supplements, May 13, 2003.

Terpstra, A.H.M., et al. The decrease in body fat in mice fed conjugated linoleic acid is due to increases in energy expenditure and energy loss in excreta. *Journal of Nutrition* (2002) 132: 940–45.

Thal, L. J., Salmon, D. P., Lasker, B., Bower, D., and Klauber, M. R. The safety and lack of efficacy of vinpocetine in Alzheimer's disease. *Journal of the American Geriatrics Society* (1989) 37: 515–20.

Tyler, V. *The Honest Herbal: A Sensible Guide to the Use of Herbs and Related Remedies.* New York: Lubrecht and Cramer, 1993.

Vasisman, N., et al. Correlation between changes in blood fatty acid composition and visual sustained attention performance in children with inattention: Effect of dietary n-3 fatty acids containing phospholipids. *American Journal of Clinical Nutrition* (2008) 87: 1170–80.

Villardita, J. C., Grioli, S., Salmeri, G., Nicoletti, F., and Pennisi, G. Multicenter clinical trial of brain phosphatidylserine in elderly patients with intellectual deterioration. *Clinical Trials Journal* (1987) 24: 84–93.

von Moltke, L. L., et al. Inhibition of human cytochromes P450 by components of Ginkgo biloba. *Journal of Pharmacy and Pharmacology* (2004) 56: 1039–44.

Vuksan, V., Sievenpiper, J. L., et al. American ginseng (Panax quinquefolius L.) reduces postprandial glycemia in nondiabetic subjects and subjects with type 2 diabetes mellitus. *Archives of International Medicine* (2000) 160: 1009–13.

Vuksan, V., Stavro, M. P., et al. Similar postprandial glycemic reductions with escalation of dose and administration time of American ginseng type 2 diabetes. *Diabetes Care* (2000), 1221–25.

Vuong, Q. V., et al. L-theanine: Properties, synthesis and isolation from tea. *Journal of the Science of Food and Agriculture* (2011) 91: 1931–39.

Wagate, C. G., et al. Screening of some Kenyan medicinal plants for antibacterial activity. *Phytotherapy Research* (2010) 24: 150–53.

Weil, Dr. Andrew. Weil website at www.drweil, August 20, 2002.

Wong, C. What is Guarana? About.com. Alternative Medicine, www.altmedicine.about.com, July 20, 2006.

Wujaiaseng China National Native Produce & Animal By-Products Import & Export Corp. Heilungkiang Native Produce Branch.

Xie, J., Guo, L., Pang, G., Wu, X., and Zhang, M. Modulation effect of Semen Ziziphi Spinosae extracts on IL-1B, IL-4, IL-6, IL-10,TNF-a and IFN-y in mouse serum. *Natural Product Research* (2011) 25: 464–67.

Yokogoshi, H., and Kobayashi, M. Hypotensive effect of gamma-glutamylmethylamide in spontaneously hypertensive rats. *Life Sciences* (1998) 62:1065–68.

Yokogoshi, H., Kobayashi, M., Mochizuki, M., and Terashima, T. Effect of theanine, r-glutamylethylamide, on brain monoamines and striatal dopamine release in conscious rats. *Neurochemical Research* (1998) 23: 667–73.

Yokogoshi, H., Mochizuki, M., and Saitoh, K. Theanine-induced reduction of brain serotonin concentration in rats. *Bioscience, Biotechnology, and Biochemistry* (1998) 62: 816–17.

Yoo, K. Y., et al. Zizyphus attenuates ischemic damage in the gerbil hippocampus via its antioxidant effect. *Journal of Medicinal Food* (2010) 13: 557–63.

Yoshikawa, T., et al. Ginkgo biloba leaf extract: Review of biological actions and clinical applications. *Antioxidants & Redox Signaling* (1999) 1: 469–80.

Zanotti, A., Valzelli, L., and Toffano, G. Chronic phosphatidylserine treatment improves spatial memory and passive avoidance in aged rats. *Psychopharmacology* (1989) 99: 316–21.

Zhang, Z., Wan, X., and Li, D. Chemistry and biological properties of theanine. In C. Ho, J.-K. Lin, and F. Shadhidi, eds., *Tea and Tea Products: Chemistry and Health-Promoting Properties*. New York: CRC Press, 2009.

Chapter 12: Artificial Sweeteners and Caffeine

American Dietetic Association Facts About Sucralose. ADA Nutrition Fact Sheet, 2006, http://www.sucralose.org/pdf/ADAFactSheet_FINAL.pdf.

Arab, L., Liu, W., and Elashoff, D. Green and black tea consumption and risk of stroke: A meta-analysis. *Stroke* (2009) 40: 1786–92.

Arnlov, J. Coffee consumption and insulin sensitivity. *JAMA* (2004) 291: 1199–1201.

BD Diabetes. Diet soda doesn't raise diabetes risk: Study. *American Journal of Clinical Nutrition* online, March 23, 2011, http://www.bd.com/us/diabetes/pageaspx?cat=7001&id=62964.

Butchko, H., et al. Aspartame: Review of safety. *Regulatory Toxicology and Pharmacology* (April 2002) 35 (Part 2): S1–S93.

Calorie Control Council. Sucralose facts: A safe food ingredient, http://www.sucralose.org/facts/default.asp, 2011.

Center for Science in the Public Interest. Caffeine Content of Food & Drugs, http://www.cspinet.org/new/cafchart.htm. Additional information: Juliano, L. M., and Griffiths, R. R. Caffeine. In J. H. Lowinson, P. Ruiz, R. B. Millman, and J. G. Langrod, eds., *Substance Abuse: A Comprehensive Textbook*. 4th ed. Baltimore: Lippincott, Williams & Wilkins, 2005, 403–21.

Chen, L., et al. Reduction in consumption of sugar-sweetened beverages is associated with weight loss: The PREMIER trial. *American Journal of Clinical Nutrition* (2009) 82: 1299–1306.

Collins, A. C., Wehner, J. M., and Wilson, W. R. Animal models of alcoholism: Genetic strategies and neurochemical mechanisms. *Biochemical Society Symposia* (1993) 59: 173–91.

Collins, L. M., Graham, J. W., Rousculp, S. S., and Hansen, W. B. Heavy caffeine use and the beginning of the substance use onset process: An illustration of latent transition analysis. In K. Bryant, M. Windle, and S. West, eds., *The Science of Prevention: Methodological Advances from Alcohol and Substance Abuse Research*. Washington, DC: American Psychological Association, 1997, 79–99.

Cornelis, M. C., et al. Genome-wide meta-analysis identifies regions on 7p21(AHR) and 15q24 (CYP1A2) as determinants of habitual caffeine consumption. *PLoS Genetics* (2011).

de Koning, G.J.M., et al. Tea and coffee consumption and cardiovascular morbidity and mortality. *Arteriosclerosis, Thrombosis, and Vascular Biology* (2010) 30: 1665–71.

de Koning, L., Malik, V. S., Rimm, E. B., Willett, W. C., and Hu, F. B. Sugar-sweetened and artificially sweetened beverage consumption and the risk of type 2 diabetes in men. *American Journal of Clinical Nutrition* (2011) 93: 1321–27.

Dhingra, R., et al. Soft drink consumption and risk of developing cardiometabolic risk factors and the metabolic syndrome in middle-aged adults in the community. *Circulation* (2007) 116: 480–88.

European Food Safety Authority Report of the Meeting on Aspartame with National Experts. *EFSA Journal* (2010), question number: EFSA-Q-2009-00488.

Ford, H. E., et al. Effects of oral ingestion of sucralose on gut hormone response and appetite in healthy normal-weight subjects. *European Journal of Clinical Nutrition* (2011) 65: 508–13.

Fowler, S. P., et al. Fueling the obesity epidemic? Artificially sweetened beverage use and long-term weight gain. *Obesity* (2008) 16: 1894–1900.

Griffiths, R. R., Juliano, L. M., and Chausmer, A. L. Caffeine pharmacology and clinical effects. In A. W. Graham, T. K. Schultz, M. F. Mayo-Smith, R. K. Ries, and B. B. Wilford, eds., *Principles of Addiction Medicine*. 3rd ed. Chevy Chase, MD: American Society of Addiction, 2003,193–224.

Griffiths, R. R., Ressig, C. J., et al. Substance abuse: Caffeine use disorders. In A. Tasman, J. *Behavioral Pharmacology Research* (2008).

Kay, J. Lieberman, M. B. First, and M. Maj, eds., *Psychiatry*. 3rd ed. Vol. 1. Chichester, UK: John Wiley and Sons, 2008, 1019–40.

Grotz, V. L., and Munro, I. C. An overview of the safety of sucralose. *Regulatory Toxicology and Pharmacology* (2009) 55: 1–5.

Juliano, L. M. Caffeine: Pharmacology and clinical effects. In R. Ries, D. Fiellin, S. Miller, and R. Saitz, eds., *Principles of Addiction Medicine*. 4th ed. Baltimore: Lippincott Williams & Wilkins, 2011.

Juliano, L. M., and Griffiths, R. R. Caffeine. In J. H. Lowinson, P. Ruiz, R. B. Millman, J. G. Langrod, eds., *Substance Abuse: A Comprehensive Textbook*. 4th ed. Baltimore: Lippincott Williams & Wilkins, Center for Science in the Public Interest, 2005, 403–21.

Juliano, L. M., and Griffiths, R. R. Caffeine-related disorders. In B. J. Sadock, V. A. Sadock, and P. Ruiz, eds., *Comprehensive Textbook of Psychiatry*. 9th ed. Philadelphia: Lippincott Williams & Wilkins, 2011.

Kendler, K. S., Myers, J. O., and Gardner, C. Caffeine intake, toxicity and dependence and lifetime risk for psychiatric and substance use disorders: An epidemiologic and co-twin control analysis. *Psychological Medicine* (2006) 36: 1717–25.

Knight, C. A., Knight, I., Mitchell, D. C., Zepp, J. E. Beverage caffeine intake in US consumers and subpopulations of interest: Estimates from the Share of Intake Panel Survey. *Food and Chemical Toxicology* (2004) 42: 1923–30.

Kowlowski, L. T., et al. Patterns of alcohol, cigarette and caffeine and other drug use in two drug abusing populations. *Journal of Substance Abuse Treatment* (1993) 10: 171–79.

Kroger, M., Meister, K., and Kava, R. Low-calorie sweeteners and other sugar substitutes: A review of the safety issues. *Comprehensive Reviews in Food Science and Food Safety* (2006) 5: 35–47.

Larsson, S. C., Virtamo, J., and Wolk, A. Coffee consumption and risk of stroke in women. *Stroke* (2011) 42: 908–12.

Magnuson, B. A., et al. Aspartame: A safety evaluation based on current use levels, regulations and toxicological and epidemiological studies. *Critical Reviews in Toxicology* (2007) 37: 629–727.

Marchione, M. Scientists take aim at soda in obesity battle. *Huntsville Times*, March 5, 2006.

Mercola, J. Eight reasons why you should avoid drinking coffee, November 5, 2010, http://www.drmercola.com/caffeine-2/8-reasons-why-you-should-avoid-drinking-coffee/.

Mercola, J. Mercola.com. Coffee addiction is harmful to your health, http://www.mercola.com/Downloads/bonus/coffee/report.aspx.

Mercola, J. The truth about caffeine (especially during pregnancy). January 2, 2008, http://articles.mercola.com/sites/articles/archive/2008/01/02/truth-caffeine-pregnancy.aspx.

O'Neil, C. Liquids make up 22 percent of American diet. *What America Drinks Report*, January 8, 2007.

Packaged Facts. Energy drinks in the US. Rockville, MD, December 1, 2007.

Painter, K. Water wars: Bottled vs tap. *USA Today*, August 26, 2007.

Reinberg, S. Fewer sugary drinks key to weight loss. ABC News online. HealthDay, April 3, 2009, http://abcnews.go.com/Health/Healthday/story?id=7244884&page=1.

Remsen, I., and Fahlberg, C. On the oxidation of orthotoluenesulphamide. *American Chemical Journal* (1880) 1: 426–28.

Roberts, A. Sucralose metabolism and pharmacokinetics in man. *Food and Chemical Toxicology* (2000) 38 (Suppl. 2): S31–S41.

Rowe, R. C. *Aspartame Handbook of Pharmaceutical Excipients*. 5th ed. American Pharmacists Association, 2009.

Samuels, A. There really is no controversy. *European Journal of Clinical Nutrition* 63, 1044 (August 2009).

Smith, B. D., and Gupta, B. S. *Arousal and Caffeine: Effects on Health and Behavior*. New York: Taylor and Francis, 2007.

Svikis, D. S., Berger, N., Haug, N., and Griffiths, R. Caffeine dependence in combination with a family history of alcoholism as a predictor of continued use of caffeine during pregnancy. *American Journal of Psychiatry* 162 (2005): 2344–51.

Svilaas, A., et al. Intakes of antioxidants in coffee, wine and vegetables are correlated with plasma carotenoids in humans. *Journal of Nutrition* (2004) 134: 562–67.

Thompson, D., et al. Teen girls sip more soda as they age. *Pediatrics* (February 24, 2006).

Vartanian, L. R., Schwartz, M. B., and Brownell, K. D. Effects of soft drink consumption on nutrition and health: A systematic review and meta-analysis. *American Journal of Health* 97 (April 2007): 667–75.

Verhoef, P., Pasman, W. J., Van Vliet, T., Urgert, R., and Katan, M. B. Contribution of caffeine to the homocysteine-raising effect of coffee: A randomized controlled trial in humans. *American Journal of Clinical Nutrition* (2002) 76: 1244–48.

Vinson, J., et al. The potential health benefits of antioxidants no. AGFD 10, 230th national meeting of the American Chemical Society, Washington, DC, August 28, 2010.

Volkow, N. Quoted in R. Ruben, Addiction has many fathers, science finds. *USA Today*, October 10, 2005.

Zhang, Z., Hu, G., Caballero, B., Appel, L., and Chen, L. Habitual coffee consumption and risk of hypertension: A systematic review and meta-analysis of prospective observational studies. *American Journal of Clinical Nutrition* (2011) 93: 1212–19.

Chapter 13: MSG

Bush, R. K., et al. Adverse reactions to food and drug additives. Chapter 6 in N. F. Adkinson Jr., ed., *Middleton's Allergy: Principles and Practice*. 7th ed. Philadelphia, PA: Mosby Elsevier, 2008.

Camacho, A., and Massieu, L. Role of glutamate transporters in the clearance and release of glutamate during ischemia and its relation to neuronal death. *Archives of Medical Research* (2006) 37: 11–18.

Fujikawa, D. G. Prolonged seizures and cellular injury: Understanding the connection. *Epilepsy & Behavior* (2005) (Suppl. 3) (2005) 3: S3–S11.

He, K., Du, S., et al. Consumption of monosodium glutamate in relation to incidence of overweight in Chinese adults: China Health and Nutrition Survey (CHNS). *American Journal of Clinical Nutrition* (2011) 93: 1328–36.

He, K., Zhao, L., et al. Association of monosodium glutamate intake with overweight in Chinese adults: The INTERMAP Study. *Obesity* (2008) 16: 1875–80.

Kokl, C. Cognitive dysfunction and diabetes mellitus. *Endocrine Reviews* (2008) 29: 494–511.

Kwok, R.H.M., et al. Chinese restaurant syndrome. *New England Journal of Medicine* (1968) 18: 796.

Lee, W.-J., Hawkins, R. A., Viña, J. R., and Peterson, D. R. Glutamine transport by the blood-brain barrier: A possible mechanism for nitrogen removal. *American Journal of Physiology—Cell Physiology* (1998) 274: C1101–7.

Lucas, D. R., and Newhouse, J. P. The toxic effect of sodium L-glutamate on the inner layer of the retina. *Archives of Ophthalmology* (1957) 58: 193–201.

Madl, J. E., and Royer, S. M. Glutamate in synaptic terminals is reduced by lack of glucose but no hypoxia in rat hippocampal slices. *Neuroscience* (1999) 94: 417–30.

McEntee, W., and Crook, T. Glutamate: Its role in learning, memory, and the aging brain. *Psychopharmacology* (1993) 111: 391–401.

Nicholls, D., and Attwell, D. The release and uptake of excitatory amino acids. *Trends in Pharmacological Sciences* (1990) 11: 462–68.

Olney, J. W. Brain lesions, obesity and other disturbances in mice treated with monosodium glutamate. *Science* (1969) 165: 719–21.

Reeds, P. J., Burrin, D. G., Stoll, B., and Jahoor, F. Intestinal glutamate metabolism. *Journal of Nutrition* (2000) 130: 9785–9825.

Ren, X., Ferreira, J. G., Yeckel, C. W., Kondoh, T., and de Araugo, I. E. Effects of ad libitum ingestion of monosodium glutamate onweight gain in C57BL6/J mice. *Digestion* (2011) 83 (Suppl.) 1: 32–36.

Schaumburg, H. H., Byck, R., Gerstl, R., and Mashman, J. H. Monosodium L-glutamate: Its pharmacology and role in Chinese restaurant syndrome. *Science* (1969) 826–28.

Skenazy, J. A., and Bigler, E. D. Neuropsychological findings in diabetes mellitus. *Journal of Clinical Psychology* (1984) 40: 246–58.

Tarasoff, L. Monosodium L-glutamate: A double-blind study and review. *Food and Chemical Toxicology* (1993) 31: 1019–35.

van den Pol, A. N., Wuarin, J. P., and Dudek, F. E. Glutamate, the dominant excitatory transmitter in neuroendocrine regulation. *Science* (1990) 250: 1276–78.

Chapter 14: Exercise

Adlard, P. A., Perreau, V. M., and Cotman, C. W. The exercise-induced expression of BDNF within the hippocampus varies across life span. *Neurobiology of Aging* (2005) 26: 511–20.

Baker, L. D., et al. Effects of aerobic exercise on mild cognitive impairment: A controlled trial. *Archives of Neurology* (2010) 67: 71–79.

Barbour, K. A., Edenfield, T. M, and Blumenthal, J. A. Exercise as a treatment for depression and other psychiatric disorders: A review. *Journal of Cardiopulmonary Rehabilitation & Prevention* (2007) 27: 359–67.

Blomstrand, E. Amino acids and central fatigue. *Amino Acids* (2001) 20: 25–34.

Boecker, H., et al. The runner's high: Opioidergic mechanisms in the human brain. *Cerebral Cortex* (1991) 18: 2523–31.

Brager, A. J., Ruby, C. L., Prosser, R. A., and Glass, J. D. Chronic ethanol disrupts circadian photic entrainment and daily locomotor activity in the mouse. *Alcoholism: Clinical & Experimental Research* (2010) 34: 1266–73.

Brand, S., et al. High exercise levels are related to favorable sleep patterns and psychological functioning in adolescents: A comparison of athletes and controls. *Journal of Adolescent Health* (2009) 46: 133–41.

Brene, S., et al. Running is rewarding and antidepressive. *Physiology & Behavior* (2007) 92: 136–40.

Broocks, A., Ahrendt, U., and Sommer, M. Physical training in the treatment of depressive disorders. *Psychiatrische Praxis* (2007) 34 (Suppl. 3): S300–S304.

Chaouloff, F. Effects of acute physical exercise on central serotonergic systems. *Medicine and Science in Sports and Exercise* (1997) 29: 58–62.

Chaouloff, F. Influence of physical exercise on 5-HT1A receptor- and anxiety-related behaviours. *Neuroscience Letters* (1994) 176: 226–30.

Chaouloff, F., Elghozi, J. L., Guezennec, Y., and Laude, D. Effects of conditioned running on plasma, liver and brain tryptophan and on brain 5-hydroxytryptamine metabolism of the rat. *British Journal of Pharmacology* (1985) 86: 33–41.

Chaouloff, F., Laude, D., Guezennec, Y., and Elghozi, J. L. Motor activity increases tryptophan, 5-hydroxyindoleacetic acid and homovanillic acid in ventricular cerebrospinal fluid of the conscious rat. *Journal of Neurochemistry* (1986) 46: 1313–16.

Cotman, C. W., Berchtold, N. C., and Christie, L.-A. Exercise builds brain health: Key roles of growth factor cascades and inflammation. *Trends in Neuroscience* (2007) 30: 464–72.

Craft, L. L., Freund, K. M., Culpepper, L., and Perna, F. M. Intervention study of exercise for depressive symptoms in women. *Journal of Women's Health* (Larchmt) (2007) 16: 1499–1509.

Czeh, B. Stress-induced changes in cerebral metabolites, hippocampal volume, and cell proliferation are prevented by antidepressant treatment with tianeptine. *Proceedings of the National Academy of Sciences* (2001) 98: 12796–801.

Davis, J. M., Alderson, N. L., and Welsh, R. S. Serotonin and central nervous system fatigue: Nutritional considerations. *American Journal of Clinical Nutrition* (2000) 72 (Suppl.): 573S–78S.

De Matos, M. G., Calmeiro, L., and Da Fonseca, D. Effect of physical activity on anxiety and depression. *Presse Medicale* (2009) 38: 734–39.

Dey, S. Physical exercise as a novel antidepressant agent: Possible role of serotonin receptor subtypes. *Physiology & Behavior* (1994) 55: 323–29.

Dey, S., Singh, R. H., and Dey, P. K. Exercise training: Significance of regional alterations in serotonin metabolism of rat brain in relation to antidepressant effect of exercise. *Physiology & Behavior* (1992) 52: 1095–99.

DiLorenzo, T. M., et al. Long-term effects of aerobic exercise on psychological outcomes. *Preventative Medicine* (1999) 28: 75–85.

Dunn, A. L. Exercise and the neurobiology of depression. *Exercise and Sport Sciences Reviews* (1991) 19: 41–98.

Dunn, A. L., Trivedi, M. H., Kampert, J. B., Clark, C. G., and Chambliss, H. O. Exercise treatment for depression: Efficacy and dose response. *American Journal of Preventative Medicine* (2005) 28: 1–8.

Dworak, M., McCarley, R. W., Kim, T., Kalinchuk, A. V., and Basheer, R. Sleep and brain energy levels: ATP changes during sleep. *Journal of Neuroscience* (2010) 30: 9007–16.

Epel, E. S., Lapidus, R., et al. Stress may add bite to appetite in women: A laboratory study of stress-induced cortisol and eating behavior. *Psychoneuroendocrinology* (2001) 26: 37–49.

Epel, E. S., McEwen, B., et al. Stress and body shape: Stress-induced cortisol secretion is consistently greater among women with central fat. *Psychosomatic Medicine* (2000) 62: 623–32.

Garber, C. E., Allsworth, J. E., Marcus, B. H., Hesser, J., and Lapane, K. L. Correlates of the stages of change for physical activity in a population survey. *American Journal of Public Health* (2008) 98: 897–904.

Gould, E., McEwen, B. S., Tanapat, P., Galea, L.A.M., and Fuchs, E. Neurogenesis in the dentate gyrus of the adult tree shrew is regulated by psychosocial stress and NMDA receptor activation. *Journal of Neuroscience* (1997) 17: 2492–98.

Hackney, A. C. Effects of endurance exercise on the reproductive system of men: The exercise-hypogonadal male condition. *Journal of Endocrinological Investigation* (2008) 31: 932–38.

Hackney, A. C., and Dobridge, J. D. Thyroid hormones and the interrelationship of cortisol and prolactin: Influence of prolonged, exhaustive exercise. *Polish Journal of Endocrinology* (2009) 60: 252–57.

Hackney, A. C., and Viro, A. Research methodology: Endocrinologic measurements in exercise science and sports medicine. *Journal of Athletic Training* (2008) 43: 631–39.

Hansen, C. J., Stevens, L. C., and Coast, J. R. Exercise duration and mood state: How much is enough to feel better? *Health Psychology* (2001) 4: 267.

Hassmén, P., Koivula, N., and Uutela, A. Physical exercise and psychological well-being: A population study in Finland. *Preventive Medicine* (2000) 30: 17–25.

Hattori, S., Naoi, M., and Nishino, H. Striatal dopamine turnover during treadmill running in the rat: Relation to the speed of running. *Brain Research Bulletin* (1994) 35: 41–49.

Herring, M. P., Puetz, T. W., O'Connor, P. J., and Dishman, R. K. Effects of exercise and weight loss on depressive symptoms among men and women and hypertension. *Journal of Psychosomatic Research* (2007) 63: 463–69.

Hill, E. E., et al. Exercise and circulating cortisol levels: The intensity threshold effect. *Journal of Endocrinological Investigation* (2008) 311: 587–91.

Hinton, E., and Taylor, S. Does placebo response mediate runner's high? *Perceptual and Motor Skills* (1986) 62: 789–90.

Hunsberger, J. G., et al. Antidepressant actions of the exercise-regulated gene. *VGF Nature Medicine* (2007) 13: 1476–82.

Jacobs, D. R., and Pereira, M. A. Physical activity, relative body weight and risk of death among women. *New England Journal of Medicine* (2004) 351: 2753–55.

Jacobs, B. L., and Fornal, C. A. Activity of serotonergic neurons in behaving animals. *Neuropsychopharmacology* (1999) 21: 9S–15S.

Jamtvedt, G., et al. A pragmatic randomized trial of stretching before and after physical activity to prevent injury and soreness. *British Journal of Sports Medicine* (2010) 44: 1002–9.

Jensen, T. S. Cerebral atrophy in young torture victims. *New England Journal of Medicine* (1982) 307: 1341.

Johnston, O., Reilly, J., and Kremer, J. Excessive exercise: From quantitative categorization to a qualitative continuum approach. *European Eating Disorders Review* (2011) 19: 237–48.

Jouvet, M. Paradoxical sleep mechanisms. *Sleep* (1994) 17: S77–S83.

Knab, A. M., and Lightfoot, J. T. Does the difference between physically active and couch potato lie in the dopamine system? *International Journal of Biological Sciences* (2010) 6: 133–50.

Krogh, J., Nordentoft, M., Sterne, J.A.C., Lawlor, D. A. The effect of exercise in clinically depressed adults: Systematic review and meta-analysis of randomized controlled trials. *Journal of Clinical Psychiatry* (2011) 72: 529–38.

Legrand, F., and Heuze, J. P. Antidepressant effects associated with different exercise conditions in participants with depression: A pilot study. *Journal of Sport & Exercise Psychology* (2007) 29: 348–64.

Lewis, B. A., et al. Comparing psychosocial predictors of physical activity adoption and maintenance. *Annals of Behavioral Medicine* (2008) 36: 186–94.

Lloyd, J. Stretches: No sports panacea. *USA Today*, October 29, 2009.

Lowery, E. G., and Thiele, T. E. Pre-clinical evidence that corticotropin-releasing factor (CRF) receptor antagonists are promising targets for pharmacological treatment of alcoholism. *CNS and Neurological Disorders—Drug Targets* (2010) 9: 77–86.

Lowry, C. A., Lightman, S. L., and Nutt, D. J. That warm fuzzy feeling: Brain serotonergic neurons and the regulation of emotion. *Journal of Psychopharmacology* (2009) 23: 392.

Magnusson, S. P. Passive properties of human skeletal muscle during stretch maneuvers. *Scandanavian Journal of Medicine & Science in Sports* (1998) 8: 65–77.

Martinsen, E. W., Medhus, A., and Sandvik, L. Effects of exercise on depression: A controlled study. *BMJ* (1985) 291: 109.

Meeusen, R., and De Meirleir, K. Exercise and brain neurotransmission. *Sports Medicine* (1995) 20: 160–88.

Meeusen, R., and Piacentini, M. F., et al. Brain neurotransmitter levels during exercise. *Deutsche Zeitschrift für Sportmedizin* (2001) 52: 361–68.

Meeusen, R., Smolders, I., et al. Endurance training effects on neurotransmitter release in rat striatum: An in vivo microdialysis. *Acta Physiologica Scandinavica* (1997) 159: 335–41.

Moses, J., Steptoe, A., Mathews, A., and Edwards, S. The effects of exercise training on mental well-being in the normal population: A controlled trial. *Journal of Psychosomatic Research* (1989) 33: 47–61.

Napolitano, M. A., et al. Mediators of physical activity behavior change: A multivariate approach. *Health Psychology* (2008) 27: 409–18.

Nicoloff, G., and Schwenk, T. S. Using exercise to ward off depression. *Physician and Sports Medicine* (1995) 23: 44–58.

Öngür, D., Drevets, W. C., and Price, J. L. Glial reduction in the subgenual prefrontal cortex in mood disorders. *Proceedings of the National Academy of Sciences* (1998) 95: 13290–95.

Paluska, S. A., and Schwenk, T. L. Physical activity and mental health: Current concepts. *Sports Medicine* (2000) 29: 167–89.

Pardridge, W. M. Blood-brain barrier transport of nutrients. *Nutrition Reviews* (1986) 44 (Suppl.) 15–25.

Piekut, D. T., and Phipps, B. Corticotropin-releasing factor—immunolabeled fibers in brain regions with localized kainite. *Neurotoxicity Acta Neuropathologica* (1999) 98: 622–28.

Pollock, K. M. Exercise in treating depression: Broadening the psychotherapist's role. *Journal of Clinical Psychology* (November 2001) 57 (11): 1289–300.

Prochaska, J. O., and DiClemente, C. C. The transtheoretical approach. In J. C. Norcross and M. R. Goldfried, eds., *Handbook of Psychotherapy Integration.* 2nd ed. New York: Oxford University Press, 2005, 147–71.

Prochaska, J. O., and Norcrosse, J. C. *Systems of Psychotherapy: A Transtheoretical Analysis.* Independence, KY: Cengage Learning, 2009.

Puterman, E., et al. The power of exercise: Buffering the effect of chronic stress on telomere length. *PLoS One* (2010) 26: 5.

Rajkowska, G., et al. Morphometric evidence for neuronal and glial prefrontal cell pathology in major depression. *Biological Psychiatry* (1999) 45: 1085–98.

Rhodes, J. S., et al. Exercise increases hippocampal neurogenesis to high levels but does not improve spatial learning in mice bred for increased voluntary wheel running. *Behavioral Neuroscience* (2003) 117: 1006–16.

Rose, A. K., Shaw, S. G., Prendergast, M. A., and Little, H. J. The importance of glucocorticoids in alcohol dependence and neurotoxicity. *Alcoholism: Clinical and Experimental Research* (2010) 34: 2100–2118.

Rosmand, R., Dallman, M. F., and Björntrop, P. Stress-related cortisol secretion in men: Relationships with abdominal obesity and endocrine, metabolic, and hemodynamic abnormalities. *Journal of Clinical Endocrinology and Metabolism* (1998) 83: 1853–59.

Salmon, P. Effects of physical exercise on anxiety, depression, and sensitivity to stress: A unifying theory. *Clinical Psychology Review* (2001) 21: 33–61.

Sapolsky, R. M. A mechanism for glucocorticoid toxicity in the hippocampus: Increased neuronal vulnerability to metabolic insults. *Journal of Neuroscience* (1985) 5: 1228–32.

Sapolsky, R. M. Depression, antidepressants, and the shrinking hippocampus. *Proceedings of the National Academy of Sciences* (2001) 98: 12320–22.

Sapolsky, R. M. Glucocorticoids, stress and their adverse neurological effects: Relevance to aging. *Experimental Gerontology* (1999) 34: 721–32.

Sapolsky, R. M. Why stress is bad for your brain. *Science* (1996) 273: 749–50.

Sapolsky, R. M., Uno, H., Rebert, C. S., and Finch, C. E. Hippocampal damage associated with prolonged glucocorticoid exposure in primates. *Journal of Neuroscience* (1990) 10: 2897–2902.

Shapiro, C. M., Bortz, R., Mitchell, D., Bartel, P., and Jooste, P. Slow wave sleep: A recovery period after exercise. *Science* (1981) 214: 1253–54.

Sheline,Y. I., Sanghavi, M., Mintun, M. A., and Gado, M. H. Depression duration but not age predicts hippocampal volume loss in medically healthy women with recurrent major depression. *Journal of Neuroscience* (1999) 19: 5034–43.

Sheline, Y. I., Wang, P. W., Gado, M. H., Csernansky, J. G., and Vannier, M. W. Hippocampal atrophy in recurrent major depression. *Proceedings of the National Academy of Sciences* (1996) 93: 3908–13.

Silva, A., et al. Sleep quality evaluation, chronotype, sleepiness and anxiety of Paralympics Brazilian athletes: Beijing 2008 Paralympics Games. *British Journal of Sports Medicine* (2010).

Sime, W. E. Exercise therapy for stress management. In P. M. Lehrer, R. L. Woolfolk, and W. E. Sime, eds., *Principles and Practice of Stress Management*. 3rd ed. Spring Street, NY: Guilford Press, 2007, 333.

Soares, J., Naffah-Mazzacoratti, M. G., and Cavalheiro, E. A. Increased serotonin levels in physically trained men. *Brazilian Journal of Medical and Biological Research* (1994) 27: 1635–38.

Starkman, M. N. Hippocampal formation volume, memory dysfunction, and cortisol levels in patients with Cushing's syndrome. *Biological Psychiatry* (1992) 32: 756–65.

Strohle, A. Physical activity exercise, depression and anxiety disorders. *Journal of Neural Transmission* (2009) 116: 777.

Tang, S. W., Chu, E., Hui, T., Helmeste, D., and Law, C. Influence of exercise on serum brain-derived neurotrophic factor concentrations in healthy human subjects. *Neuroscience Letters* (2008) 431: 62–65.

Trivedi, M. H. TREAD: Treatment with exercise augmentation for depression: Study rationale and design. *Clinical Trials* (2006) 3: 291–305.

Trivedi, M. H., Greer, T. L., Church, T. S., et al. Exercise as an augmentation treatment for nonremitted major depressive disorder: A randomized, parallel dose comparison. *Journal of Clinical Psychiatry* (2011) 72: 677–84.

Trivedi, M. H., Greer, T. L., Grannemann, B. D., Chambliss, H. O., and Jordan, A. N. Exercise as an augmentation strategy for treatment of major depression. *Journal of Psychiatric Practice* (2006) 12: 205–13.

Uno, H., et al. Neurotoxicity of glucocorticoids in the primate brain. *Hormones and Behavior* (1994) 28: 336–48.

Williams, D. M., Matthews, C., Rutt, C., Napolitano, M. A., and Marcus, B. H. Interventions to increase walking behavior. *Medicine and Science in Sports and Exercise* (2008) (7 Suppl.) 40: S567– S73.

Wilson, W. M., and Marsden, C. A. Extracellular dopamine in the nucleus accumbens of the rat during treadmill running. *Acta Physiologica Scandinavia* (1995) 155: 465–66.

Wittert, G. A., Livesey, J. H., Espinger, E. A., Donald, R. A. Adaptation of the hypothalamopituitary adrenal axis to chronic exercise stress in humans. *Medicine and Science in Sports and Exercise* (1996) 28: 1015–19.

Chapter 15: Sleep

AHRQ. New AHRQ comparative effectiveness review of sleep apnea diagnosis and treatment. *Sleep Research Society*, August 12, 2011, http://www.sleepresearchsociety.org.

Brower, K. J. Insomnia, alcoholism and relapse. *Sleep Medicine Reviews* (2003) 7: 523–39.

Colace, C. Dreaming in addiction: A study on the motivation bases of dreaming process. *Neuropsychoanalysis* (2004) 6: 165–79.

Conroy, D., et al. Perception of sleep in recovering alcohol-dependent patients with insomnia: Relationship with future drinking. *Alcoholism: Clinical and Experimental Research* (2006) 30: 1992–99.

Moorecroft, W. H. *Understanding Sleep and Dreaming*. New York: Plenum Publishers, 2003, 170–75.

Obermeyer, W. H., and Benca, R. M. Effects of drugs on sleep. *Neurologic Clinics* (1996) 14: 827–40.

Passos, G. S., et al. Nonpharmacologic treatment of chronic insomnia. *Journal of Clinical Sleep Medicine* (2007) 29: 279–82.

Richardson, G., and Zee, P. Insomnia: Primary care edition. *Clinical Symposia* (2006) 56: 1.

Starr, A. *Freud: A Very Short Introduction*. Oxford: Oxford University Press, 1989.

Zhang, L., Samet, J., Caffo, B., Bankman, I., and Punjabi, N. M. Power spectral analysis of EEG activity during sleep in cigarette smokers. *Chest* (2008) 133: 427–32.

Chapter 16: Meditation and Yoga

Ainsworth, B. E., et al. Compendium of physical activities: An update of activity codes and MET intensities. *Medicine and Science in Sports and Exercise* (2000) 32 (Suppl.): S498–S516.

Badra, L. J., et al. Respiratory modulation of human autonomic rhythms. *American Journal of Physiology—Heart Circulatory Physiology* (2001): H2674–88.

Bera, T. K., Wagh, C., and Madhuri, T. Yoga and aesthetics in sports: A research review. *SAI Scientific Journal* 22, no. 3 (July 1999): 5–7.

Bohn, M. Meditation changes the brain: Meditative experience translated into the science of brain waves. Meditation@suite101, December 4, 2008, http://martin-bohn.suite101.com/meditation-changes-the-brain-a80996.

Brefczynski-Lewis, J. A., Lutz, A., Schaefer, H. S., Levinson, D. B., and Davidson, R. J. Neural correlates of attention expertise in long-term meditation practitioners. *Proceedings of the National Academy of Sciences* (2007) 104: 1148–88.

Brown, C. A., and Jones, A.K.P. Meditation experience predicts less negative appraisal of pain: Electrophysiological evidence for the involvement of anticipatory neural responses. *Pain* (2010) 150: 428–38.

Carson, J. W., et al. A pilot randomized controlled trial of the Yoga of Awareness program in the management of fibromyalgia. *Pain* (2010) 151: 530.

Castillo-Richmond, A., et al. Effects of the transcendental meditation program on carotid atherosclerosis in hypertensive African American women. *Ethnicity & Disease* (2000) 10: 309.

Catton, T. Awakening the spirit: Meditation, mindfulness, and the twelve steps. Sixteenth Annual Counseling Skills Conference, Las Vegas, Nevada, October 1, 2010.

Chawkin, K. TM activates default mode network, the brain's ground state. EurekAlert! Article retrieved from http://theuncarvedblog.com/2010/03/04/tm-activates-dmn-the-brains-ground-state/.

Cherkin, D. C., Sherman, K. J., Deyo, R. A., and Shekelle, P. G. A review of the evidence for the effectiveness, safety and cost of acupuncture, massage therapy and spinal manipulation for back pain. *Annals of Internal Medicine* (2003) 128: 898–906.

Cooper, M. J., and Aygen, M. M. Transcendental meditation in the management of hypercholesterolemia. *Journal of Human Stress* (1979) 5: 24–27.

Coull, J. T. Neural correlates of attention and arousal: Insights from electrophysiology, functional neuroimaging and psychopharmacology. *Progress in Neurobiology* (1998) 55: 343–61.

Cowen, V. S. Functional fitness improvements after a worksite-based yoga initiative. *Journal of Body Work and Movement Therapies* (2010) 14: 50–54.

Creswell, J. D., Way, B. M., Eisenberger, N. I., and Lieberman, M. D. Neural correlates of dispositional mindfulness during affect labeling. *Psychosomatic Medicine* (2007) 69: 560–65.

Dagenais, S., Caro, J., and Haldeman, S. A systematic review of low back pain cost of illness studies in the United States and internationally. *Spine* (2008) 8: 8–20.

D'Aquili, E. G. *The Mystical Mind: Probing the Biology of Religious Experience.* Theology and the Sciences. Minneapolis: Augsburg Fortress, 1999.

Davidson, R. J. Affective neuroscience and psychophysiology: Toward a synthesis. *Psychophysiology* (2003) 40: 655–65.

Davidson, R. J. Affective style and affective disorders: Perspectives from affective neuroscience. *Cognition and Emotion* (1998) 12: 307–30.

Davidson, R. J. Affective style, psychopathology and resilience: Brain mechanisms and plasticity. *American Psychologist* (2000) 55: 1196–214.

Davidson, R. J. Anxiety and affective style: Role of prefrontal cortex and amygdala. *Biological Psychiatry* (2002) 51: 68–80.

Davidson, R. J. Buddha's brain: Neuroplasticity and meditation. *IEEE Signal Processing Magazine*, January 2008.

Davidson, R. J. Panel: The affect of emotions: Laying the groundwork in childhood; Understanding positive and negative emotions. University of Wisconsin-Madison, January 2000. Library of Congress, http://www.loc.gov/loc/brain/emotion/Davidson.html.

Davidson, R. J. Seven sins in the study of emotion: Correctives from affective neuroscience. *Brain and Cognition* (2003) 52: 129–32.

Davidson, R. J. Toward a biology of positive affect and compassion. In R. J. Davidson and A. Harrington, eds., *Visions of Compassion: Western Scientist and Tibetan Buddhist Examine Human Nature*, ed. New York: Oxford University Press, 2002, 107–30.

Davidson, R. J. Well-being and affective style: Neural substrates and biobehavioral correlates. *Philosophical Transaction of the Royal Society* (2004) 359: 1395–1411.

Davidson, R. J. What does the prefrontal cortex "do" in affect? Perspectives on frontal EEG asymmetry research. *Biological Psychology* (2004) 67: 219–33.

Davidson, R. J., and Irwin, W. The functional neuroanantomy of emotion and affective style. *Trends in Cognitive Science* (1999) 3: 11–21.

Davidson, R. J., Coe, C. C., Dolski, I., and Donzella, B. Individual differences in prefrontal activation asymmetry predict natural killer cells activity at rest and in response to challenge. *Brain, Behavior, and Immunity* (1999) 13: 93–108.

Davidson, R. J., Jackson, D. C., and Kalin, N. H. Emotion, plasticity, context and regulation: Perspectives from affective neuroscience. *Psychological Bulletin* (2000) 126: 890–906.

Davidson, R. J., Kabat-Zinn, J., et al. Alterations in brain and immune function produced by mindfulness meditation. *Psychosomatic Medicine* (2003) 65: 564–70.

Ditto, B., Eclache, M., and Goldman, N. Short-term autonomic and cardiovascular effects of mindfulness body scan meditation. *Annals of Behavioral Medicine* (2006) 32: 227–34.

Dusek, J. A., et al. Association between oxygen consumption and nitric oxide production during the relaxation response. *Medical Science Monitor* (2006) 12: CR1–10.

Eckberg, D. L., Nerhed, C., and Wallin, B. G. Respiratory modulation of muscle sympathetic and vagal cardiac outflow in man. *Journal of Physiology* (1985) 365: 181–96.

Engel, A. K., Fries, P., König, P., Brecht, M., and Singer, W. Temporal binding, binocular rivalry and consciousness. *Consciousness and Cognition* (1999) 8: 128–51.

Fetterman, M. Yoga copyright raises questions of ownership: India takes action to keep traditional knowledge public. *USA Today*, June 29, 2006.

Framson, C., et al. Development and validation of the mindful eating questionnaire. *Journal of the American Dietetic Association* (2009) 109: 1439–44.

Garfinkel, M. S., et al. Yoga-based intervention for carpal tunnel syndrome: A randomized trial. *JAMA* (1998) 280: 1601–3.

Goldberg, N. Yoga boosts health in heart failure patients. Annual meeting of the American Heart Association in Orlando, November 6, 2007.

Grace, K. Your source of yoga basics and information. Elysium Yoga, http://www.elysiumyoga.com/category/benefits/.

Grant, J. A., and Rainville, P. Pain sensitivity and analgesic effects of mindful states in Zen meditators: A cross-sectional study. *Psychosomatic Medicine* (2009) 71: 106–14.

Grant, J. A., Courtemanche, J., and Rainville, P. A non-elaborative mental stance and decoupling of executive and pain-related cortices predicts low pain sensitivity in Zen meditators. *Pain* (January 2011) 152: 150–56.

Grepmair, L., et al. Promoting mindfulness in psychotherapists in training influences the treatment results of their patients: A randomized, double-blind, controlled study. *Psychotherapy and Psychosomatics* (2007) 76: 332–38.

Griffen, K. *One Breath at a Time: Buddhism and the Twelve Steps*. Emmaus, PA: Rodale, 2004.

Hayes, S. C. *Mindfulness and Acceptance: Expanding the Cognitive Behavioral Tradition*. New York: Guilford Press, 2004.

Hughes, J. R. Gamma, fast, and ultrafast waves of the brain: Their relationships with epilepsy and behavior. *Epilepsy & Behavior* (2008) 13: 25–31.

Innes, K. E., Bourguignon, C., and Taylor, A. G. Risk indices associated with the insulin resistance syndrome, cardiovascular disease and possible protection with yoga: A systematic review. *Journal of the American Board of Family Practitioners* (2005) 18: 491–519.

Jacobs, G. D. *Ancestral Mind*. New York: Penguin, 2004.

Jacobs, G. D. Cognitive behavior therapy and pharmacotherapy for insomnia: A randomized controlled trial and direct comparison. *Archives of Internal Medicine* (2004) 164: 1888–96.

Jacobs, G. D., and Freedman, R. EEG spectral analysis of relaxation techniques. *Applied Psychophysiology and Biofeedback* (2004) 29: 245–54.

Jain, S. C., Uppal, A., Bhatnagar, S. O., and Talukdar, B. A study of response pattern of non-insulin dependent diabetics to yoga therapy. *Diabetes Residency and Clinical Practice* (1993) 19: 69–74.

Janig, W. The autonomic nervous system and its coordination by the brain. In R. J. Davidson, K. R. Scherer, and H. H. Goldsmith, eds., *Handbook of Affective Sciences*. New York: Oxford University Press, 2003.

John, P. J., Sharma, N., Sharma, C. M., and Kankane, A. Effectiveness of yoga therapy in the treatment of migraine without aura: A randomized controlled trial. *Headache* (2007) 47: 654–61.

Joseph, C. N., et al. Slow breathing improves arterial baroreflex sensitivity and decreases blood pressure in essential hypertension. *Hypertension* (2005) 45: 714–18.

Josipovic, Z. Duality and nonduality in meditation research. *Consciousness and Cognition* (2010) 19: 1119–21.

Jung, Y. H., et al. Influence of brain-derived neurotrophic factor and catechol O-methyl transferase (COMT) on effects of meditation on plasma catecholamines and stress. *Stress* (2012) 15: 97–104.

Kabat-Zinn, J. *Arriving at Your Own Door: 108 Lessons in Mindfulness*. New York: Hyperion, 2005.

Lazar, S. W., Bush, G., et al. Functional brain mapping of the relaxation response and meditation. *Neuroreport* (2000) 11: 1581–85.

Lazar, S. W., Kerr, C. E., et al. Meditation experience is associated with increased cortical thickness. *Neuroreport* (2005) 16: 1893–97.

Lehmann, D., et al. Brain sources of EEG gamma frequency during volitionally meditation-induced altered states of consciousness and experience of the self. *Psychiatry Research* (2001) 30: 111–21.

Linehan, M. M. *Cognitive Behavioral Treatment of Borderline Personality Disorder*. New York: Guilford Press, 1993.

Linehan, M. M. Dialectical behavior therapy for patients with borderline personality disorder and drug dependence. *American Journal of Addiction* (1999) 8: 279–92.

Lloyd, J. It is no stretch to say yoga has benefited this skater: For Olympic medalist Sasha Cohen, it keeps her strong, balanced. *USA Today*, January 13, 2009, 4D.

Lou, H., et al. A 150-H2O PET study of meditation and the resting state of normal consciousness. *Human Brain Mapping* (1999) 7: 98–105.

Love, R. Fear of yoga: Today, the Hindu practice of health and spirituality is loved by everybody—including the press, but it took a couple of centuries to get there. *Columbia Journalism Review*, November 1, 2006.

Luders, E., Toga, A. W., Lepore, N., and Gaser, C. The underlying anatomical correlates of long-term meditation: Larger hippocampal and frontal volumes of gray matter. *Neuroimage* (2009) 45: 672–78.

Luo, X., Pietrobon, R., Sun, S. X., Liu, G. G., and Hey, L. Estimates and patterns of direct health care expenditures among individuals with back pain in the United States. *Spine* (2004) 29: 79–86.

Lutz, A., Brefczynski-Lewis, J., Johnstone, T., and Davidson, R. J. Regulation of neural circuitry of emotion by compassion meditation: Effects of meditative expertise. *PLoS ONE* (2008) 3: e1987.

Lutz, A., Greischar, N. L., Rawlings, N. B., Ricard, M., and Davidson, R. J. Long-term mediators self-induce high-amplitude gamma synchrony during mental practice. *Proceedings of the National Academy of Sciences* USA (2004) 101: 16369–73.

Lutz, A., Slagter, H. A., Dunne, J. D., and Davidson, R. J. Attention regulation and monitoring in meditation. *Trends in Cognitive Science* (2008) 12: 163–69.

MacLean, K. Meditation appears to boost attention span. *Psychological Science* (July 22, 2010).

Maddern, J. *Yoga Burns Fat.* Minneapolis: Fair Winds, 2002.

Manjunath, N. K., et al. Influence of yoga and Ayurveda on self-rated sleep in geriatric population. *Indian Journal of Medical Research* (2005) 121: 683–90.

Manna, A., et al. Neural correlates of focused attention and cognitive monitoring in meditation. *Brain Research Bulletin* (2010) 29: 82: 46–56.

Matthew, R. J. *The True Path: Western Science and the Quest for Yoga.* New York: Basic Books, 2001.

Mirescu, C., Peters, J. D., Noiman, L., and Gould, E. Sleep deprivation inhibits adult neurogenesis in the hippocampus by elevating glucocorticoids. *Proceedings of the National Academy of Sciences* (2006) 103: 19170–75.

Moore, J., Lorig, K., Von Korff, M., Gonzalez, V., and Laurent, D. *The Back Pain Helpbook.* Redding, MA: Perseus Books, 2005.

Nagendra, R. P., Sulekha, S., Tubaki, B. R., et al. Efficacy of mindfulness meditation practice on sleep architecture. Nineteenth European Sleep Research Society Conference, Glasgow, 2008. *Journal of Sleep Research* 17 (2008): 251–51.

Newberg, A. B., et al. Cerebral blood flow differences between long-term meditators and non-meditators. *Consciousness and Cognition* (2010) 19: 899–905.

Newberg, A., D'Aquili, E., and Rause, V. *Why God Won't Go Away: Brain Science and the Biology of Belief.* New York: Ballantine Books, 2002, 90.

Nimgade, A. Increased expenditures for other health conditions after an incident of low back pain. *Spine* (2010) 35: 769–77.

O'Nuallain, S. Zero power and selflessness: What meditation and conscious perception have in common. *Cognitive Sciences* (2009) 4: 49–64.

Ornish, D., Brown, S. E., et al. Can lifestyle changes reverse coronary atherosclerosis? The Lifestyle Heart Trial. *Lancet* (1990) 336: 129–33.

Ornish, D. M., Gotto, A. M., Miller, R. R., Rochelle, D., McAllister, G. K. Effects of a vegetarian diet and selected yoga techniques in the treatment of coronary artery disease. *Lancet* (1990) 336: 741–42.

Ornish, D., Scherwitz, L. W., et al. Intensive lifestyle changes for reversal of coronary heart disease: Five-year follow-up of the Lifestyle Heart Trial. *Journal of the American Medical Association* (1998) 280: 2001–7.

Pagnoni G., and Cekic, M. Age effects on gray matter volume and attentional performance in Zen meditation. *Neurobiology of Aging* (2007) 28: 1623–27.

Paul-Labrador, M., et al. Effects of a randomized controlled trial of transcendental meditation on components of the metabolic syndrome with coronary heart disease. *Archives of International Medicine* (2006) 166: 1218–24.

Posner, M. Meditation a quick fix for stress. *Proceedings of the National Academy of Sciences* (October 11, 2007).

Raffone, A. The exploration of meditation in the neuroscience of attention and consciousness. *Cognitive Processing* (2010) 11: 1–7.

Raub, J. A. Psychophysiologic effects of Hatha Yoga on musculoskeletal and cardiopulmonary function: A literature review. *Journal of Alternative and Complementary Medicine* (2002) 8: 797–812.

Roberts, K. C., et al. Mindfulness and health behaviors: Is paying attention good for you? *Journal of American College Health* (2010) 59: 165–73.

Rubia, K. The neurobiology of meditation and its clinical effectiveness in psychiatric disorders. *Biological Psychology* (2009) 82: 1–11.

Saper, R. B., et al. Yoga for chronic low back pain in a predominantly minority population: A pilot randomized controlled trial. *Alternative Therapies in Health and Medicine* (2009) 15: 18–27.

Schmid, A. A., et al. Preliminary evidence of yoga and balance and endurance outcomes for veterans with stroke. American College of Sports Medicine meeting in Denver, January 4, 2011.

Schneider, R., et al. Long-term effects of stress reduction on mortality in persons >55 years of age with systemic hypertension. *American Journal of Cardiology* (2005) 95: 1060–64.

Sharma, R. K. Contributions of yogic exercises in the field of sports. *International Referred Research Journal* (2009) 2 (26).

Sherman, K. J., et al. Comparing yoga, exercise and a self-care book for chronic low back pain: A randomized controlled trial. *Annals of Internal Medicine* (2005) 143: 849–56.

Sorosky, S., Stilp, S., and Akuthota, V. Yoga and Pilates in the management of low back pain. *Current Reviews in Musculoskeletal Medicine* (2008) 1: 39–47.

Springen, K. The price of pain. *Newsweek*, February 12, 2008.

Srinivasan, N., and Baijal, S. Concentrative meditation enhances pre-attentive processing: A mismatch negativity study. *Neuroreport* (2007) 18: 1709–12.

Stein, J. Just say Om. *Time*, August 4, 2003, 49–56.

Telles, S. Short-term health impact of a yoga and diet change program on obesity. *Medical Science Monitor* (2010) 16: CR35–40.

Thuse, M. P. Yogasana and their contribution towards positive health. *Indian Streams Research Journal* (2011) 1: 57–60.

Travis, F., et al. Transcendental meditation activates default mode network, the brain's natural ground state. *Cognitive Processing* 11 (1) (2010).

Weissman, D. H., Roberts, K. C., Visscher, K. M., and Woldorff, M. J. The neural bases of momentary lapses in attention. *Nature Neuroscience* (2006) 9: 971–78.

Wenger, M. A., and Bagchi, B. K. Studies of autonomic functions in practitioners of Yoga in India. *Behavioral Sciences* (1961) 6: 312–23.

Williams, K., et al. Evaluation of the effectiveness and efficacy of Iyengar yoga therapy on chronic low back pain. *Spine* (2009) 34: 2066–76.

Yang, K., et al. Utilization of 3-month yoga program for adults at high risk for type 2 diabetes: A pilot study. *Evidence-Based and Complementary Alternative Medicine: eCAM* (2009).

Yoga Journal. Yoga Journal releases 2008 "Yoga in America" market study. Available online at http://www.yogajournal.com/advertise/press_releases/10.

Chapter 17: Get the Message

Bruce, B., ed. *Mayo Clinic Guide to Pain Relief.* Rochester, MN: Mayo Foundation for Medical Education and Research, 2008, 211–31.

Coan, J. A., Schaefer, H. S., and Davidson, R. J. Lending a hand: Social regulation of the neural response to threat. *Psychological Science* (2006) 17: 1032–39.

Field, T. Massage therapy effects. *American Psychologist* (1998) 53: 1270–81.

Field, T., Schanberg, S., et al. Bulimic adolescents benefit from massage therapy. *Adolescence* (1998) 33: 555–63.

Grewen, K. M., and Amico, J. A. More frequent partner hugs and higher oxytocin levels are linked to lower blood pressure and heart rate in premenopausal women. *Biological Psychology* (2005): 5–21.

Grewen, K. M., Anderson, B. J., Girdler, S. S., and Light, K. C. Warm partner contact is related to lower cardiovascular reactivity. *Behavioral Medicine* (2003) 29: 123–30.

Hart, S., et al. Anorexia nervosa symptoms are reduced by massage therapy. *Eating Disorders: Journal of Treatment and Prevention* (2001) 9: 217–28.

Hou, W. H., Chiang, P. T., Hsu, T. Y., Chiu, S. Y., and Yen, Y. C. Treatment effects of massage therapy in depressed people: A meta-analysis. *Journal of Clinical Psychiatry* (2010) 71: 894–901.

Mitchinson, A. R., et al. Acute postoperative pain management using massage as an adjuvant therapy: A randomized trial. *Archives of Surgery* (2007) 142: 1158–67.

Rapaport, M. H., Schettler, P., and Bresee, C. A preliminary study of the effects of a single session of Swedish massage on hypothalamic-pituitary-adrenal and immune function in normal individuals. *Journal of Alternative and Complementary Medicine* (2010) 16: 1079–88.

Shaffer, A. 12 little instant health boosts. *Prevention*, October 12, 2010.

Chapter 18: Addictions or Eating Disorders

Arborelius, L., Owens, M. J., Plotsky, P. M., and Nemeroff, C. B. The role of corticotropin-releasing factor in depression and anxiety disorders. *Journal of Endocrinology* (1999) 160: 1–12.

Aureli, F., and Yates, K. Distress prevention by grooming others in crested black macaques. *Biology Letters* (February 23, 2010) 6: 27–29.

Baxter, L. R., et al. Reduction of prefrontal cortex glucose metabolism common to three types of depression. *Archives of General Psychiatry* (1989) 46: 243–50.

Beauregard, M., and Paquette, V. Neural correlates of a mystical experience in Carmelite nuns. *Neuroscience Letters* 405, 3 (2006).

Begley, S. Scans of monks' brains show meditation alters structure, function. *Wall Street Journal*, November 5, 2004, B1.

Bellafato, M. President of the International Association of Eating Disorder Professionals. Personal communication. March 1991.

Bergh, C., and Sodersten, P. Anorexia nervosa, self-starvation and the reward of stress. *Nature Medicine* (1996) 2: 1–21.

Berridge, C. W., et al. Stress and coping: Asymmetry of dopamine effects within prefrontal cortex. In K. Hugdahl and R. J. Davidson, eds., *The Asymmetrical Brain*. Cambridge: MIT Press, 1998, 69–103.

Blum, K., et al. Reward deficiency syndrome: A biogenetic model for the diagnosis and treatment of impulsive, addictive and compulsive behaviors. *Psychoactive Drugs* (2000): 32 (Suppl.): 1–112.

Brassareo, V., and Di Chiara, G. Modulation of feeding-induced activation of mesolimbic dopamine transmission by appetitive stimuli and its relation to motivational state. *European Journal of Neuroscience* (1999) 11: 4839–93.

Bremner, J. D., et al. MRI-based measurement of hippocampal volume in post-traumatic stress disorder related to childhood physical and sexual abuse: A preliminary report. *Biological Psychiatry* (1997) 41: 23–32.

Bryner, J. Brain shrinkage in anorexia is reversible. *LiveScience*, May 26, 2010.

Charney, M. J., et al. *Neurobiological and clinical consequences of stress: From normal adaptation to PTSD*. Philadelphia: Lippincott-Raven, 1995.

Chilton, F. H. *Inflammation Nation: The First Clinically Proven Eating Plan to End Our Nation's Secret Epidemic*. New York: Touchstone, 2005.

Chowdhury, U., et al. Early onset anorexia nervosa: Is there evidence of limbic system imbalance? *International Journal of Eating Disorders* (2003) 33: 388–96.

Christensen, L. Effects of eating behavior on mood: A review of the literature. *International Journal of Eating Disorders* (1993) 14: 171–83.

Cloninger, C. R. The psychobiological regulation of social cooperation. *Nature Medicine* (1995) 1: 623–24.

Coffey, S. F., Schumacher, J. A., Brimo, M. L., and Brady, K. T. Exposure therapy for substance abusers with PTSD. *Behavior Modification* (2005) 29: 10–38.

Davidson, R. J. Affective neuroscience and psychophysiology: Toward a synthesis. *Psychophysiology* (2003) 40: 655–65.

Davidson, R. J. Affective style and affective disorders: Perspectives from affective neuroscience. *Cognition and Emotion* (1998) 12: 307–30.

Davidson, R. J. Affective style, psychopathology and resilience: Brain mechanisms and plasticity. *American Psychology* (2000) 55: 1196–24.

Davidson, R. J. Anxiety and affective style: Role of prefrontal cortex and amygdala. *Biological Psychiatry* (2002) 51: 68–80.

Davidson, R. J. Buddha's brain: Neuroplasticity and meditation. *IEEE Signal Processing Magazine*, January 2008.

Davidson, R. J. Panel: The affect of emotions: Laying the groundwork in childhood; Understanding positive and negative emotions. University of Wisconsin-Madison, January 2000. Library of Congress, http://www.loc.gov/loc/brain/emotion/Davidson.html.

Davidson, R. J. Seven sins in the study of emotion: Correctives from affective neuroscience. *Brain and Cognition* (2003) 52: 129–32.

Davidson, R. J., Jackson, D. C., and Kalin, N. H. Emotion, plasticity, context and regulation: Perspectives from affective neuroscience. *Psychological Bulletin* (2000) 126: 890–906.

Delgado, P. L., et al. Serotonin function and the mechanism of antidepressant action. *Archives of General Psychiatry* (1990) 47: 411–16.

Di Chiara, G., et al. Drug addiction as a disorder of associative learning: Role of nucleus accumbens shell/extended amygdala dopamine. In J. F. McGinty, ed., *Advancing from the Ventra Striatum to the Extended Amygdala. Annals of the New York Academy of Science* (1999) 877: 461–85.

Duman, R. S., et al. Neural plasticity to stress and antidepressant treatment. *Society of Biological Psychiatry* (1999) 46: 1181–91.

Dunbar, R. *Grooming, Gossip, and the Evolution of Language*. London: Farber & Farber, 1996.

Duvvuri, V., and Kaye, W. H. *Anorexia Nervosa Focus* (Fall 2009) 7 (4): 455–62.

Ehlers, C. L., Chaplin, R. I., and Kaneko, W. M. Effects of chronic corticosterone treatment on electrophysiological and behavioral measures in the rat. *Psychoneuroendocrinology* (1992) 17: 691–99.

Eison, A. S., and Mullins, U. L. Regulation of central 5-HT2A receptors: A review of in vivo studies. *Behavioural Brain Research* (1996) 73: 177–81.

Ellison, A. R., and Fong, J. Imaging in eating disorders. In H. W. Hoek, J. Treasure, and M. A.

Katzman, eds., *Neurobiology in the Treatment of Eating Disorders*. New York: John Wiley, 1998, 255–69.

Epstein, L. H., et al. Food reinforcement, the dopamine D2 receptor genotype and energy intake in obese and nonobese humans. *Behavioral Neuroscience* (2007) 121 (5): 877–87.

Foa, E. B., Keane, T. M., Friedman, M. J., and Cohen, J. A., eds. *Effective Treatments for PTSD: Practice Guidelines from the International Society for Traumatic Stress Studies*. 2nd ed. New York: Guilford Press, 2010.

Frank, G. K., et al. Increased dopamine D2/D3 receptor binding after recovery from anorexia nervosa measured by positron emission tomography and [11c]raclopride. *Biological Psychiatry* (2005) 58: 908–12.

Fraser, O. N., Stahl, D., and Aureli, F. Stress reduction through consolation in chimpanzees. *Proceedings of the National Academy of Sciences* (2008) 105: 8557–62.

Friedman, M. J., Charney, D. S., and Deutch, A. Y. *Neurobiological and clinical consequences of stress: From normal adaptation to PTSD.* Philadelphia: Lippincott-Raven, 1995.

Friedman, M. J. Post-traumatic stress disorder: An overview. US Department of Veteran Affairs, http://www.ptsd.va.gov/professional/pages/ptsd-overview.asp.

Friedrich, J., et al. Psychophysical numbing: When lives are valued less as the lives at risk increase. *Journal of Consumer Psychology* (1999) 8: 277–99.

Gallup, G. G., Jr., and Maser, J. D. Tonic immobility: Evolutionary underpinnings of human catalepsy and catatonia. In M.E.P. Seligman and J. D. Masser, *Psychopathology: Experimental Models.* San Francisco: W. H. Freeman, 1977.

Gould, E., Beylin, A., Tanapat, P., Reeves, A., Shors, T. J. Learning enhances adult neurogenesis in the hippocampal formation. *Nature Neuroscience* (1999) 2: 260–65.

Gould, E., McEwen, B. S., Tanapat, P., Galea, L.A.M., Fuchs, E. Neurogenesis in the dentate gyrus of the adult tree shrew is regulated by psychosocial stress and NMDA receptor activation. *Journal of Neuorscience* (1997) 17: 2492–98.

Gould, E., Tanapat, P., McEwen, B. S., Flügge, G., Fuchs, E. Proliferation of granule cell precursors in the dentate gyrus of adult monkeys is diminished by stress. *Proceedings of the National Academy of Sciences* USA (1998) 95: 3168–71.

Grunder, J. L., and Cochran-Black, D. L. Comparing patient outcomes using cognitive behavioral therapy vs selective serotonin reuptake inhibitors in the treatment of body dysmorphic disorder: An evidence-based literature review. *Proceedings of the Third Annual GRASP Symposium,* Wichita State University, 2007.

Gumert, M. D. Payment for sex in a macaque mating market. *Animal Behaviour* (2007) 74: 1655–67.

Haidt, J. *The Happiness Hypothesis.* Cambridge, MA: Basic Books, 2006.

Hariri, A. Serotonin receptors mediate stress. *Neuroscience* (November 2005).

Heim, C., and Nemeroff, C. B. The impact of early adverse experiences on brain systems involved in the pathophysiology of anxiety and affective disorders. *Society of Biological Psychiatry* (1999) 46: 1–15.

Heim, C., Newport, D. J., et al. Increased sensitivity of the hypothalamic-pituitary-adrenal axis to psychosocial stress in adult survivors of childhood abuse. *Society for Neuroscience Abstracts* (1998) 28: 201.

Hill, A. J. The psychology of food craving. *Proceedings of the Nutrition Society* (2007) 66: 277–85.

Holmes, P., et al. Further delineating the applicability of acceptance and change to private responses: The example of dialectical behavior therapy. *Behavior Analyst Today* (2005) 7: 301–11.

Hull, A. M. Neuroimaging findings in post-traumatic stress disorder: Systematic review. *British Journal of Psychiatry* (2002) 181: 102–10.

Interlandi, J. What addicts need. *Newsweek*, March 3, 2008, 37–41.

Jeyakumar, M., et al. Central nervous system inflammation is a hallmark of pathogenesis in mouse models of GM1 and GM2 gangliosidosis. *Brain* (2003) 126: 974–87.

Kalin, N. H., Shelton, S. E., and Davidson, R. J. The role of the central nucleus of the amygdala in mediating fear and anxiety in the primate. *Journal of Neuroscience* (2004) 24: 5506–15.

Kalus, O., et al. The role of serotonin in depression. *Psychiatric Annals* (1989) 19: 348–53.

Katzman, D. K., et al. Cerebral gray matter and white matter volume deficits in adolescent girls with anorexia nervosa. *Journal of Pediatrics* (1996) 129: 794–803.

Kaufman, O., et al. Lateralized processing of pleasant and unpleasant emotions from single-unit recordings in human prefrontal cortex and amygdala. Paper presented at the 8th Annual Meeting of the Cognitive Neuroscience Society, New York, March 25–27, 2001.

Kaye, W. H., and Frank, G. Overactive dopamine receptors may help explain anorexia nervosa symptoms. *Biological Psychology*, July 11, 2005. Article available at http://www.news-medical.net/news/2005/07/11/11621.aspx.

Kaye, W. H., and Strober, M. Neurobiology of eating disorders. In D. Charney, E. Nestler, and W. Bunney, eds., *Neurobiological Foundations of Mental Illness*. New York: Oxford University Press, 1997, 891–906.

Kaye, W. H., Fudge, J. L., and Paulus, M. New insights into symptoms and microcircuit function of anorexia nervosa. *Nature Reviews Neuroscience* (2009) 10: 573–84.

Kindt, M. Beta-blocker blocks feelings of bad memories. *Nature Neuroscience* (February 16, 2009).

Kitayama, I., et al. Chronic immobilization stress: Evidence for decreases of serotonin immunoreactivity and for increases of glucocorticoid receptor immunoreactivity in various brain regions of the rat. *Journal of Neural Transmission* (1989) 77: 93–130.

Klein, S. *The Science of Happiness*. New York: Marlowe and Co., 2002.

Koob, G. Neuroadaptive mechanisms of addiction: Studies on the extended amygdala. *European Neuropharmacology* (2003) 13: 442–52.

Lang, K. C. Primate factsheets: Olive baboon (Papio anubis) behavior. *Primate Info Net* (April 18, 2006).

Lanius, R. A., Bluhm, R., Lanius, U., and Pain, C. A review of neuroimaging studies of hyperarousal and dissociation in PTSD: Heterogeneity of response to symptom provocation. *Journal of Psychiatric Research* (2005).

Lanius, R., Lanius, U., Fisher, J., and Ogden, P. Psychological trauma and the brain: Towards a neurobiological treatment model. In P. Ogden, K. Minton, and C. Pain, eds., *Trauma and the Body: A Sensorimotor Approach to Psychotherapy*. New York: W. W. Norton, 2006.

LeDoux, J. E. *Synaptic Self: How Our Brains Become Who We Are*. New York: Viking, 2002.

LeDoux, J. E. *The Emotional Brain*. New York: Simon and Schuster, 1996.

Levine, P. *Waking the Tiger: Healing Trauma; The Innate Capacity to Transform Overwhelming Experiences.* Berkeley, CA: North Atlantic Books, 1997.

Liberzon, I., and Phan, K. L. Brain-imaging studies of post-traumatic stress disorders. *CNS Spectrums* (2003) 8: 641–50.

Linehan, M. M., and Dimeff, L. Dialectical Behavior Therapy in a nutshell. *California Psychologist* (2001) 34: 10–13.

Lipton, P. Ischemic cell death in brain neurons. *Physiological Reviews* (1999) 79: 1431–1568.

Liston, C., McEwen, B. S., and Casey, B. J. Psychosocial stress reversibly disrupts prefrontal processing and attentional control. *Proceedings of the National Academy of Science* (2009) 106: 912–17.

Lyubomirsky, S. *The How of Happiness.* London: Penguin Books, 2007.

Lyubomirsky, S., Sheldon, K. M., and Schkade, D. Pursuing happiness: The architecture of sustainable change. *Review of General Psychology* (2005) 9: 111–31.

Mayo Clinic. Selective serotonin reuptake inhibitors (SSRIs). Mayo Clinic online, December 10, 2008, www.mayoclinic.com.

McEwen, B. S. Stress and hippocampal plasticity. *Annual Review of Neuroscience* (1999) 22: 105–22.

McFarland, D., ed. *The Oxford Companion to Animal Behavior.* New York: Oxford University Press, 1987.

Meggs, W. J. *The Inflammation Cure.* Chicago: Contemporary Books, 2004.

Meltzer, H. Role of serotonin in depression. *Annals of New York Academy of Science* (1990) 600: 486–500.

Milkman, H., and Sunderwirth, S. *Craving for Ecstasy.* Lexington, MA: Lexington Books, 1987.

Milkman, H., and Sunderwirth, S. *Pathways to Pleasure: The Consciousness and Chemistry of Optimal Living.* Lexington, MA: Lexington Books, 1993.

Morey, R., et al. Brain scans might help spot PTSD. World Psychiatric Association meeting in Florence, Italy, April 3, 2009.

Murphy, F. C., et al. Functional neuroanatomy of emotions: A meta-analysis. *Cognitive, Affective and Behavioral Neuroscience* (2003) 3: 207–33.

Nemeroff, C. B. Recent findings in the pathophysiology of depression. *Focus* (2008) 6: 3–14.

Nestler, E. J. Common molecular and cellular substrates of addiction and memory. *Neurobiology of Learning and Memory* (2002) 78 (3): 637–47.

Nestler, E. J., and Aghajanian, G. K. Molecular and cellular basis of addiction. *Science* (1997) 278: 58–63.

Novin, D., et al. In the activity stress paradigm (AS) there are close relations between vital signs which allows us to predict longevity in rats with unfailing accuracy. *Obesity Research* (1995) 3 (Suppl. 3): 375S.

O'Connor, R. *Undoing Depression: What Therapy Doesn't Teach You and Medication Can't Give You*. New York: Little, Brown and Company, 1999.

Ogden, P. A. Psychology of action: The role of the body in trauma treatment. *IAEDP Connections* (June/July 2006).

Ogden, P., Minton, K., and Pain, C. *Trauma and the Body: A Sensorimotor Approach to Psychotherapy*. New York: W. W. Norton, 2006.

Obrecht, D. Switching addictions: Changing seats on the *Titanic*. Ezine Articles online, June 30, 2008. Article available at http://ezinearticles.com.

Parsons, L. H., and Justice, A. B., Jr. Serotonin and dopamine sensitization in the nucleus accumbens, ventral tegmental area and dorsal raphe nucleus following repeated cocaine administration. *Journal of Neurochemistry* (1993) 61: 1611–19.

Pelchat, M. L. Food cravings in young and elderly adults. *Appetite* (1997) 28: 103–13.

Pelchat, M. L., Johnson, A., Chan, R., Valdez, J., and Ragland, J. D. Brain regions activated by food craving overlap with areas implicated in drug craving. Innovations Report, May 11, 2004, http://www.innovations-report.com/.

Pelchat, M. L., Johnson, A., Chan, R., Valdez, J., and Ragland, J. D. Images of desire: Food craving activation during fMRI. *NeuroImage* (2004) 23: 1486–93.

Peterson, D. Social stress may kill off new brain cells. *Journal of Neuroscience* (March 14, 2007).

Pollice, C., Kaye, W. H., Greeno, C. G., and Weltzin, T. E. Relationship of depression, anxiety and obsessionality to state of illness in anorexia nervosa. *International Journal of Eating Disorders* (1997) 21: 367–76.

Preskorn, S. H., et al. Selective serotonin reuptake inhibitors. In S. H. Preskorn, C. Y. Stanga, J. *Antidepressants: Past, Present and Future*. Berlin: Springer. 241–62.

P. Feighner, and R. Ross, eds., *Antidepressants: Past, Present and Future*. Berlin: Springer, 2004, 241–62.

Prochnau, W., and Parker, L. *Miracle on the Hudson: The Survivors of Flight 1549 Tell Their Extraordinary Stories of Courage, Faith, and Determination*. New York: Ballantine, 2009.

Quirk, G. J., Likhtik, E., Pelletier, J. G., and Paré, D. Stimulation of medial prefrontal cortex decreases the responsiveness of central amygdala output neurons. *Journal of Neuroscience* (2003) 23: 8800–807.

Rasmussen-Torvik, L. J., and McAlpine, D. D. Genetic screening for SSRI drug response among those with major depression: Great promise and unseen perils. *Depression and Anxiety* (2007) 24: 350–57.

Restak, R. M. *The Modular Brain*. New York: Macmillan, 1994.

Roberto, C. Brain shrinkage in anorexia is reversible. *International Journal of Eating Disorders* (May 2010).

Ross, C. A. *The Trauma Model: A Solution to the Problem of Comorbidity in Psychiatry*. Richardson, TX: Manitou Communications, Inc., 2000.

Ruden, R. A., and Byalick, M. *The Craving Brain*. New York: HarperCollins, 1997.

Sadasivan, S., et al. Amino acid starvation-induced autophagic cell death in PC-12 cells: Evidence for activation of caspase-3 but not calpain-1. *Apoptosis* (2006) 11 (9).

Sapolsky, R. M. Stress, glucocorticoids, and damage to the nervous system: The current state of confusion. *Stress* (1996) 46: 1181–91.

Schwartz, B. Pitfalls on the road to a positive psychology of hope. In B. Schwartz and J. Gillham, eds., *The Science of Optimism and Hope: Research Essays in Honor of Martin E. P.* Seligman. Philadelphia: Templeton Foundation Press, 2000, 399–412.

Seligman, M.E.P. *Authentic Happiness*. New York: Free Press, 2002.

Seligman, M.E.P. Why is there so much depression today? The waxing of the individual and the waning of the commons. In R. Ingram, ed., *Contemporary Psychological Approaches to Depression: Theory, Research and Treatment*. New York: Plenum, 1990, 1–9.

Sheline, Y. I., Sanghavi, M., Mintun, M. A., and Gado, M. H. Depression duration but not age predicts hippocampal volume loss in medically healthy women with recurrent major depression. *Journal of Neuroscience* (1999) 19: 5034–43.

Shultz, W. Predictive reward signal of dopamine neurons. *Journal of Neurophysiology* (1998) 80: 1–27.

Sloviter, R. S., Sollas, A. L., and Neubort, S. Hippocampal dentate granule cell degeneration after adrenalectomy in the rat is not reversed by dexamethasone. *Brain Research* (1995) 682: 227–30.

Spoont, M. R. Modulatory role of serotonin in neural information processing: Implications for human psychopathology. *Psychological Bulletin* (1992) 112: 330–50.

Stein, D. J., Daniels, W.M.U., Savitz, J., and Harvey, B. H. Brain-derived neurotrophic factor: The neurotrophin hypothesis of psychopathology. *CNS Spectrums* (2008) 13: 945–49.

Stein, M. B., Koverola, C., Hanna, C., Torchia, M. G., and McClarty, B. Hippocampal volume in women victimized by childhood sexual abuse. *Psychological Medicine* (1997) 27: 951–59.

Sternberg, E. M. *The Balance Within: The Science Connecting Health and Emotions*. New York: W. H. Freeman & Co., 2001, 192.

Sullenberger, C. *Highest Duty: My Search for What Really Matters*. New York: William Morrow, 2009.

Tanex, K. Neuroimaging and neurocircuitry in post-traumatic stress disorder: What is currently known? *Current Psychiatry Reports* (2003) 5: 369–83.

Tan, S., Sagara, Y., Liu, Y., Maher, P., and Schubert, D. The regulation of reactive oxygen species production during programmed cell death. *Journal of Cell Biology* (1998) 141 (6): 1423–32.

Thakker-Varia, S., et al. The neuropeptide VGF produces antidepressant-like behavioral effects and enhances proliferation in the hippocampus. *Journal of Neuroscience* (2007) 27: 12156–67.

Thanos, P., et al. Food restriction increases pleasure in rats. *Synapse* (2007) 62: 50–61.

Thiele, T. E., et al. Overlapping peptide control of alcohol administration. *Alcoholism: Clinical & Experimental Research* (2004) 28: 288–94.

Tomarken, A. J., Davidson, R. J., Wheeler, R. E., and Doss, R. C. Individual differences in anterior brain asymmetry and fundamental dimensions of emotion. *Journal of Personality and Social Psychology* (1992) 62: 676–87.

Urry, H. L., et al. Making a life worth living: Neural correlates of well-being. *Psychological Science* (2004) 15: 367–72.

van der Kolk, B. A. The body keeps the score: Memory and the evolving psychobiology of posttraumatic stress. *Harvard Psychiatric Review* 1 (1994).

van der Kolk, B. A. The neurobiology of childhood trauma and abuse. *Child & Adolescent Psychiatric Clinics of North America* (2003) 12: 293–317.

van der Kolk, B. A., and Fisler, R. E. The biologic basis of posttraumatic stress. *Primary Care* (1993) 20 (2): 417–32.

van der Kolk, B. A., McFarlane, A. C., and Weisaeth, L., eds. *Traumatic Stress: The Effects of Overwhelming Experience on Mind, Body, and Society.* New York: Guilford Press, 1996.

Van Honk, J., and Schutter, D.J.L. From affective valence to motivational direction: The frontal asymmetry of emotion revised. *Psychological Science* (2006) 17: 963–65.

Wagner, A. Brain activity points to origins of anorexia. *American Journal of Psychiatry* (December 3, 2007).

Wang, G.-J., Volkow, N. D., Thanos, P. K., and Fowler, J. S. Similarity between obesity and drug addiction as assessed by neurofunctional imaging: A concept review. *Journal of Addictive Diseases* (2004) 23: 39–53.

Wiskott, L., Rasch, M. J., and Kempermann, G. A functional hypothesis for adult hippocampal neurogenesis: Avoidance of catastrophic interference in the dentate gyrus. *Hippocampus* (2006) 16: 329–43.

Wurtman, R. Ways that foods can affect the brain. *Nutritional Reviews* (Suppl. 1986): 2–5.

Chapter 19: Change Your Mind

Hagan, S. *Buddhism: Plain and Simple.* New York: Broadway Books, 1997.

Lyubomirsky, S. *The How of Happiness.* London: Penguin Books, 2007.

Marston, C. Motivating the "What's in it for me?" *Workforce.* Hoboken, NJ: John Wiley, 1970.

Marston, W. *The Emotions of Normal People.* Minneapolis, MN: Persona Press, 1979.

Martin, P. R. *Martin's Magic Motivation Book.* New York: St. Martin's Press, 1984.

Rohm, R. *Positive Personality Profiles.* Atlanta, GA: Personality Insights, 1993.

Walton, S. *Sam Walton: Made in America.* New York: Bantam, 1992.

Warren, R. E., and Baker, J. E. *Life's Healing Choices.* New York: Howard Books, 2007.

Zimmerman, G. L., Olsen, C. G., and Bosworth, M. F. A "Stages of Change" approach to helping patients change behavior. *American Family Physician* (March 1, 2001).

Chapter 20: A Final Note

Almario, R. U., Vonghavaravat, V., Wong, R., and Kasim-Karakas, S. E. Effects of walnut consumption on plasma fatty acids and lipoproteins in combined hyperlipidemia. *American Journal of Clinical Nutrition* (2000) 74: 72–79.

Amaral, J. S., Alves, M. R., Seabra, R. M., and Oliveira, B. P. Vitamin E composition of walnuts (Juglans regia L.): A 3-year comparative study of different cultivars. *Journal of Agricultural and Food Chemistry* (2005) 53: 5467–72.

Bendinelli, B., et al. Fruit, vegetables, and olive oil and risk of coronary heart disease in Italian women: The EPICOR Study. *American Journal of Clinical Nutrition* (2011) 93: 275–28.

Beunza, J-J., et al. Adherence to the Mediterranean diet, long-term weight change, and incident overweight or obesity: The Seguimiento Universidad de Navarra (SUN) cohort. *American Journal of Clinical Nutrition* (2010) 92: 1484–93.

Cosmluescu, S. N., Baciu, A., Achim, G., Botu, M., and Trandafir, I. Mineral composition of fruits in different walnut (*Juglans regia L.*) cultivars. *Notulae Botanicae Horti Agrobotanici Cluj-Napoca* (2009) 37: 156–60.

De Lorgeni, M., et al. Mediterranean alpha-linolenic acid rich diet in secondary prevention of coronary heart disease. *Lancet* (1994) 11: 1454–59.

FDA approves health claims for walnuts. *Health News* (2004) 10 (6): 6.

Feart, C., et al. Adherence to a Mediterranean diet, cognitive decline, and risk of dementia. *JAMA* (2009) 302: 638–48.

Knopman, D. S. Mediterranean diet and late-life cognitive impairment: A taste of benefit. *JAMA* (2009) 302: 686–87.

Lavedrine, F., Zmirou, D., Ravel, A., Balducci, F., and Alary, J. Blood cholesterol and walnut consumption: A cross-sectional survey in France. *Preventative Medicine* (1999) 28: 333–39.

Ma, Y., et al. Effects of walnut consumption on endothelial function in type 2 diabetic subjects: A randomized controlled crossover trial. *Diabetes Care* (2010) 33: 227–32.

Martínez, M. L., Labuckas, D. O., Lamarque, A. L., and Maestri, D. M. Fatty acid composition of some walnut (*Juglans regia L.*) cultivars from east Anatolia. *Grasas y Aceites* (2005) 328: 328–31.

Müller, R., and Rappert, S. Pyrazines: Occurrence, formation and biodegradation. *Applied Microbiology and Biotechnology* (2010) 85: 1315–20.

Negi, A. S., et al. Antiproliferative and antioxidant activities of *Juglans regia* fruit extracts. *Pharmaceutical Biology* (2011) 49: 669–73.

Ozkhan, G., and Koyuncu, M. A. Physical and chemical compositon of some walnut (*Juglans regia L.*) genotypes grown in Turkey. *Grasas y Aceites* (2005) 56: 141–46.

Sabate, J., et al. Effect of walnuts on serum lipid levels and blood pressure in normal men. *New England Journal of Medicine* (1993) 328: 603–7.

Sanchez-Villegas, A., et al. Association of the Mediterranean dietary pattern with the incidence of depression: The Seguimiento Universidad de Navarra/University of Navarra follow-up (SUN) cohort. *Archives of General Psychiatry* (2009) 66: 1090–98.

Savage, G. P. Chemical composition of walnuts (*Juglans regia L.*) grown in New Zealand. *Plant Food for Human Nutrition* (2001) 56: 75–82.

Scarmeas, N., et al. Mediterranean diet and mild cognitive impairment. *Archives of Neurology* (2009) 66: 216–25.

Simon, J. A., Fong, J., Bernert, J. T., Jr., and Browner, W. S. Serum fatty acids and the risk of stroke. *Stroke* (1995) 26: 778–82.

USDA Nutrient Database for Standard Reference, Release 17. Nutrient Data Laboratory Home Page, 2011. http://www.nal.usda.gov/fnic/foodcomp. USDA SR-21.

Willis, L. M., Shukitt-Hale, B., Cheng, V., and Joseph, J. A. Dose-dependent effects of walnuts on motor and cognitive function in aged rats. *British Journal of Nutrition* (2009) 101: 1140–44.

Woods, R. *The New Whole Foods Encyclopedia: A Comprehensive Resource for Healthy Eating.* New York: Penguin Books, 2009.

Zambon, D., et al. Substituting walnuts for monounsaturated fat improves the serum lipid profile of hypercholesterolemic men and women: A randomized crossover trial. *Annals of Internal Medicine* (2000) 132: 538–46.

Index

354 ❖ Index